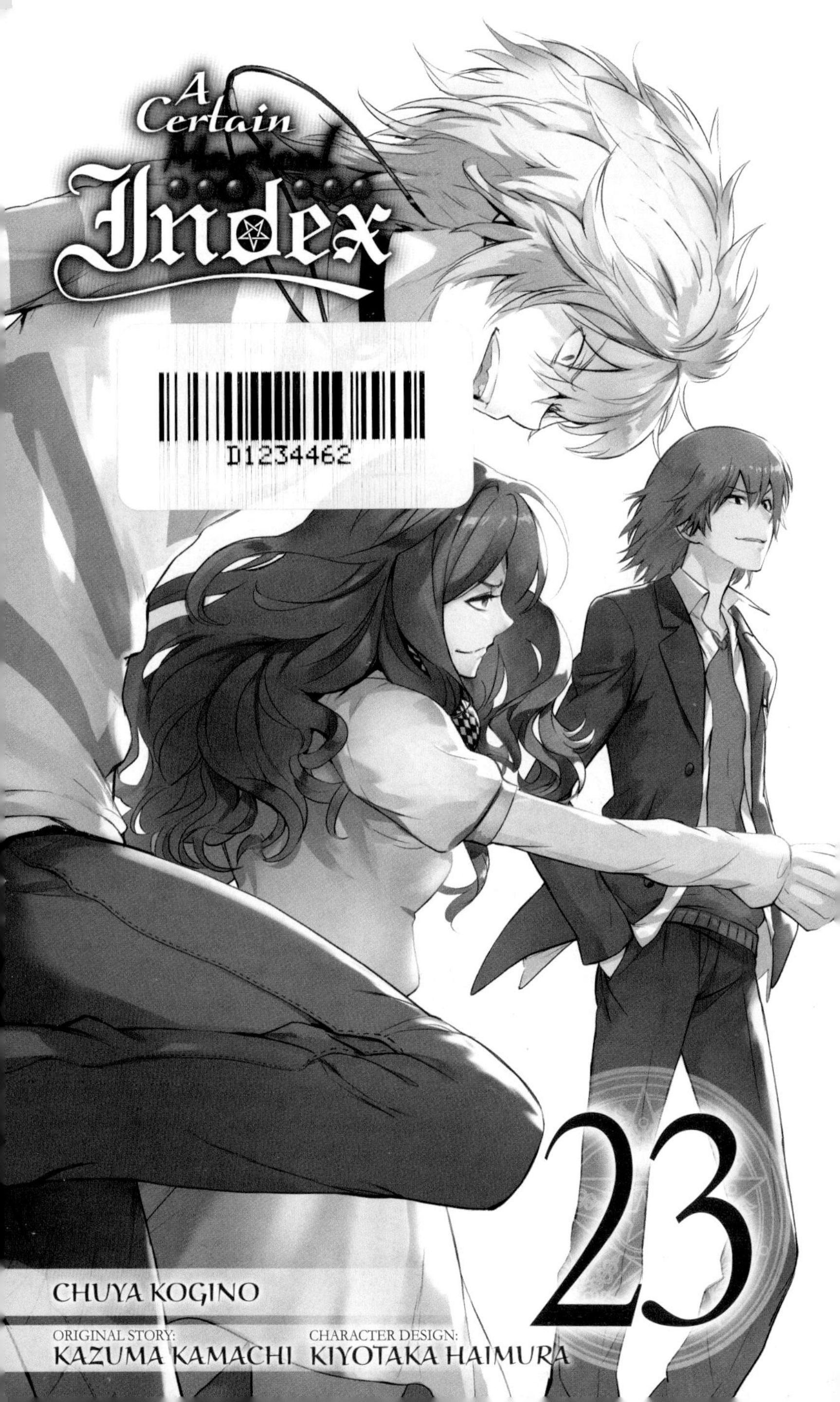

# A Certain Magical Index

23

CHUYA KOGINO

ORIGINAL STORY:
KAZUMA KAMACHI

CHARACTER DESIGN:
KIYOTAKA HAIMURA

A CERTAIN MAGICAL INDEX 23 TABLE OF CONTENTS

Index Librorum Prohibitorum

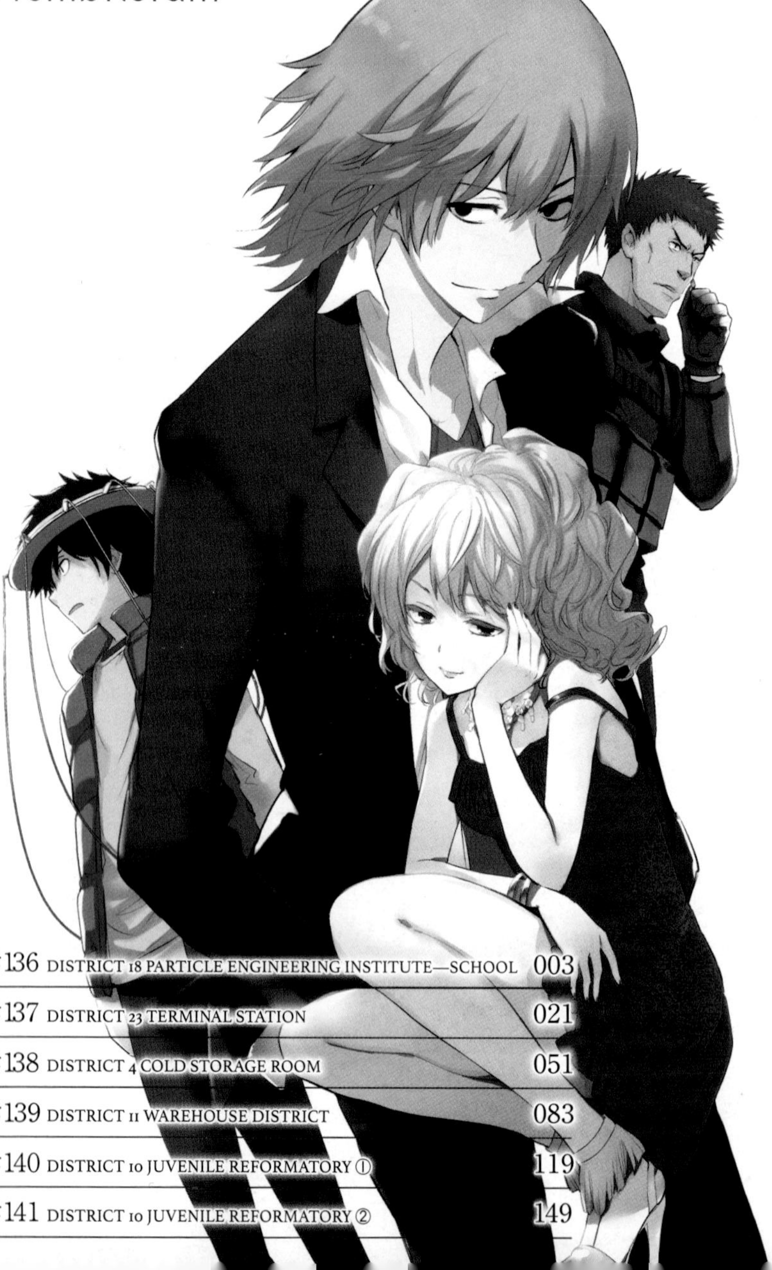

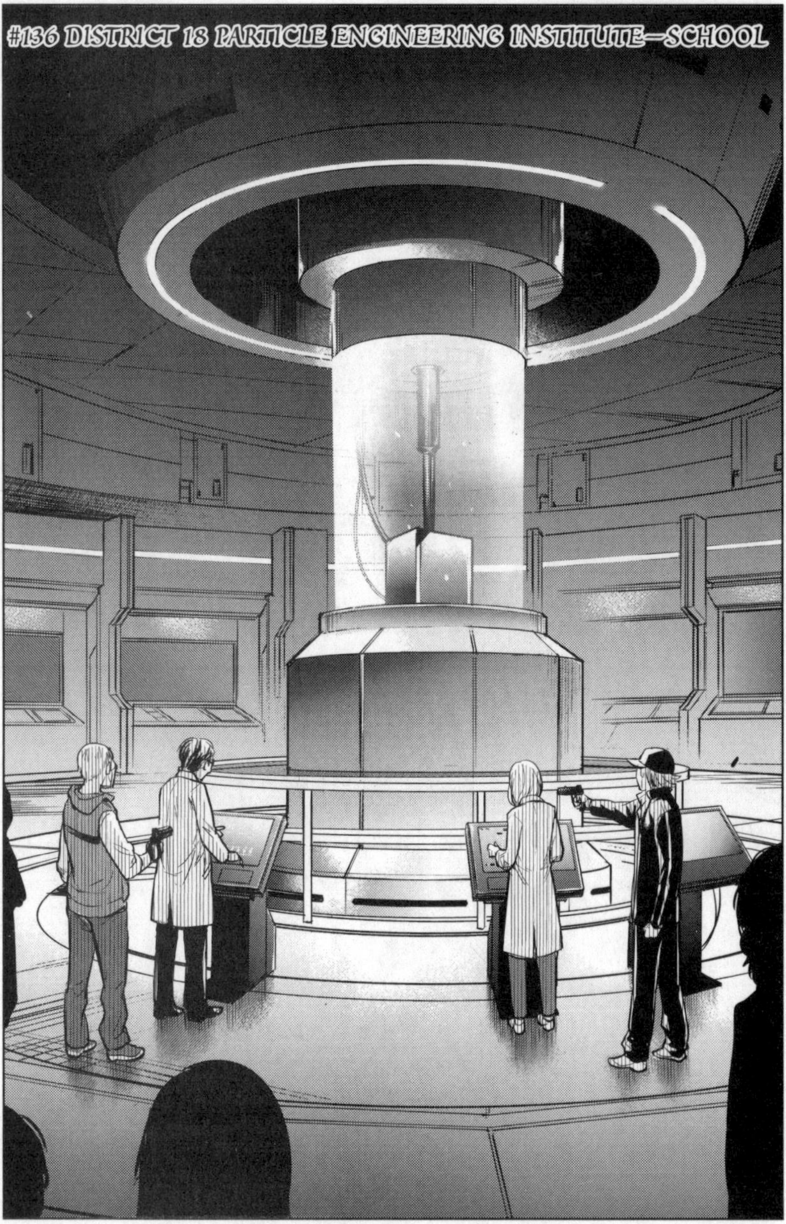
#136 DISTRICT 18 PARTICLE ENGINEERING INSTITUTE—SCHOOL

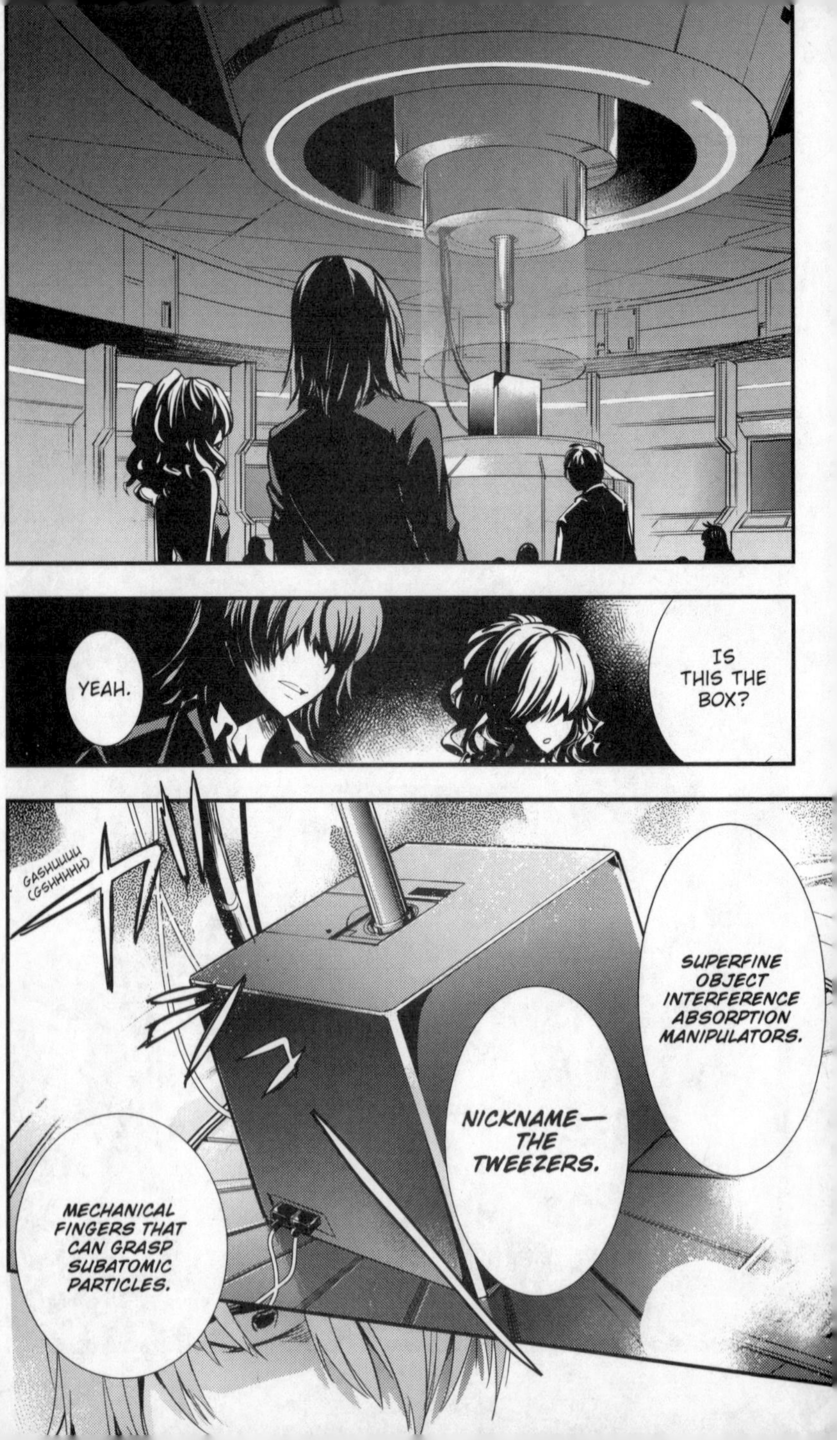
IS THIS THE BOX?
YEAH.
SUPERFINE OBJECT INTERFERENCE ABSORPTION MANIPULATORS.
GASHUUUU (GSHHHHH)
NICKNAME—THE TWEEZERS.
MECHANICAL FINGERS THAT CAN GRASP SUBATOMIC PARTICLES.

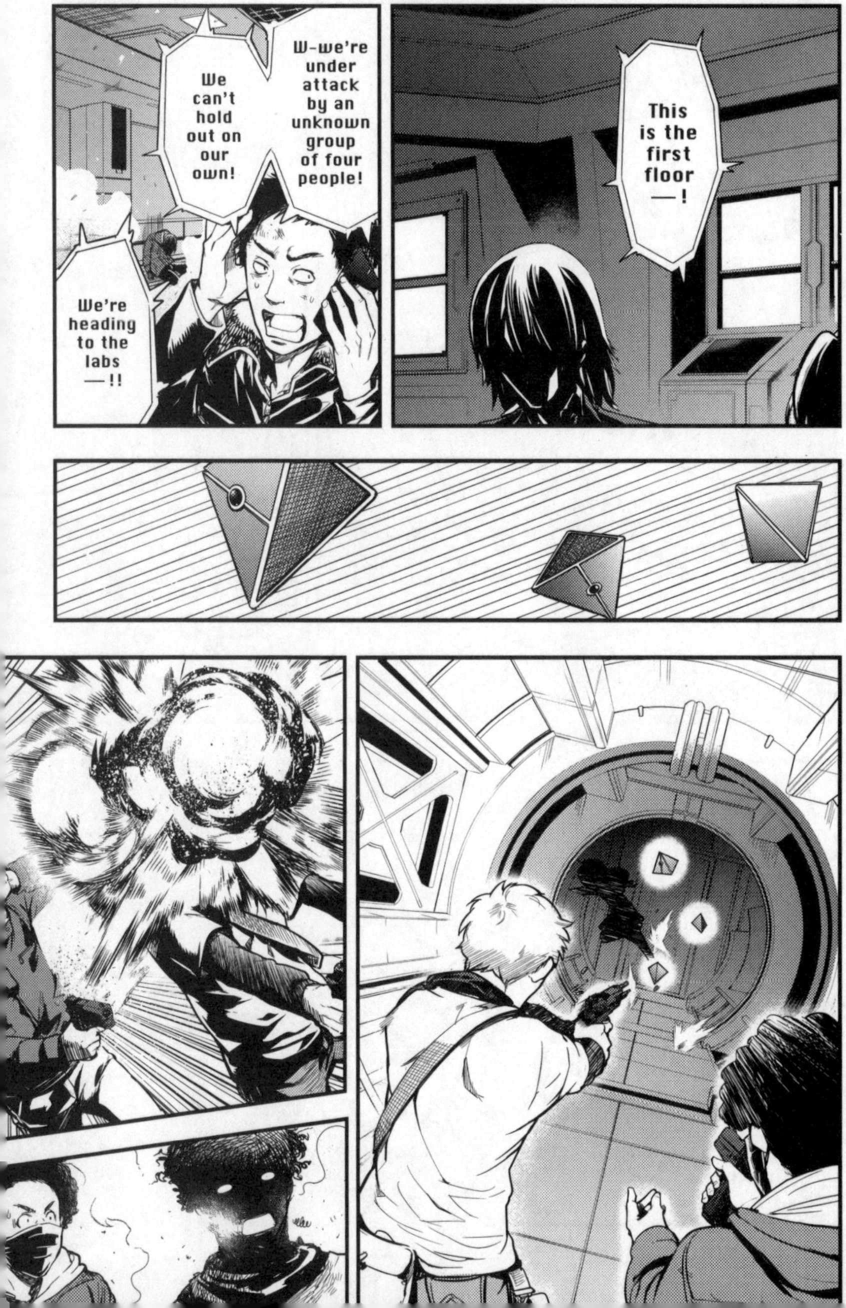
This is the first floor—!
W-we're under attack by an unknown group of four people!
We can't hold out on our own!
We're heading to the labs—!!

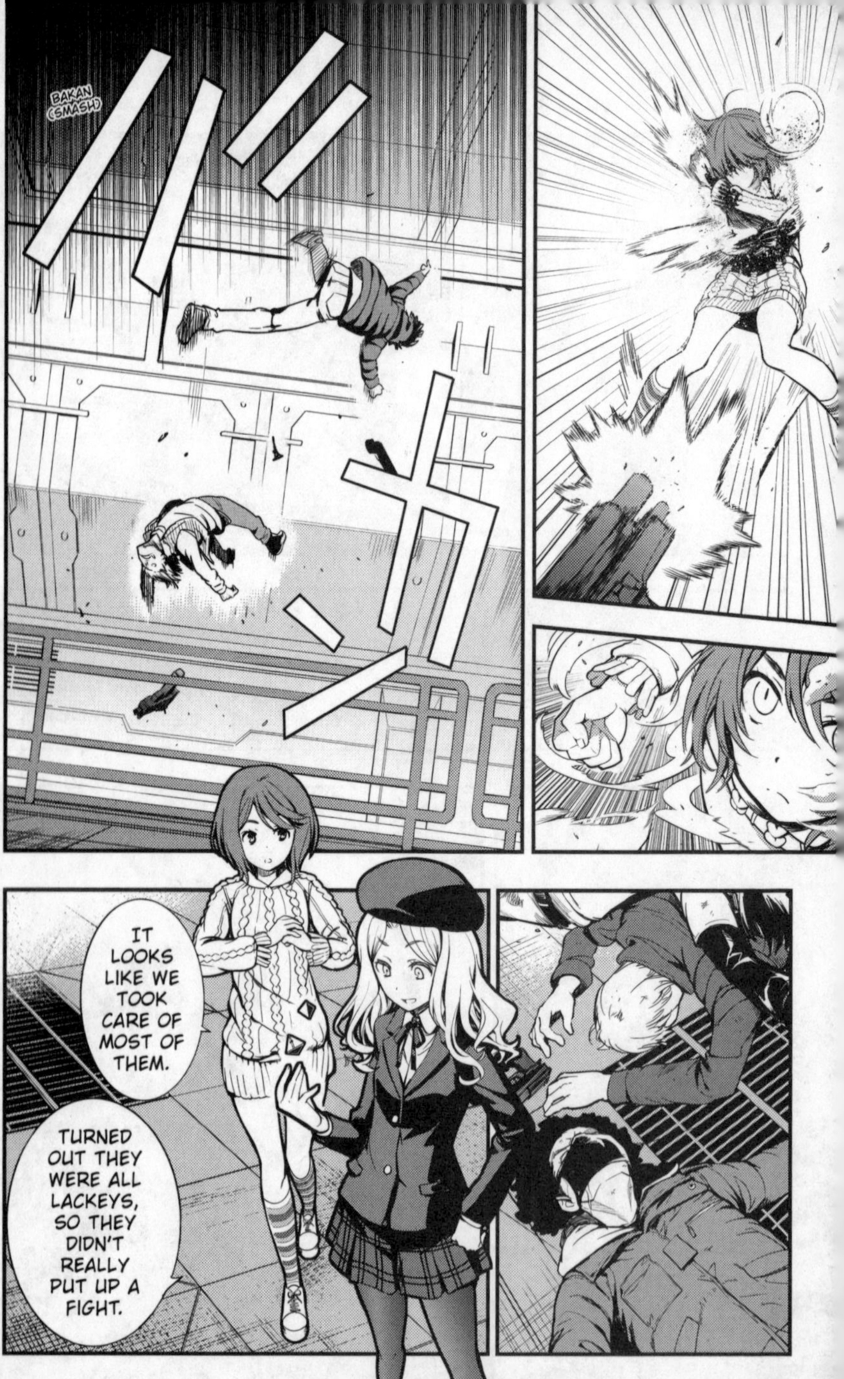
BAKAN (SMASH)
IT LOOKS LIKE WE TOOK CARE OF MOST OF THEM.
TURNED OUT THEY WERE ALL LACKEYS, SO THEY DIDN'T REALLY PUT UP A FIGHT.

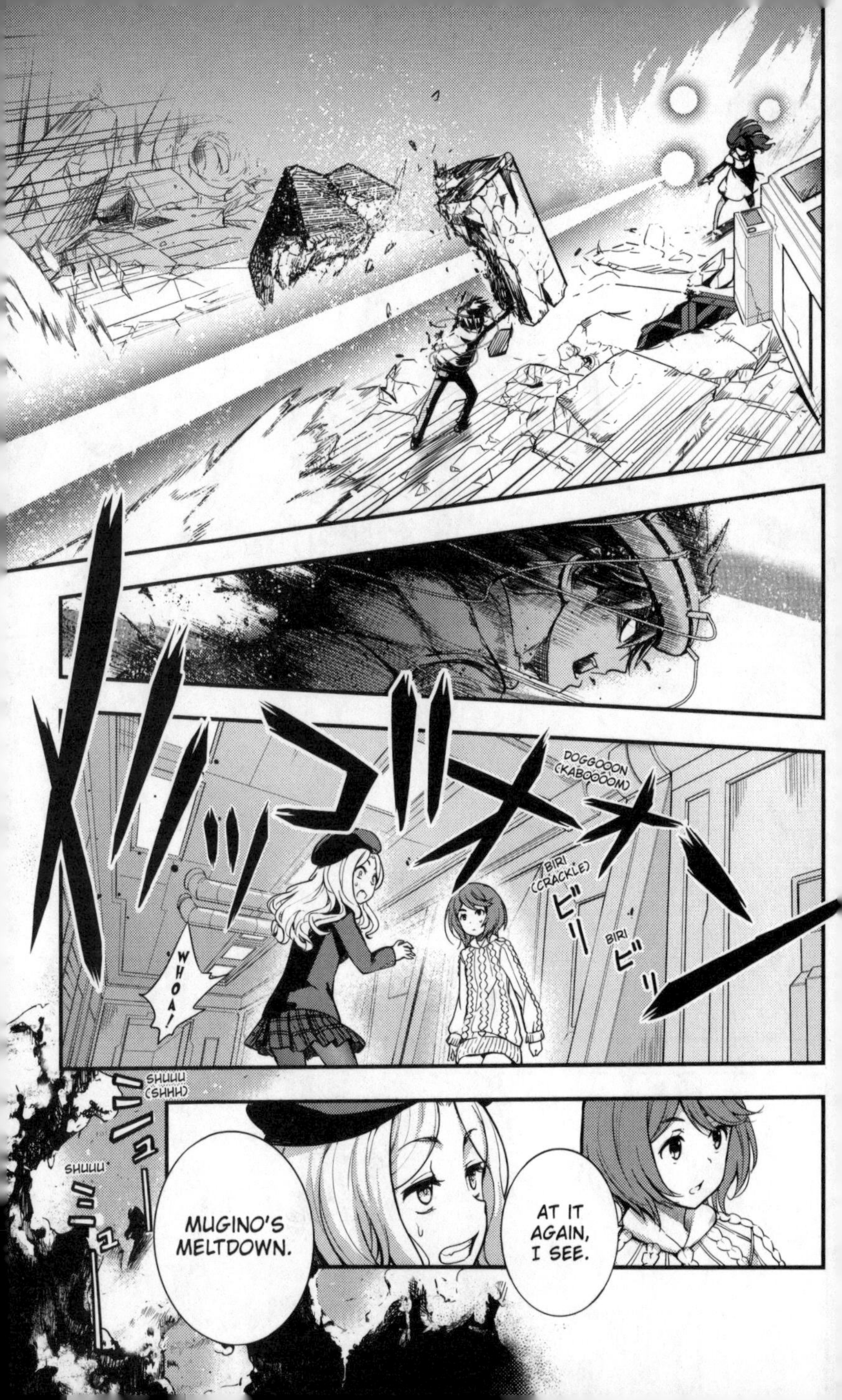
DOGGOOON (KABOOOOM)
BIRI (CRACKLE)
BIRI
WHOA!
SHUUU (SHHH)
SHUUU
AT IT AGAIN, I SEE.
MUGINO'S MELTDOWN.

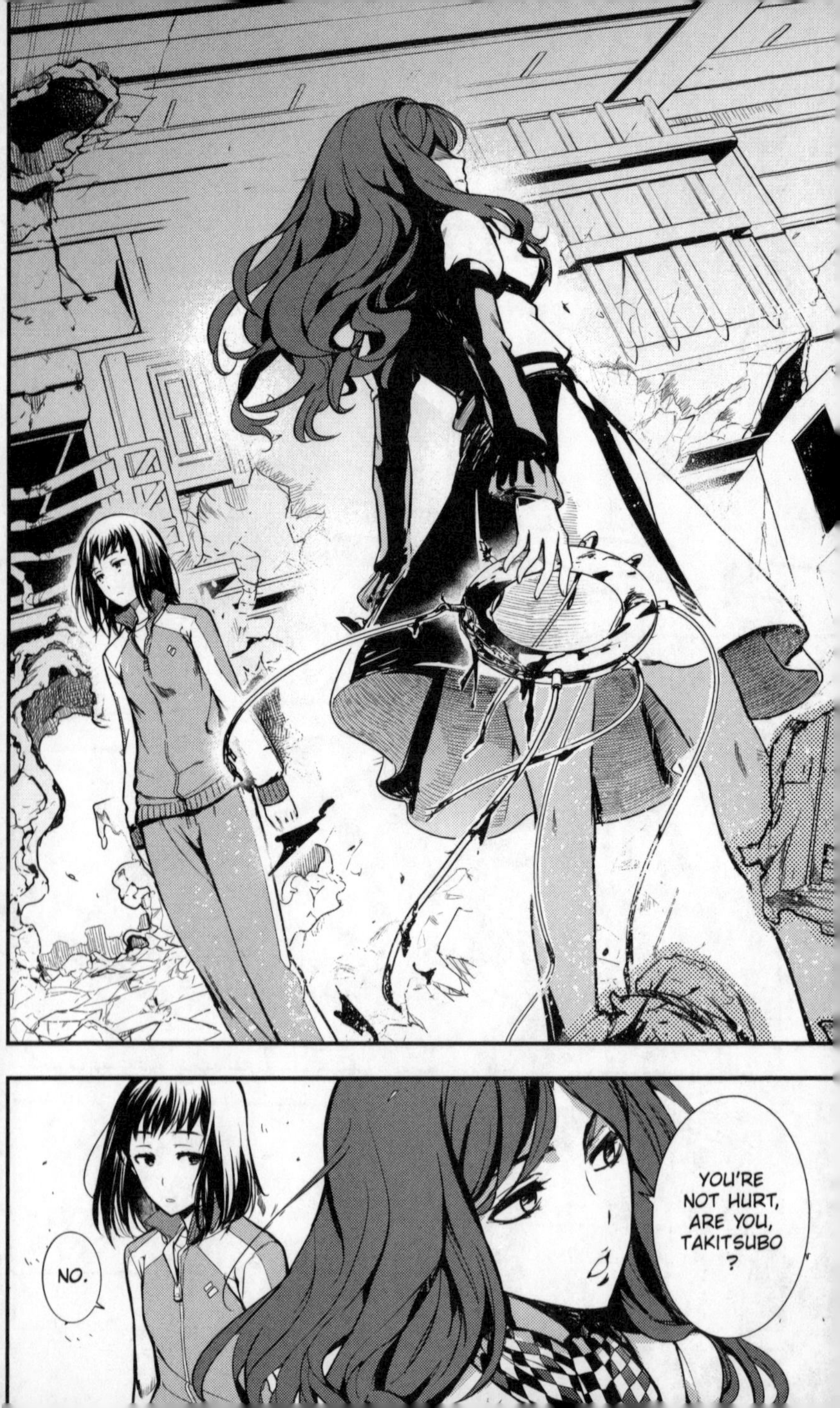
YOU'RE NOT HURT, ARE YOU, TAKITSUBO?
NO.

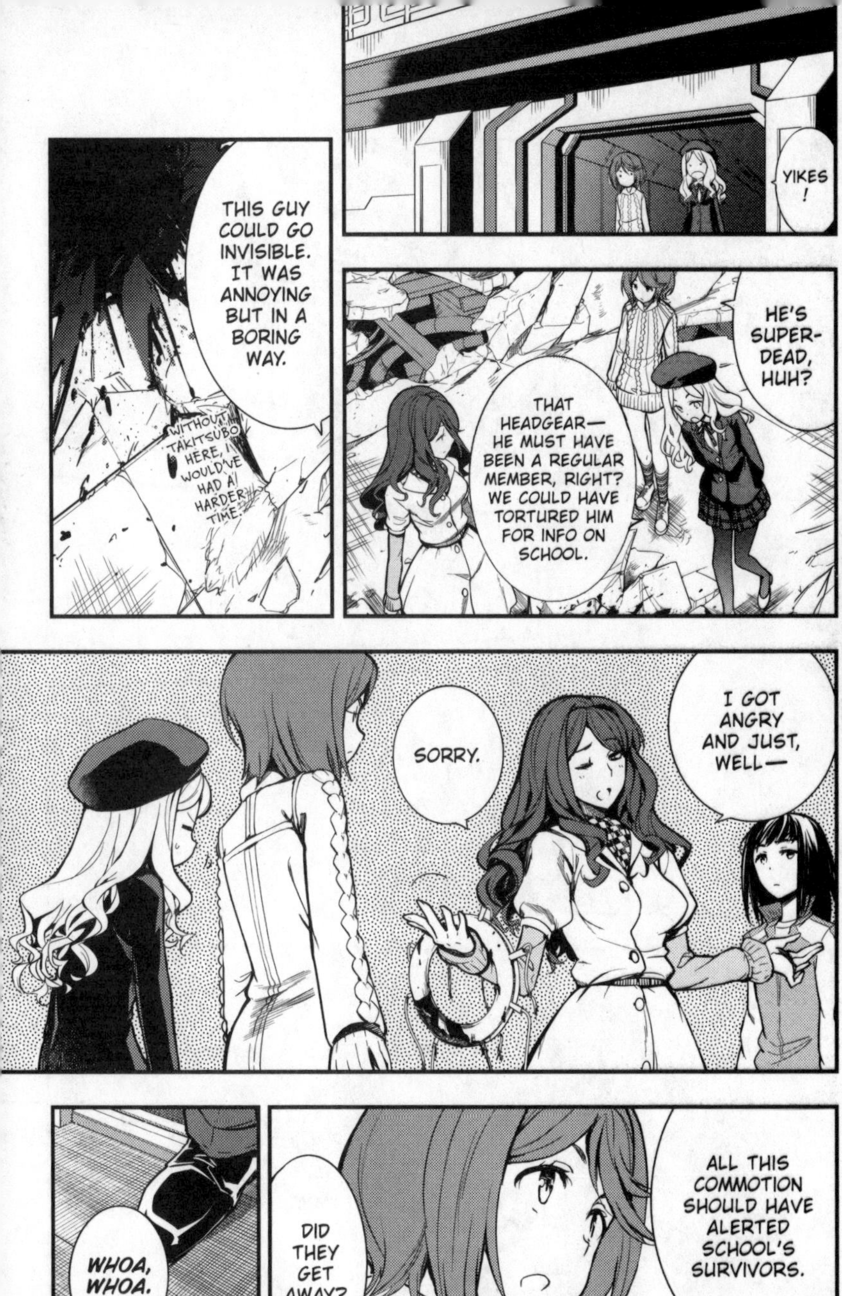
YIKES!
HE'S SUPER-DEAD, HUH?
THAT HEADGEAR—HE MUST HAVE BEEN A REGULAR MEMBER, RIGHT? WE COULD HAVE TORTURED HIM FOR INFO ON SCHOOL.
THIS GUY COULD GO INVISIBLE. IT WAS ANNOYING BUT IN A BORING WAY.
WITHOUT TAKITSUBO HERE, I WOULD'VE HAD A HARDER TIME.
I GOT ANGRY AND JUST, WELL—
SORRY.
ALL THIS COMMOTION SHOULD HAVE ALERTED SCHOOL'S SURVIVORS.
DID THEY GET AWAY?
WHOA, WHOA.

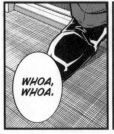

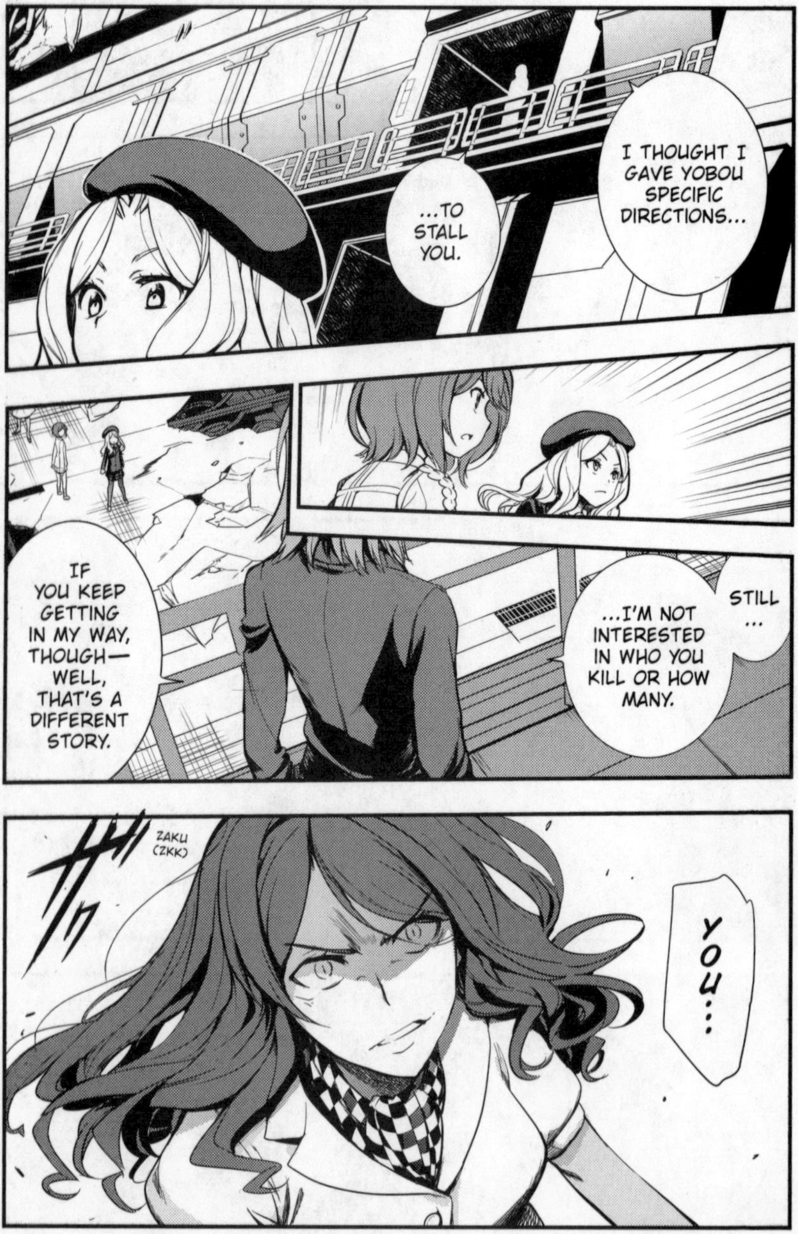
I THOUGHT I GAVE YOBOU SPECIFIC DIRECTIONS...
...TO STALL YOU.
STILL ...
...I'M NOT INTERESTED IN WHO YOU KILL OR HOW MANY.
IF YOU KEEP GETTING IN MY WAY, THOUGH— WELL, THAT'S A DIFFERENT STORY.
YOU...
ZAKU (ZKK)

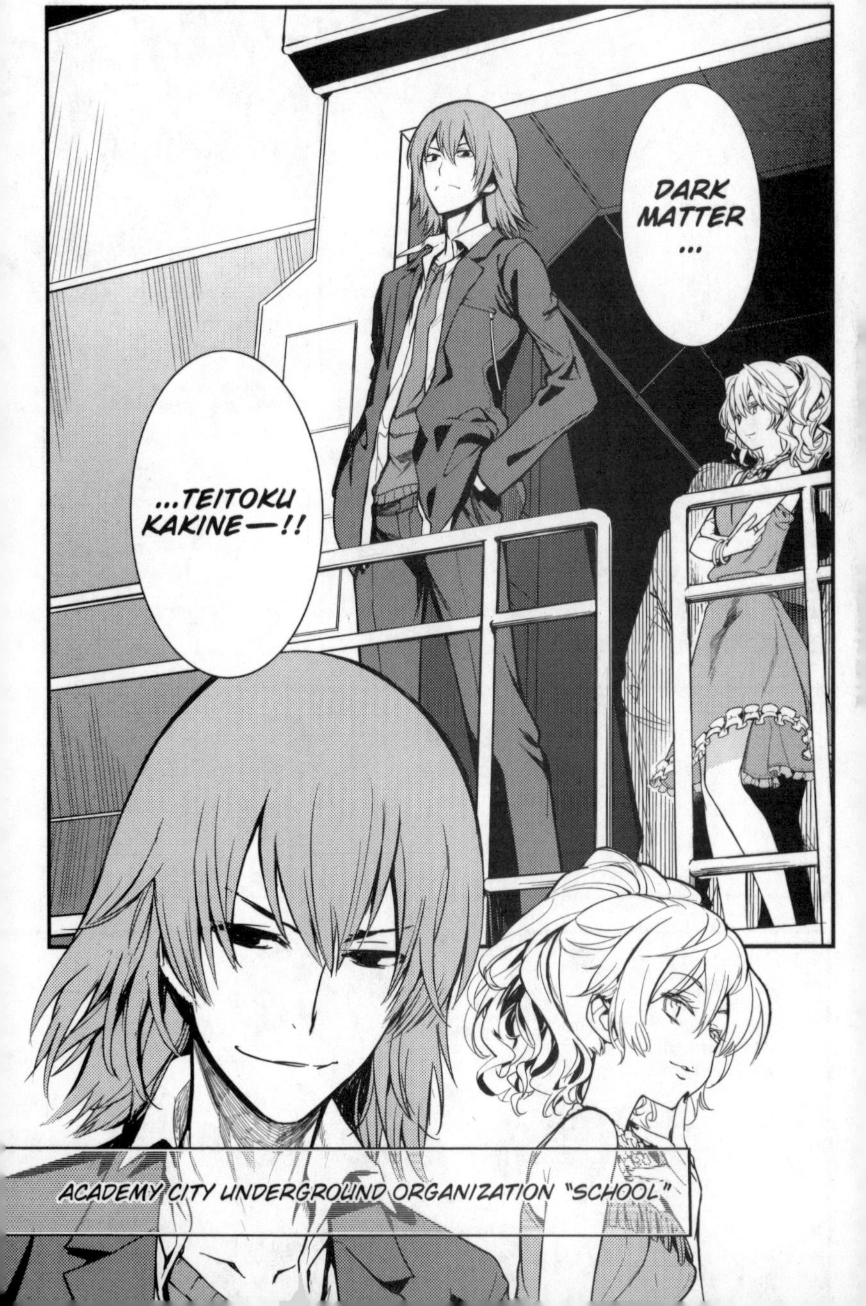
DARK MATTER ...
...TEITOKU KAKINE—!!
ACADEMY CITY UNDERGROUND ORGANIZATION "SCHOOL"

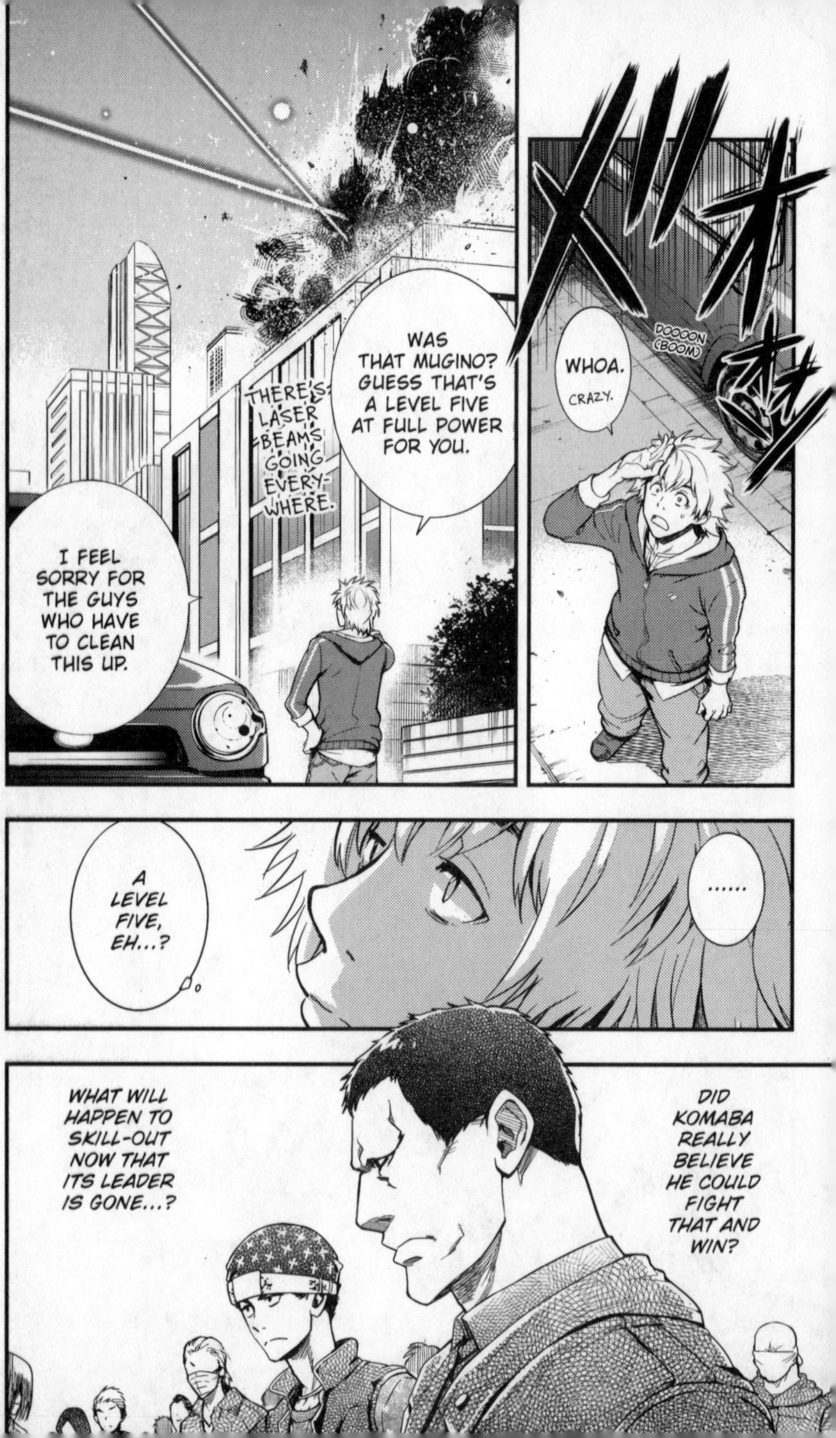
WHOA.
CRAZY.
DOOOON (BOOM)
WAS THAT MUGINO? GUESS THAT'S A LEVEL FIVE AT FULL POWER FOR YOU.
THERE'S LASER BEAMS GOING EVERY-WHERE.
I FEEL SORRY FOR THE GUYS WHO HAVE TO CLEAN THIS UP.
......
A LEVEL FIVE, EH...?
DID KOMABA REALLY BELIEVE HE COULD FIGHT THAT AND WIN?
WHAT WILL HAPPEN TO SKILL-OUT NOW THAT ITS LEADER IS GONE...?

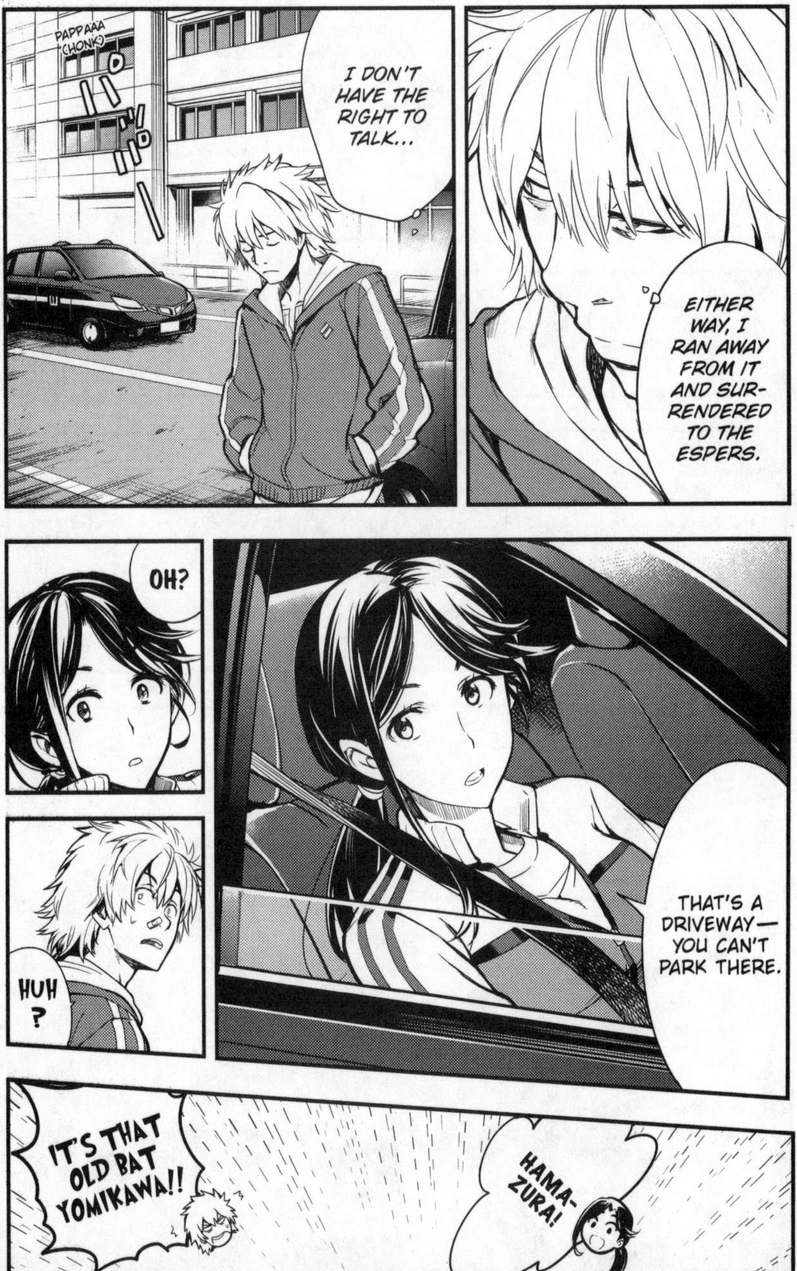
EITHER WAY, I RAN AWAY FROM IT AND SUR-RENDERED TO THE ESPERS.
I DON'T HAVE THE RIGHT TO TALK...
PAPPAAA (HONK)
THAT'S A DRIVEWAY— YOU CAN'T PARK THERE.
OH?
HUH?
HAMA-ZURA!
IT'S THAT OLD BAT YOMIKAWA!!

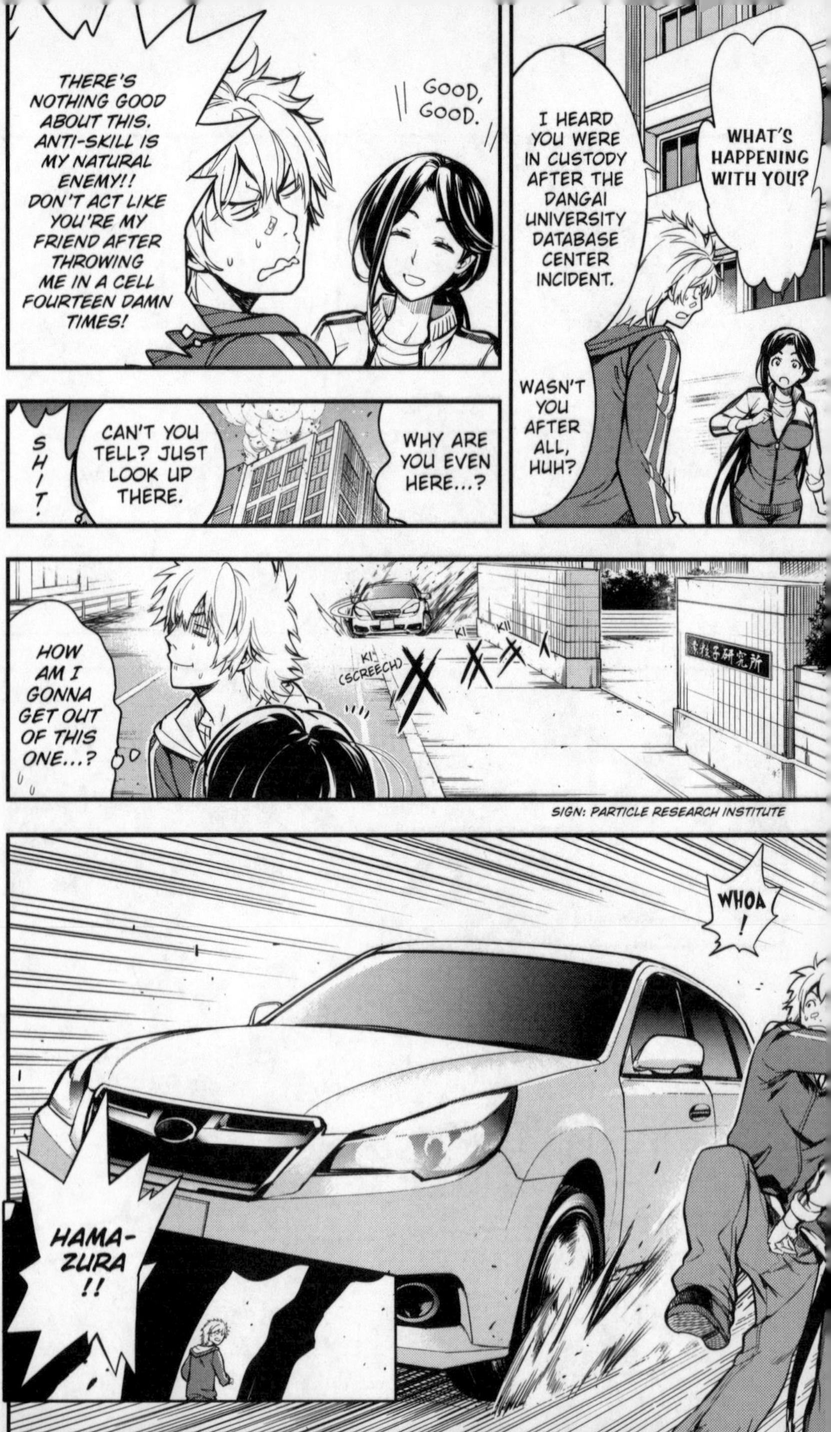

WHAT'S HAPPENING WITH YOU?
I HEARD YOU WERE IN CUSTODY AFTER THE DANGAI UNIVERSITY DATABASE CENTER INCIDENT.
WASN'T YOU AFTER ALL, HUH?
GOOD, GOOD.
THERE'S NOTHING GOOD ABOUT THIS. ANTI-SKILL IS MY NATURAL ENEMY!! DON'T ACT LIKE YOU'RE MY FRIEND AFTER THROWING ME IN A CELL FOURTEEN DAMN TIMES!
WHY ARE YOU EVEN HERE...?
CAN'T YOU TELL? JUST LOOK UP THERE.
SHIT!
KII
KI
KI (SCREECH)
HOW AM I GONNA GET OUT OF THIS ONE...?
SIGN: PARTICLE RESEARCH INSTITUTE
WHOA!
HAMA-ZURA!!

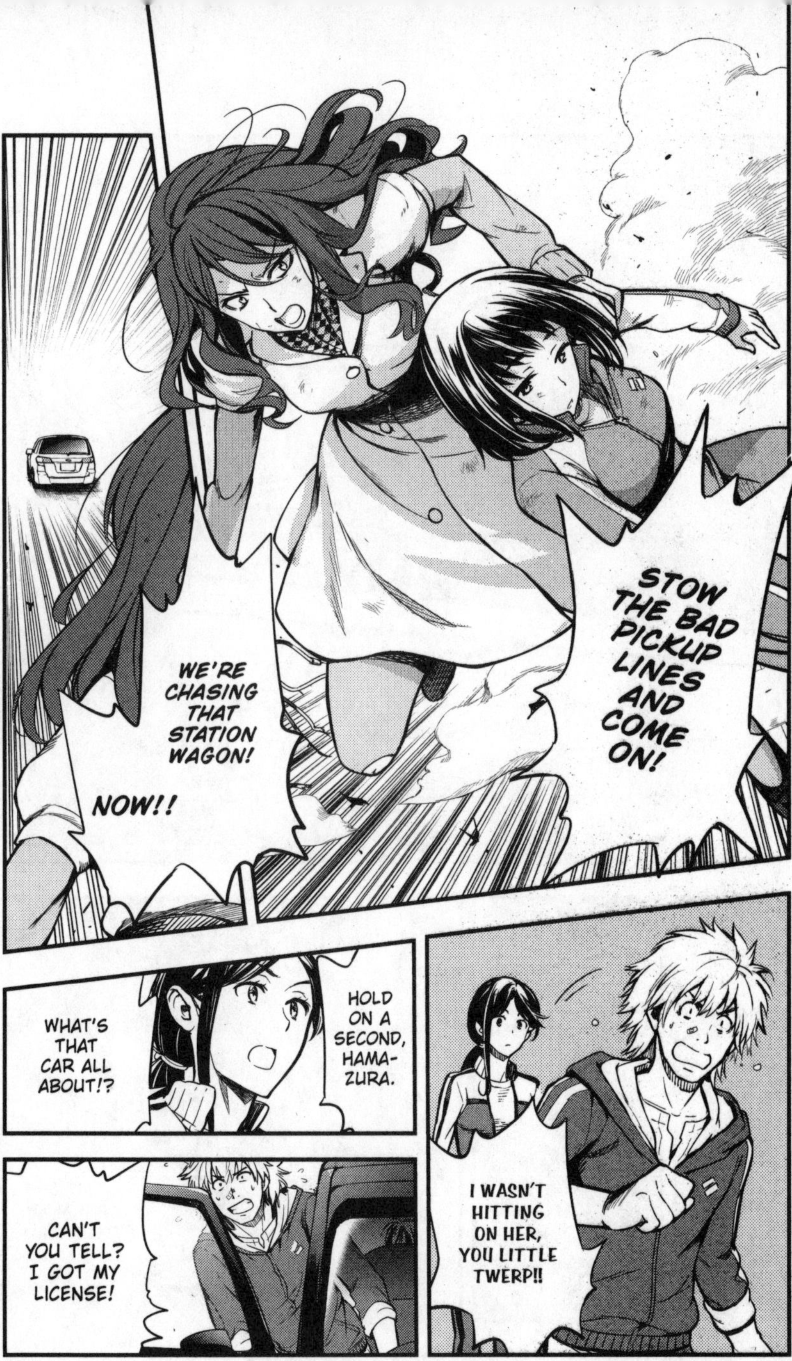
STOW THE BAD PICKUP LINES AND COME ON!
WE'RE CHASING THAT STATION WAGON!
NOW!!
I WASN'T HITTING ON HER, YOU LITTLE TWERP!!
HOLD ON A SECOND, HAMA-ZURA.
WHAT'S THAT CAR ALL ABOUT!?
CAN'T YOU TELL? I GOT MY LICENSE!

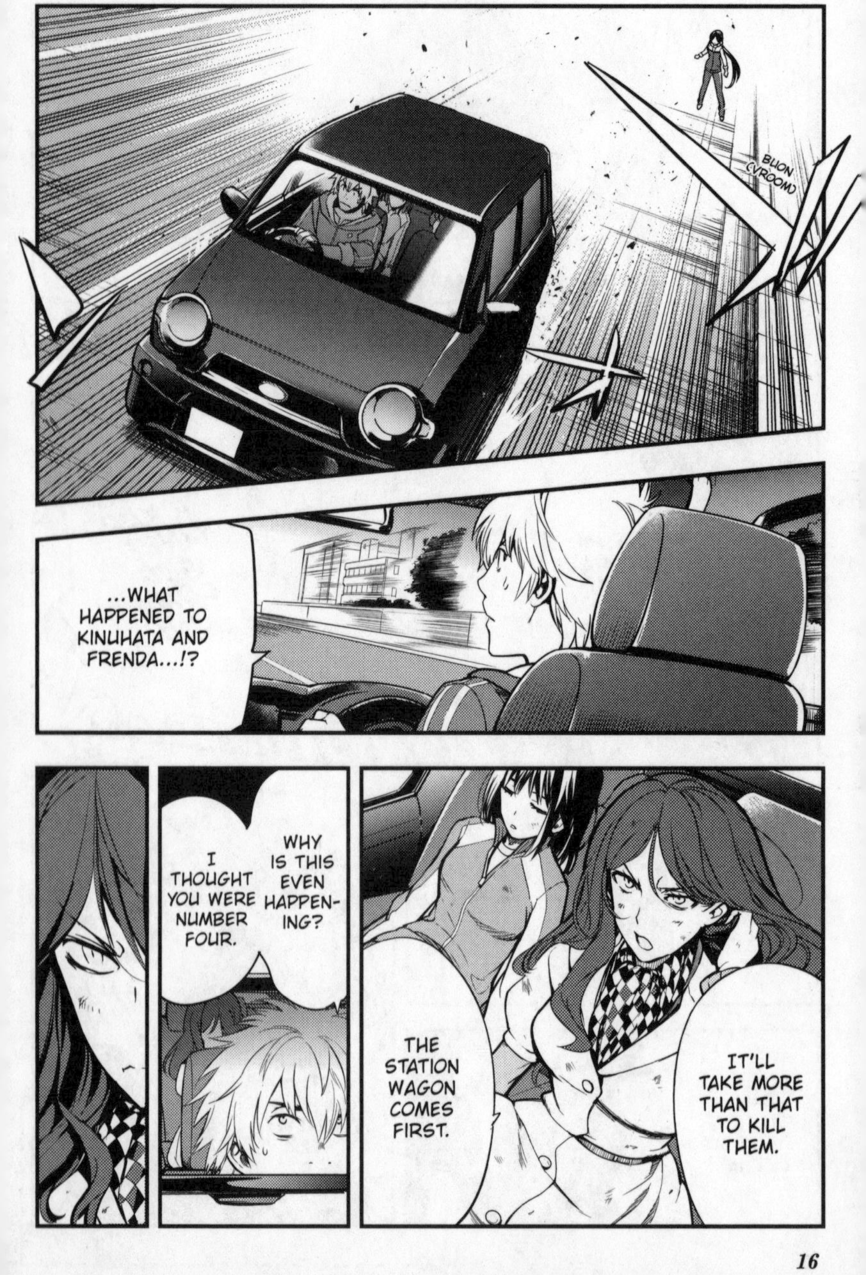
BUON (VROOM)
...WHAT HAPPENED TO KINUHATA AND FRENDA...!?
IT'LL TAKE MORE THAN THAT TO KILL THEM.
THE STATION WAGON COMES FIRST.
WHY IS THIS EVEN HAPPEN-ING?
I THOUGHT YOU WERE NUMBER FOUR.

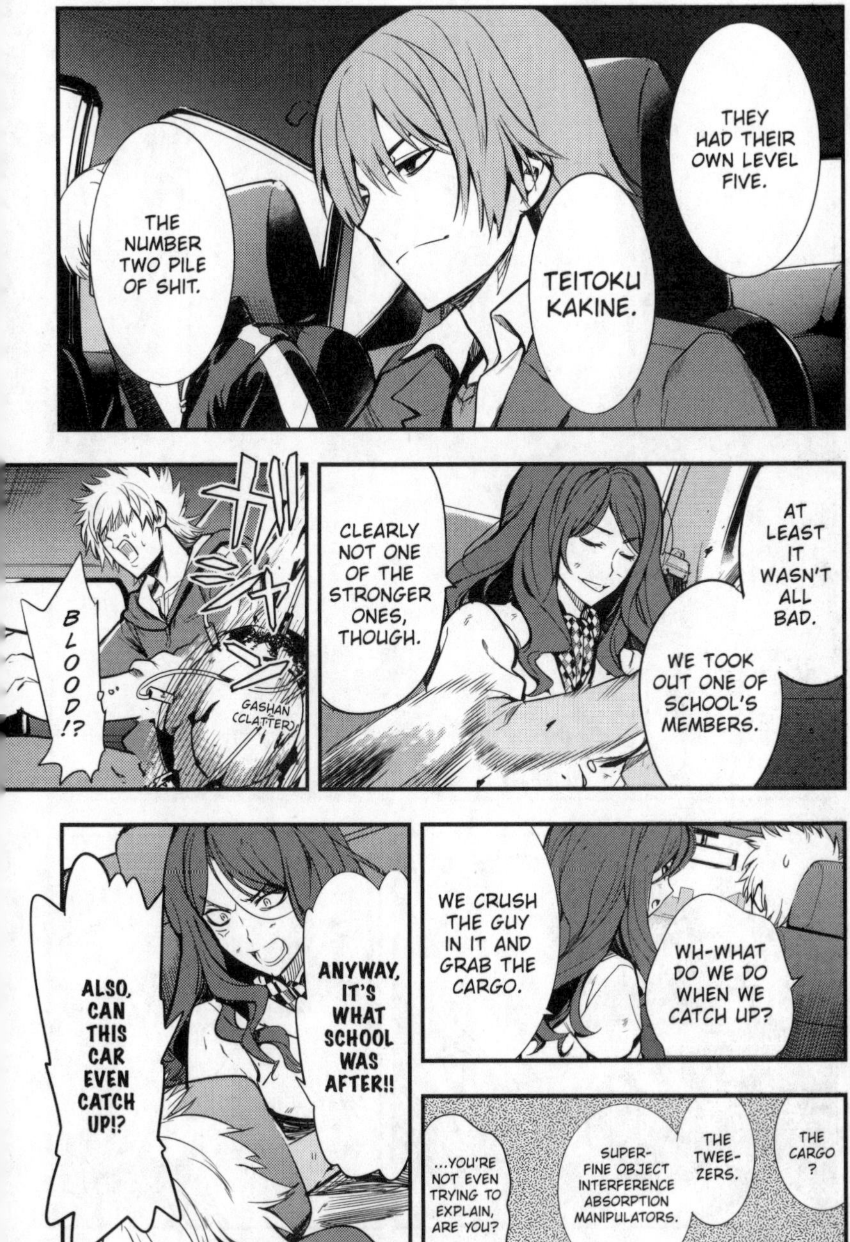
THEY HAD THEIR OWN LEVEL FIVE.
TEITOKU KAKINE.
THE NUMBER TWO PILE OF SHIT.
AT LEAST IT WASN'T ALL BAD.
WE TOOK OUT ONE OF SCHOOL'S MEMBERS.
CLEARLY NOT ONE OF THE STRONGER ONES, THOUGH.
BLOOD!?
GASHAN (CLATTER)
WH-WHAT DO WE DO WHEN WE CATCH UP?
WE CRUSH THE GUY IN IT AND GRAB THE CARGO.
THE CARGO?
THE TWEE-ZERS.
SUPER-FINE OBJECT INTERFERENCE ABSORPTION MANIPULATORS.
...YOU'RE NOT EVEN TRYING TO EXPLAIN, ARE YOU?
ANYWAY, IT'S WHAT SCHOOL WAS AFTER!!
ALSO, CAN THIS CAR EVEN CATCH UP!?

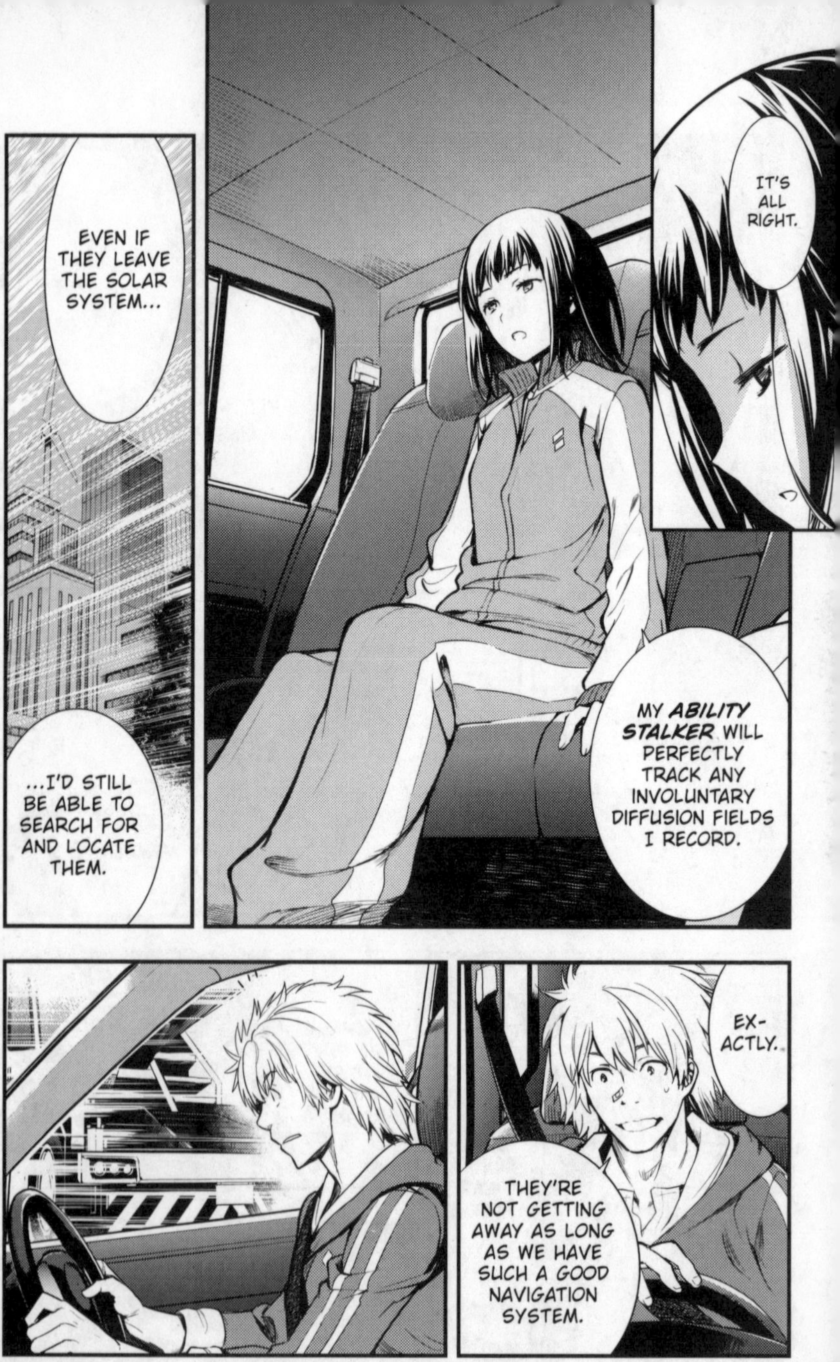
IT'S ALL RIGHT.
MY ***ABILITY STALKER*** WILL PERFECTLY TRACK ANY INVOLUNTARY DIFFUSION FIELDS I RECORD.
EVEN IF THEY LEAVE THE SOLAR SYSTEM...
...I'D STILL BE ABLE TO SEARCH FOR AND LOCATE THEM.
EX-ACTLY.
THEY'RE NOT GETTING AWAY AS LONG AS WE HAVE SUCH A GOOD NAVIGATION SYSTEM.

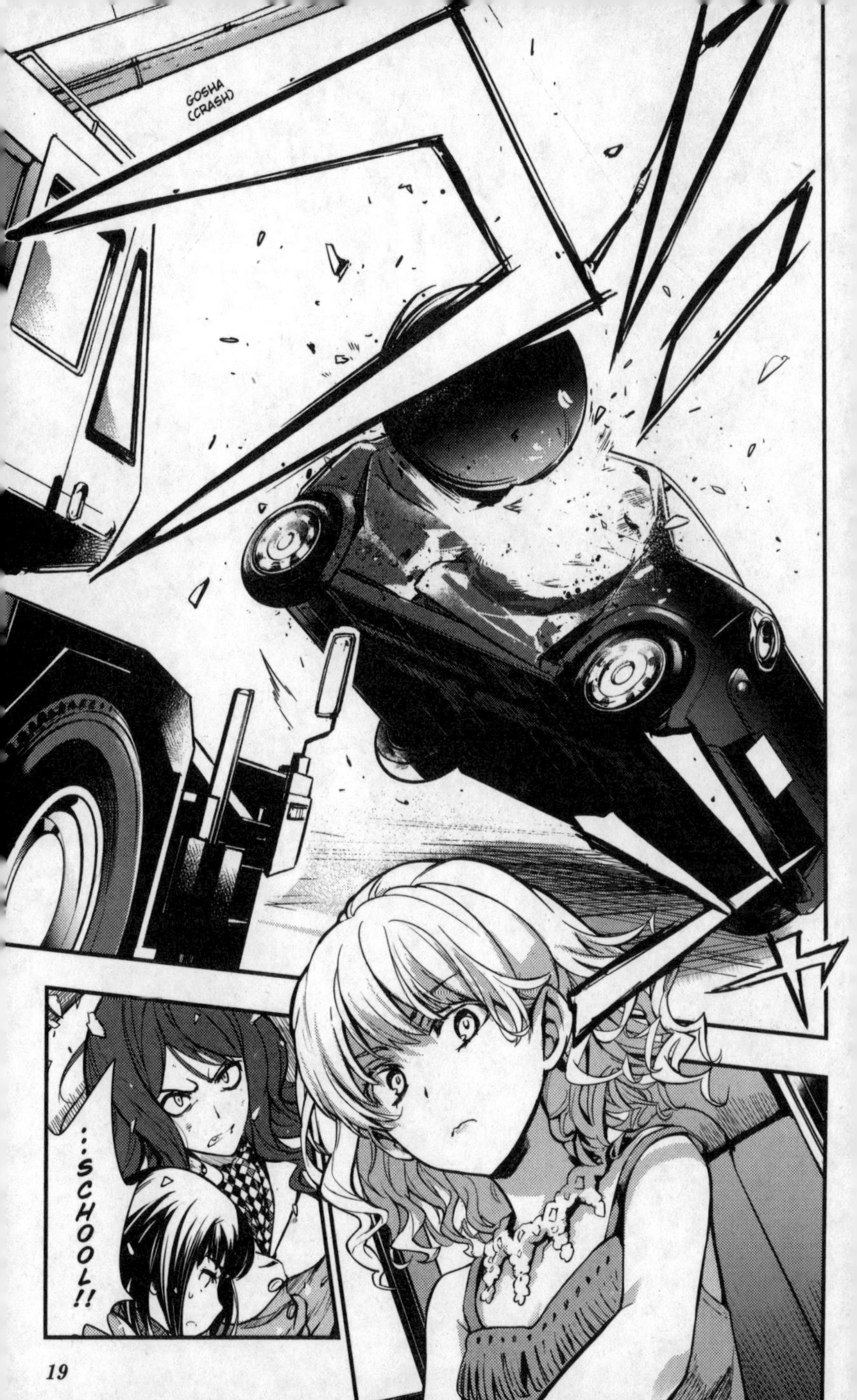

GOSHA (CRASH)
...SCHOOL!!

# A Certain Magical Index

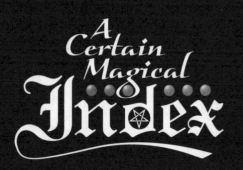

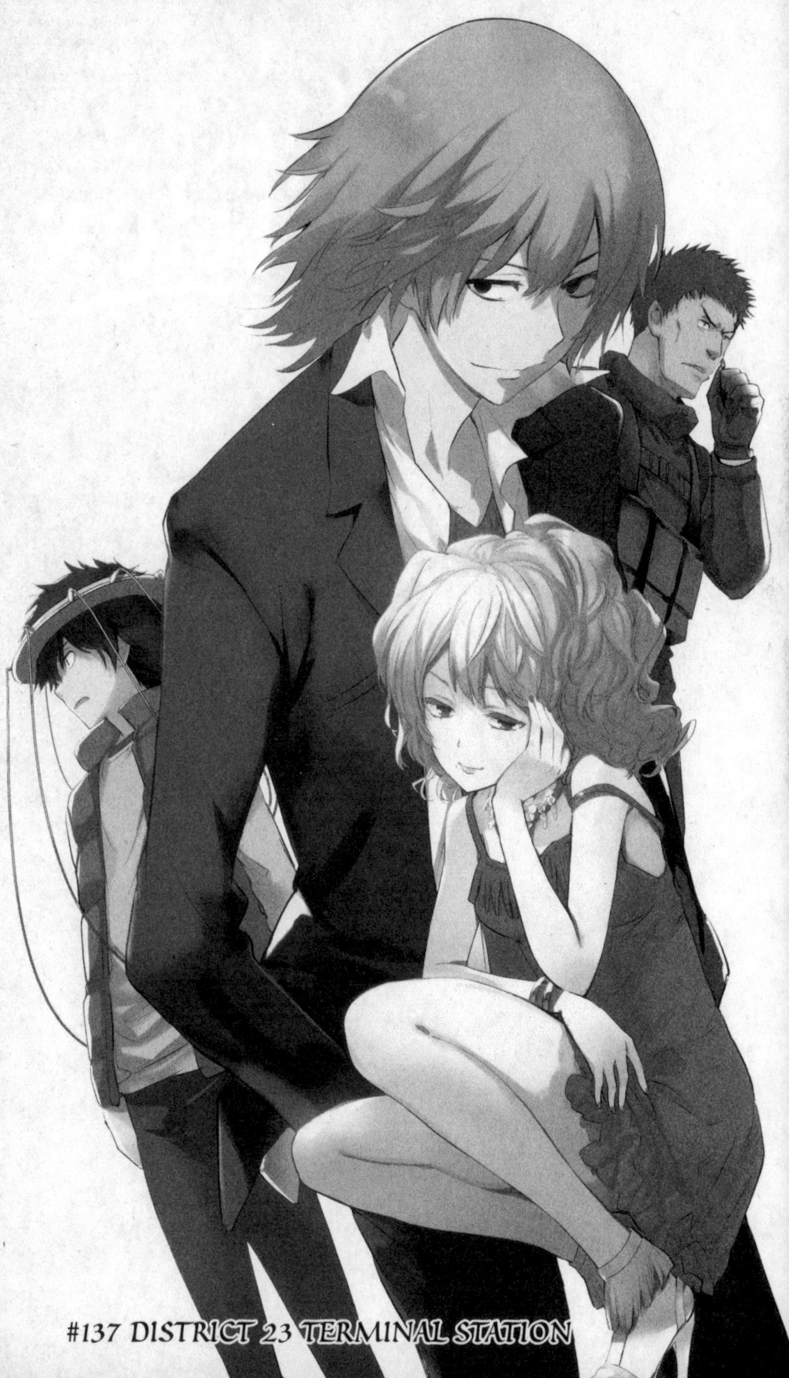
#137 DISTRICT 23 TERMINAL STATION

# A Certain Magical Index

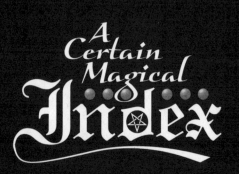

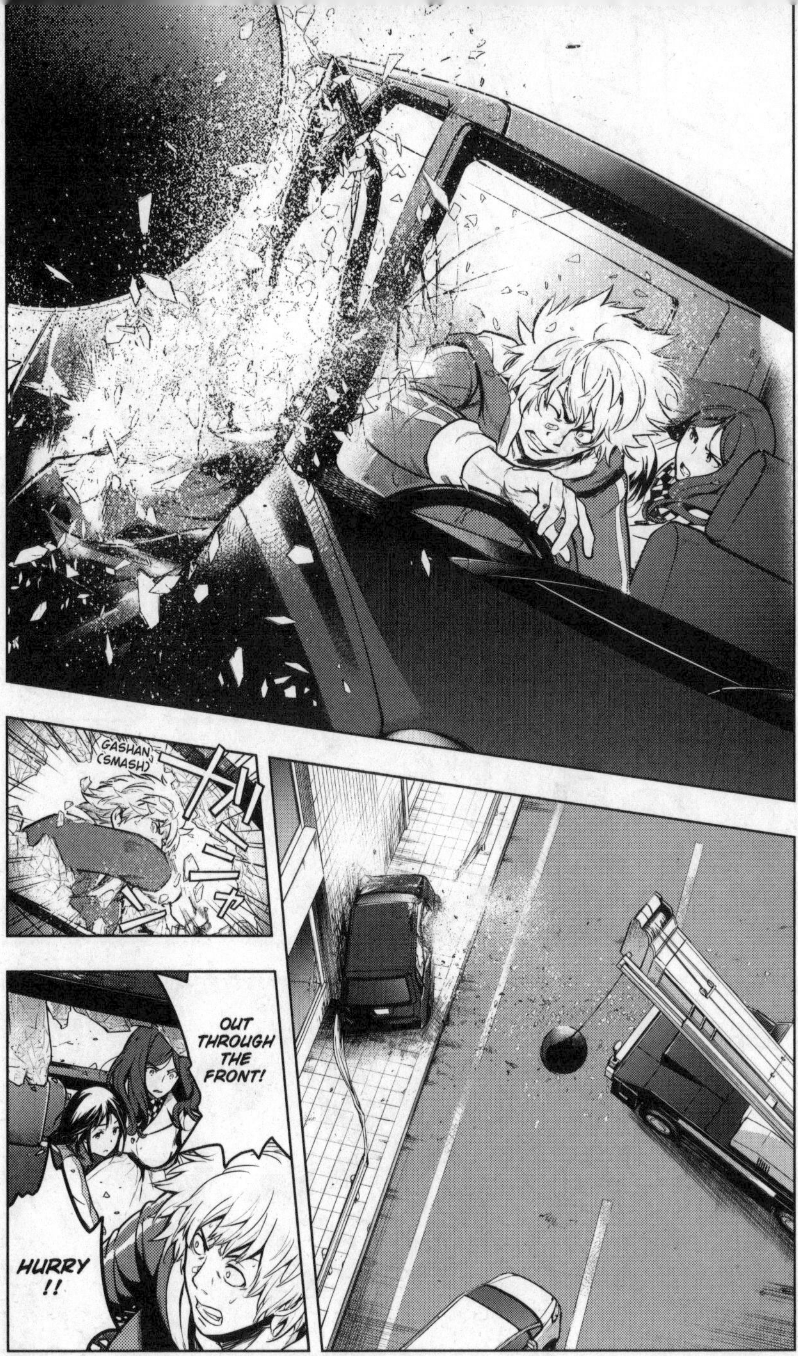
GASHAN (SMASH)
OUT THROUGH THE FRONT!
HURRY !!

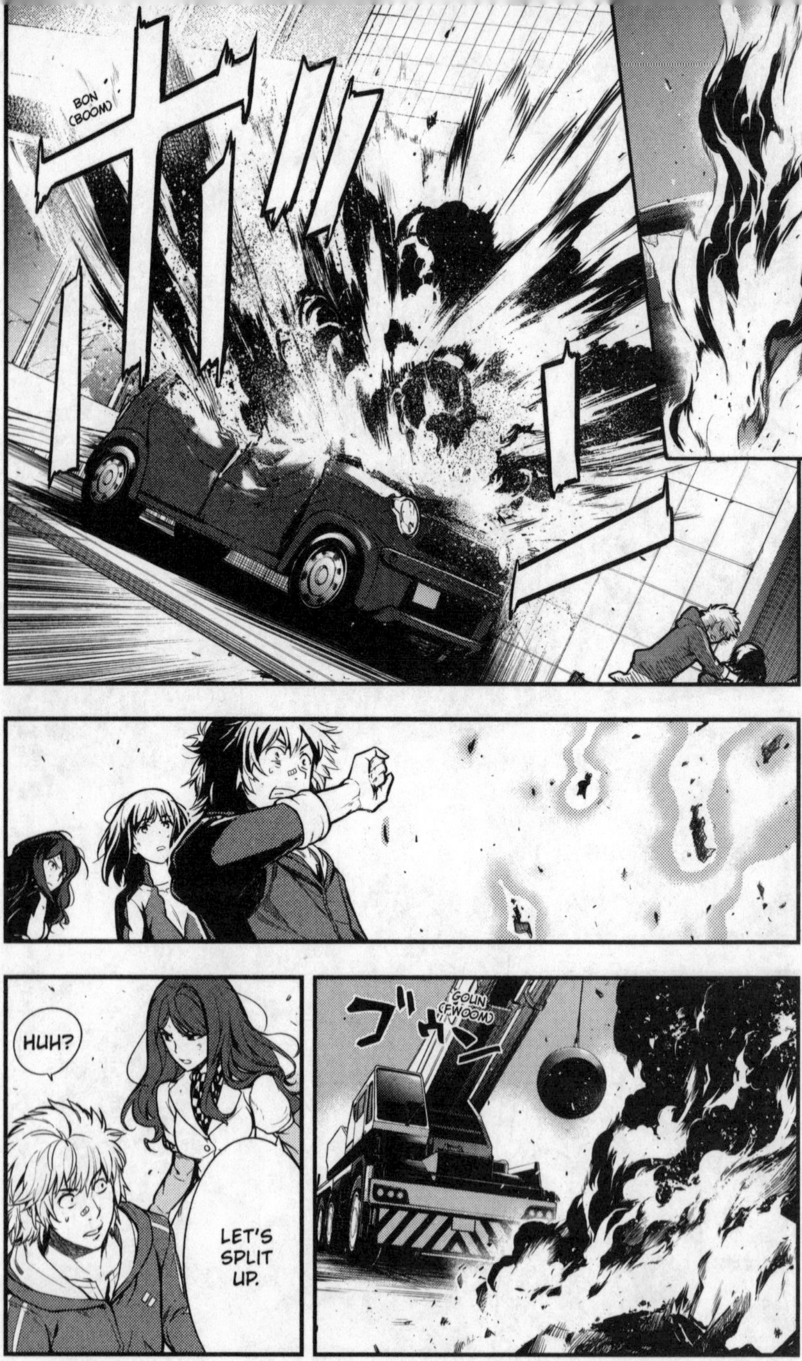
BON (BOOM)
GOUN (FWOOM)
HUH?
LET'S SPLIT UP.

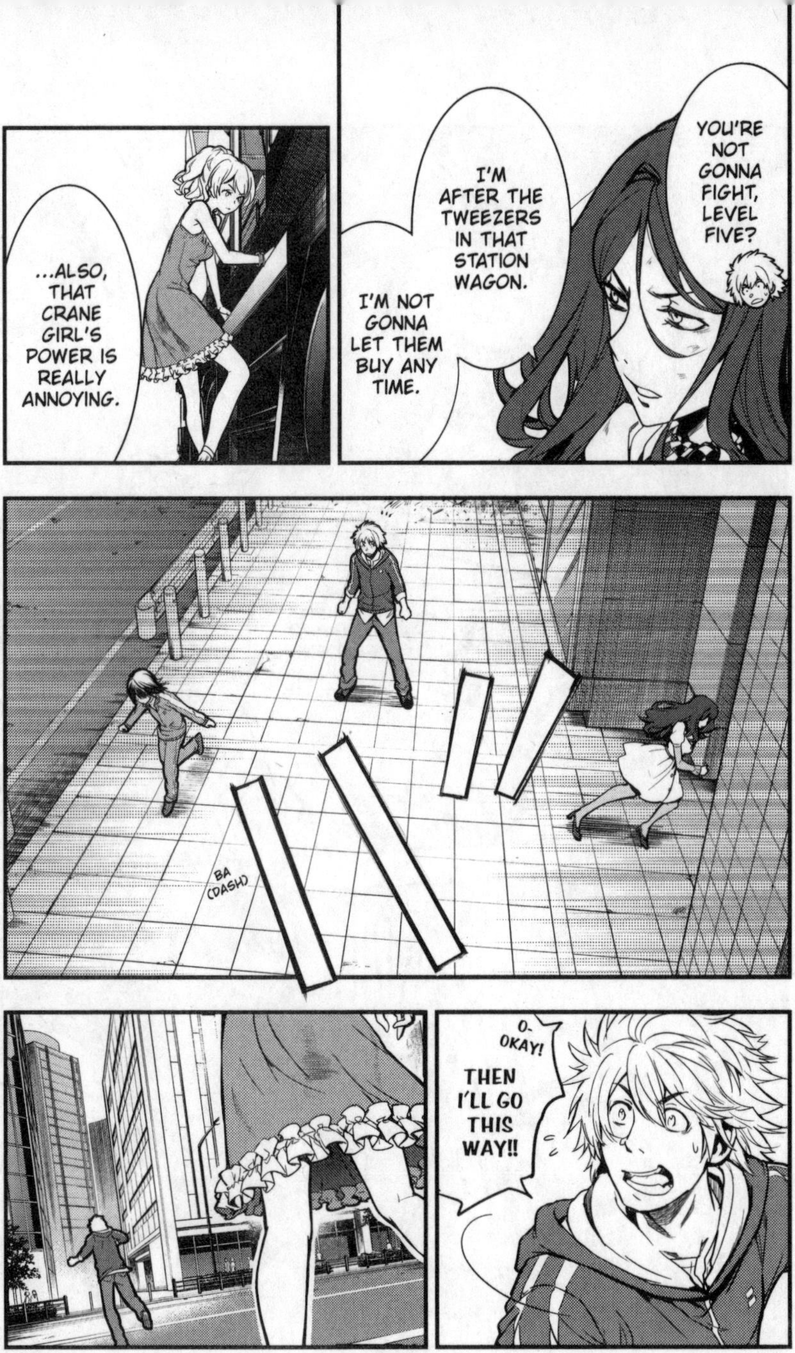
YOU'RE NOT GONNA FIGHT, LEVEL FIVE?
I'M AFTER THE TWEEZERS IN THAT STATION WAGON.
I'M NOT GONNA LET THEM BUY ANY TIME.
...ALSO, THAT CRANE GIRL'S POWER IS REALLY ANNOYING.
BA (DASH)
O-OKAY!
THEN I'LL GO THIS WAY!!

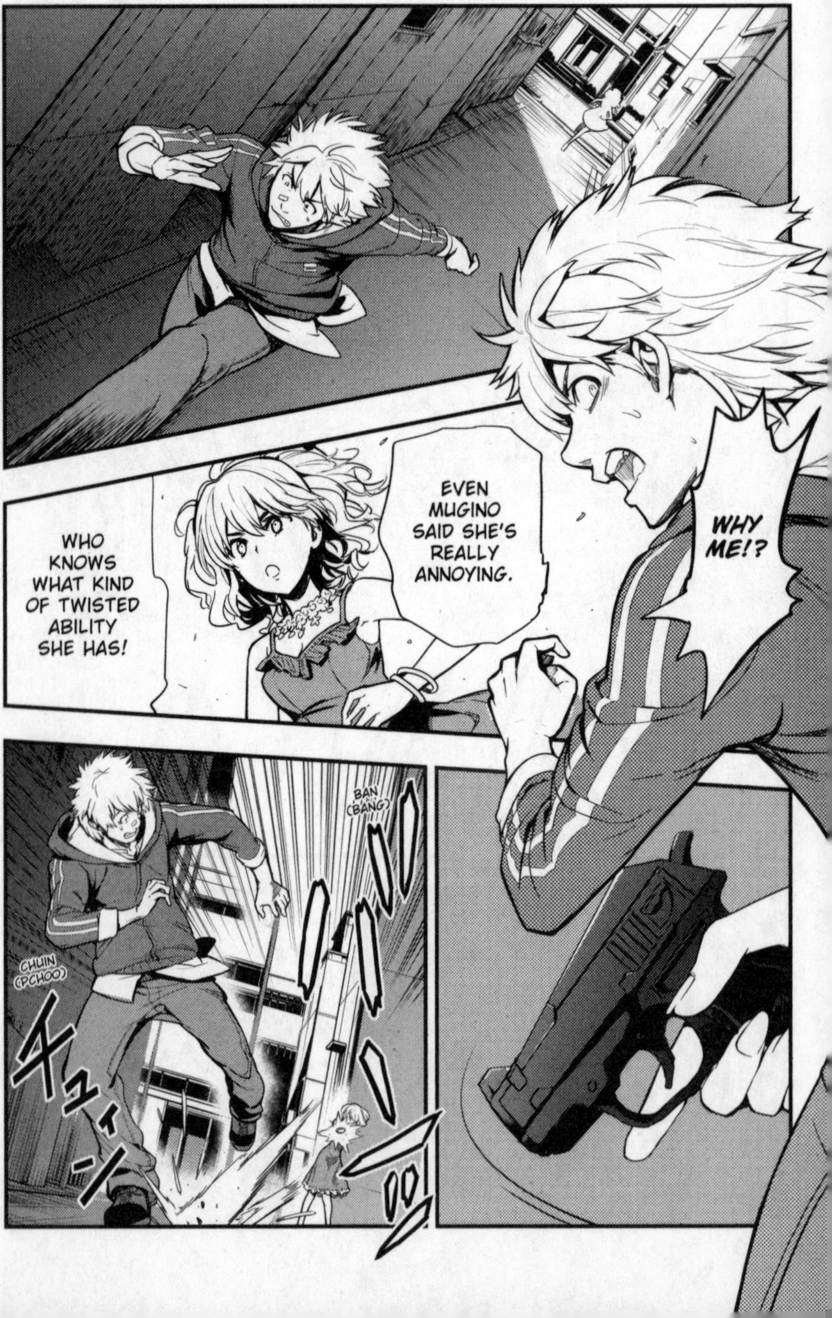
WHY ME!?
EVEN MUGINO SAID SHE'S REALLY ANNOYING.
WHO KNOWS WHAT KIND OF TWISTED ABILITY SHE HAS!
BAN (BANG)
CHUIN (PCHOO)

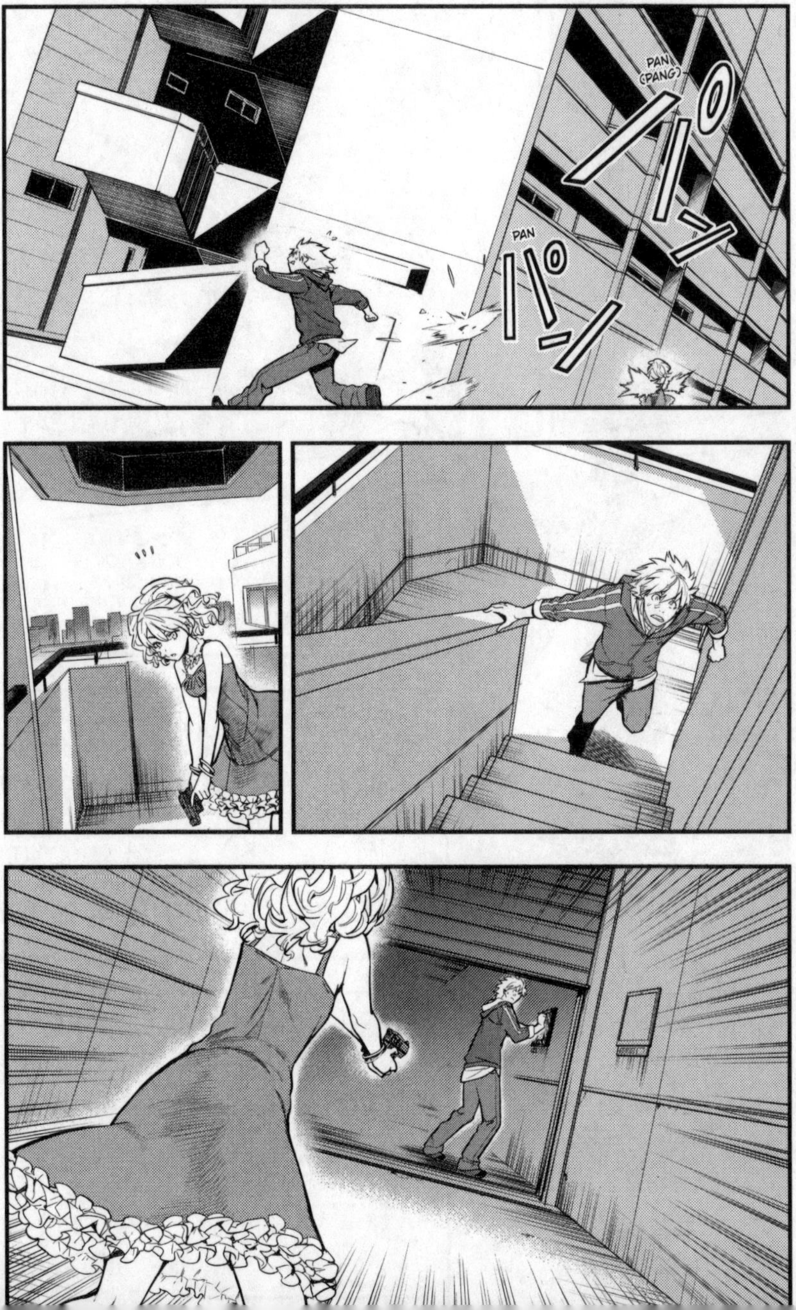
PAN (PANG)
パーン
PAN
パーン

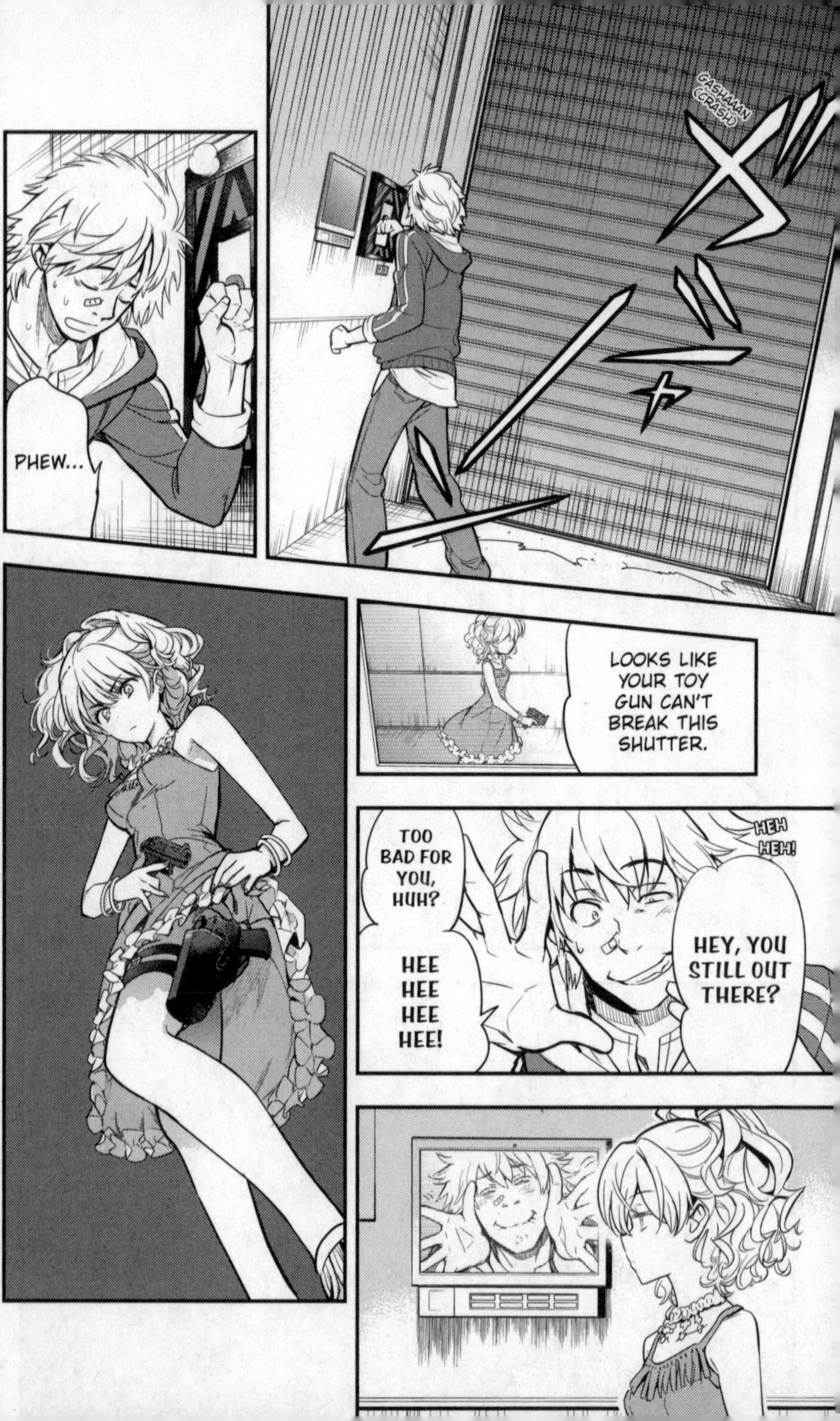
GASHAAAN (CRASH)
PHEW...
LOOKS LIKE YOUR TOY GUN CAN'T BREAK THIS SHUTTER.
HEH HEH!
HEY, YOU STILL OUT THERE?
TOO BAD FOR YOU, HUH?
HEE HEE HEE HEE!

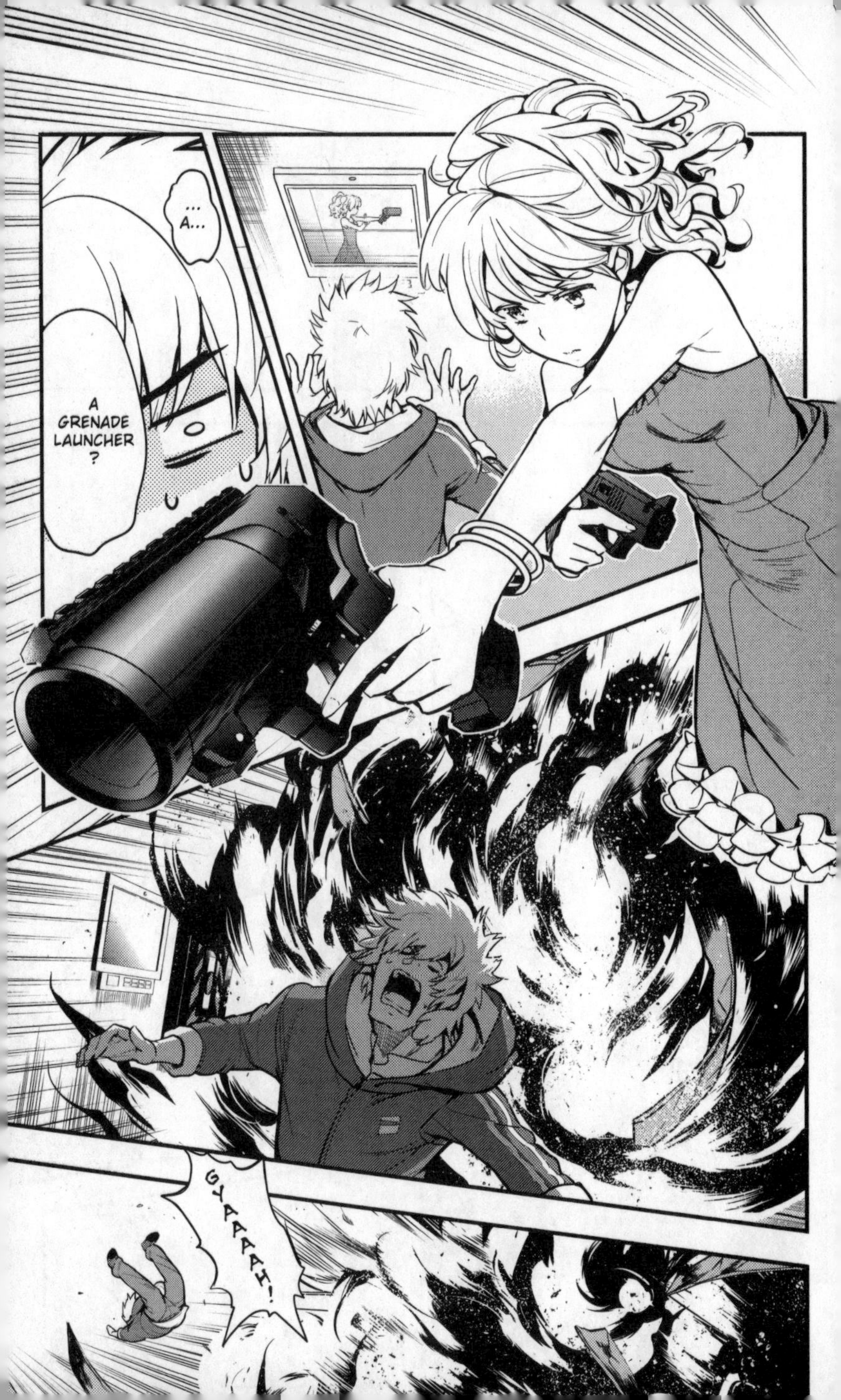
...A...
A GRENADE LAUNCHER?
GYAAAAAH!

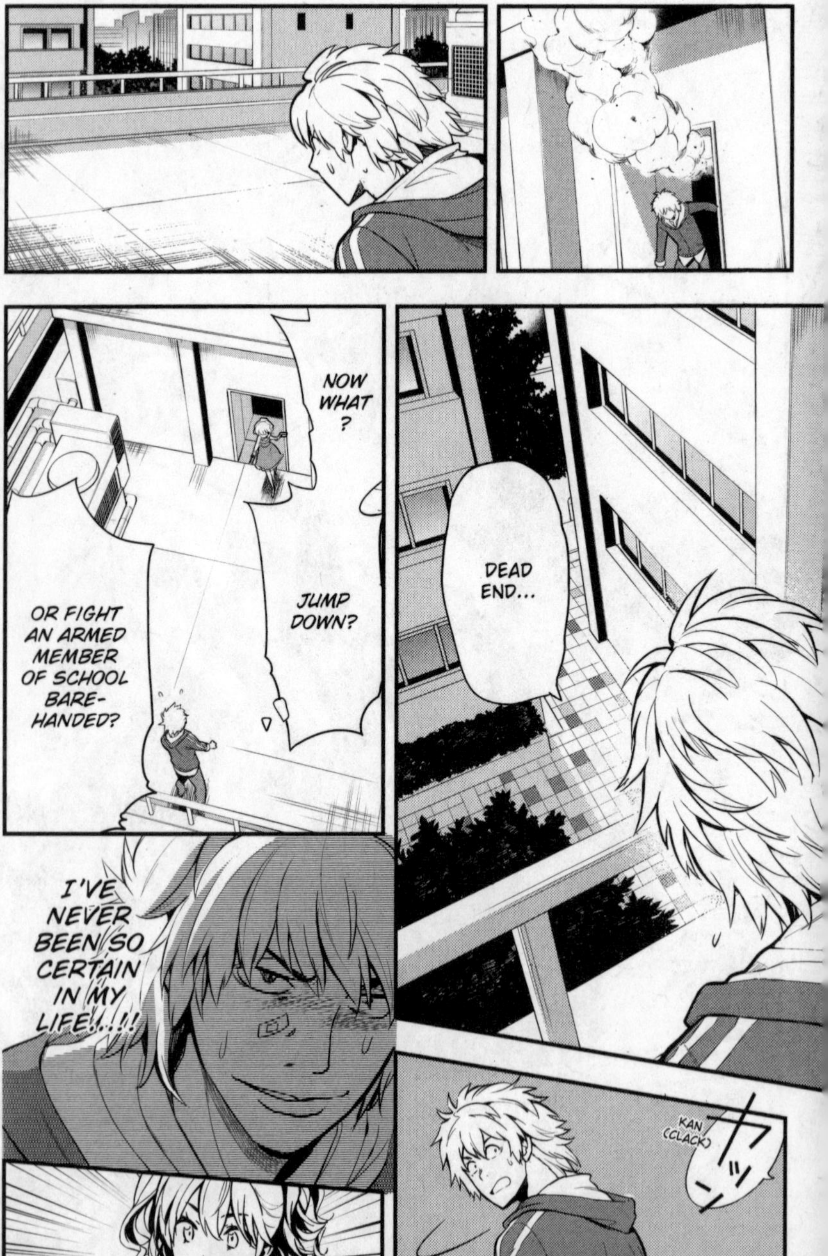
DEAD END...
NOW WHAT?
JUMP DOWN?
OR FIGHT AN ARMED MEMBER OF SCHOOL BARE-HANDED?
I'VE NEVER BEEN SO CERTAIN IN MY LIFE!!!!!
KAN (CLACK)

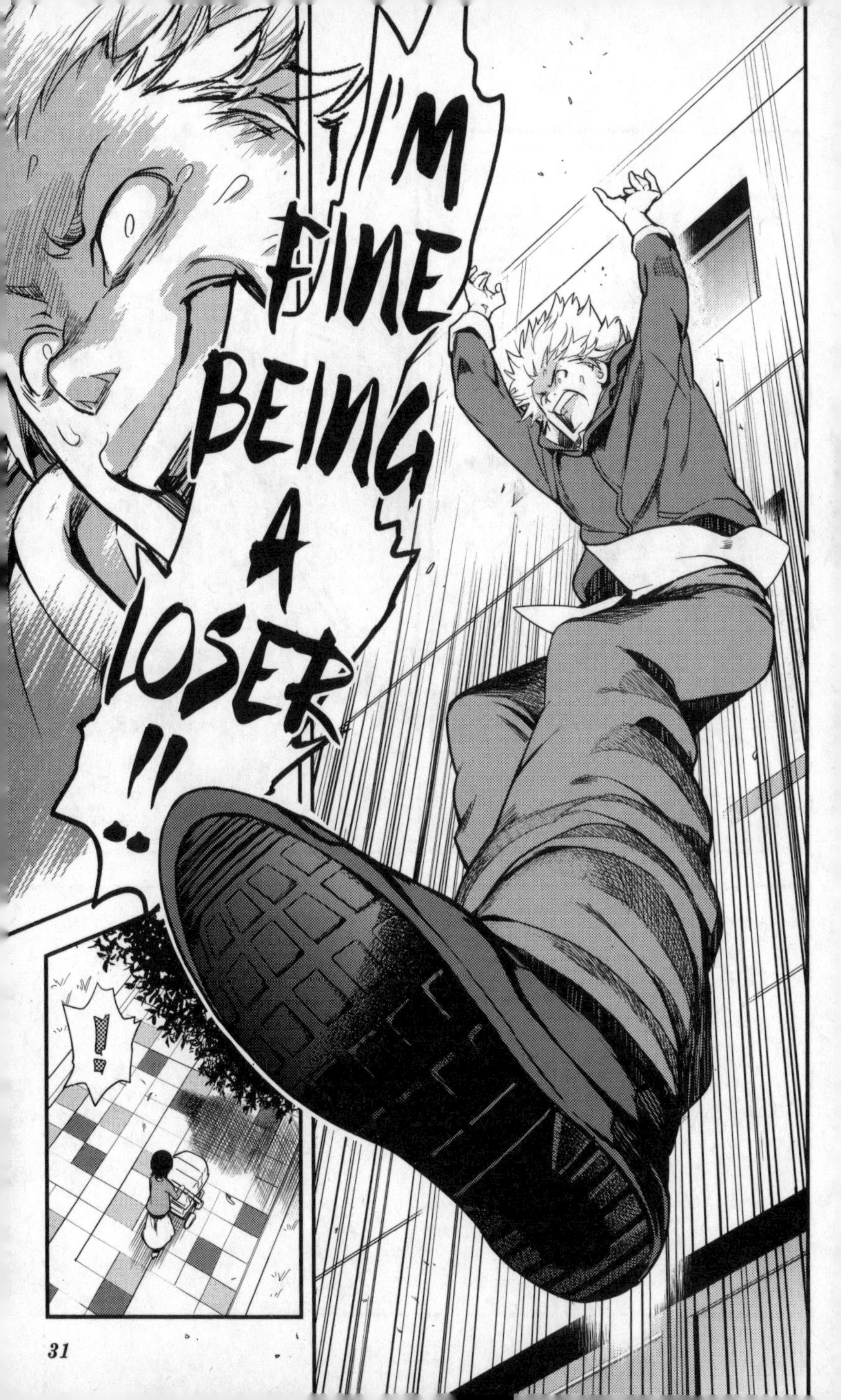
I'M FINE BEING A LOSER!!
!

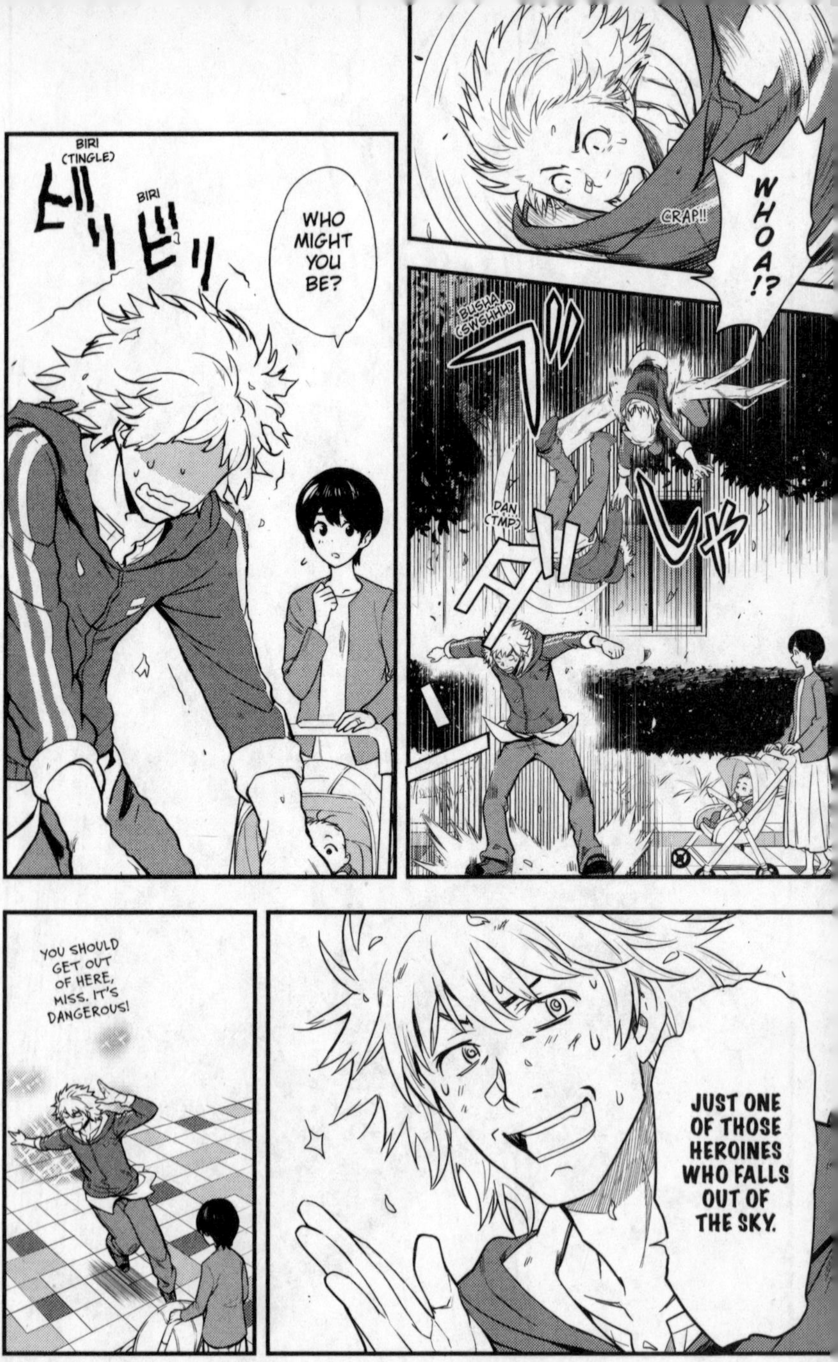
WHOA!?
CRAP!!
BUSHA (SWSHH)
DAN (TMP)
BIRI (TINGLE)
BIRI
WHO MIGHT YOU BE?
JUST ONE OF THOSE HEROINES WHO FALLS OUT OF THE SKY.
YOU SHOULD GET OUT OF HERE, MISS. IT'S DANGEROUS!

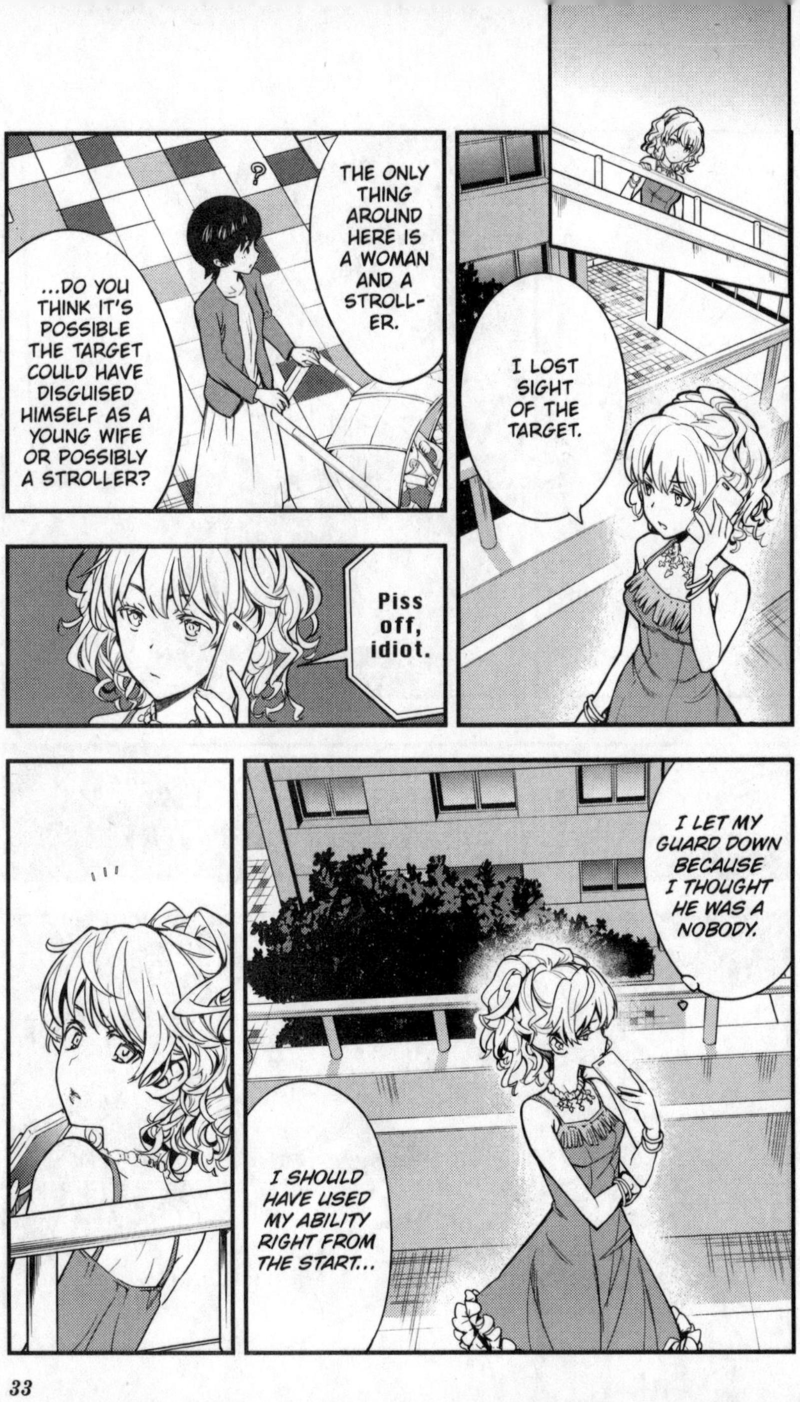
I LOST SIGHT OF THE TARGET.
THE ONLY THING AROUND HERE IS A WOMAN AND A STROLL-ER.
...DO YOU THINK IT'S POSSIBLE THE TARGET COULD HAVE DISGUISED HIMSELF AS A YOUNG WIFE OR POSSIBLY A STROLLER?
Piss off, idiot.
I LET MY GUARD DOWN BECAUSE I THOUGHT HE WAS A NOBODY.
I SHOULD HAVE USED MY ABILITY RIGHT FROM THE START...

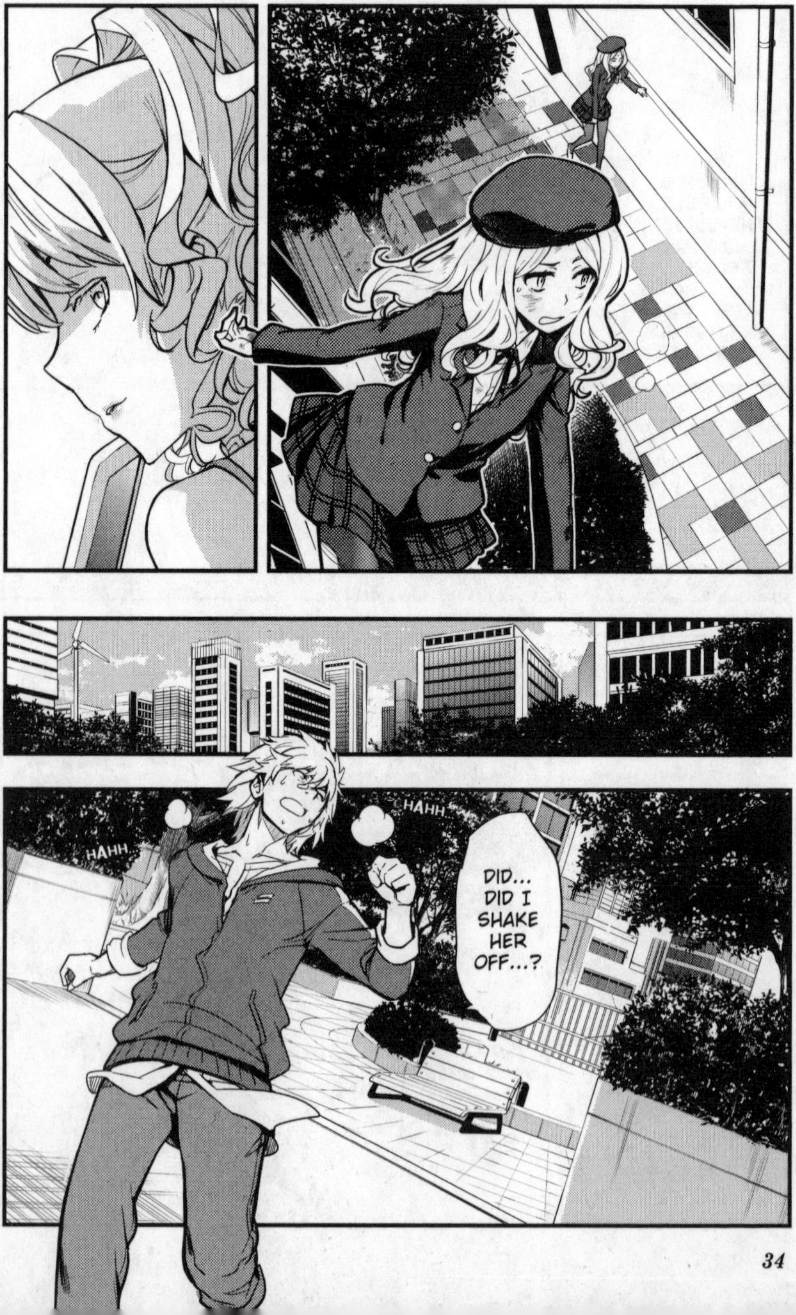
HAHH
HAHH
DID... DID I SHAKE HER OFF...?

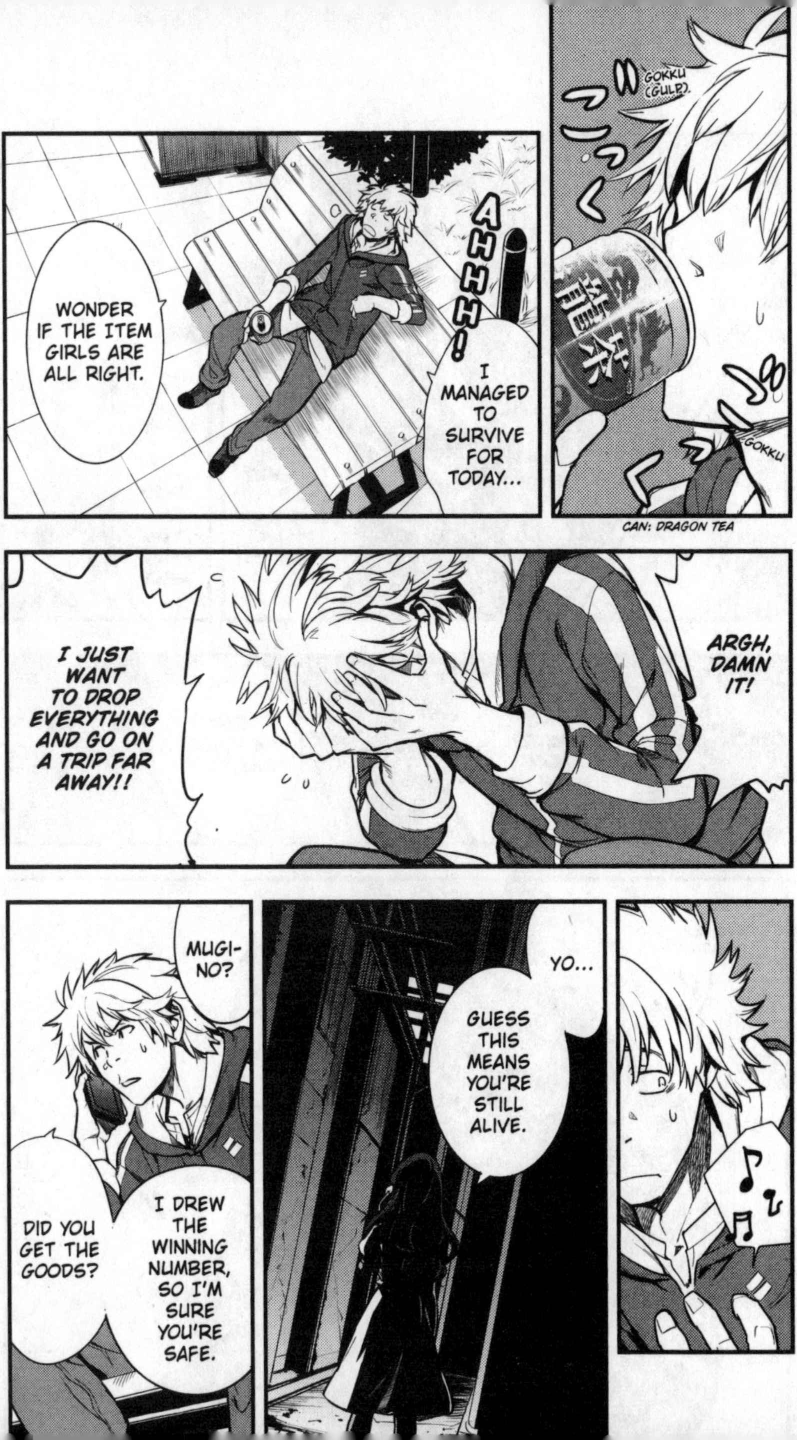
GOKKU (GULP)
GOKKU
CAN: DRAGON TEA
AHHHH!
I MANAGED TO SURVIVE FOR TODAY...
WONDER IF THE ITEM GIRLS ARE ALL RIGHT.
ARGH, DAMN IT!
I JUST WANT TO DROP EVERYTHING AND GO ON A TRIP FAR AWAY!!
YO...
GUESS THIS MEANS YOU'RE STILL ALIVE.
MUGI-NO?
I DREW THE WINNING NUMBER, SO I'M SURE YOU'RE SAFE.
DID YOU GET THE GOODS?

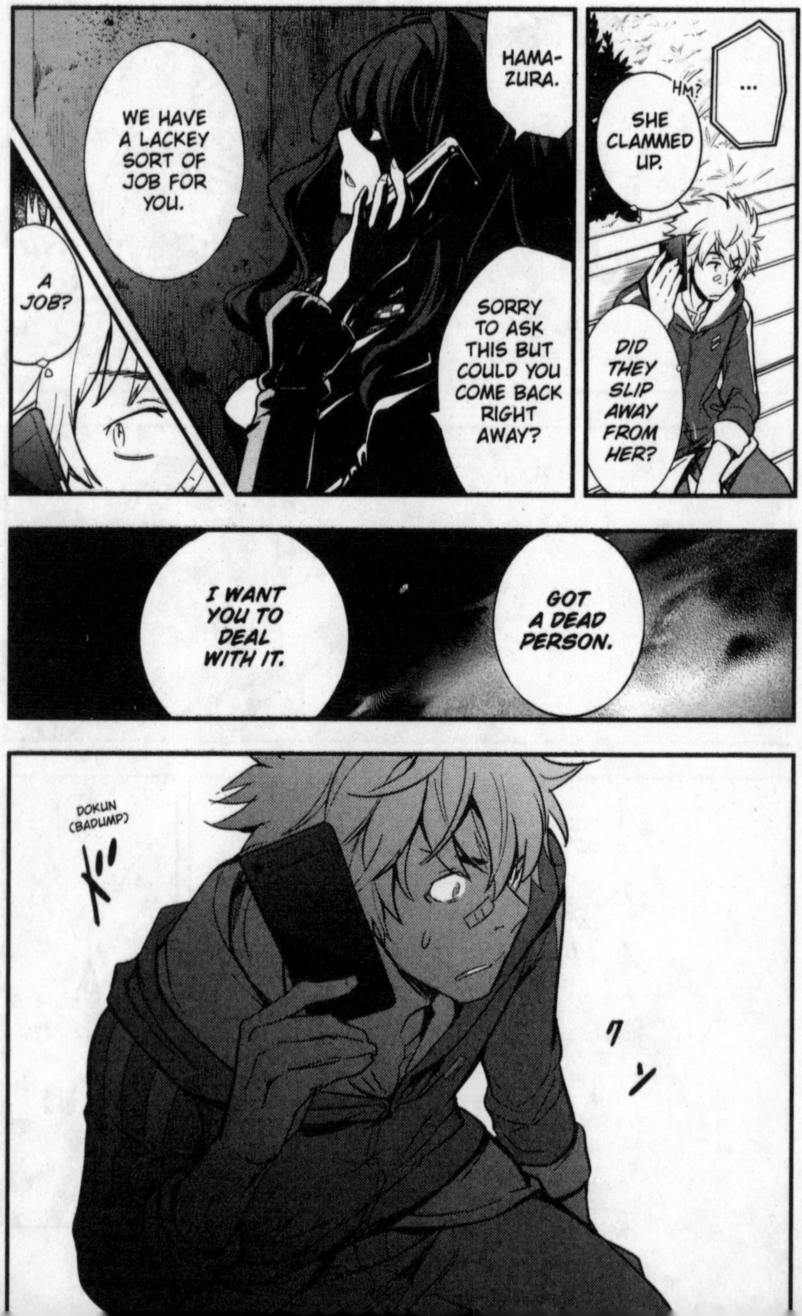
...
HM?
SHE CLAMMED UP.
DID THEY SLIP AWAY FROM HER?
HAMA-ZURA.
SORRY TO ASK THIS BUT COULD YOU COME BACK RIGHT AWAY?
WE HAVE A LACKEY SORT OF JOB FOR YOU.
A JOB?
GOT A DEAD PERSON.
I WANT YOU TO DEAL WITH IT.
クン
DOKUN (BADUMP)
ドッ

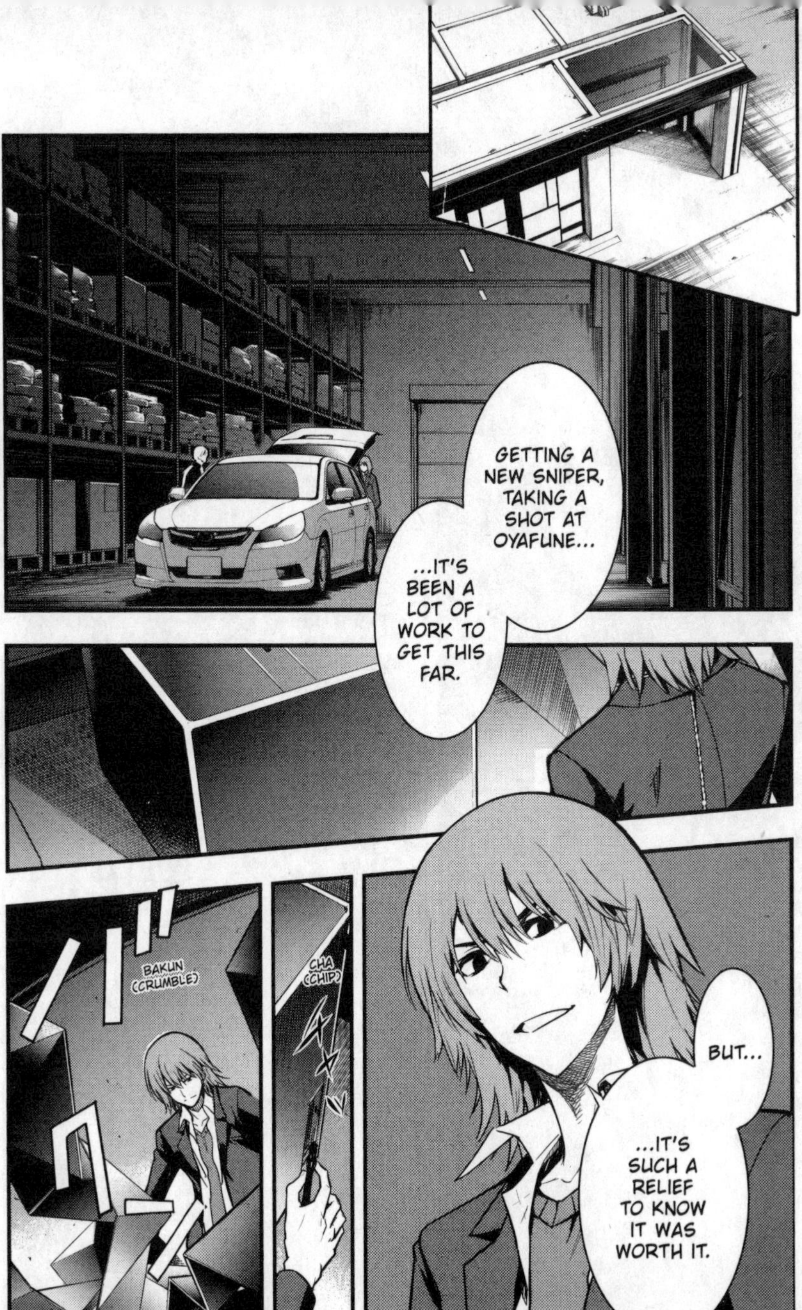
GETTING A NEW SNIPER, TAKING A SHOT AT OYAFUNE...
...IT'S BEEN A LOT OF WORK TO GET THIS FAR.
BUT...
...IT'S SUCH A RELIEF TO KNOW IT WAS WORTH IT.
CHA (CHIP)
BAKUN (CRUMBLE)

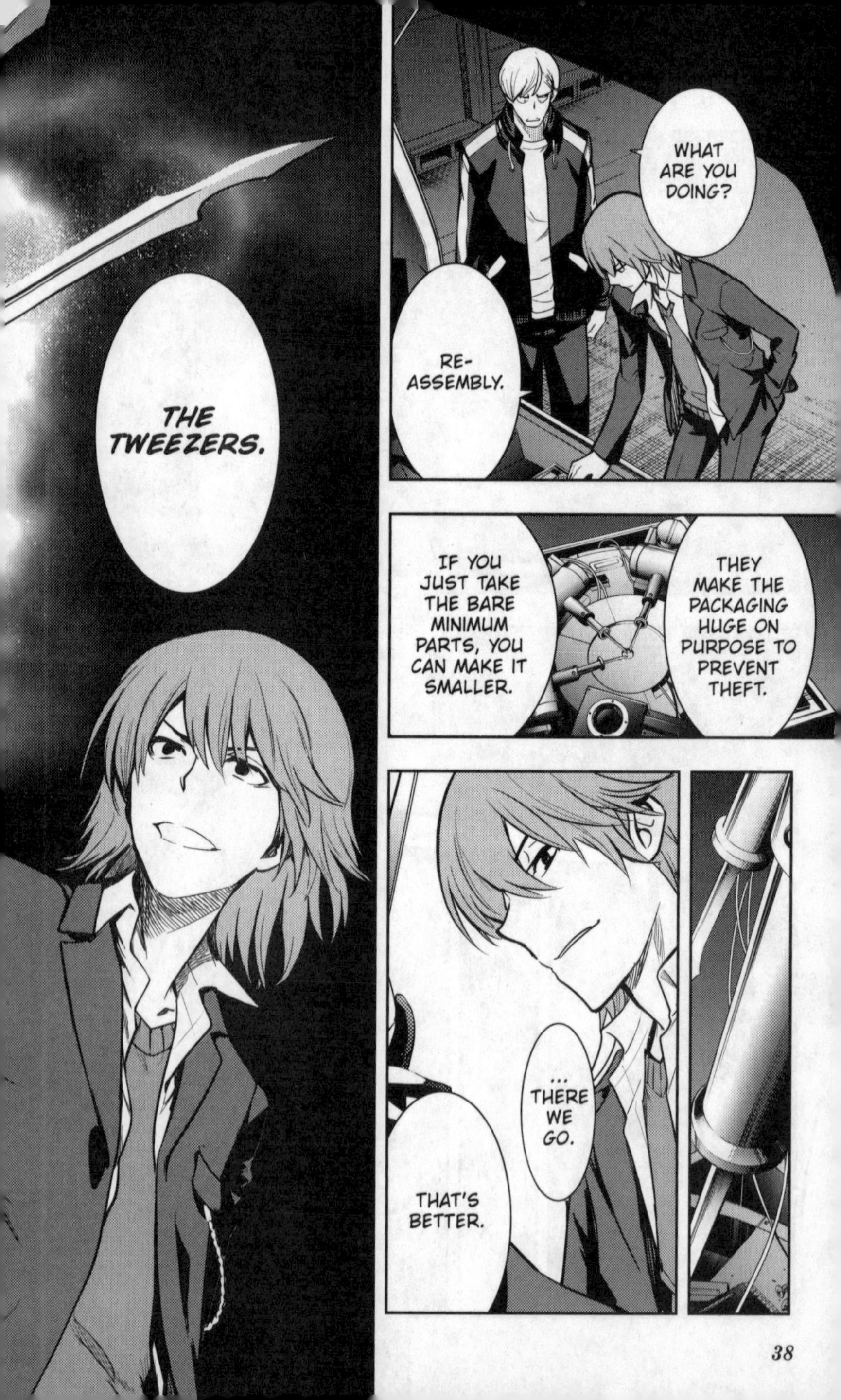
WHAT ARE YOU DOING?
RE-ASSEMBLY.
THEY MAKE THE PACKAGING HUGE ON PURPOSE TO PREVENT THEFT.
IF YOU JUST TAKE THE BARE MINIMUM PARTS, YOU CAN MAKE IT SMALLER.
... THERE WE GO.
THAT'S BETTER.
THE TWEEZERS.

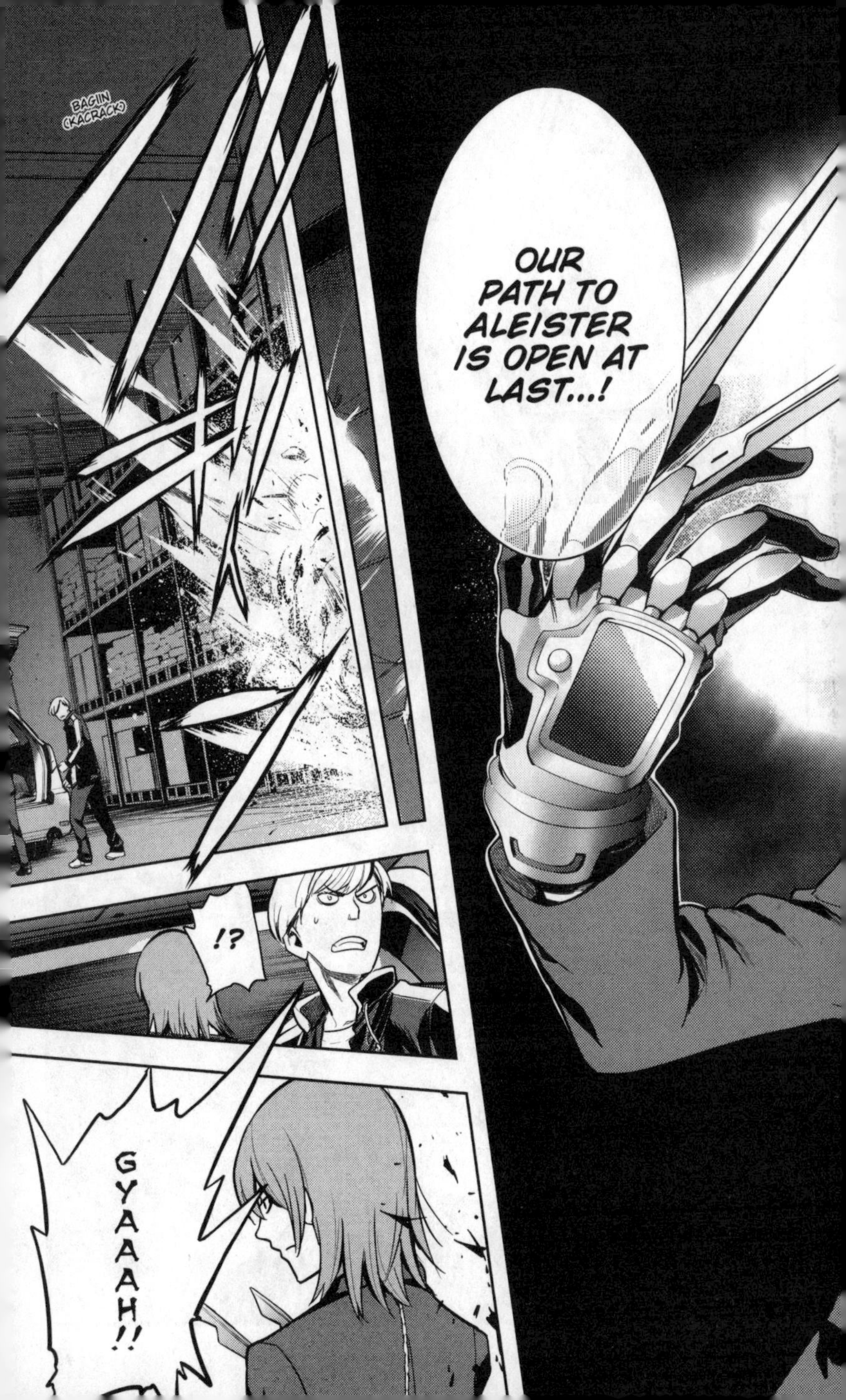
OUR PATH TO ALEISTER IS OPEN AT LAST...!
BAGIIN (KACRACK)
!?
GYAAAH!!

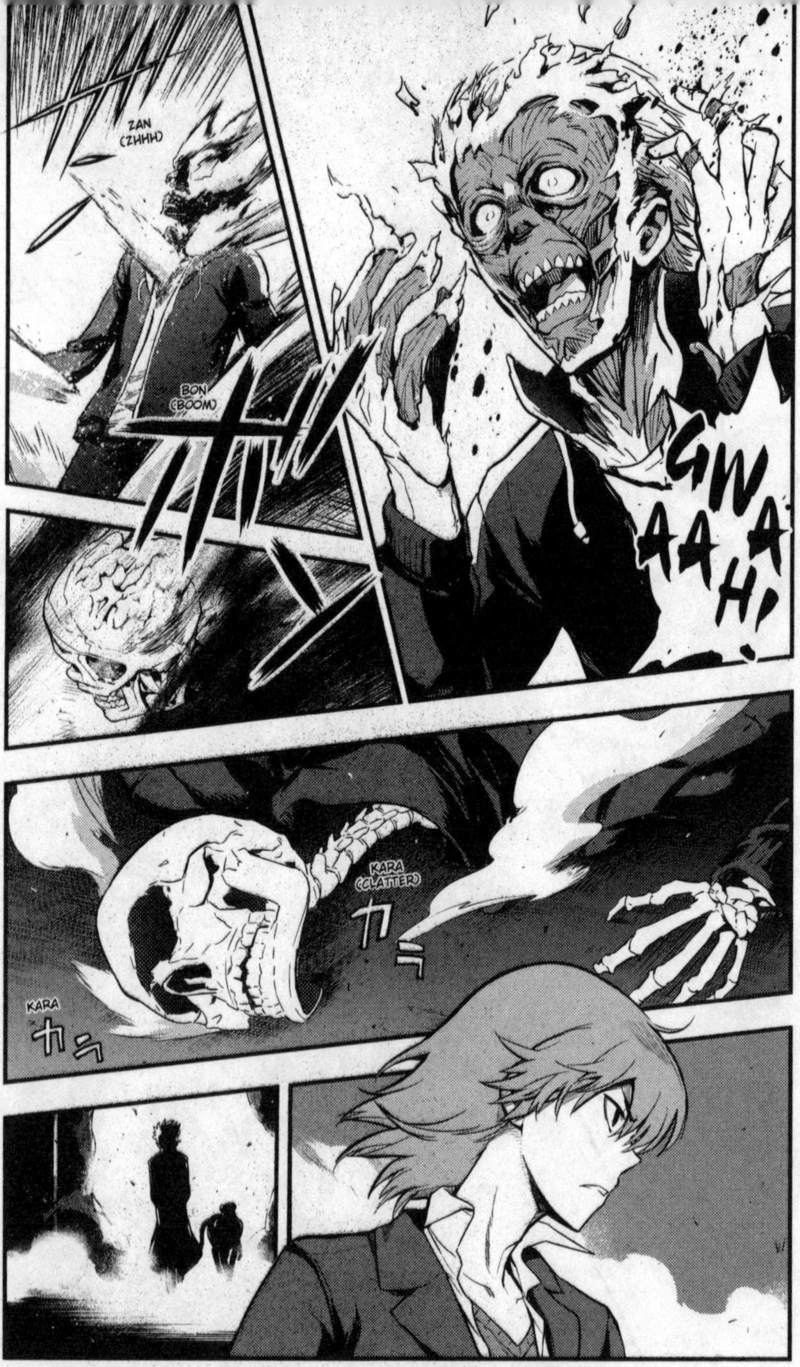
GWAAAAH!
ZAN (ZHHH)
BON (BOOM)
KARA (CLATTER)
カラ
KARA
カラ

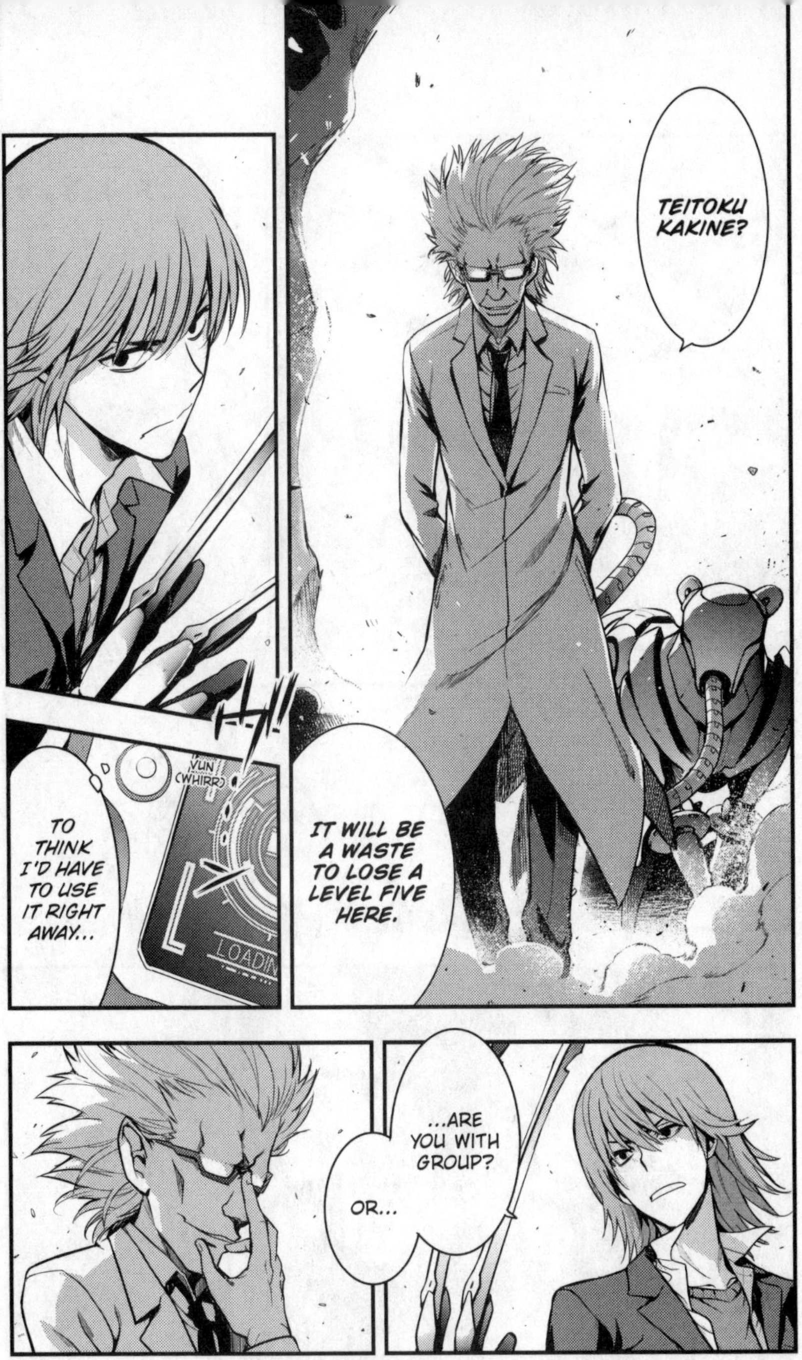
TEITOKU KAKINE?
IT WILL BE A WASTE TO LOSE A LEVEL FIVE HERE.
VUN (WHIRR)
TO THINK I'D HAVE TO USE IT RIGHT AWAY...
LOADIN
...ARE YOU WITH GROUP?
OR...

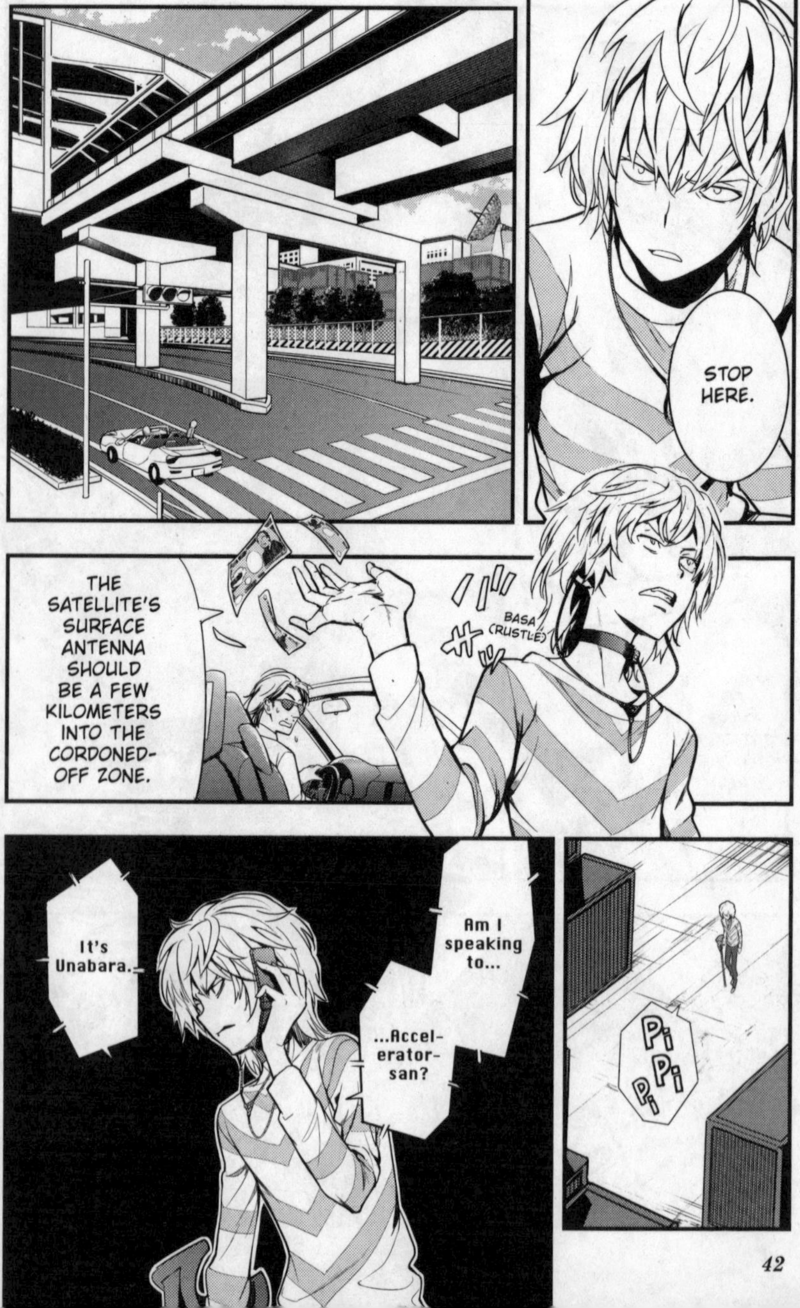
STOP HERE.
BASA (RUSTLE)
THE SATELLITE'S SURFACE ANTENNA SHOULD BE A FEW KILOMETERS INTO THE CORDONED-OFF ZONE.
Pi Pi Pi
It's Unabara.
Am I speaking to...
...Accel-erator-san?

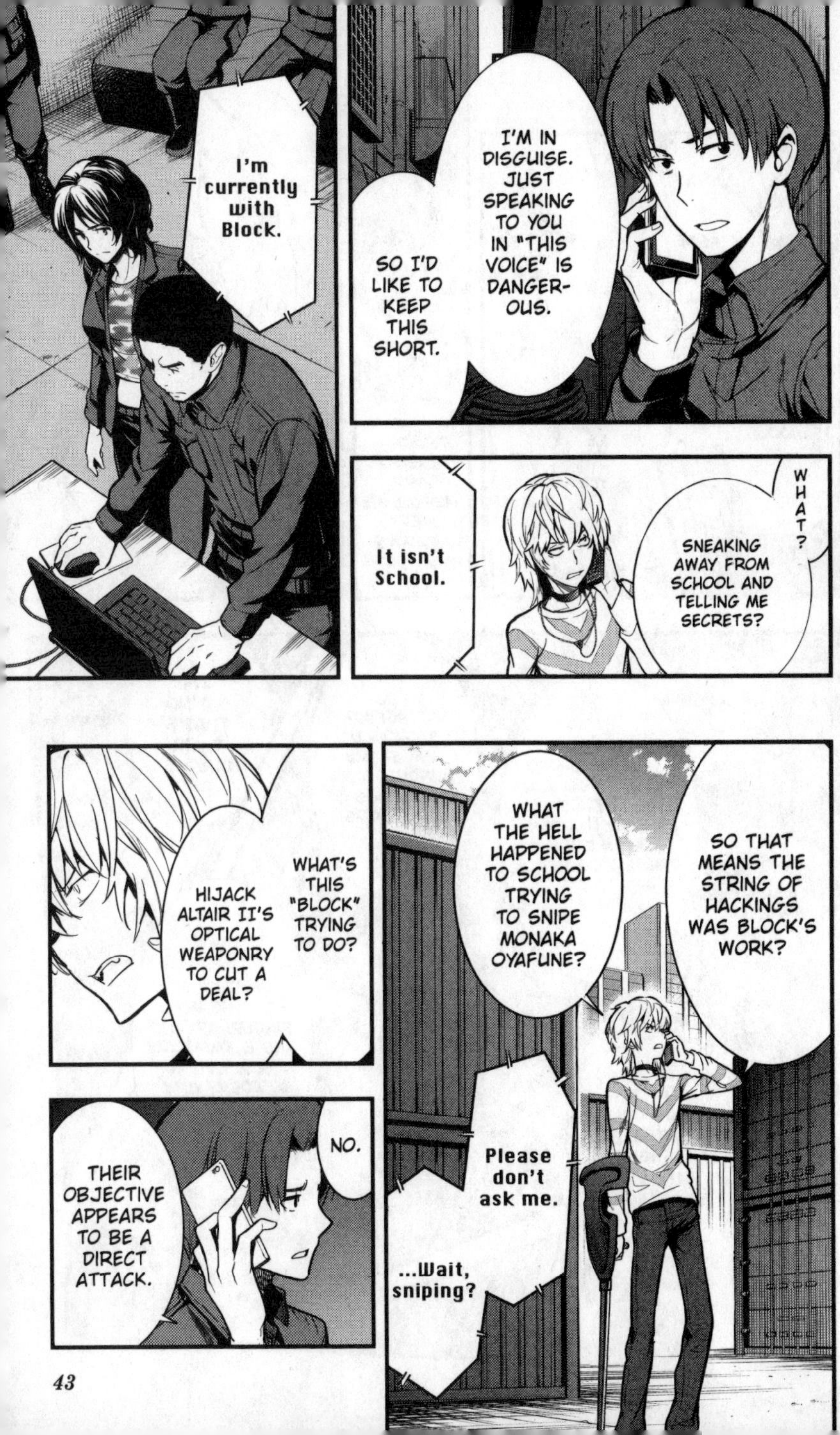
I'M IN DISGUISE. JUST SPEAKING TO YOU IN "THIS VOICE" IS DANGEROUS.
SO I'D LIKE TO KEEP THIS SHORT.
WHAT?
SNEAKING AWAY FROM SCHOOL AND TELLING ME SECRETS?
It isn't School.
I'm currently with Block.
SO THAT MEANS THE STRING OF HACKINGS WAS BLOCK'S WORK?
WHAT THE HELL HAPPENED TO SCHOOL TRYING TO SNIPE MONAKA OYAFUNE?
Please don't ask me.
...Wait, sniping?
WHAT'S THIS "BLOCK" TRYING TO DO?
HIJACK ALTAIR II'S OPTICAL WEAPONRY TO CUT A DEAL?
NO.
THEIR OBJECTIVE APPEARS TO BE A DIRECT ATTACK.

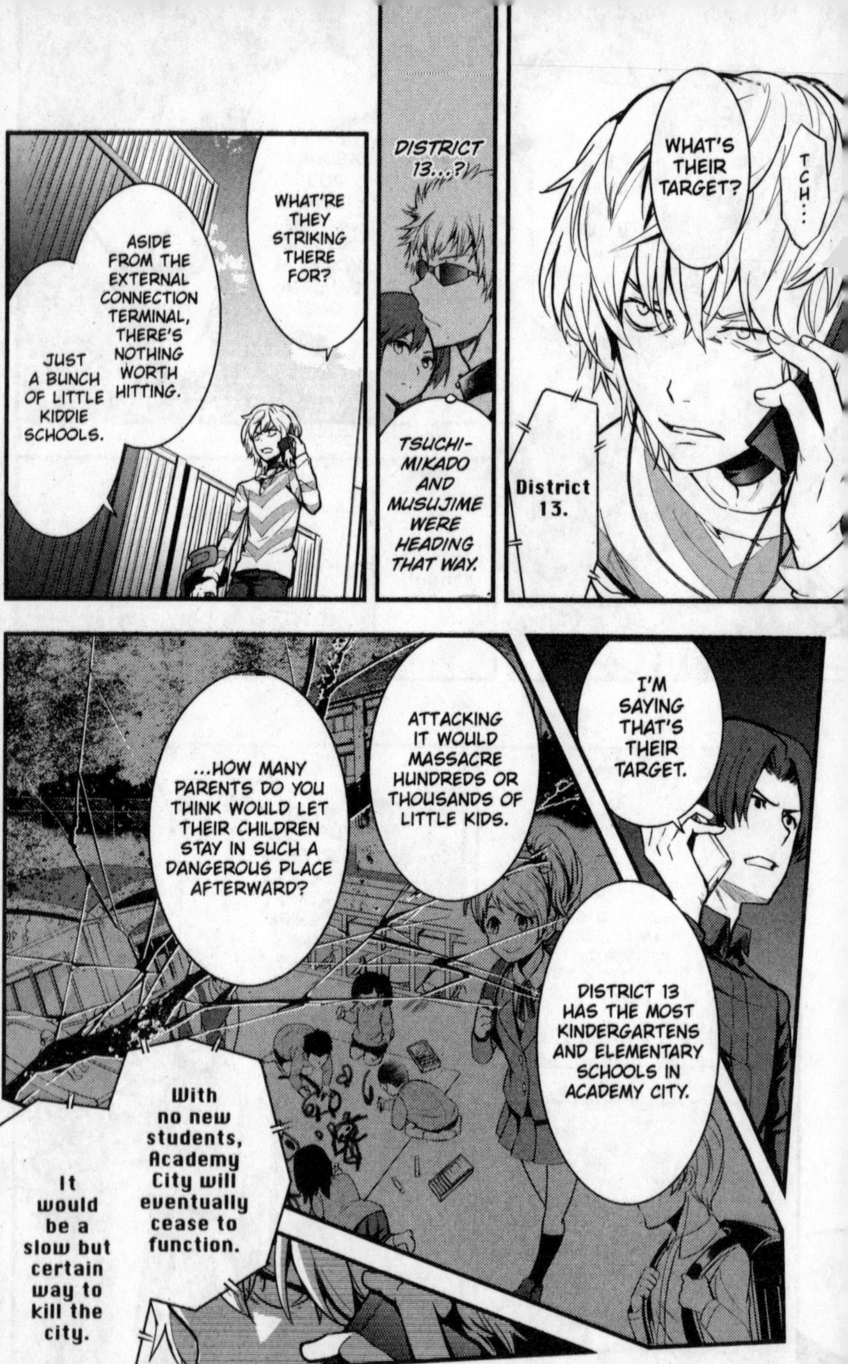
TCH...
WHAT'S THEIR TARGET?
District 13.
DISTRICT 13...?!
TSUCHIMIKADO AND MUSUJIME WERE HEADING THAT WAY.
WHAT'RE THEY STRIKING THERE FOR?
ASIDE FROM THE EXTERNAL CONNECTION TERMINAL, THERE'S NOTHING WORTH HITTING.
JUST A BUNCH OF LITTLE KIDDIE SCHOOLS.
I'M SAYING THAT'S THEIR TARGET.
DISTRICT 13 HAS THE MOST KINDERGARTENS AND ELEMENTARY SCHOOLS IN ACADEMY CITY.
ATTACKING IT WOULD MASSACRE HUNDREDS OR THOUSANDS OF LITTLE KIDS.
...HOW MANY PARENTS DO YOU THINK WOULD LET THEIR CHILDREN STAY IN SUCH A DANGEROUS PLACE AFTERWARD?
With no new students, Academy City will eventually cease to function.
It would be a slow but certain way to kill the city.

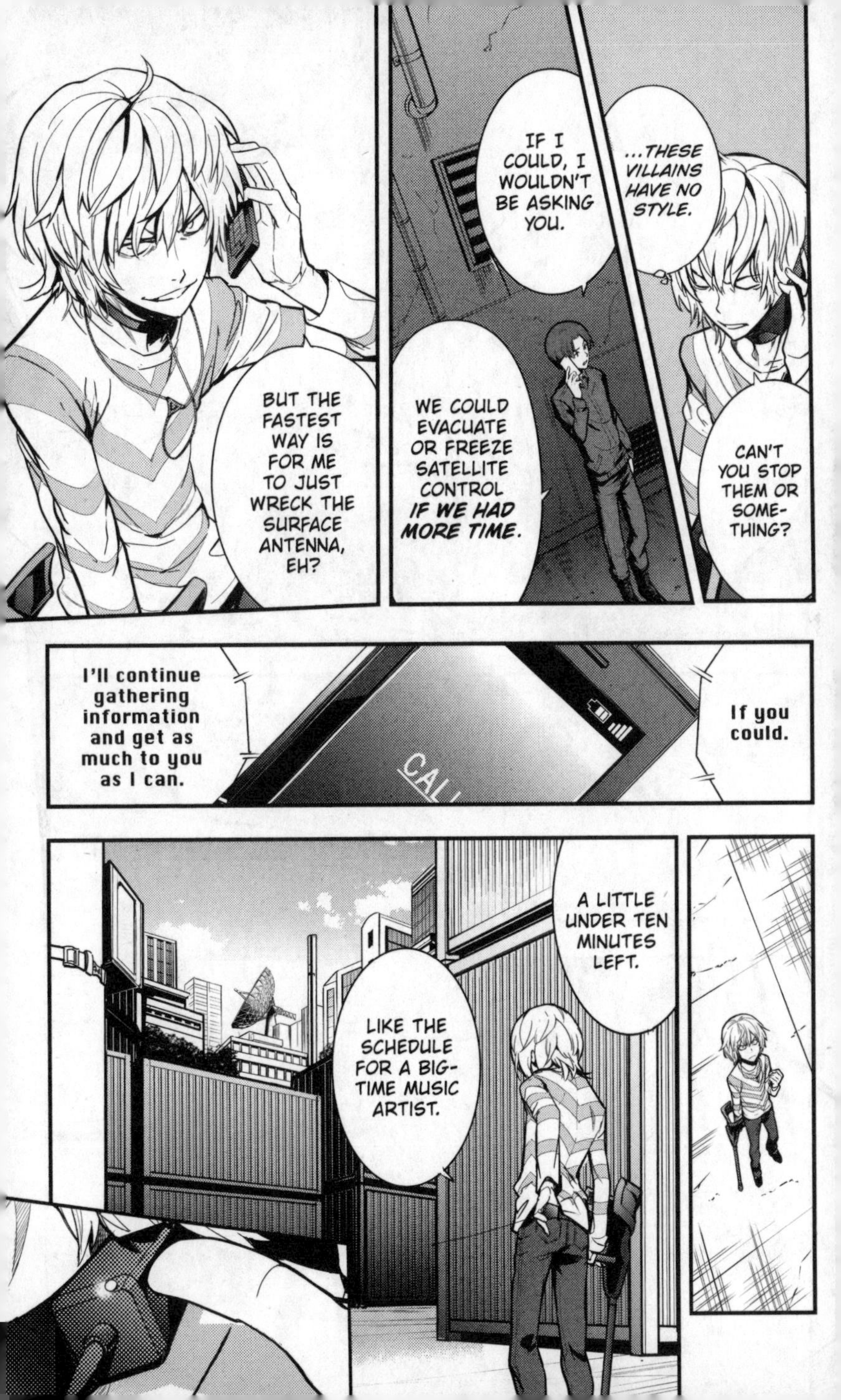
...THESE VILLAINS HAVE NO STYLE.
CAN'T YOU STOP THEM OR SOME-THING?
IF I COULD, I WOULDN'T BE ASKING YOU.
WE COULD EVACUATE OR FREEZE SATELLITE CONTROL *IF WE HAD MORE TIME.*
BUT THE FASTEST WAY IS FOR ME TO JUST WRECK THE SURFACE ANTENNA, EH?
I'll continue gathering information and get as much to you as I can.
If you could.
A LITTLE UNDER TEN MINUTES LEFT.
LIKE THE SCHEDULE FOR A BIG-TIME MUSIC ARTIST.

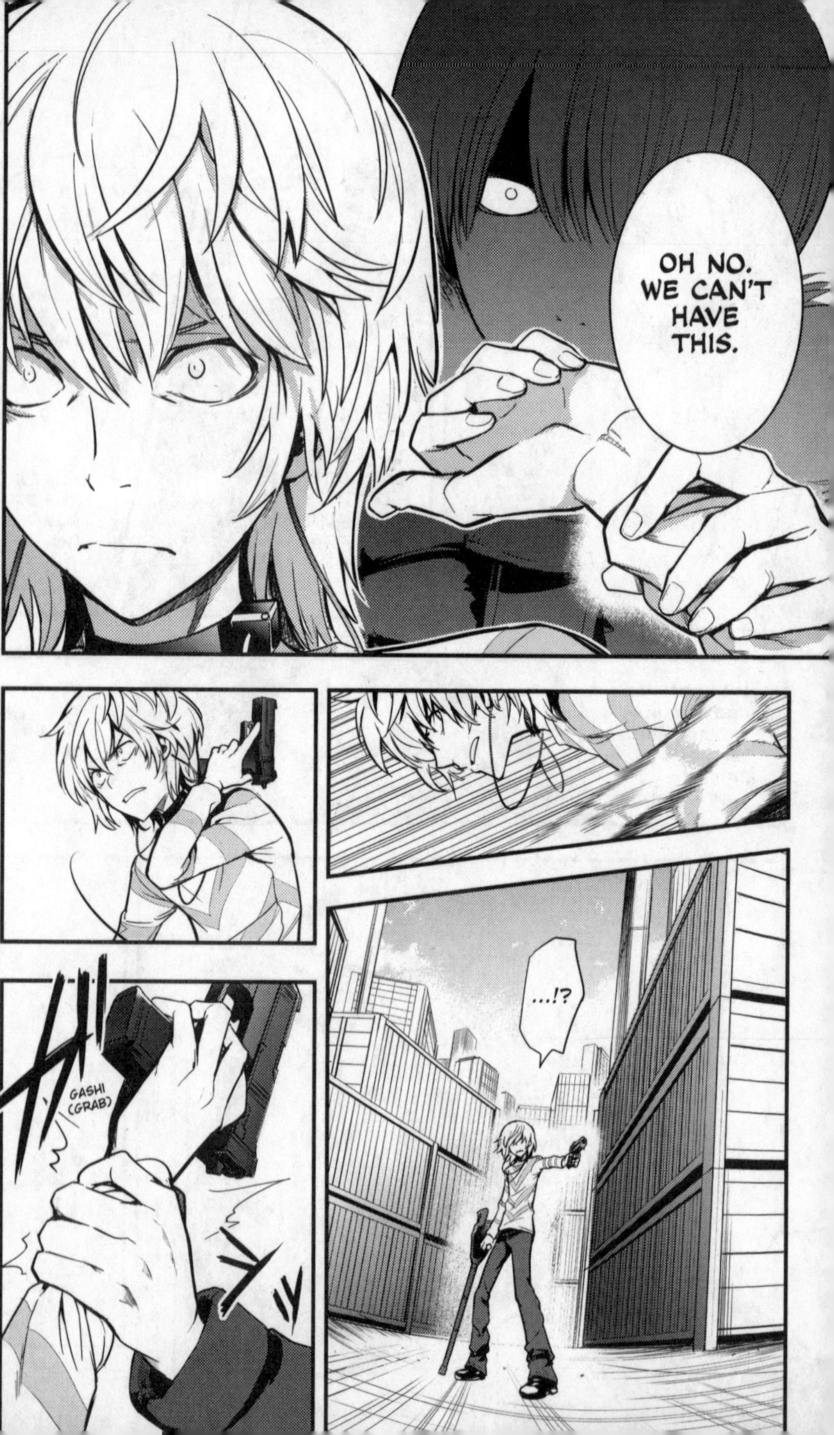
OH NO. WE CAN'T HAVE THIS.
...!?
GASHI (GRAB)

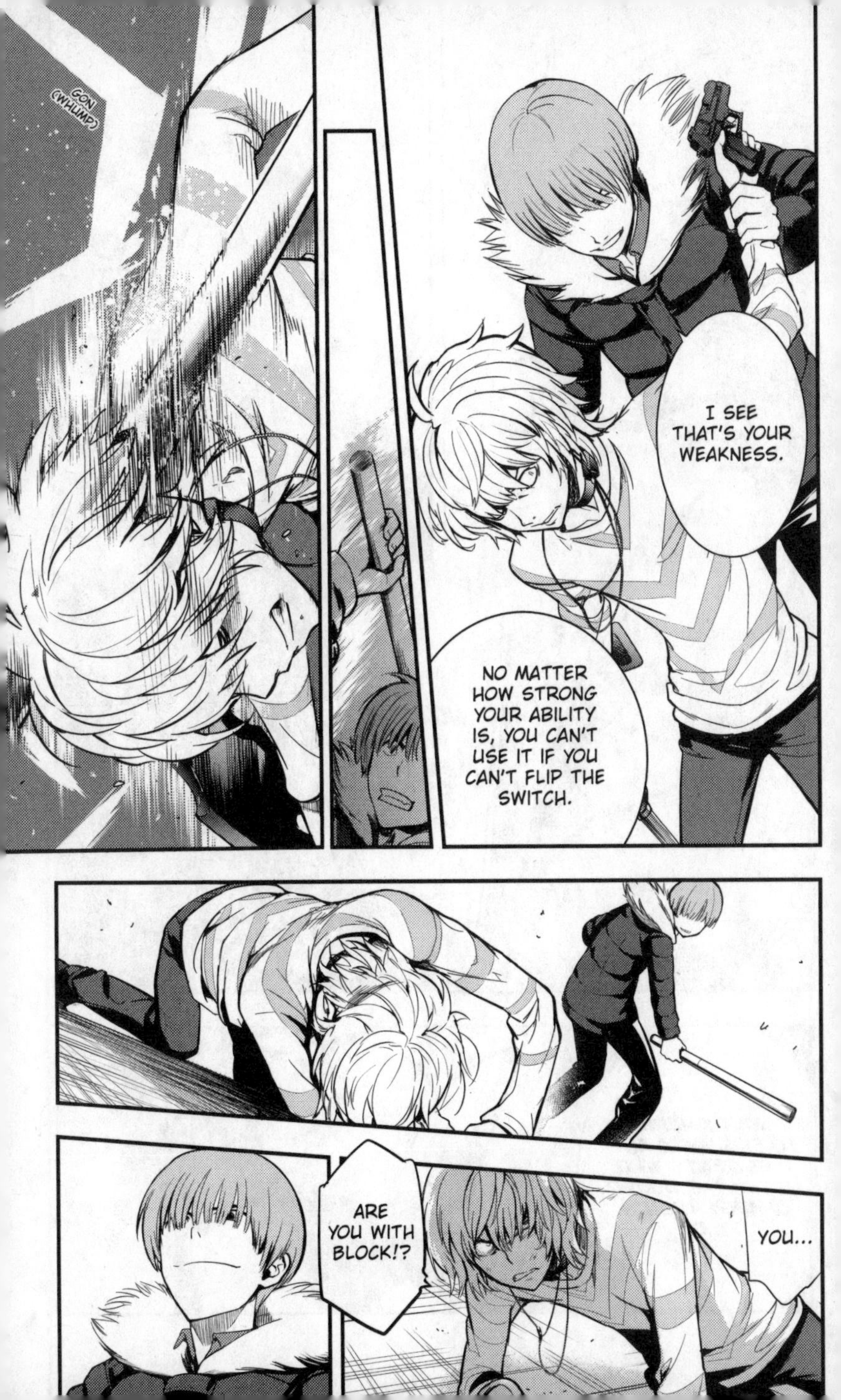
I SEE THAT'S YOUR WEAKNESS.
NO MATTER HOW STRONG YOUR ABILITY IS, YOU CAN'T USE IT IF YOU CAN'T FLIP THE SWITCH.
GON (WHUMP)
YOU...
ARE YOU WITH BLOCK!?

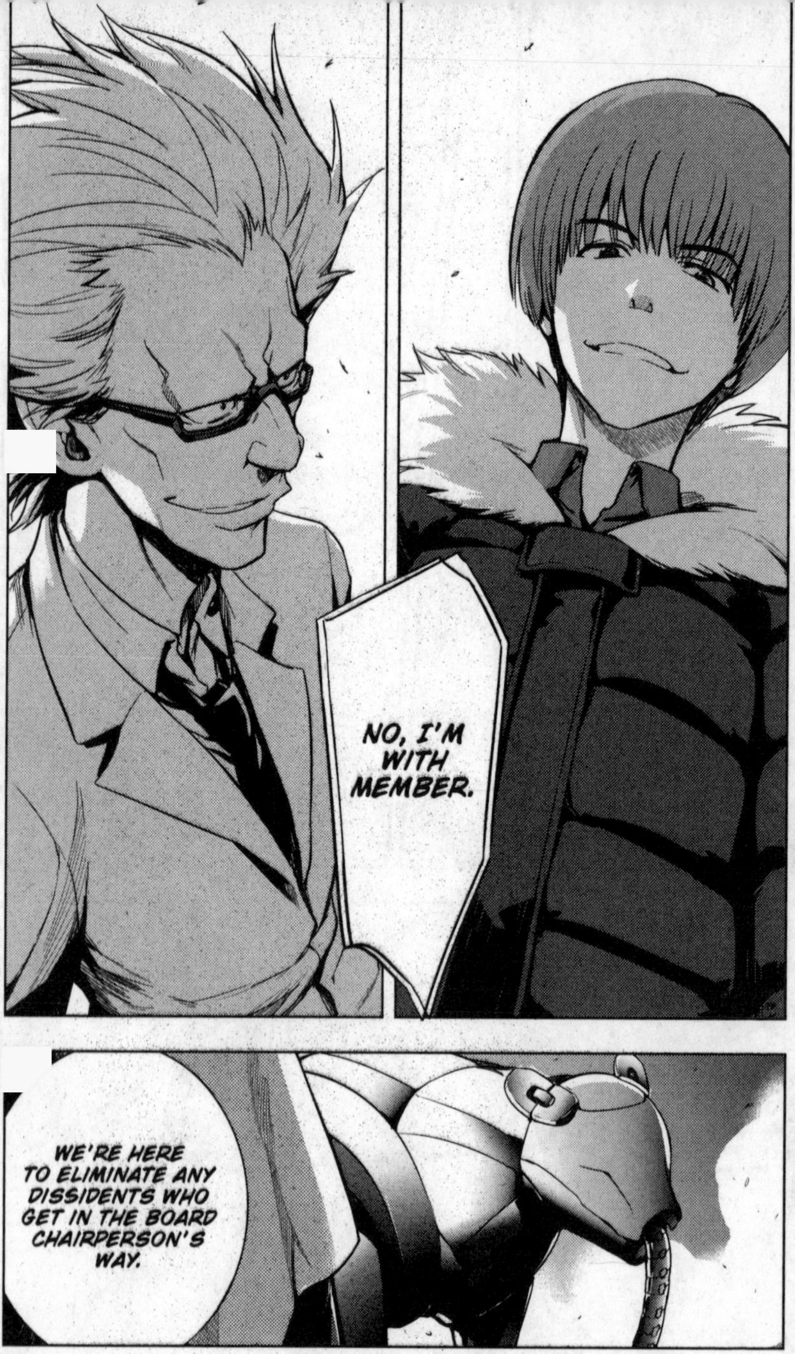
NO, I'M WITH MEMBER.
WE'RE HERE TO ELIMINATE ANY DISSIDENTS WHO GET IN THE BOARD CHAIRPERSON'S WAY.

A
Certain
Magical
Index

A Certain Magical Index

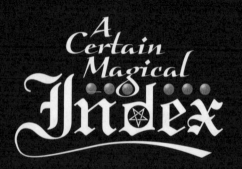

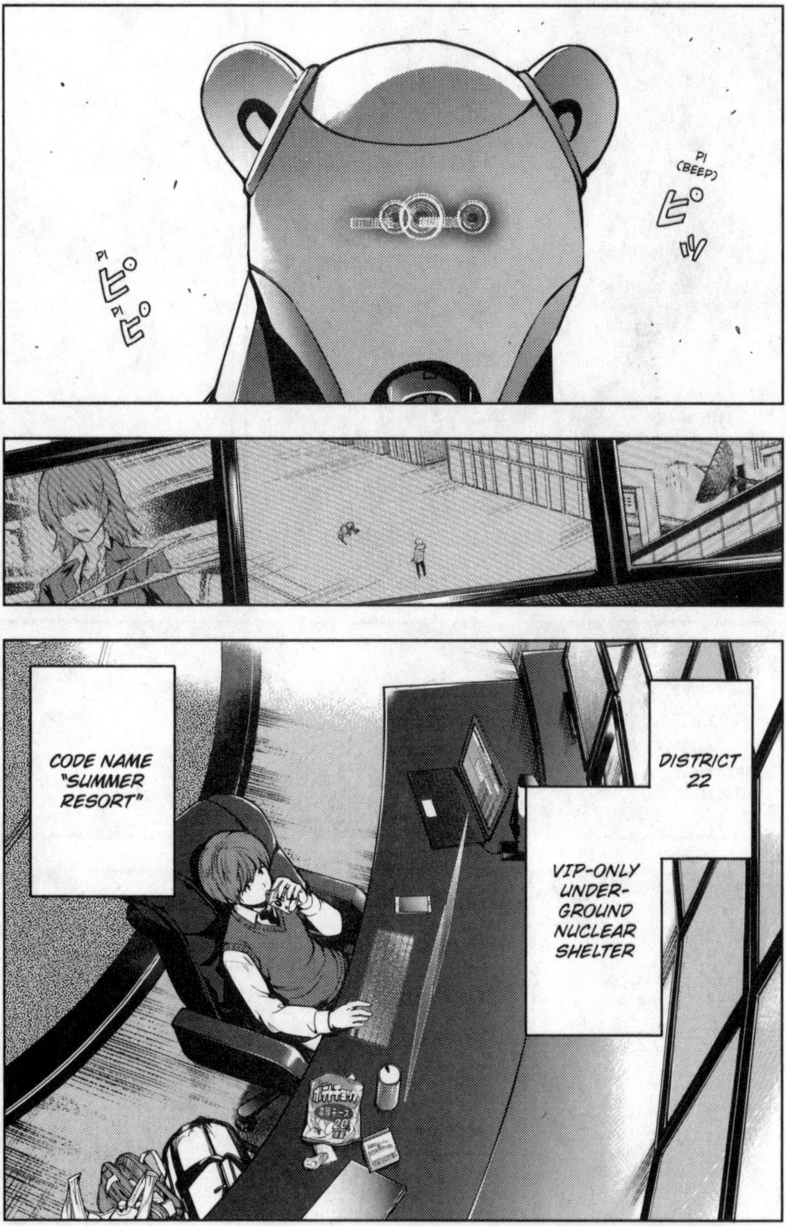
PI (BEEP)
PI
PI
DISTRICT 22
VIP-ONLY UNDER-GROUND NUCLEAR SHELTER
CODE NAME "SUMMER RESORT"
BAG: POTATO CHIPS / RICH CHEESE

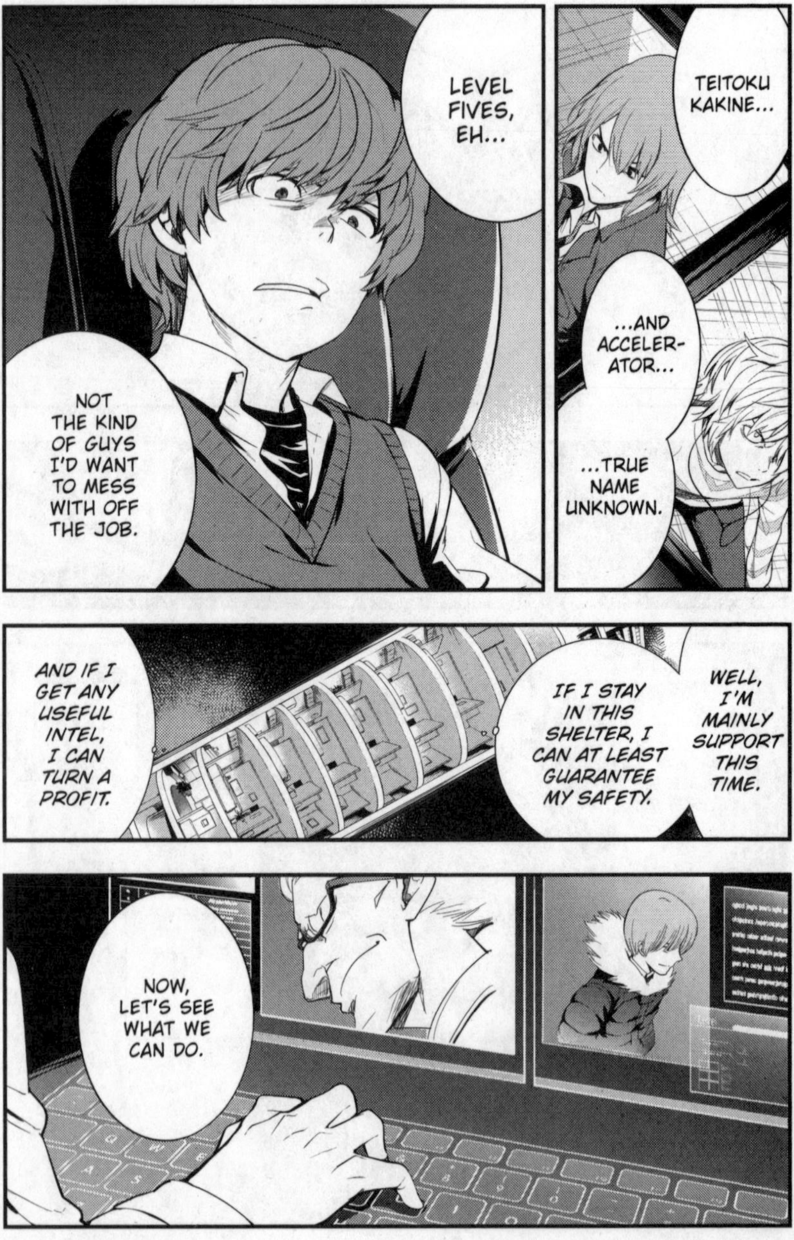
TEITOKU KAKINE...
...AND ACCELERATOR...
...TRUE NAME UNKNOWN.
LEVEL FIVES, EH...
NOT THE KIND OF GUYS I'D WANT TO MESS WITH OFF THE JOB.
WELL, I'M MAINLY SUPPORT THIS TIME.
IF I STAY IN THIS SHELTER, I CAN AT LEAST GUARANTEE MY SAFETY.
AND IF I GET ANY USEFUL INTEL, I CAN TURN A PROFIT.
NOW, LET'S SEE WHAT WE CAN DO.

# #138 DISTRICT 4 COLD STORAGE ROOM

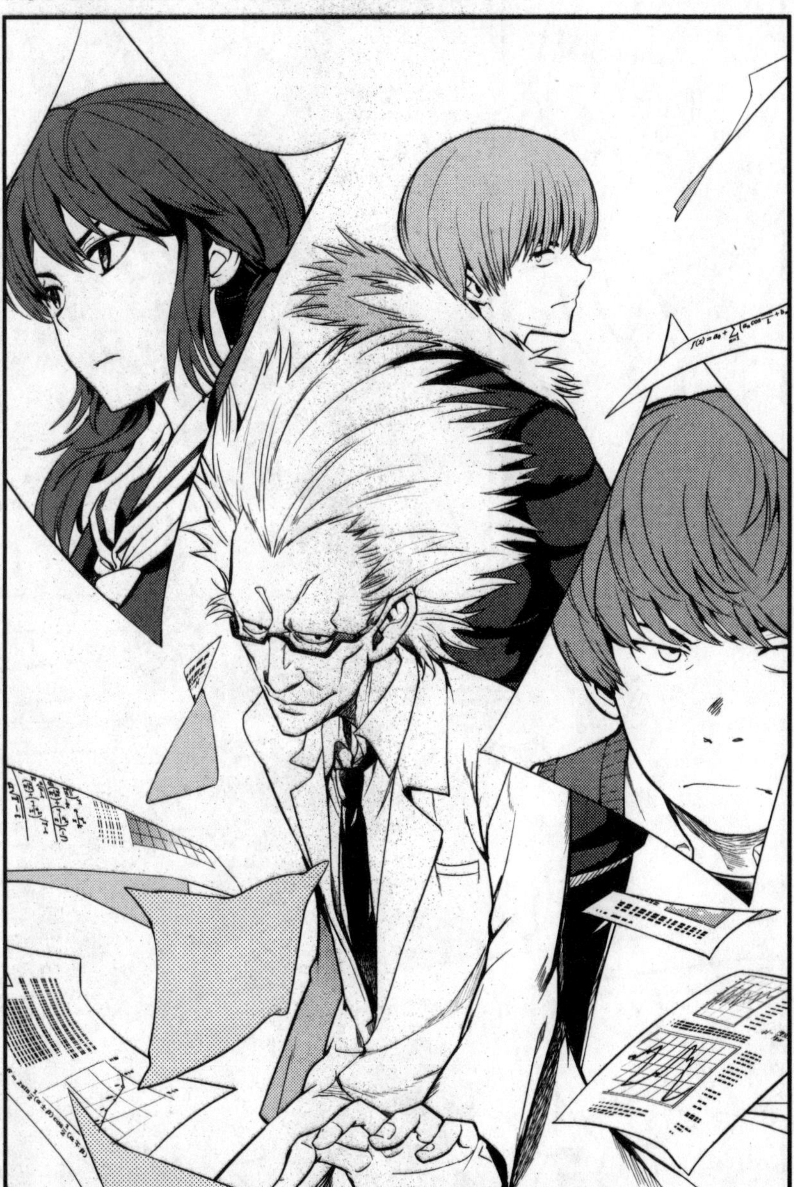

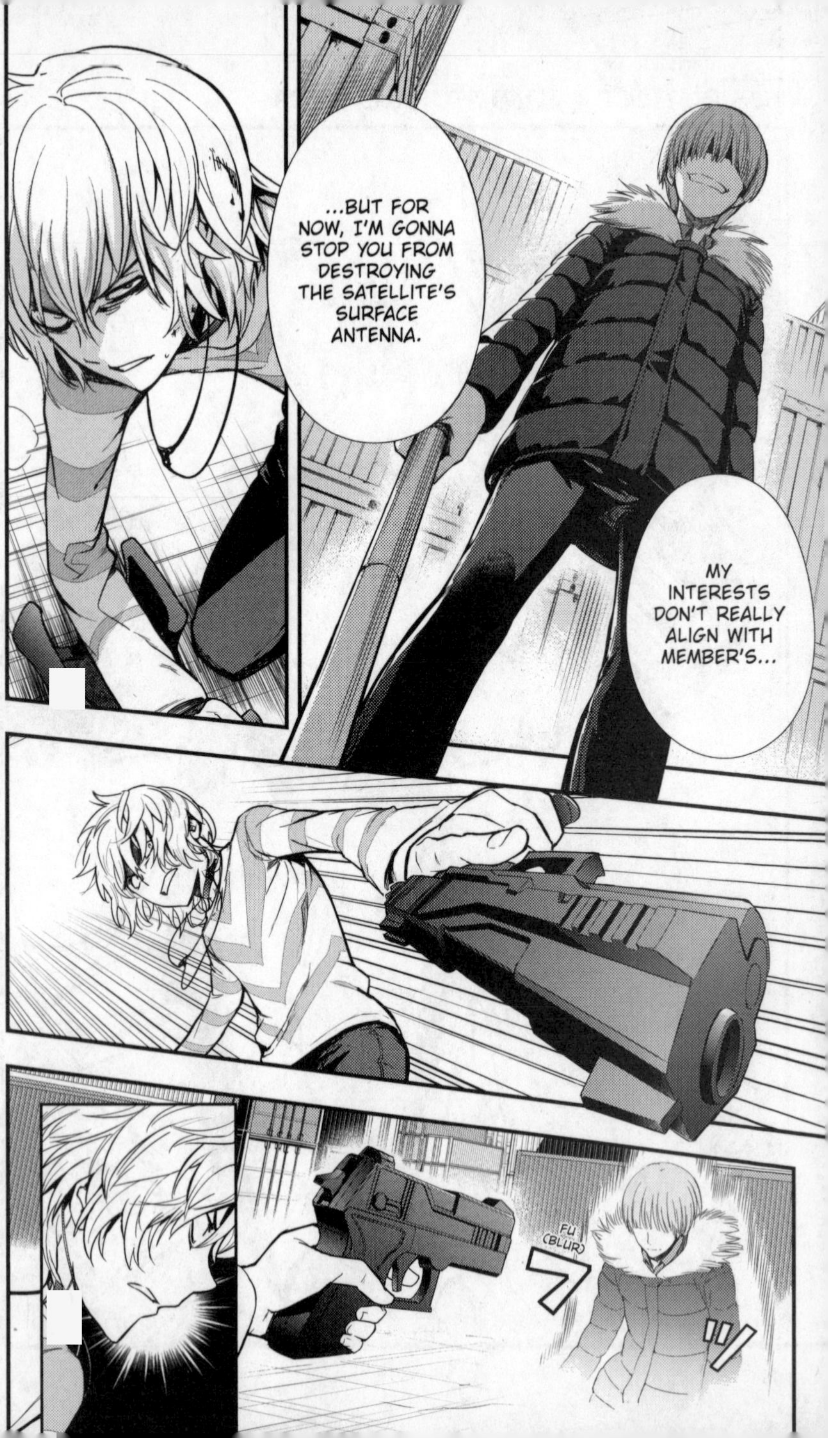
MY INTERESTS DON'T REALLY ALIGN WITH MEMBER'S...
...BUT FOR NOW, I'M GONNA STOP YOU FROM DESTROYING THE SATELLITE'S SURFACE ANTENNA.
FU (BLUR)

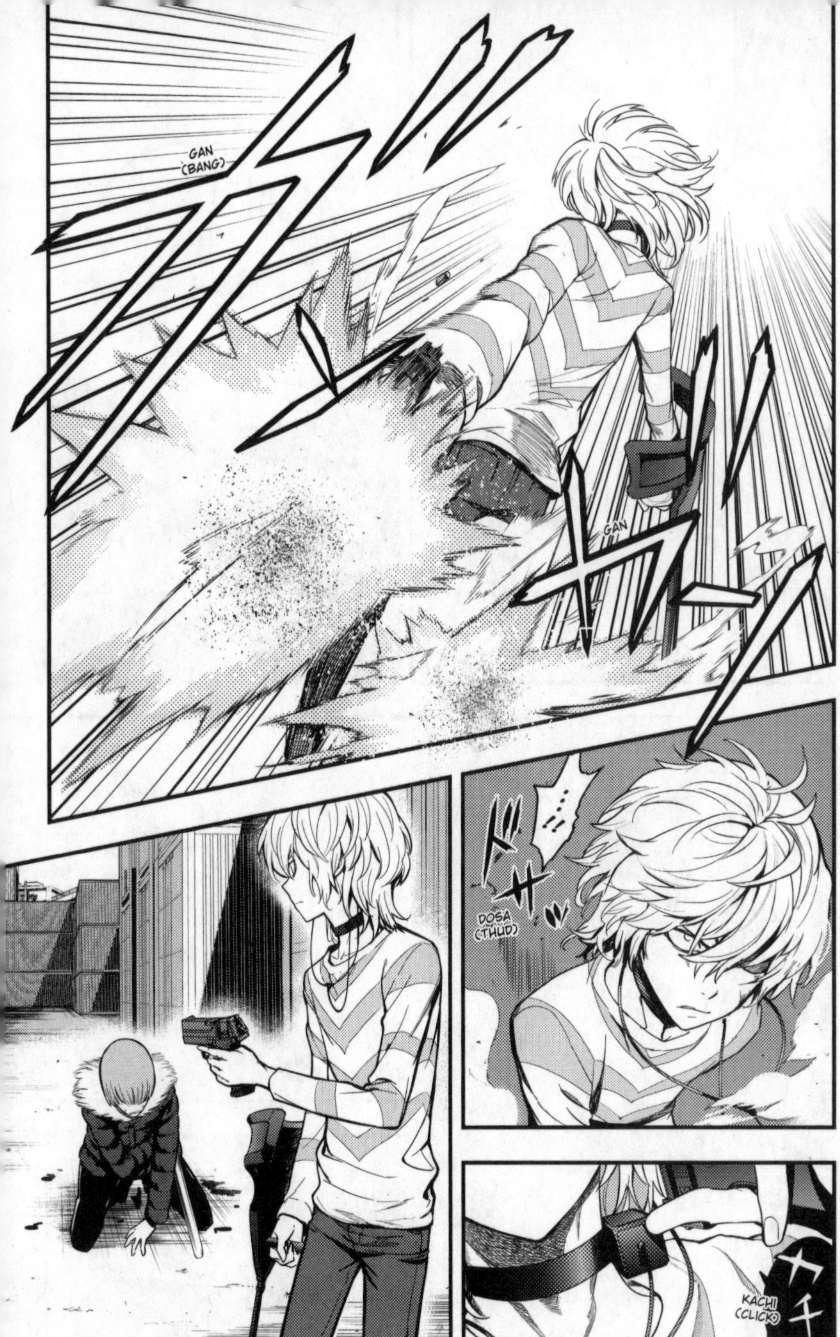
GAN (BANG)
GAN
…!!
DOSA (THUD)
KACHI (CLICK)

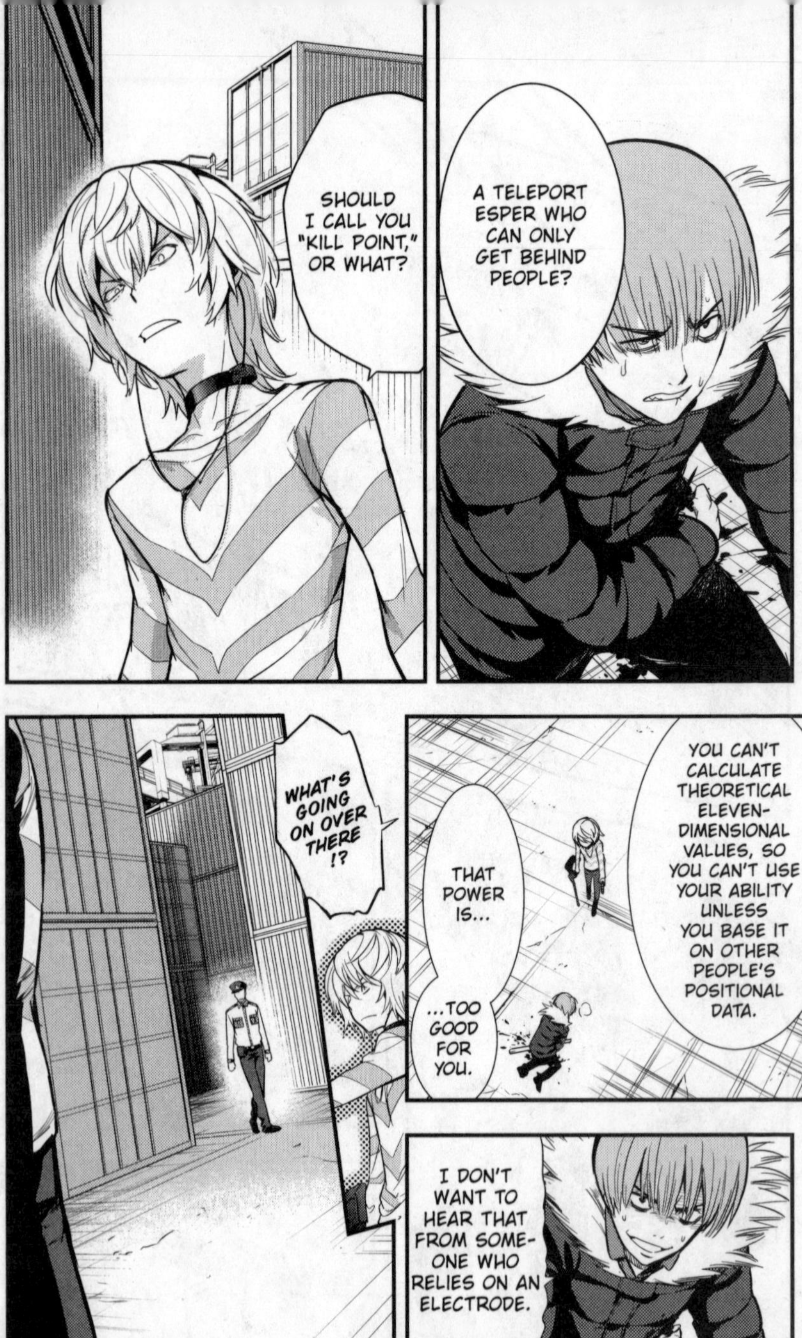
A TELEPORT ESPER WHO CAN ONLY GET BEHIND PEOPLE?
SHOULD I CALL YOU "KILL POINT," OR WHAT?
YOU CAN'T CALCULATE THEORETICAL ELEVEN-DIMENSIONAL VALUES, SO YOU CAN'T USE YOUR ABILITY UNLESS YOU BASE IT ON OTHER PEOPLE'S POSITIONAL DATA.
THAT POWER IS...
...TOO GOOD FOR YOU.
I DON'T WANT TO HEAR THAT FROM SOME-ONE WHO RELIES ON AN ELECTRODE.
WHAT'S GOING ON OVER THERE !?

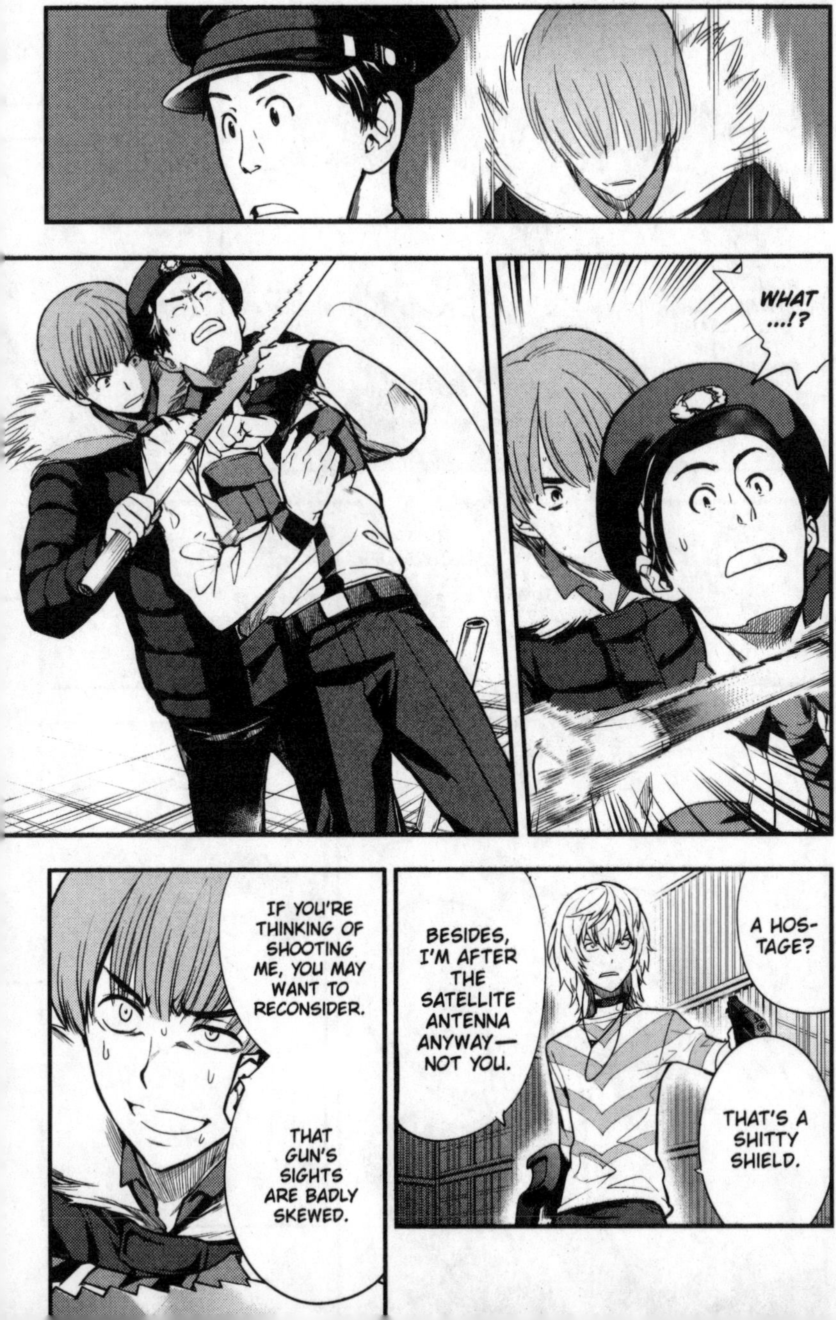
WHAT ...!?
A HOS-TAGE?
THAT'S A SHITTY SHIELD.
BESIDES, I'M AFTER THE SATELLITE ANTENNA ANYWAY— NOT YOU.
IF YOU'RE THINKING OF SHOOTING ME, YOU MAY WANT TO RECONSIDER.
THAT GUN'S SIGHTS ARE BADLY SKEWED.

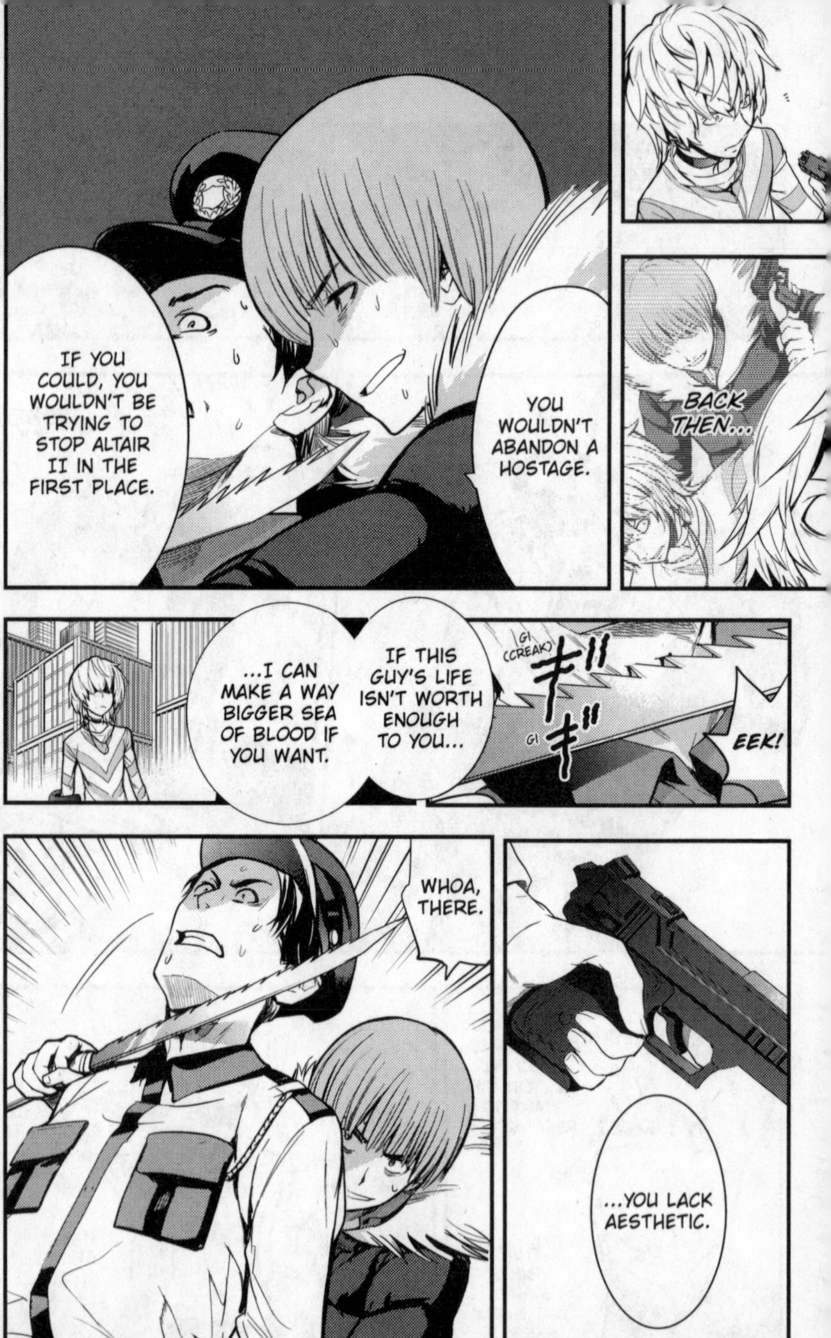
BACK THEN...
YOU WOULDN'T ABANDON A HOSTAGE.
IF YOU COULD, YOU WOULDN'T BE TRYING TO STOP ALTAIR II IN THE FIRST PLACE.
GI (CREAK)
GI
EEK!
IF THIS GUY'S LIFE ISN'T WORTH ENOUGH TO YOU...
...I CAN MAKE A WAY BIGGER SEA OF BLOOD IF YOU WANT.
...YOU LACK AESTHETIC.
WHOA, THERE.

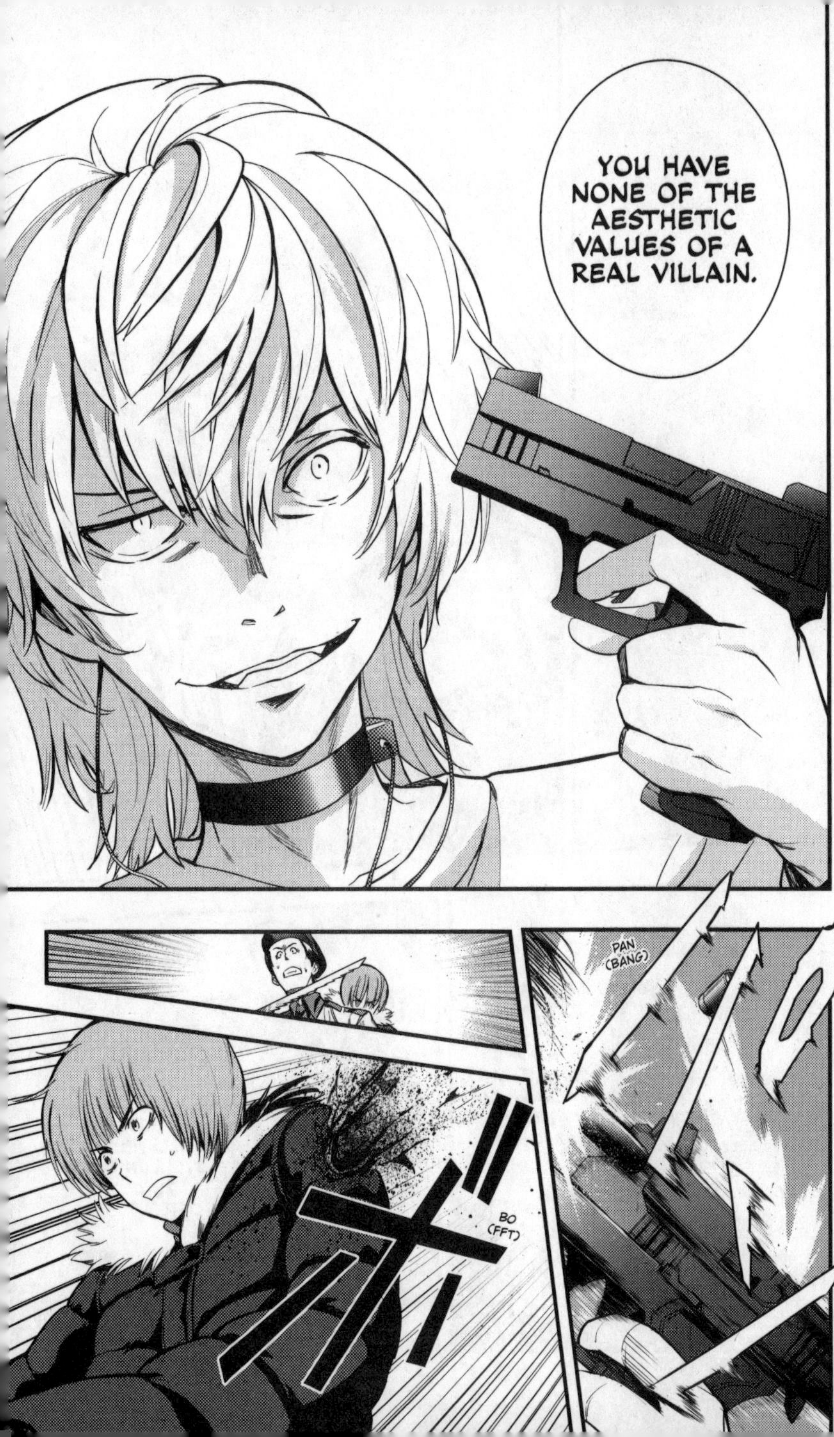
YOU HAVE NONE OF THE AESTHETIC VALUES OF A REAL VILLAIN.
PAN (BANG)
BO (FFT)

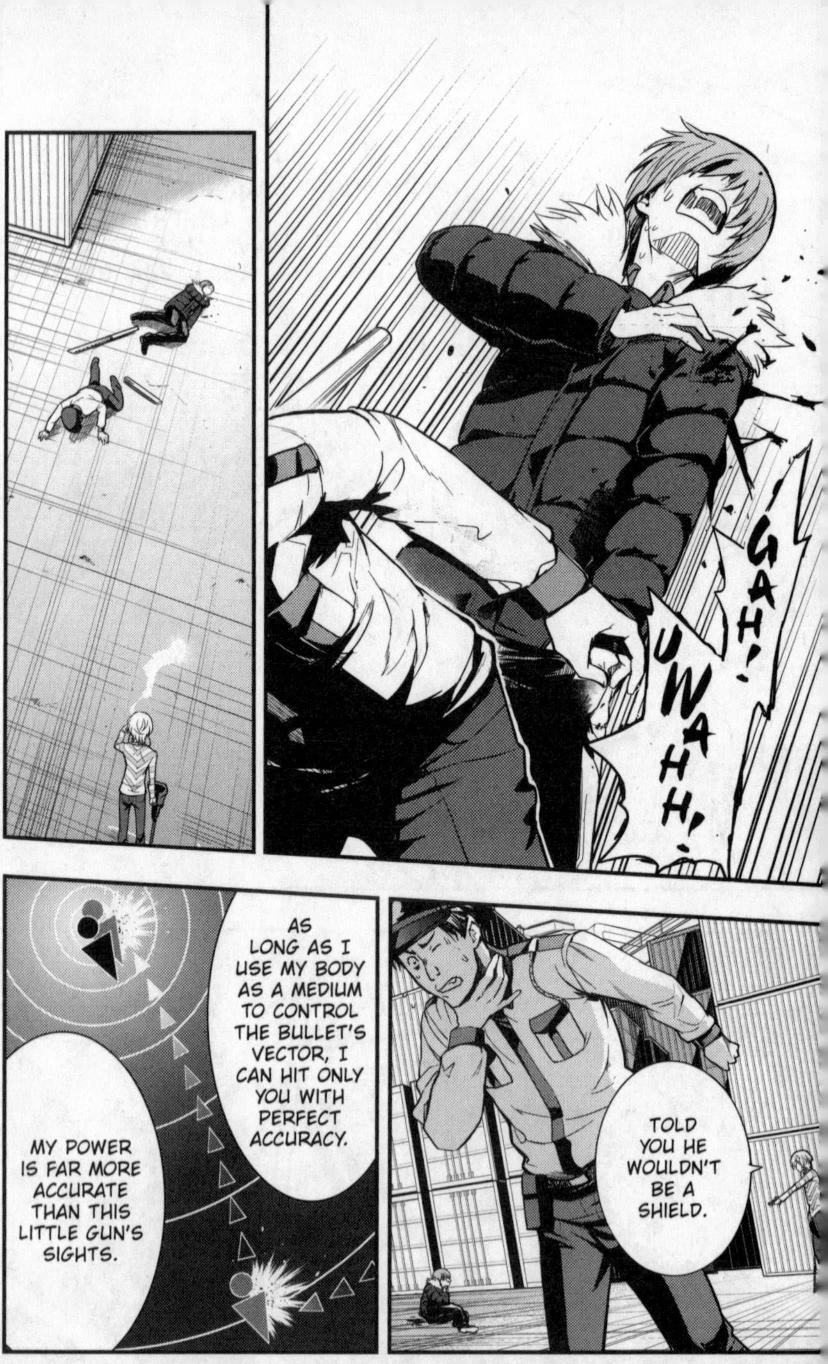
GAH!
UWAHH!
TOLD YOU HE WOULDN'T BE A SHIELD.
AS LONG AS I USE MY BODY AS A MEDIUM TO CONTROL THE BULLET'S VECTOR, I CAN HIT ONLY YOU WITH PERFECT ACCURACY.
MY POWER IS FAR MORE ACCURATE THAN THIS LITTLE GUN'S SIGHTS.

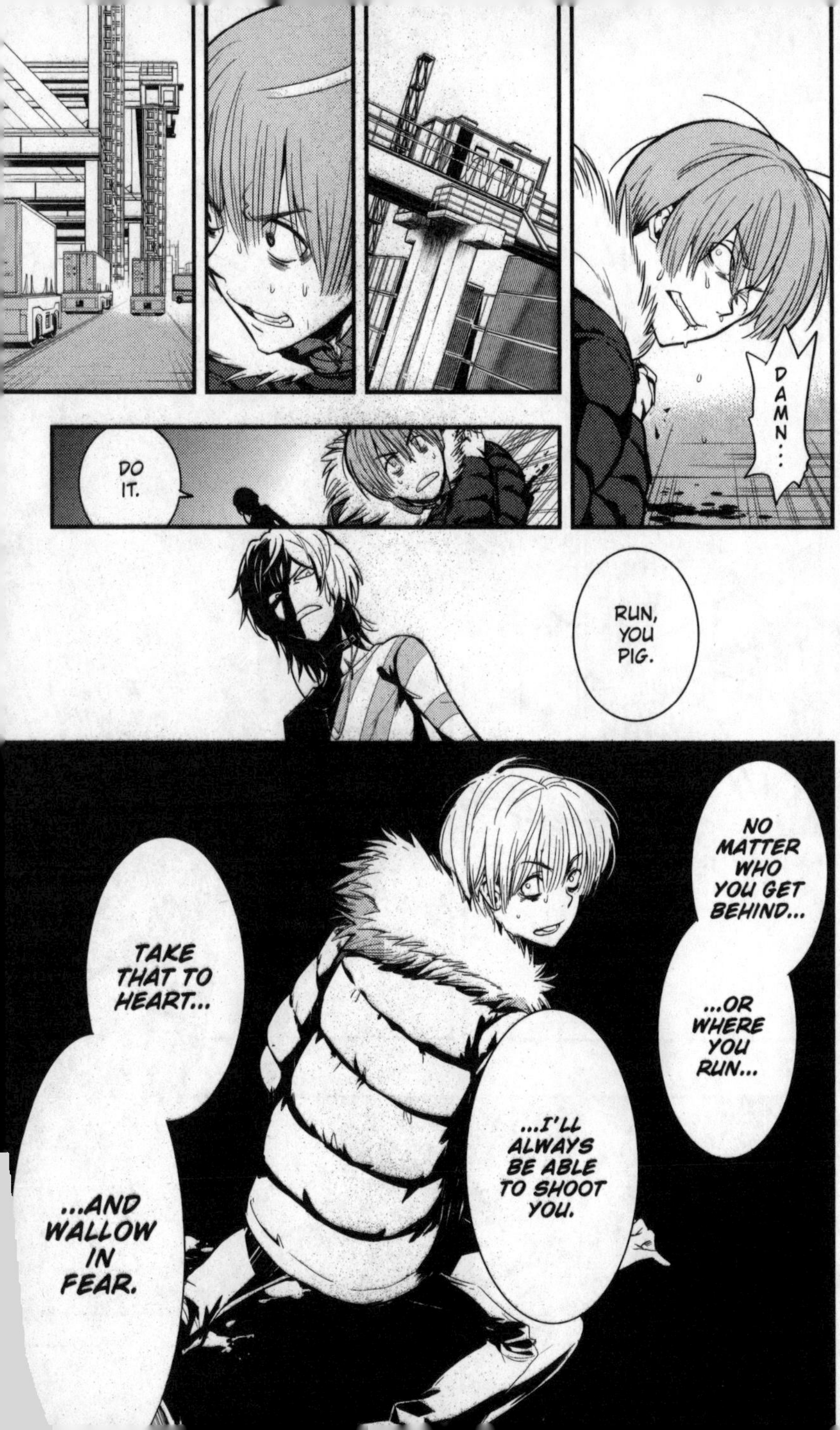
DAMN...
DO IT.
RUN, YOU PIG.
NO MATTER WHO YOU GET BEHIND...
...OR WHERE YOU RUN...
...I'LL ALWAYS BE ABLE TO SHOOT YOU.
TAKE THAT TO HEART...
...AND WALLOW IN FEAR.

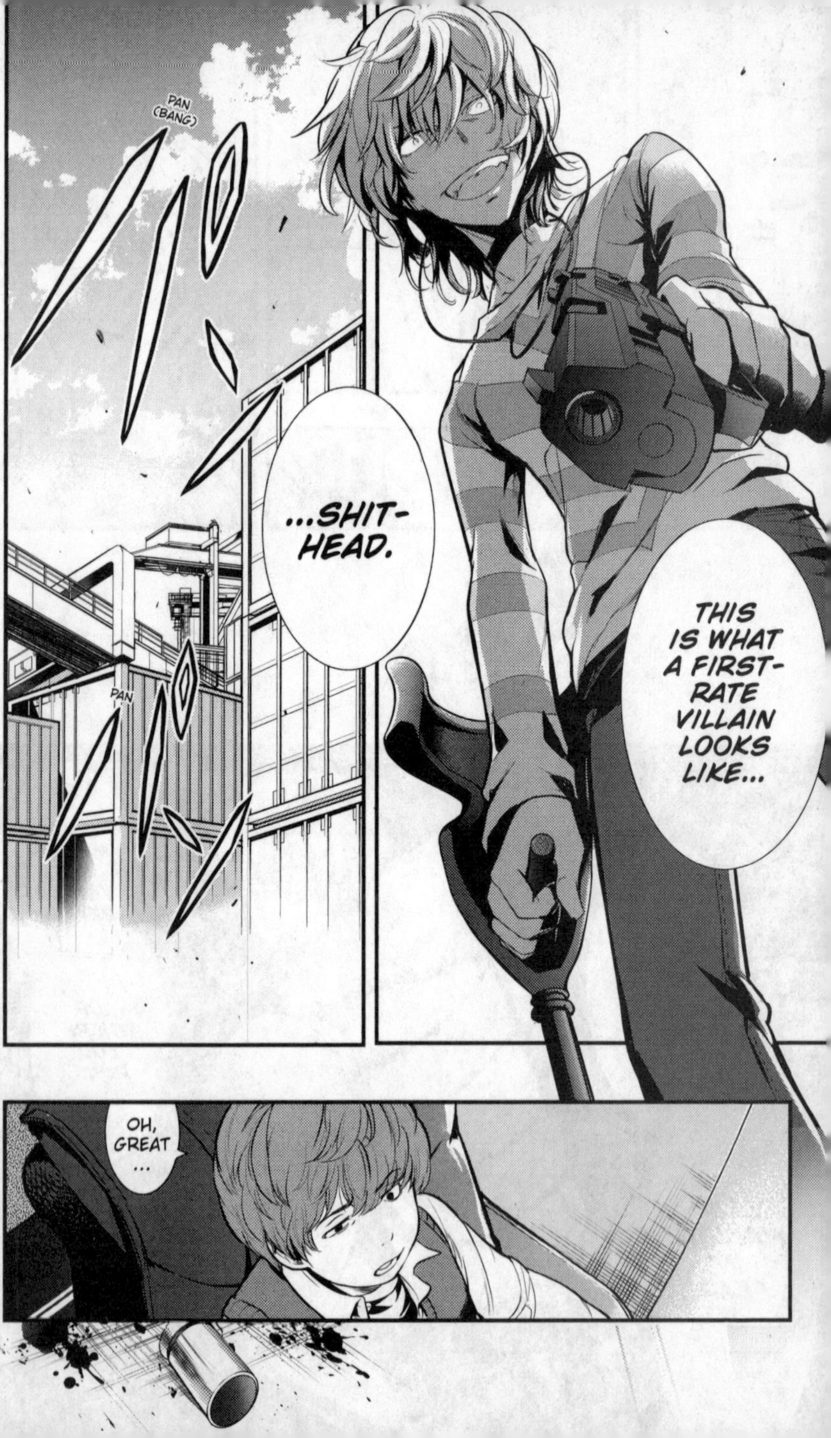
THIS IS WHAT A FIRST-RATE VILLAIN LOOKS LIKE...
PAN (BANG)
PAN
...SHIT-HEAD.
OH, GREAT ...

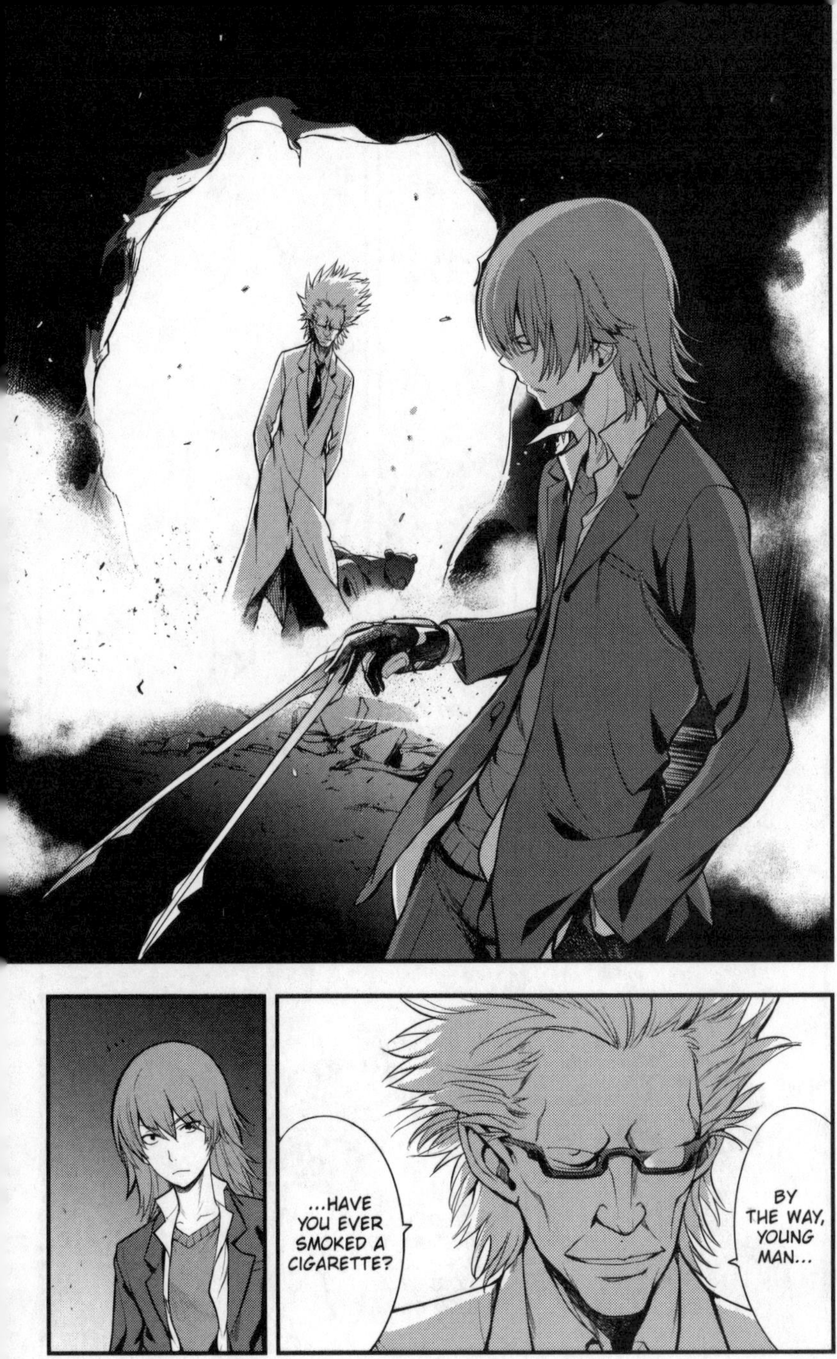
BY THE WAY, YOUNG MAN...
...HAVE YOU EVER SMOKED A CIGARETTE?

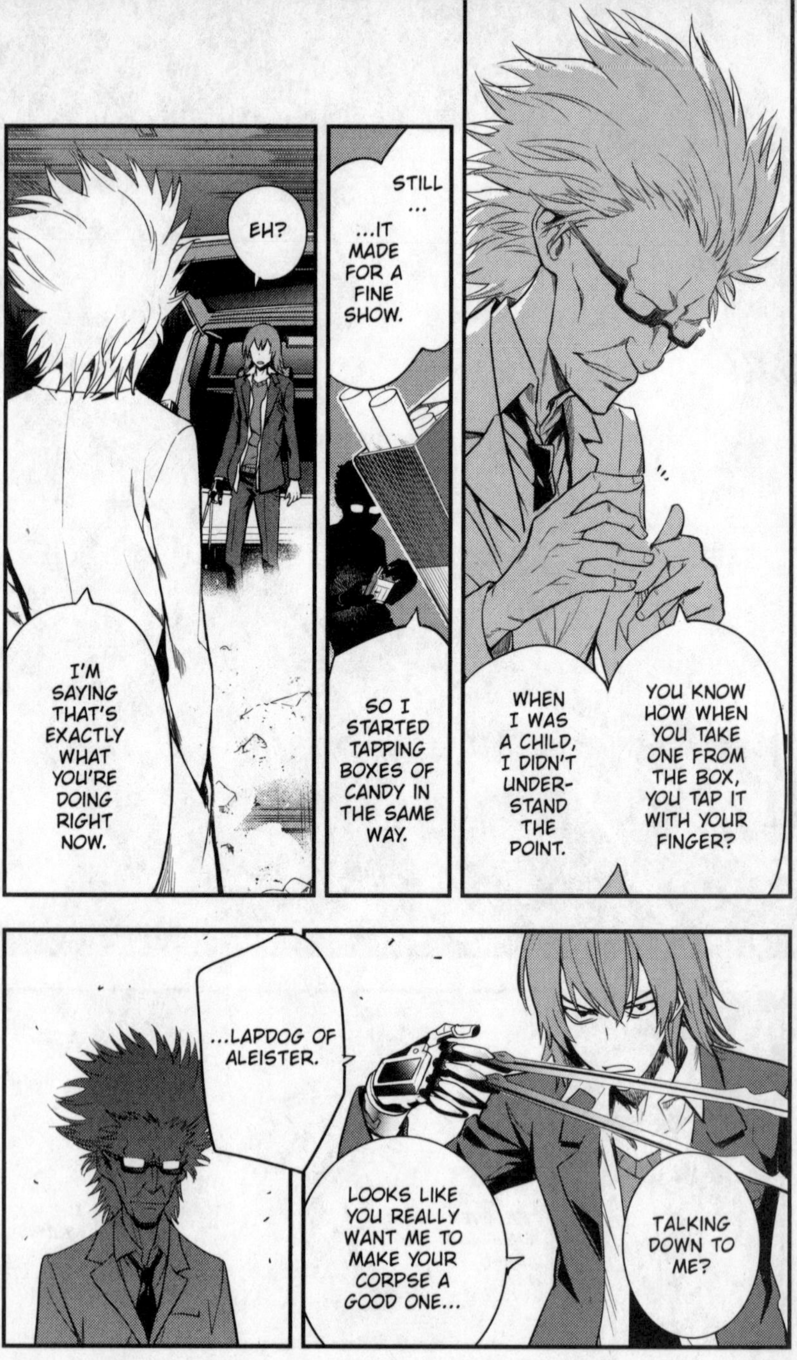
YOU KNOW HOW WHEN YOU TAKE ONE FROM THE BOX, YOU TAP IT WITH YOUR FINGER?
WHEN I WAS A CHILD, I DIDN'T UNDER-STAND THE POINT.
STILL ...
...IT MADE FOR A FINE SHOW.
SO I STARTED TAPPING BOXES OF CANDY IN THE SAME WAY.
EH?
I'M SAYING THAT'S EXACTLY WHAT YOU'RE DOING RIGHT NOW.
TALKING DOWN TO ME?
LOOKS LIKE YOU REALLY WANT ME TO MAKE YOUR CORPSE A GOOD ONE...
...LAPDOG OF ALEISTER.

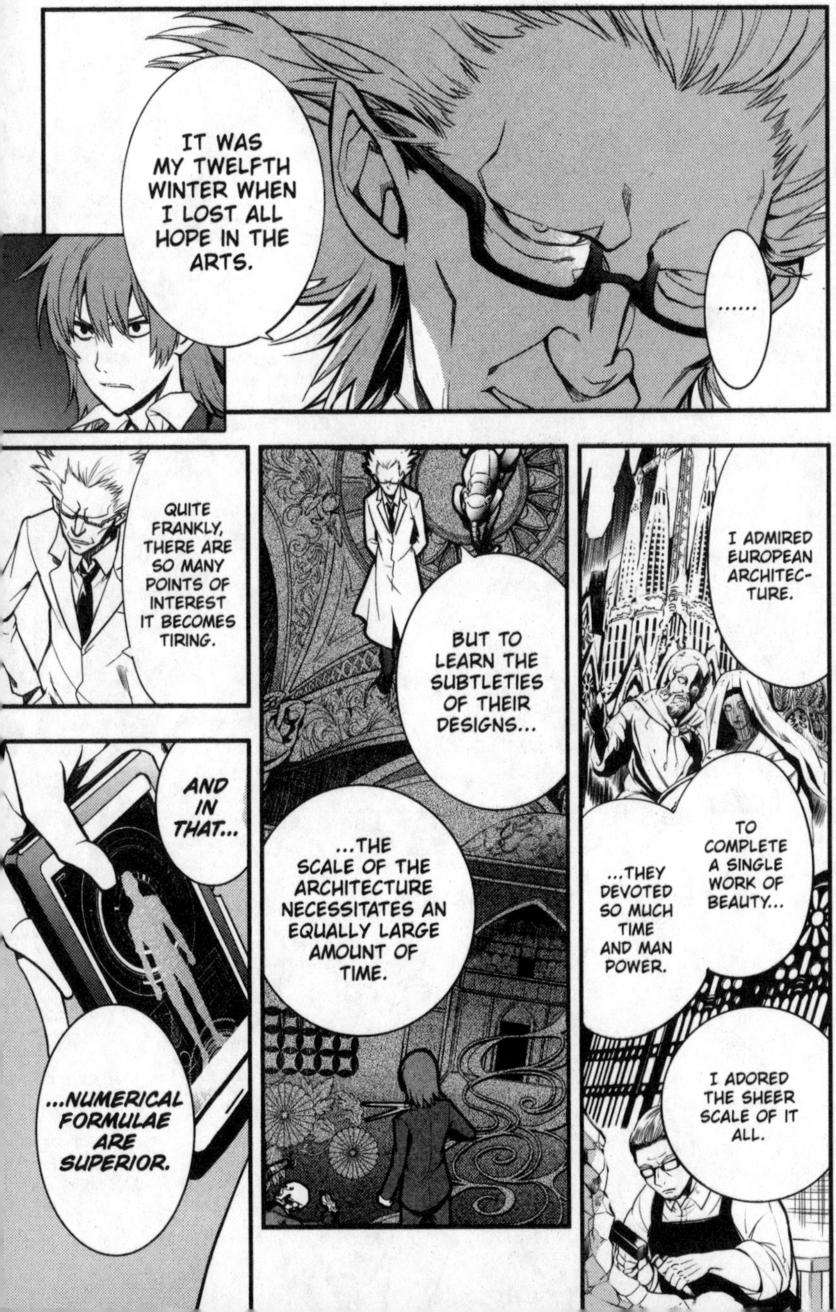
......
IT WAS MY TWELFTH WINTER WHEN I LOST ALL HOPE IN THE ARTS.
I ADMIRED EUROPEAN ARCHITEC-TURE.
TO COMPLETE A SINGLE WORK OF BEAUTY...
...THEY DEVOTED SO MUCH TIME AND MAN POWER.
I ADORED THE SHEER SCALE OF IT ALL.
BUT TO LEARN THE SUBTLETIES OF THEIR DESIGNS...
...THE SCALE OF THE ARCHITECTURE NECESSITATES AN EQUALLY LARGE AMOUNT OF TIME.
QUITE FRANKLY, THERE ARE SO MANY POINTS OF INTEREST IT BECOMES TIRING.
*AND IN THAT...*
*...NUMERICAL FORMULAE ARE SUPERIOR.*

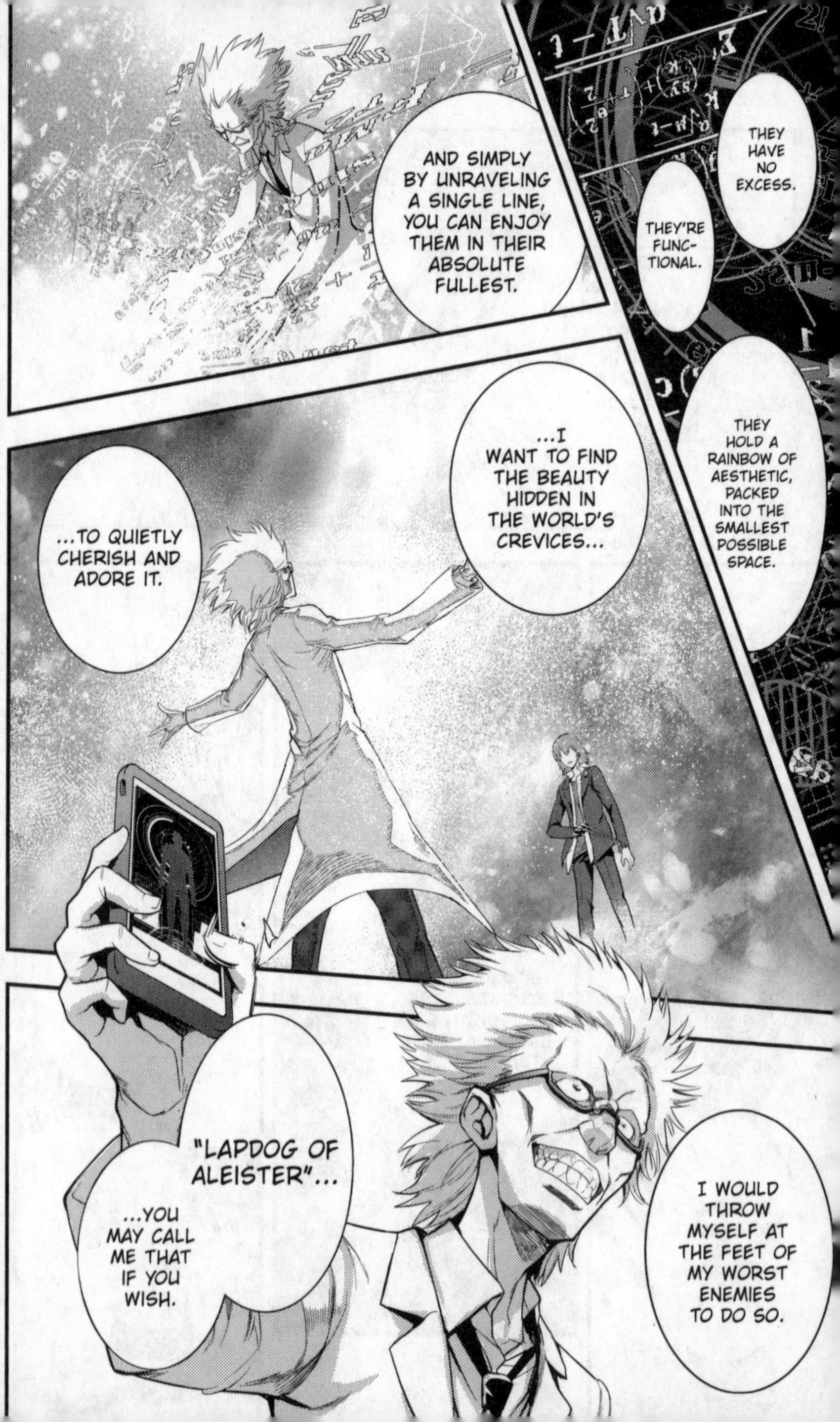
THEY HAVE NO EXCESS.
THEY'RE FUNC-TIONAL.
THEY HOLD A RAINBOW OF AESTHETIC, PACKED INTO THE SMALLEST POSSIBLE SPACE.
AND SIMPLY BY UNRAVELING A SINGLE LINE, YOU CAN ENJOY THEM IN THEIR ABSOLUTE FULLEST.
...I WANT TO FIND THE BEAUTY HIDDEN IN THE WORLD'S CREVICES...
...TO QUIETLY CHERISH AND ADORE IT.
I WOULD THROW MYSELF AT THE FEET OF MY WORST ENEMIES TO DO SO.
"LAPDOG OF ALEISTER"...
...YOU MAY CALL ME THAT IF YOU WISH.

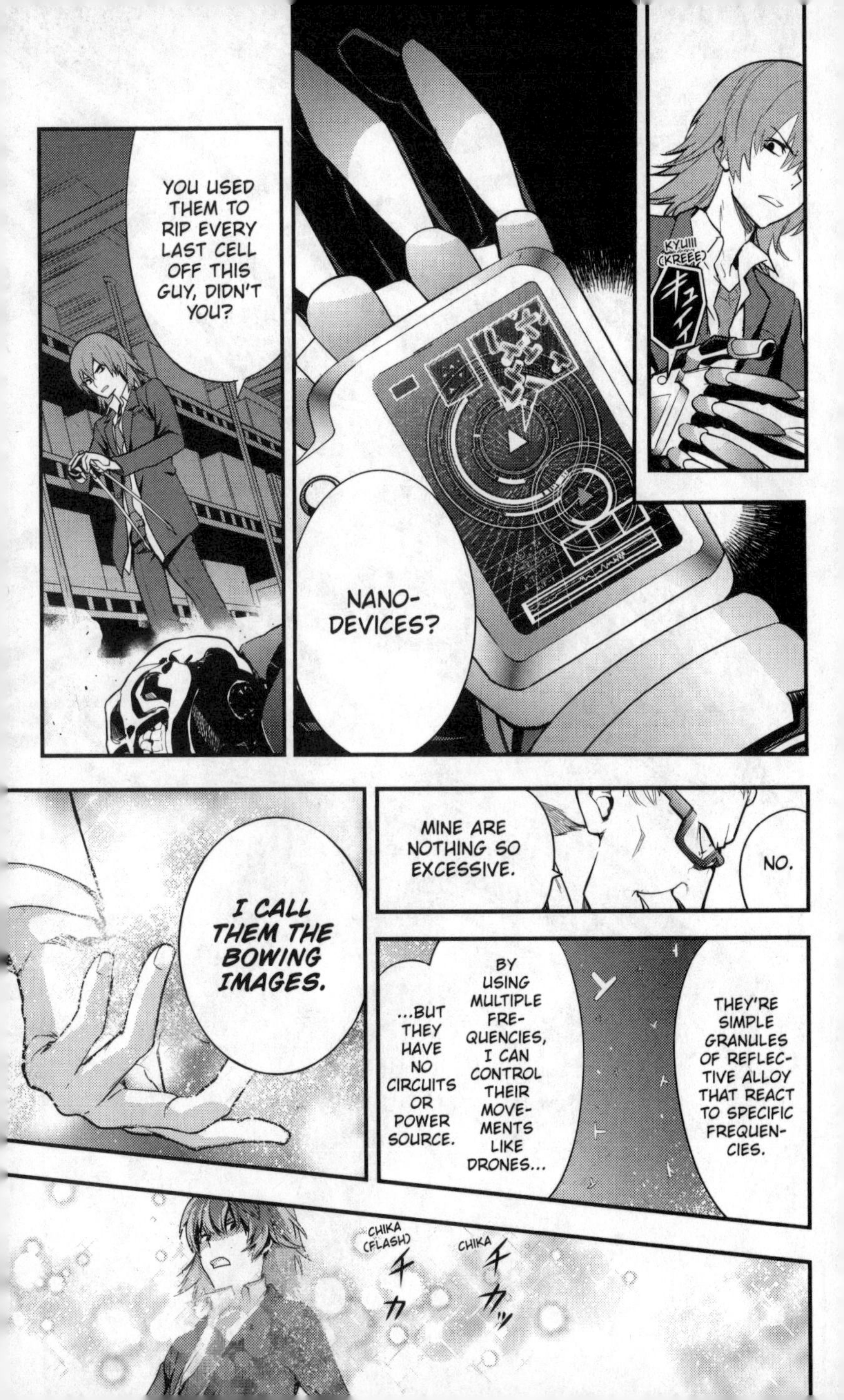
KYUIII (KREEE)
キュイイ
NANO-DEVICES?
YOU USED THEM TO RIP EVERY LAST CELL OFF THIS GUY, DIDN'T YOU?
NO.
MINE ARE NOTHING SO EXCESSIVE.
THEY'RE SIMPLE GRANULES OF REFLECTIVE ALLOY THAT REACT TO SPECIFIC FREQUENCIES.
BY USING MULTIPLE FREQUENCIES, I CAN CONTROL THEIR MOVEMENTS LIKE DRONES...
...BUT THEY HAVE NO CIRCUITS OR POWER SOURCE.
I CALL THEM THE BOWING IMAGES.
CHIKA
チカッ
CHIKA (FLASH)
チカ

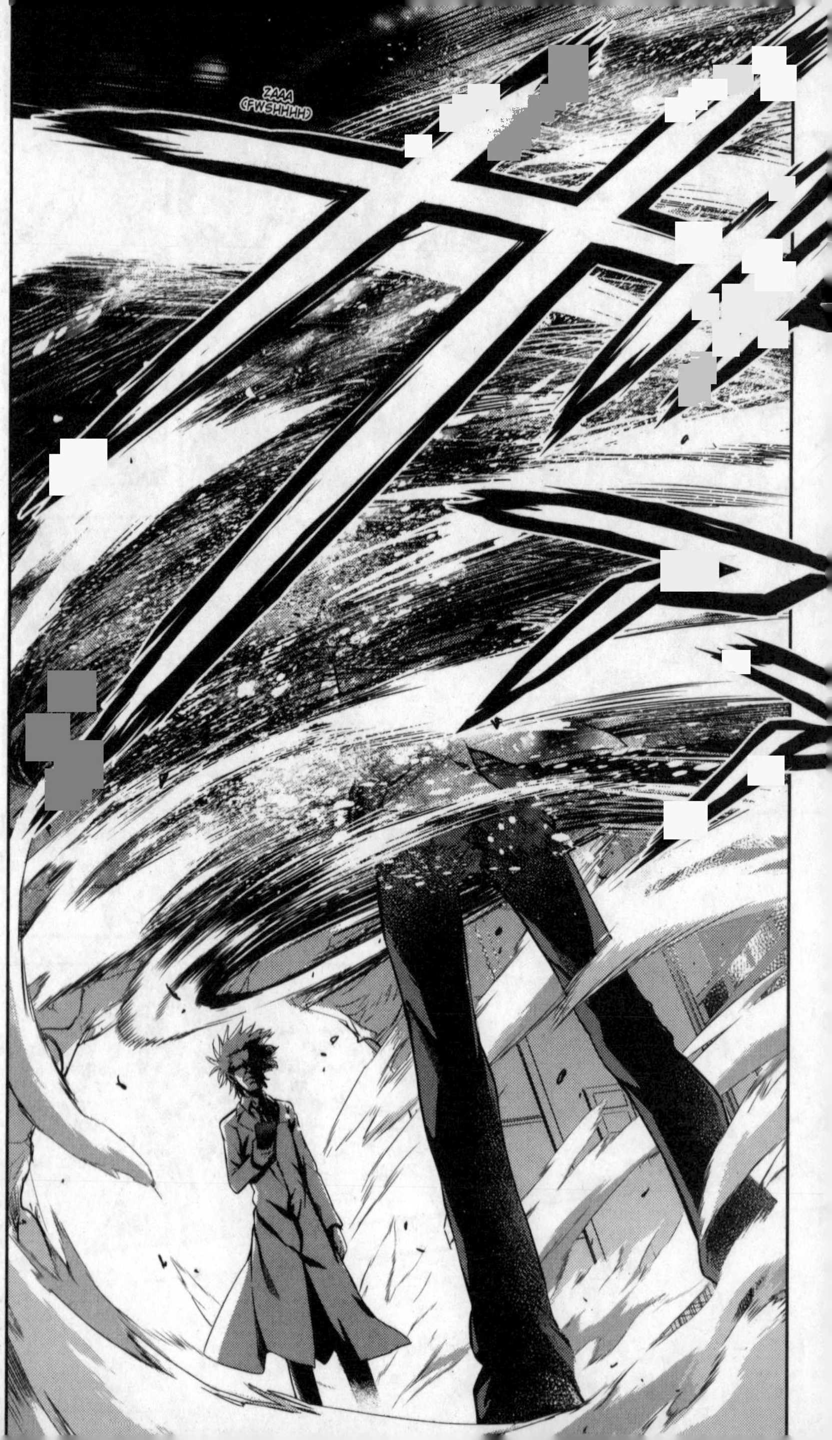
ZAAA
(FWSHHHH)

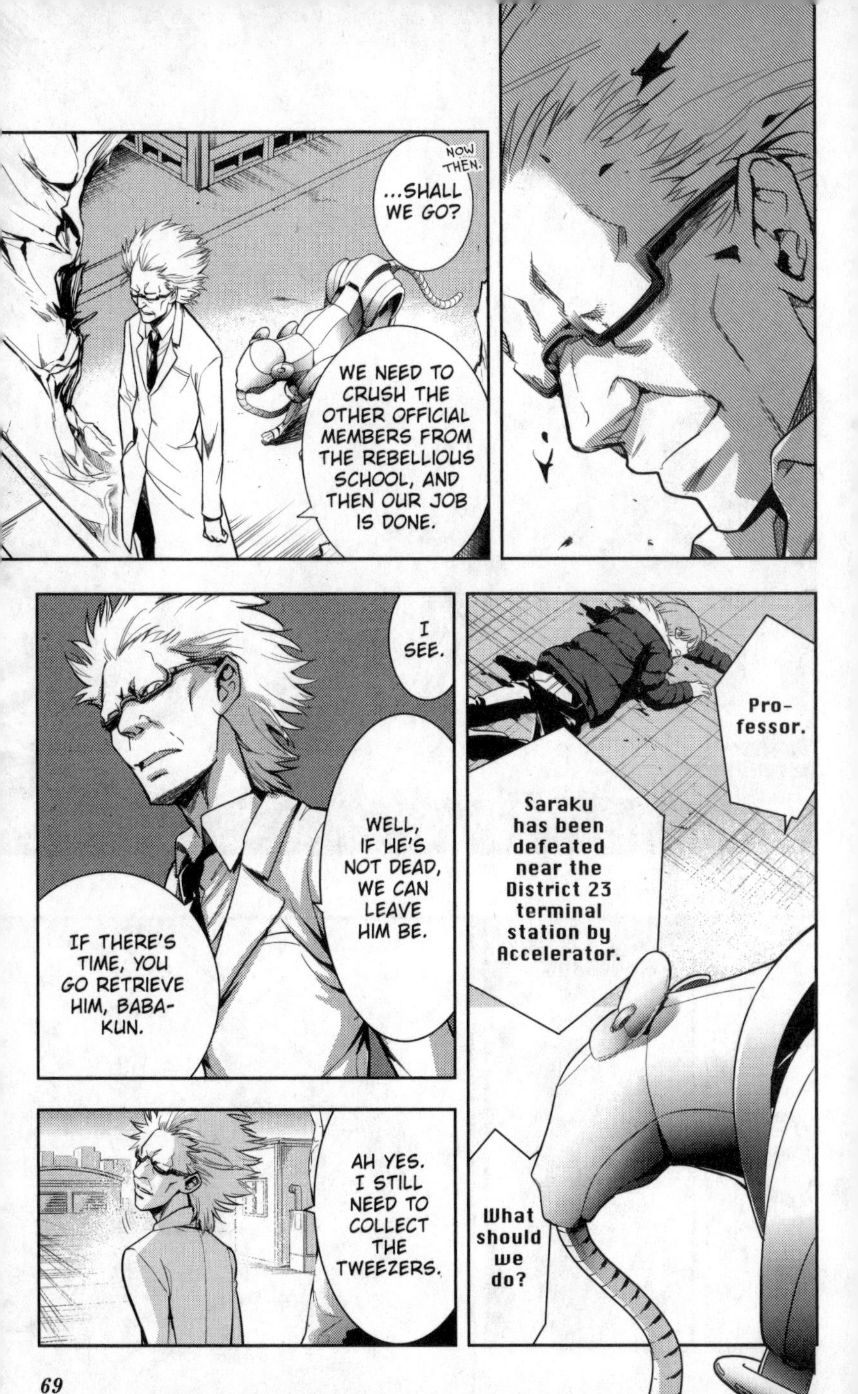
NOW THEN.
...SHALL WE GO?
WE NEED TO CRUSH THE OTHER OFFICIAL MEMBERS FROM THE REBELLIOUS SCHOOL, AND THEN OUR JOB IS DONE.
Professor.
Saraku has been defeated near the District 23 terminal station by Accelerator.
What should we do?
I SEE.
WELL, IF HE'S NOT DEAD, WE CAN LEAVE HIM BE.
IF THERE'S TIME, YOU GO RETRIEVE HIM, BABA-KUN.
AH YES. I STILL NEED TO COLLECT THE TWEEZERS.

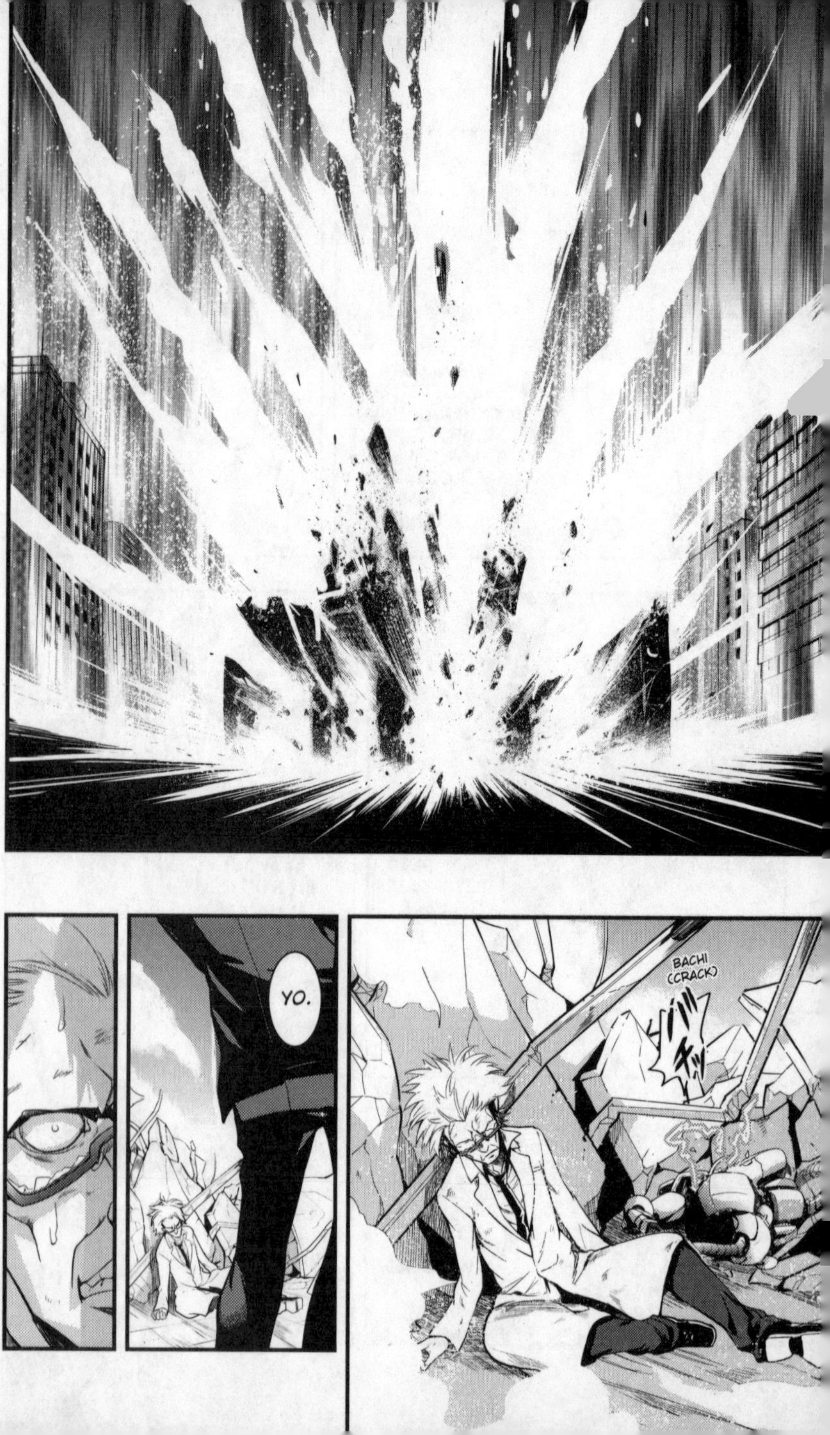
BACHI (CRACK)
YO.

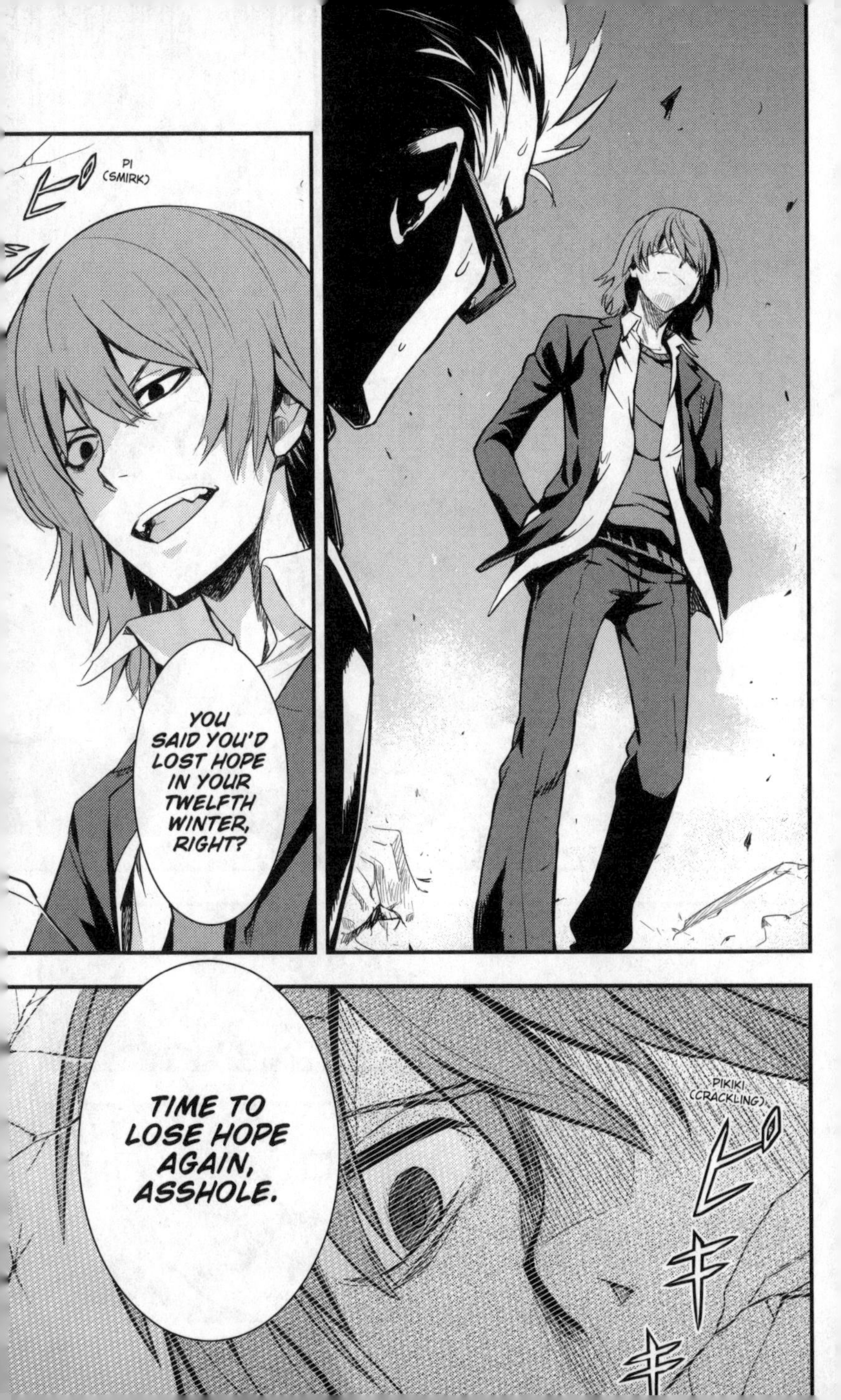
ピ
PI (SMIRK)
YOU SAID YOU'D LOST HOPE IN YOUR TWELFTH WINTER, RIGHT?
TIME TO LOSE HOPE AGAIN, ASSHOLE.
ピキキ
PIKIKI (CRACKLING)

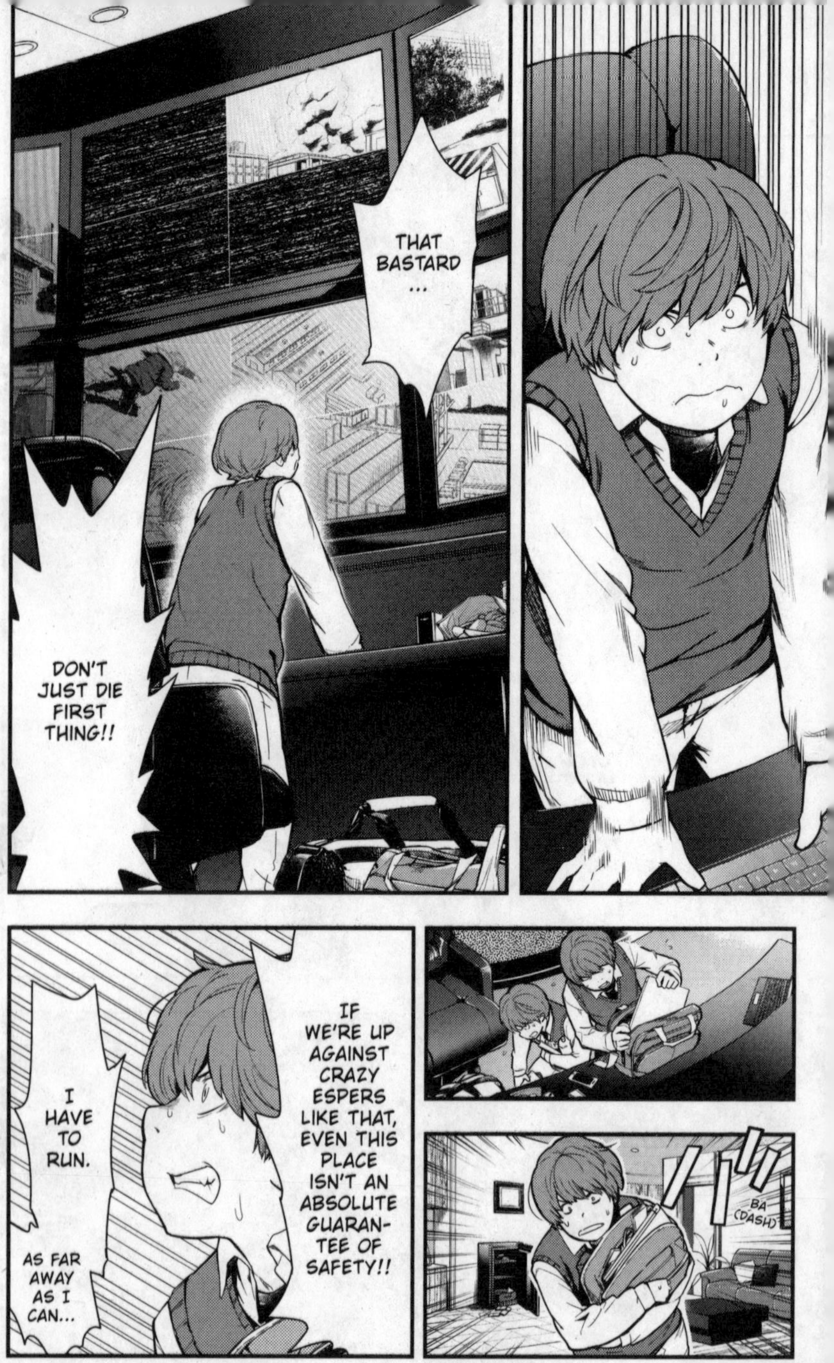
THAT BASTARD...
DON'T JUST DIE FIRST THING!!
BA (DASH)
IF WE'RE UP AGAINST CRAZY ESPERS LIKE THAT, EVEN THIS PLACE ISN'T AN ABSOLUTE GUARANTEE OF SAFETY!!
I HAVE TO RUN.
AS FAR AWAY AS I CAN...

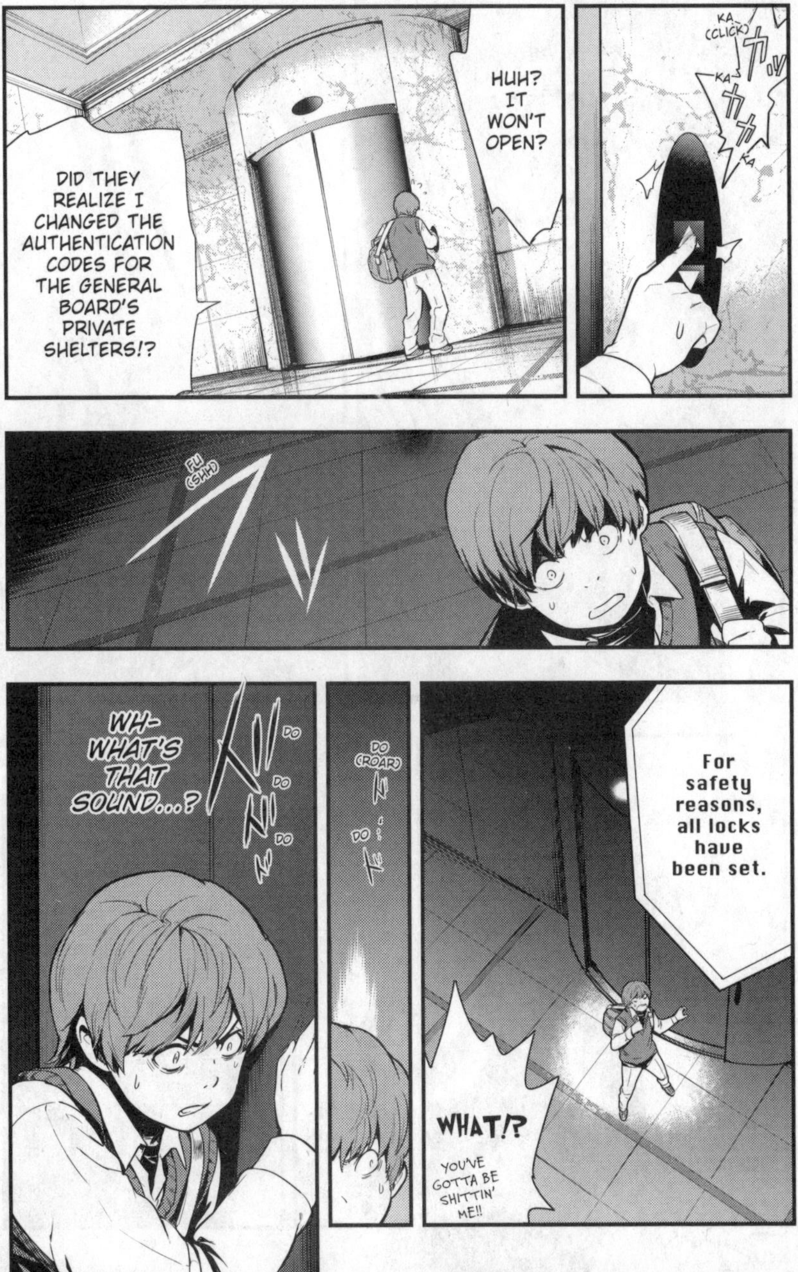
KA (CLICK)
KA
KA
HUH? IT WON'T OPEN?
DID THEY REALIZE I CHANGED THE AUTHENTICATION CODES FOR THE GENERAL BOARD'S PRIVATE SHELTERS!?
FU (SHH)
For safety reasons, all locks have been set.
DO (ROAR)
DO
WHAT!?
YOU'VE GOTTA BE SHITTIN' ME!!
DO
DO
DO
WH- WHAT'S THAT SOUND...?

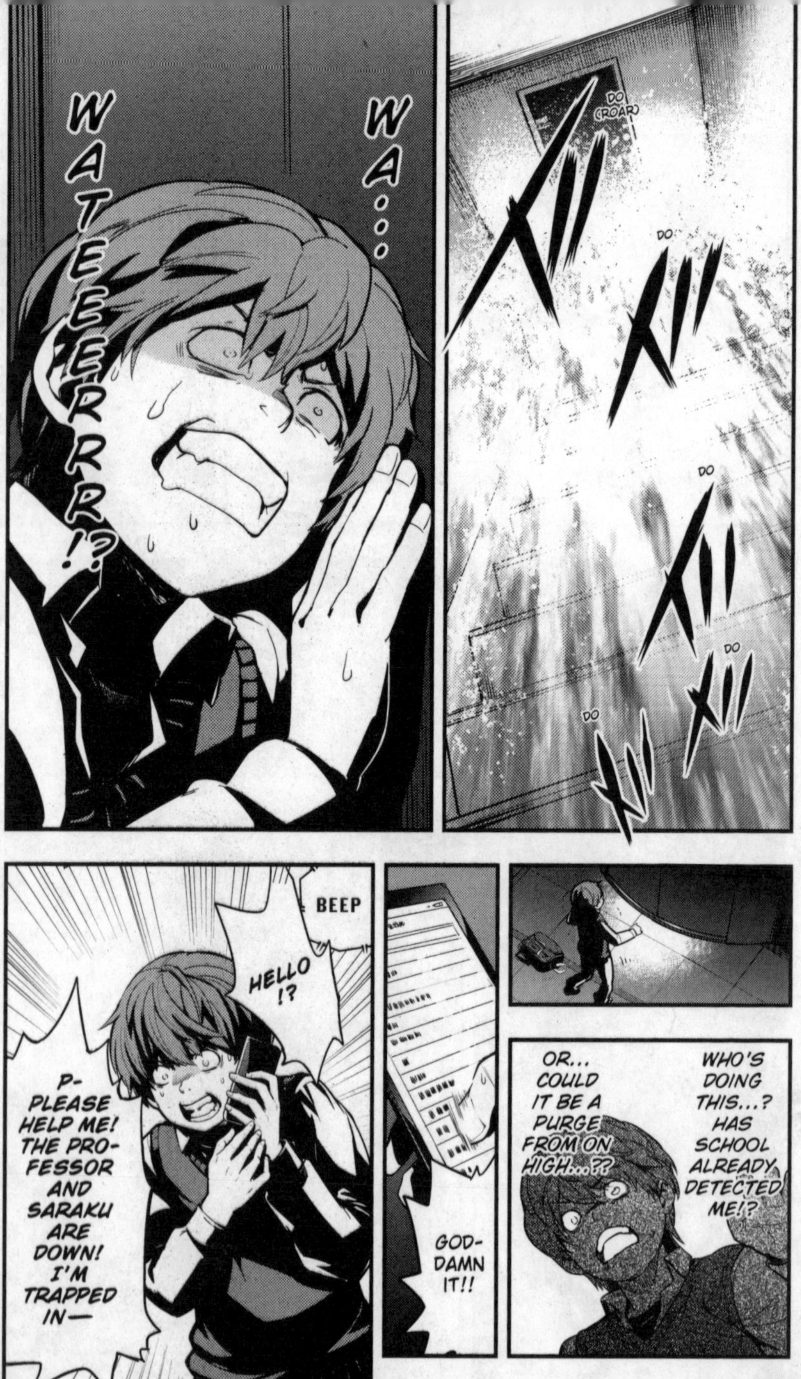
DO (ROAR)
DO
DO
DO
DO
WA...
WATEEEERRRR!?
WHO'S DOING THIS...? HAS SCHOOL ALREADY DETECTED ME!?
OR... COULD IT BE A PURGE FROM ON HIGH...??
GOD-DAMN IT!!
BEEP
HELLO!?
P-PLEASE HELP ME! THE PROFESSOR AND SARAKU ARE DOWN! I'M TRAPPED IN—

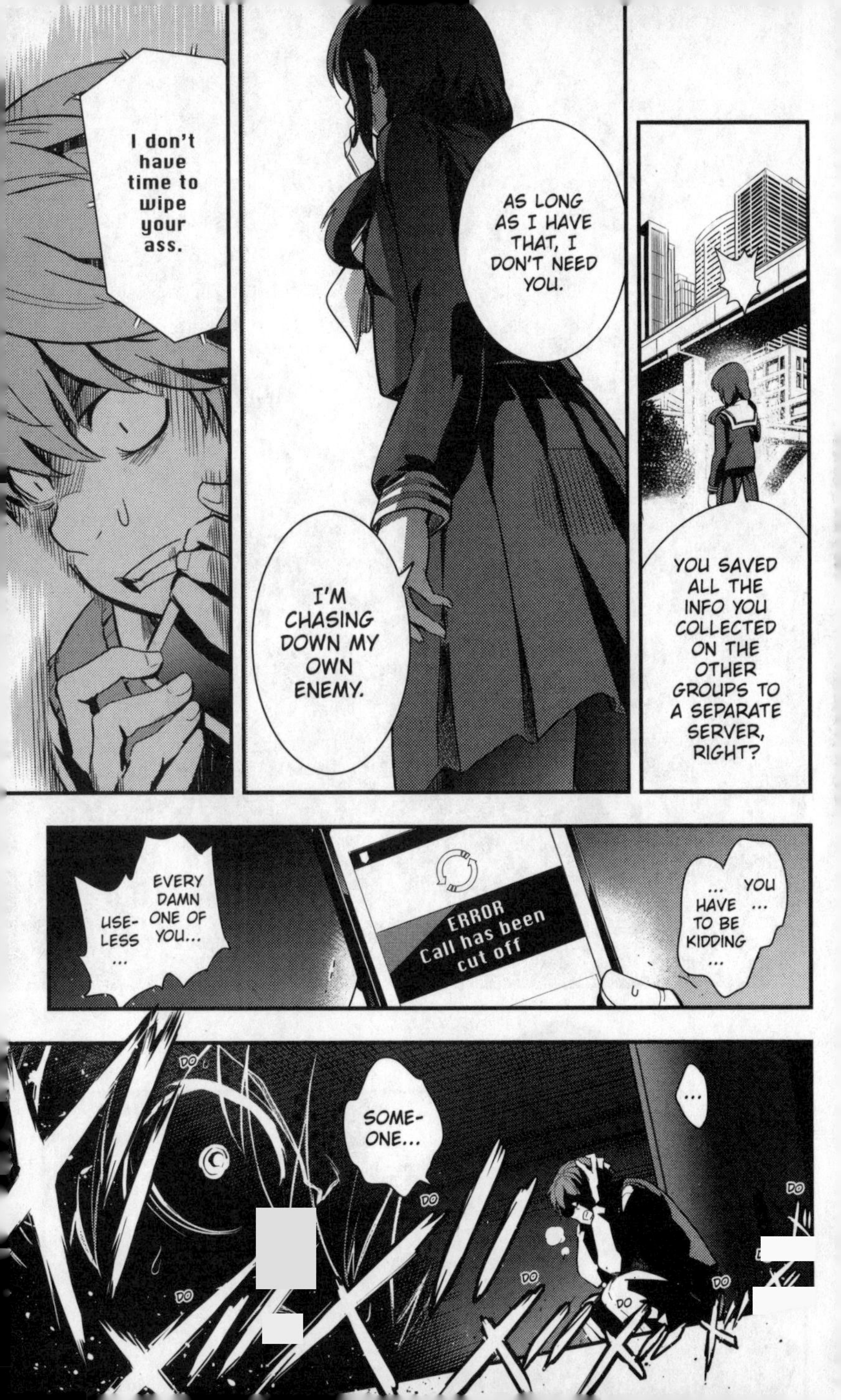
YOU SAVED ALL THE INFO YOU COLLECTED ON THE OTHER GROUPS TO A SEPARATE SERVER, RIGHT?
AS LONG AS I HAVE THAT, I DON'T NEED YOU.
I'M CHASING DOWN MY OWN ENEMY.
I don't have time to wipe your ass.
... YOU HAVE ... TO BE KIDDING ...
ERROR
Call has been cut off
EVERY DAMN ONE OF YOU... USE-LESS ...
...
SOME-ONE...
DO
DO
DO
DO
DO
DO
DO

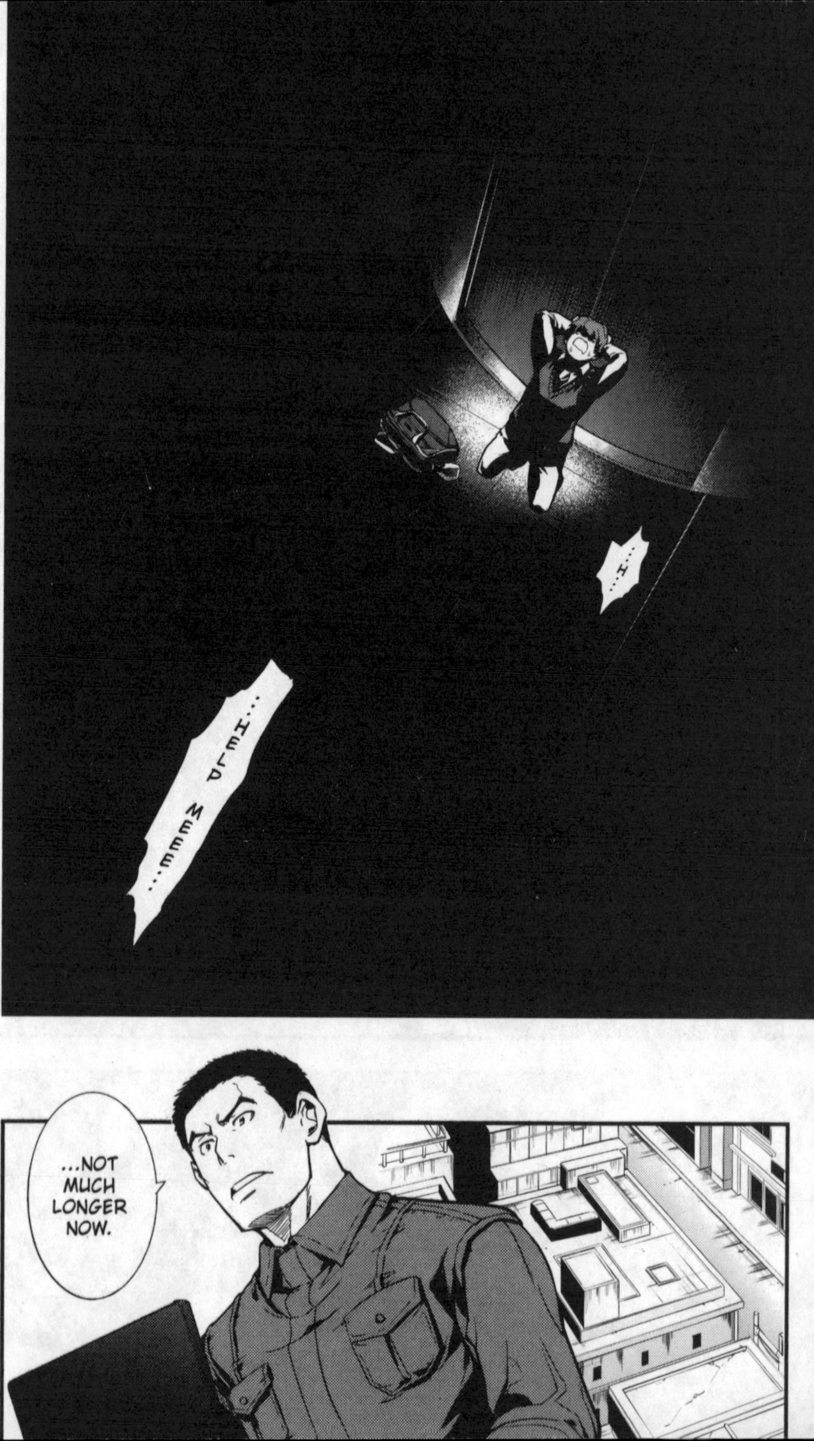
...H...
...HELP MEEE...
...NOT MUCH LONGER NOW.

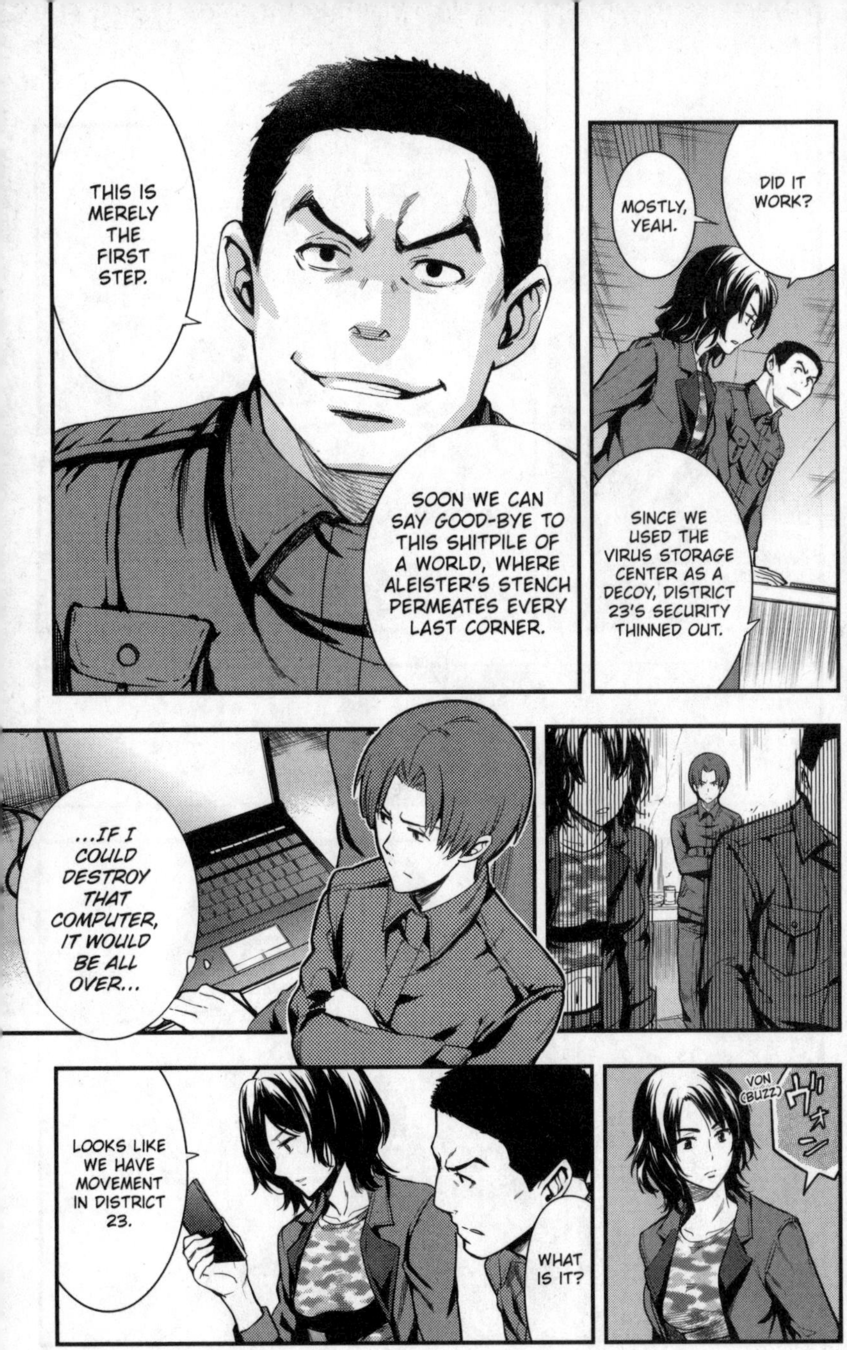
DID IT WORK?
MOSTLY, YEAH.
SINCE WE USED THE VIRUS STORAGE CENTER AS A DECOY, DISTRICT 23'S SECURITY THINNED OUT.
THIS IS MERELY THE FIRST STEP.
SOON WE CAN SAY GOOD-BYE TO THIS SHITPILE OF A WORLD, WHERE ALEISTER'S STENCH PERMEATES EVERY LAST CORNER.
...IF I COULD DESTROY THAT COMPUTER, IT WOULD BE ALL OVER...
VON (BUZZ)
WHAT IS IT?
LOOKS LIKE WE HAVE MOVEMENT IN DISTRICT 23.

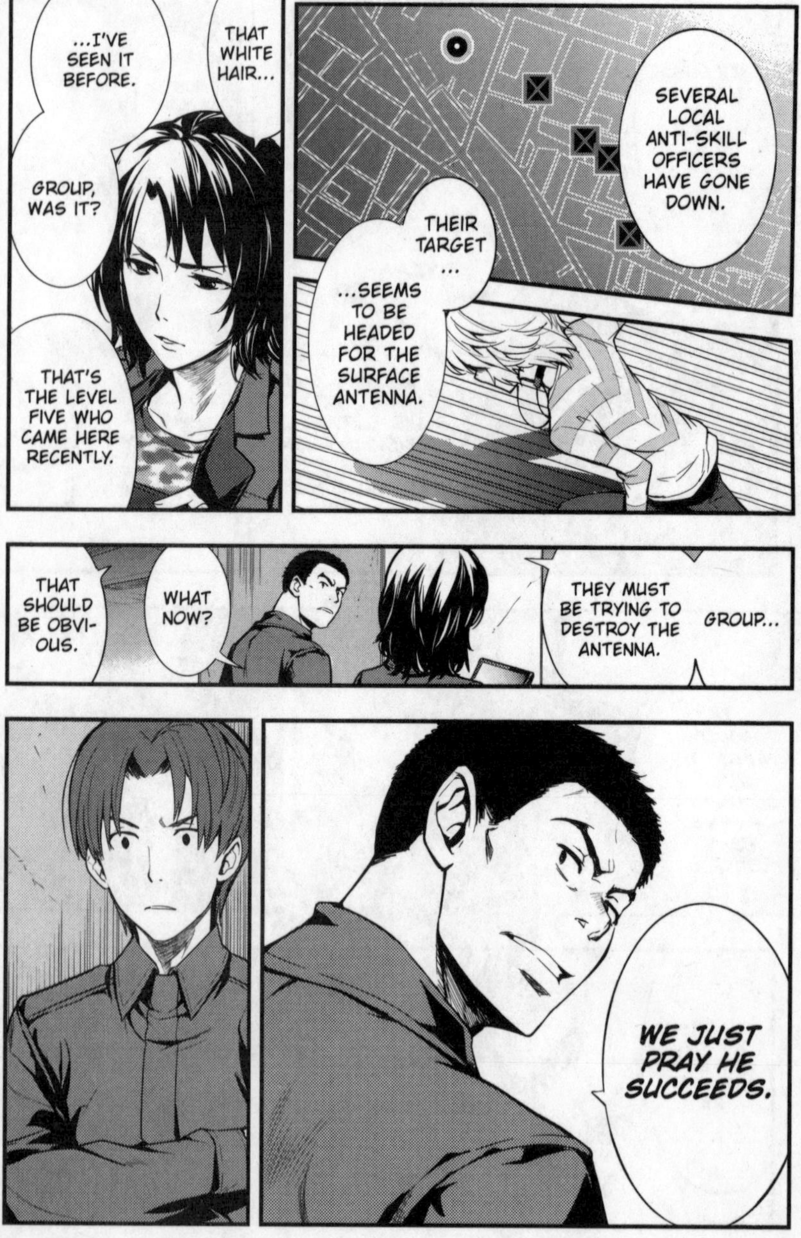

SEVERAL LOCAL ANTI-SKILL OFFICERS HAVE GONE DOWN.
THEIR TARGET ...
...SEEMS TO BE HEADED FOR THE SURFACE ANTENNA.
THAT WHITE HAIR...
...I'VE SEEN IT BEFORE.
GROUP, WAS IT?
THAT'S THE LEVEL FIVE WHO CAME HERE RECENTLY.
GROUP...
THEY MUST BE TRYING TO DESTROY THE ANTENNA.
WHAT NOW?
THAT SHOULD BE OBVI-OUS.
WE JUST PRAY HE SUCCEEDS.

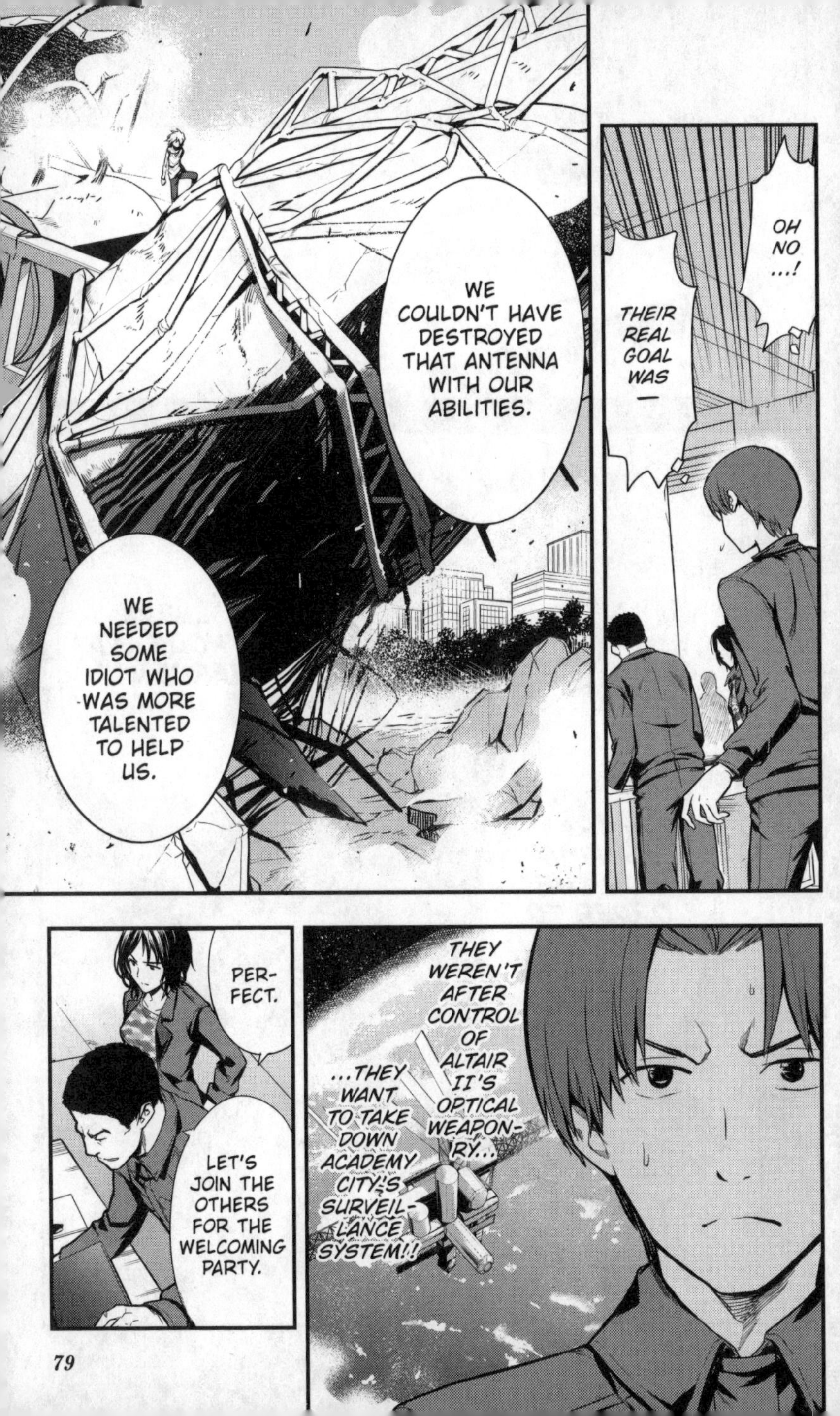

OH NO ...!
THEIR REAL GOAL WAS —
WE COULDN'T HAVE DESTROYED THAT ANTENNA WITH OUR ABILITIES.
WE NEEDED SOME IDIOT WHO WAS MORE TALENTED TO HELP US.
THEY WEREN'T AFTER CONTROL OF ALTAIR II'S OPTICAL WEAPON-RY...
...THEY WANT TO TAKE DOWN ACADEMY CITY'S SURVEIL-LANCE SYSTEM!!
PER-FECT.
LET'S JOIN THE OTHERS FOR THE WELCOMING PARTY.

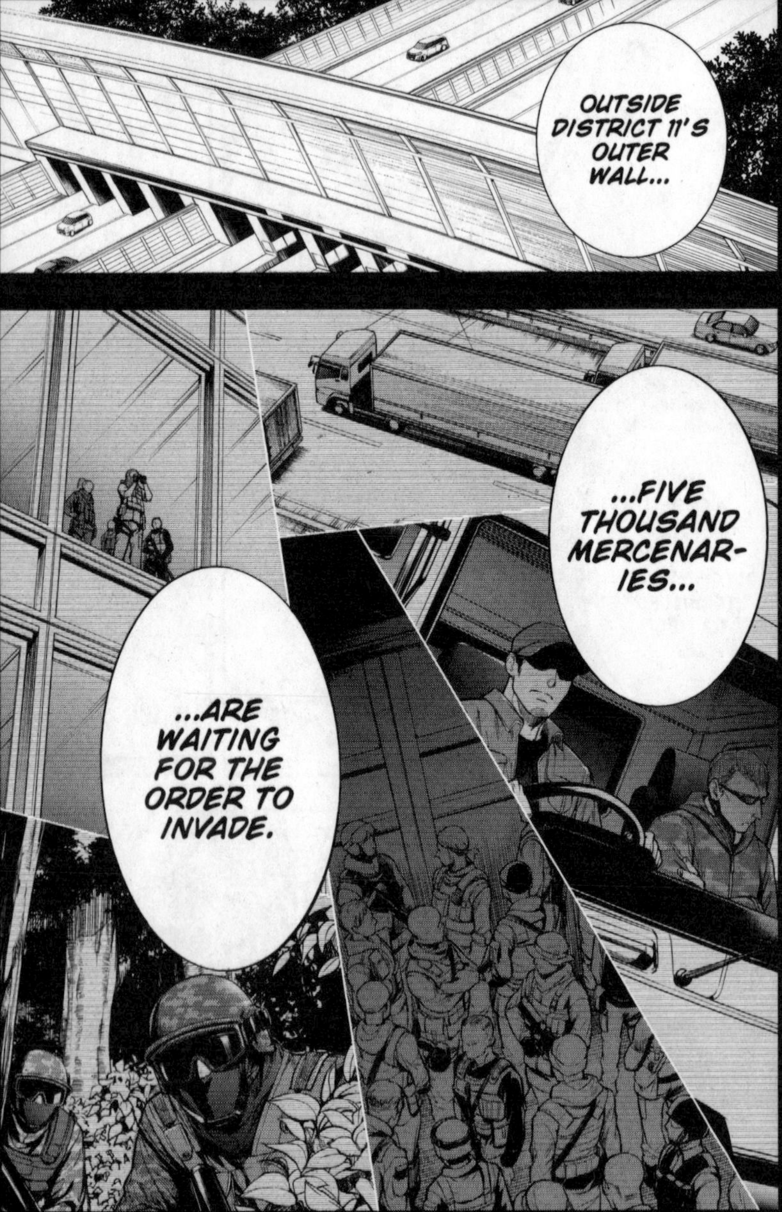
OUTSIDE DISTRICT 11'S OUTER WALL...
...FIVE THOUSAND MERCENAR-IES...
...ARE WAITING FOR THE ORDER TO INVADE.

Transmission data from "UNDER_LINE"

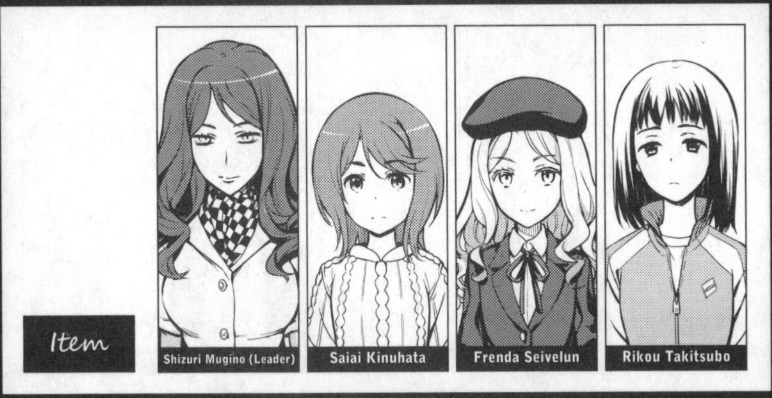
Item
Shizuri Mugino (Leader)
Saiai Kinuhata
Frenda Seivelun
Rikou Takitsubo

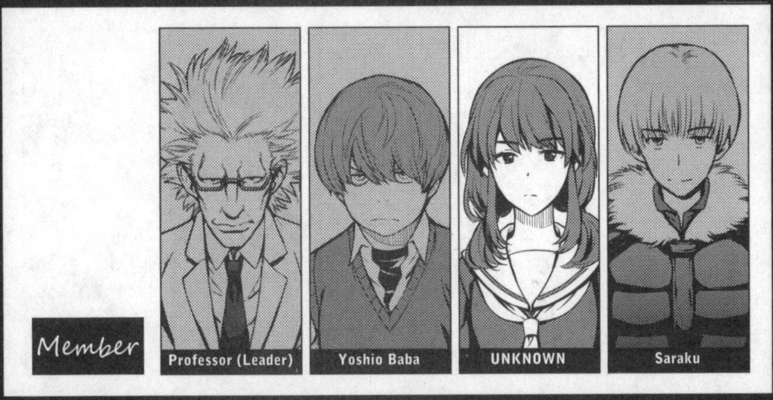
Member
Professor (Leader)
Yoshio Baba
UNKNOWN
Saraku

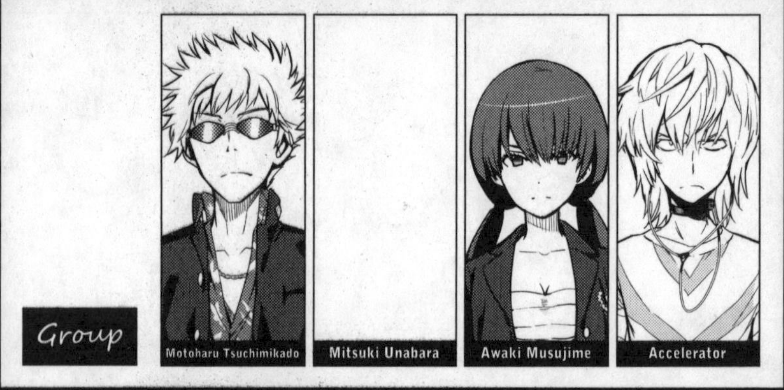
Group
Motoharu Tsuchimikado
Mitsuki Unabara
Awaki Musujime
Accelerator

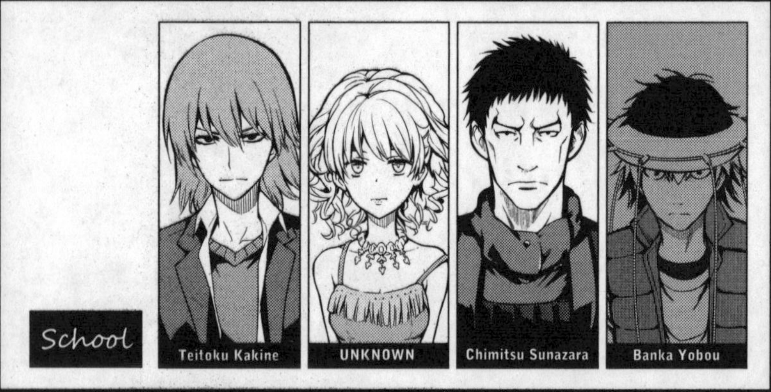
School
Teitoku Kakine
UNKNOWN
Chimitsu Sunazara
Banka Yobou

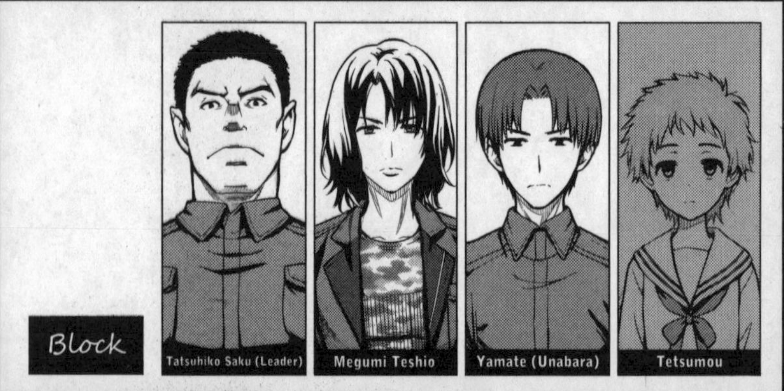
Block
Tatsuhiko Saku (Leader)
Megumi Teshio
Yamate (Unabara)
Tetsumou

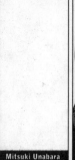

# #139 DISTRICT 11 WAREHOUSE DISTRICT

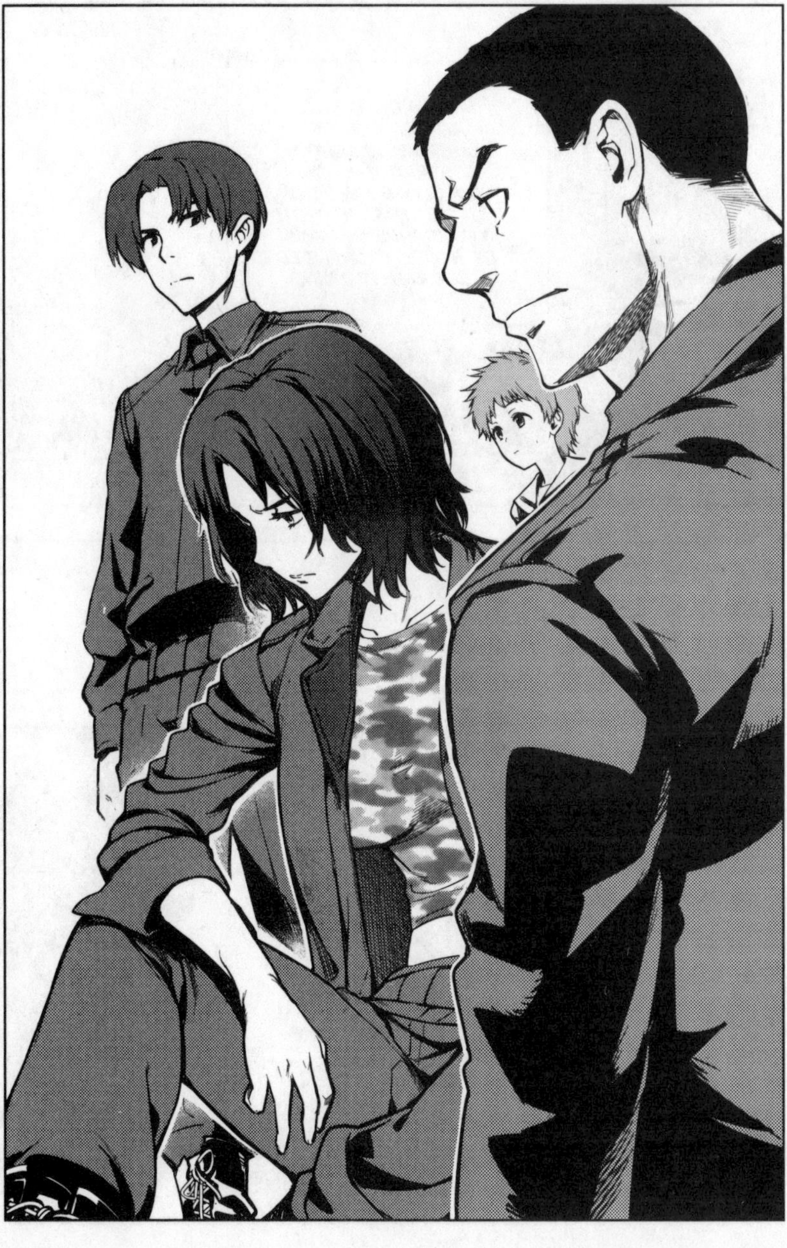

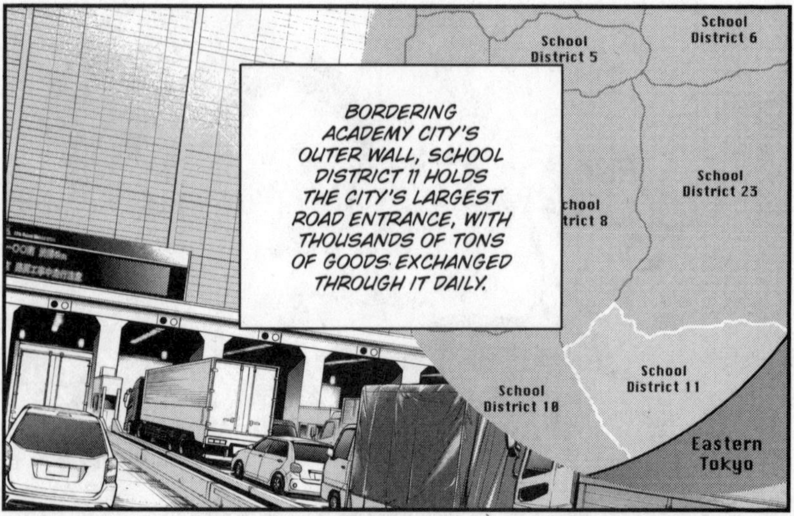
BORDERING ACADEMY CITY'S OUTER WALL, SCHOOL DISTRICT 11 HOLDS THE CITY'S LARGEST ROAD ENTRANCE, WITH THOUSANDS OF TONS OF GOODS EXCHANGED THROUGH IT DAILY.
School District 6
School District 5
School District 23
School District 11
School District 10
Eastern Tokyo

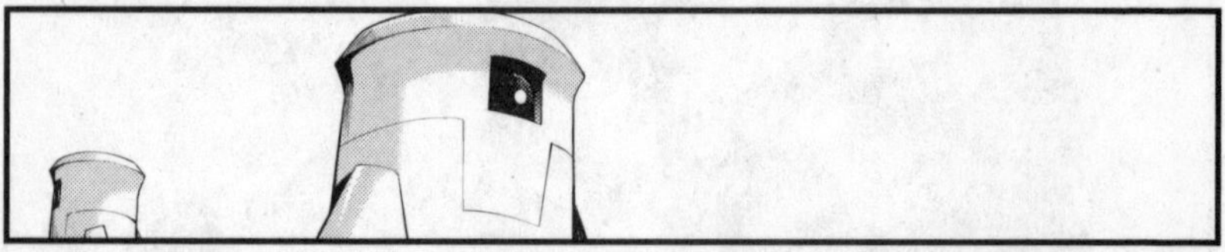

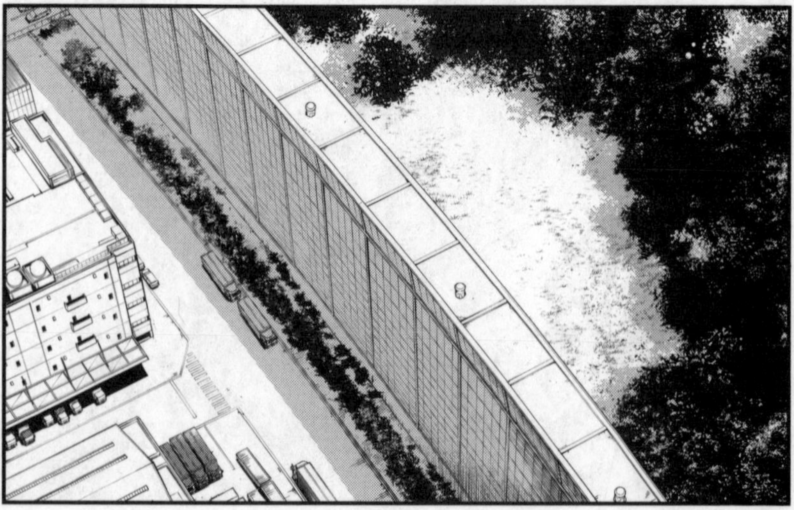

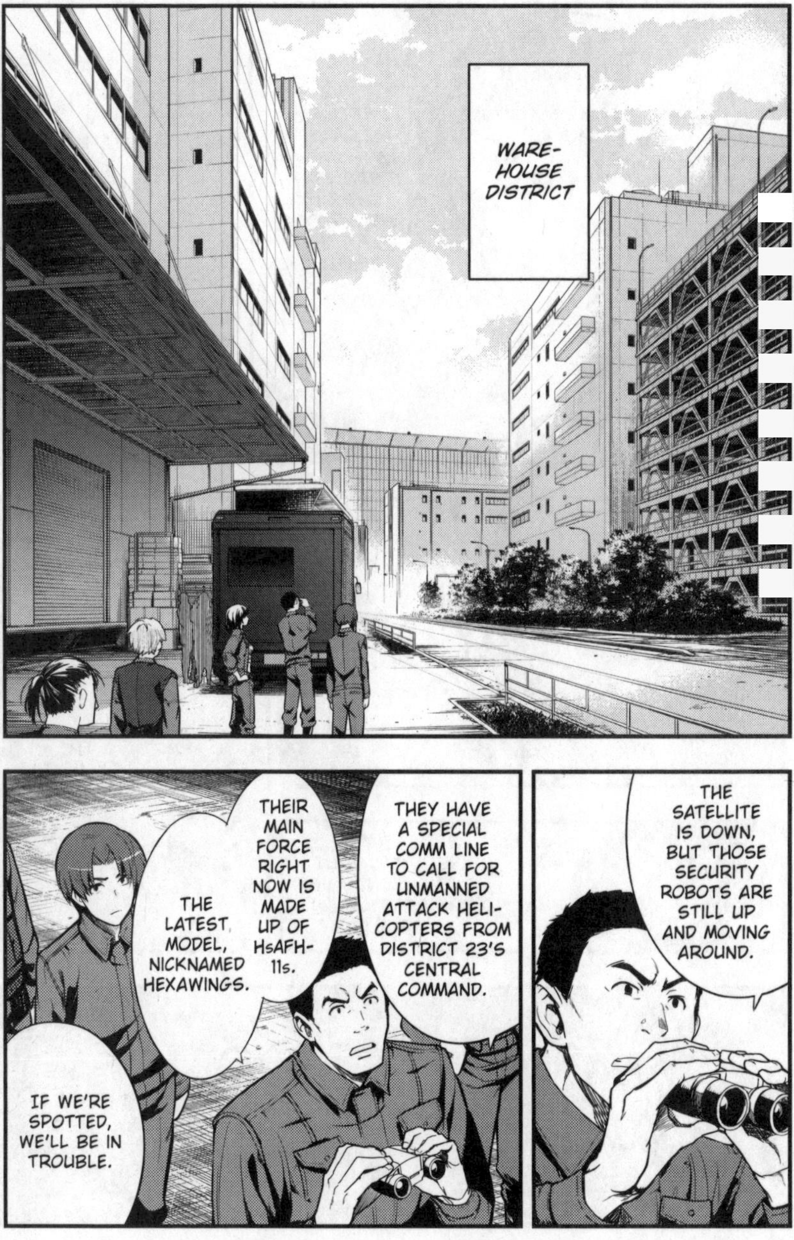
WARE-HOUSE DISTRICT
THE SATELLITE IS DOWN, BUT THOSE SECURITY ROBOTS ARE STILL UP AND MOVING AROUND.
THEY HAVE A SPECIAL COMM LINE TO CALL FOR UNMANNED ATTACK HELI-COPTERS FROM DISTRICT 23'S CENTRAL COMMAND.
THEIR MAIN FORCE RIGHT NOW IS MADE UP OF HsAFH-11s.
THE LATEST MODEL, NICKNAMED HEXAWINGS.
IF WE'RE SPOTTED, WE'LL BE IN TROUBLE.

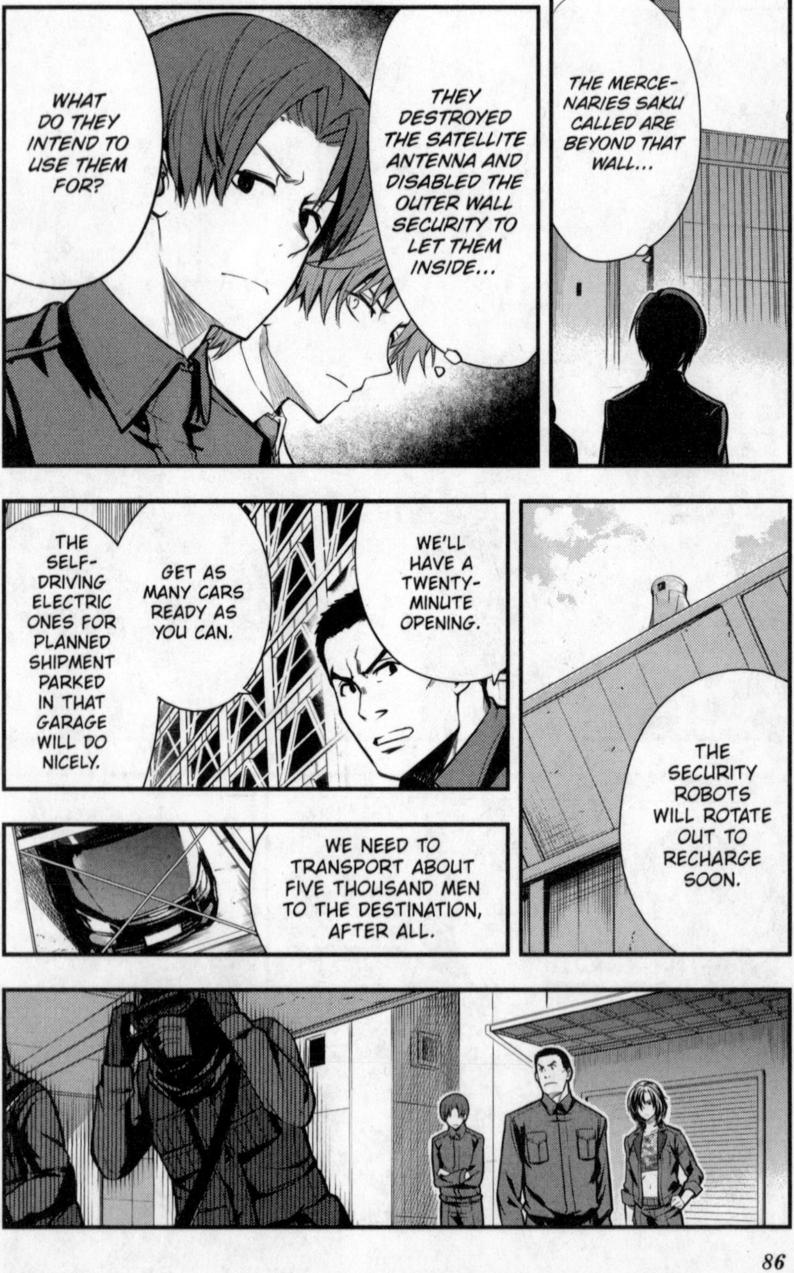
THE MERCENARIES SAKU CALLED ARE BEYOND THAT WALL...
THEY DESTROYED THE SATELLITE ANTENNA AND DISABLED THE OUTER WALL SECURITY TO LET THEM INSIDE...
WHAT DO THEY INTEND TO USE THEM FOR?
THE SECURITY ROBOTS WILL ROTATE OUT TO RECHARGE SOON.
WE'LL HAVE A TWENTY-MINUTE OPENING.
GET AS MANY CARS READY AS YOU CAN.
THE SELF-DRIVING ELECTRIC ONES FOR PLANNED SHIPMENT PARKED IN THAT GARAGE WILL DO NICELY.
WE NEED TO TRANSPORT ABOUT FIVE THOUSAND MEN TO THE DESTINATION, AFTER ALL.

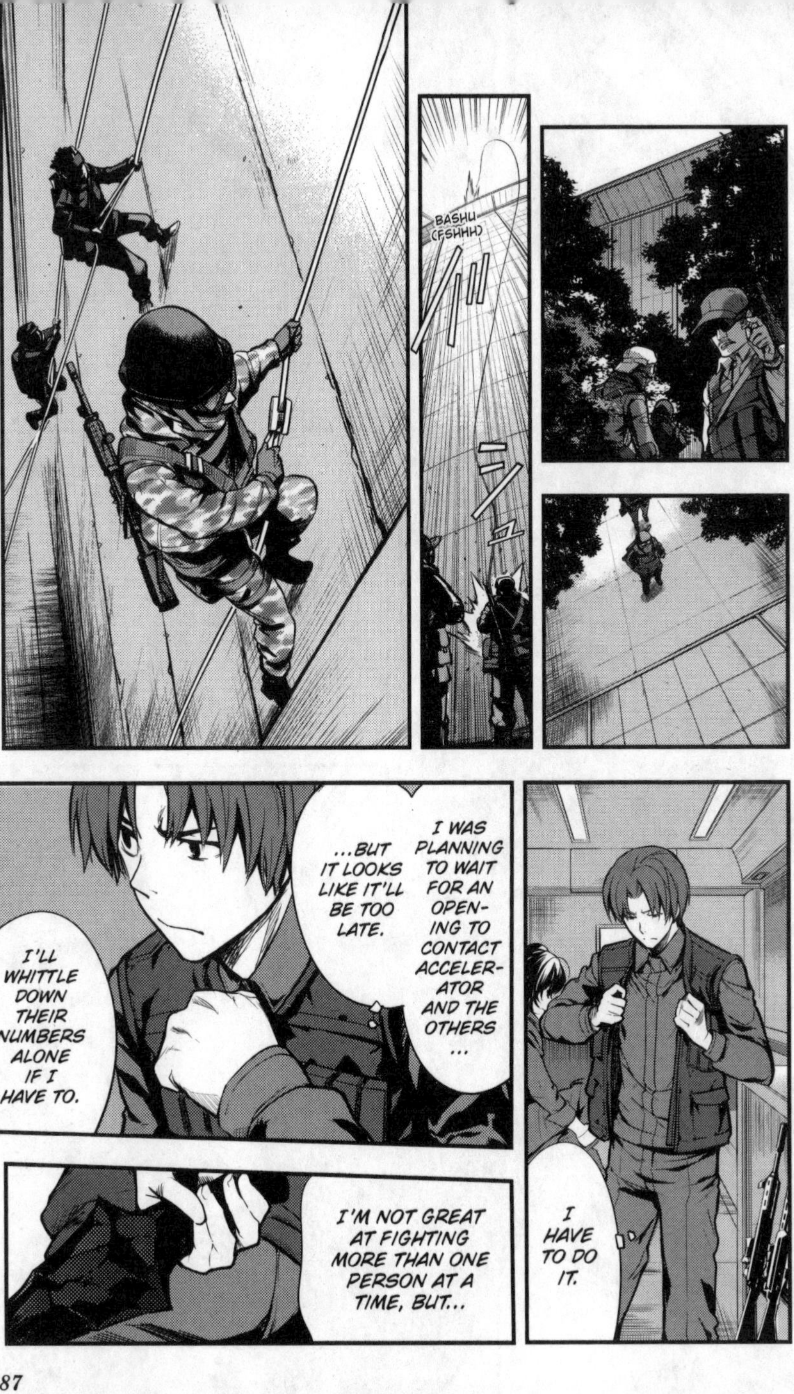
BASHU (FSHHH)
I HAVE TO DO IT.
I WAS PLANNING TO WAIT FOR AN OPEN-ING TO CONTACT ACCELER-ATOR AND THE OTHERS...
...BUT IT LOOKS LIKE IT'LL BE TOO LATE.
I'LL WHITTLE DOWN THEIR NUMBERS ALONE IF I HAVE TO.
I'M NOT GREAT AT FIGHTING MORE THAN ONE PERSON AT A TIME, BUT...

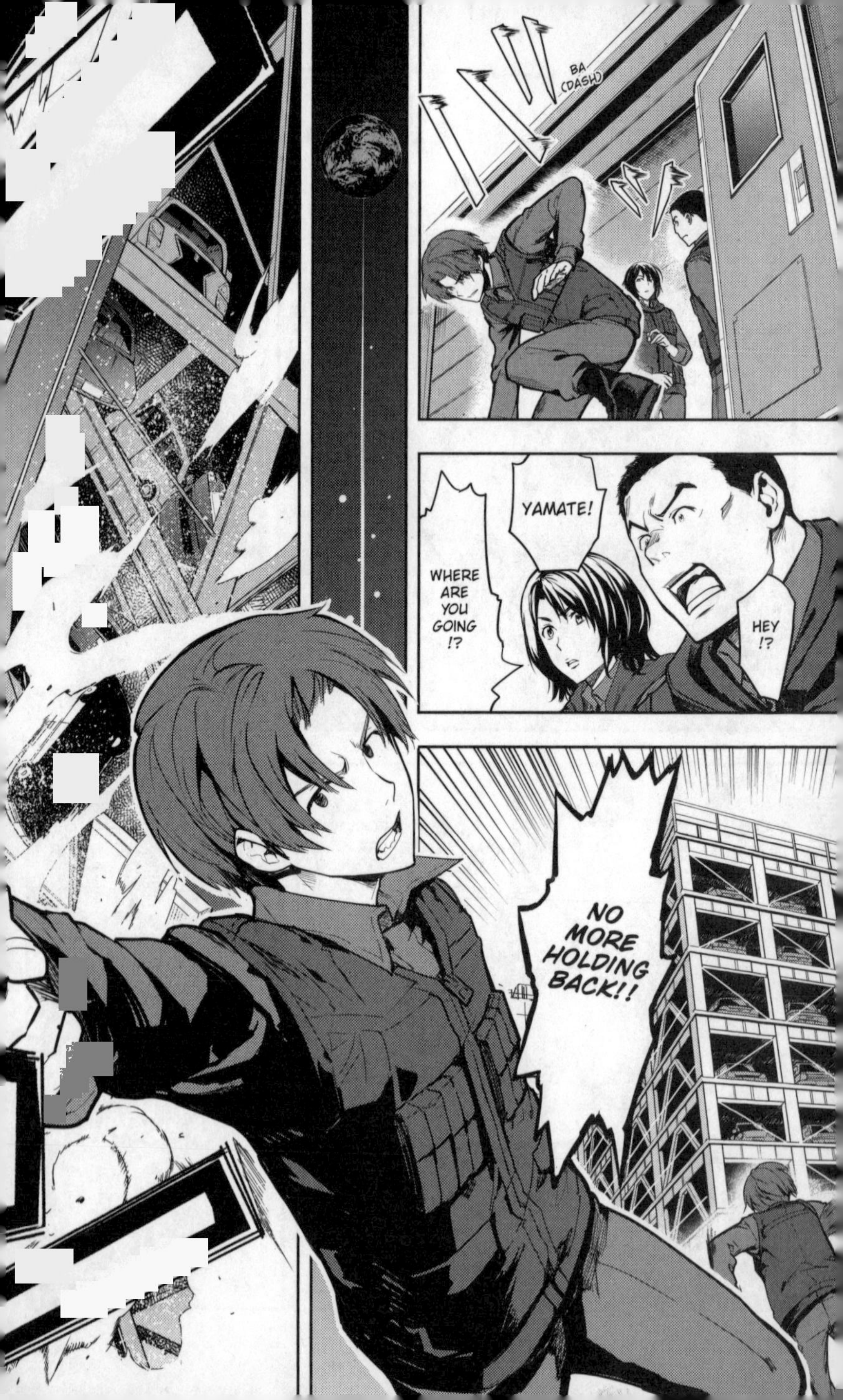
BA (DASH)
HEY!?
YAMATE!
WHERE ARE YOU GOING!?
NO MORE HOLDING BACK!!

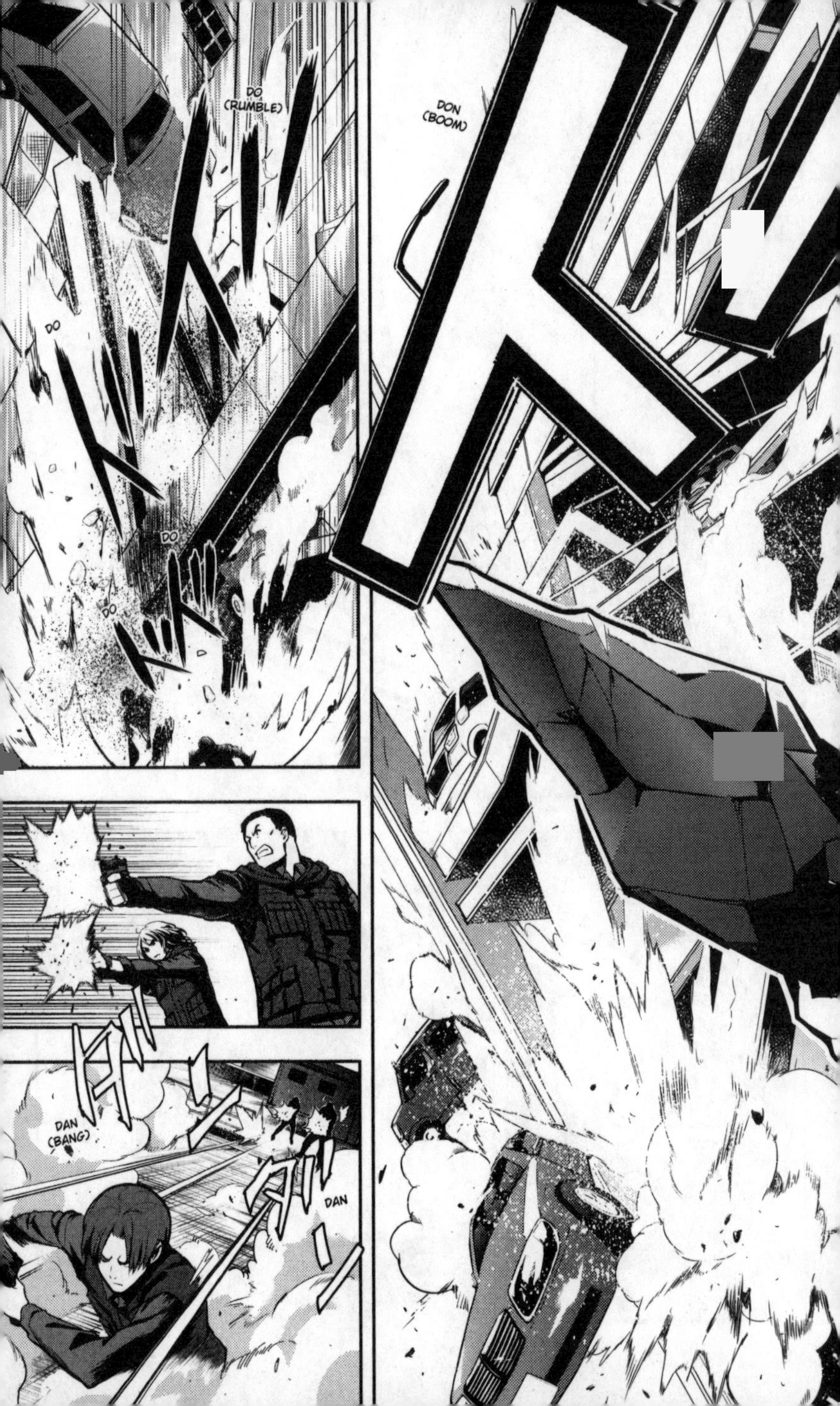
DON
(BOOM)
DO
(RUMBLE)
DO
DO
DO
DAN
(BANG)
DAN

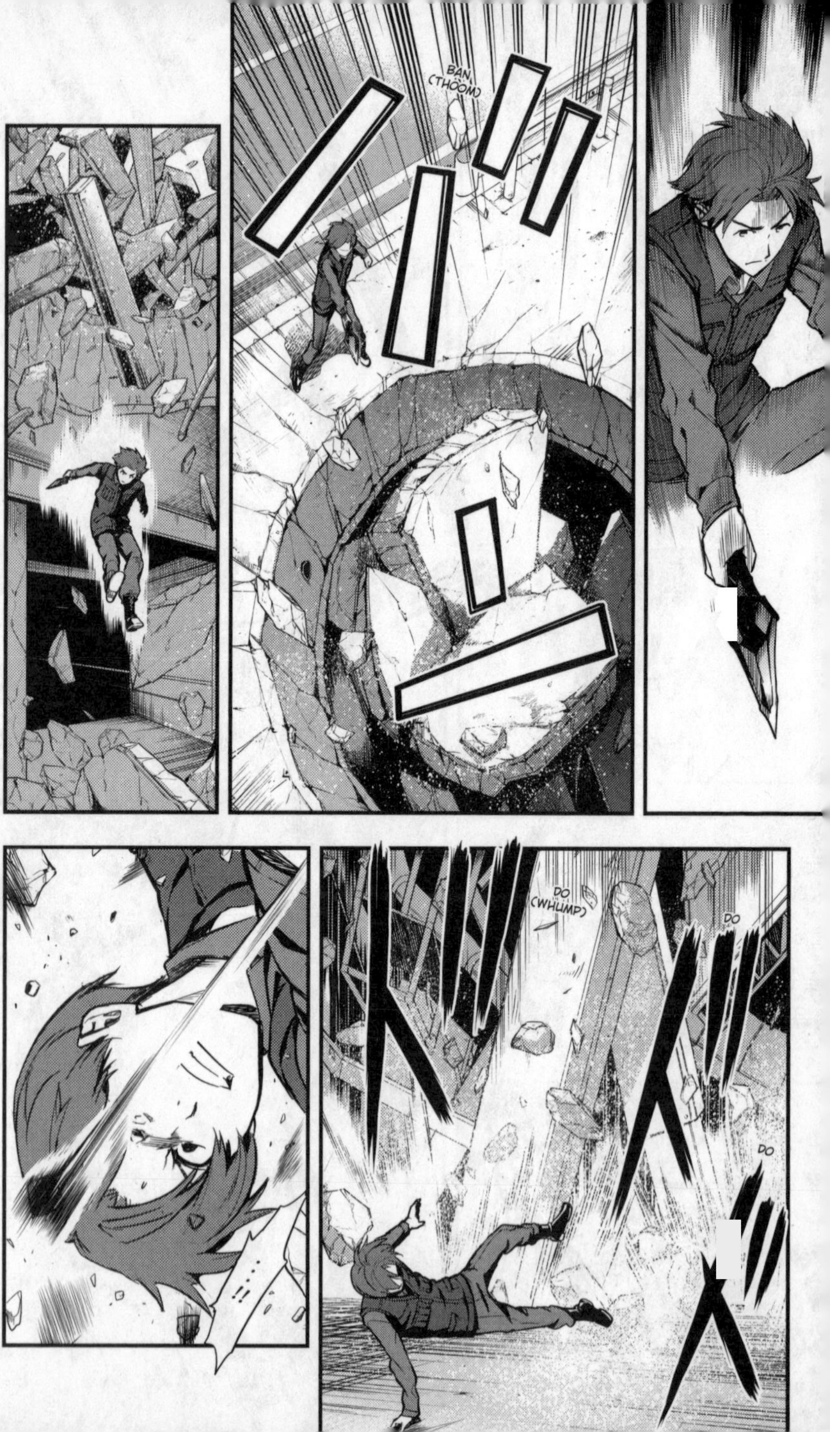
BAN (THOOM)
DO (WHUMP)
DO
DO
!!

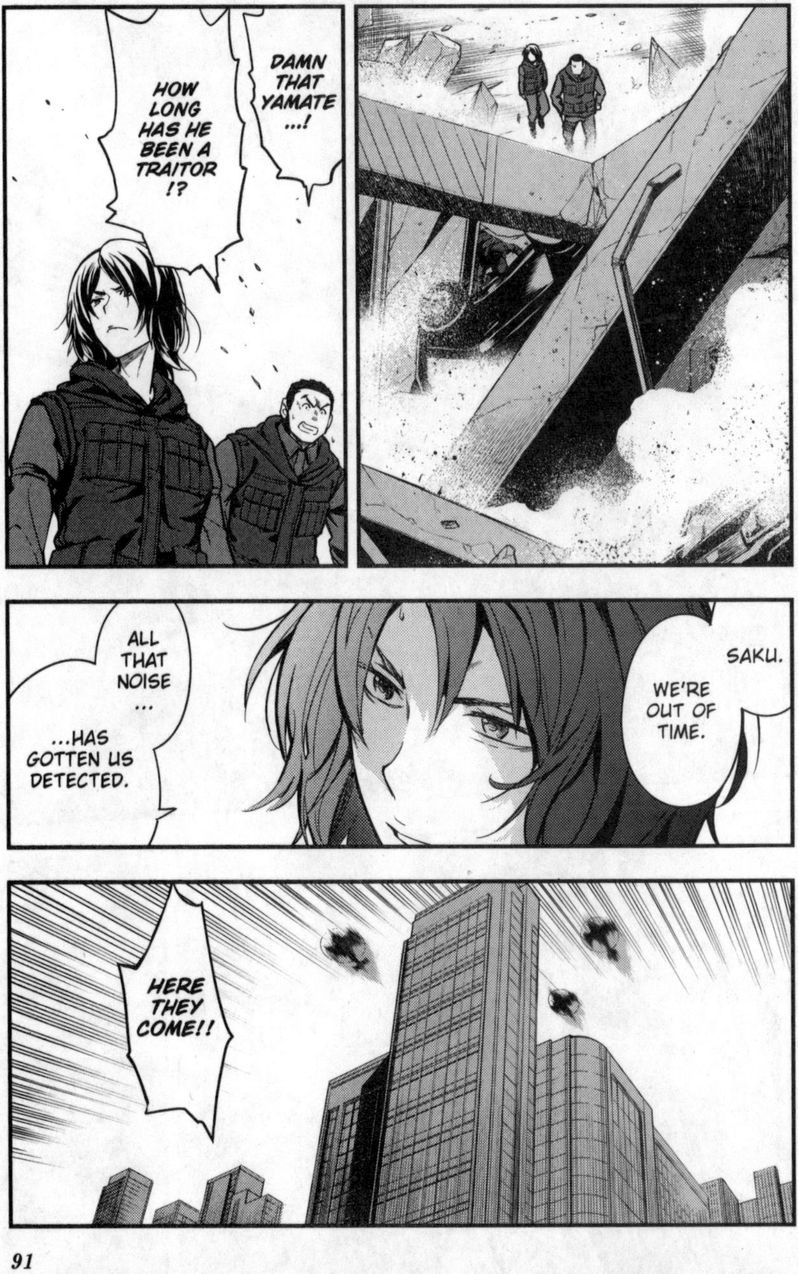
DAMN THAT YAMATE ...!
HOW LONG HAS HE BEEN A TRAITOR !?
SAKU.
WE'RE OUT OF TIME.
ALL THAT NOISE ...
...HAS GOTTEN US DETECTED.
HERE THEY COME!!

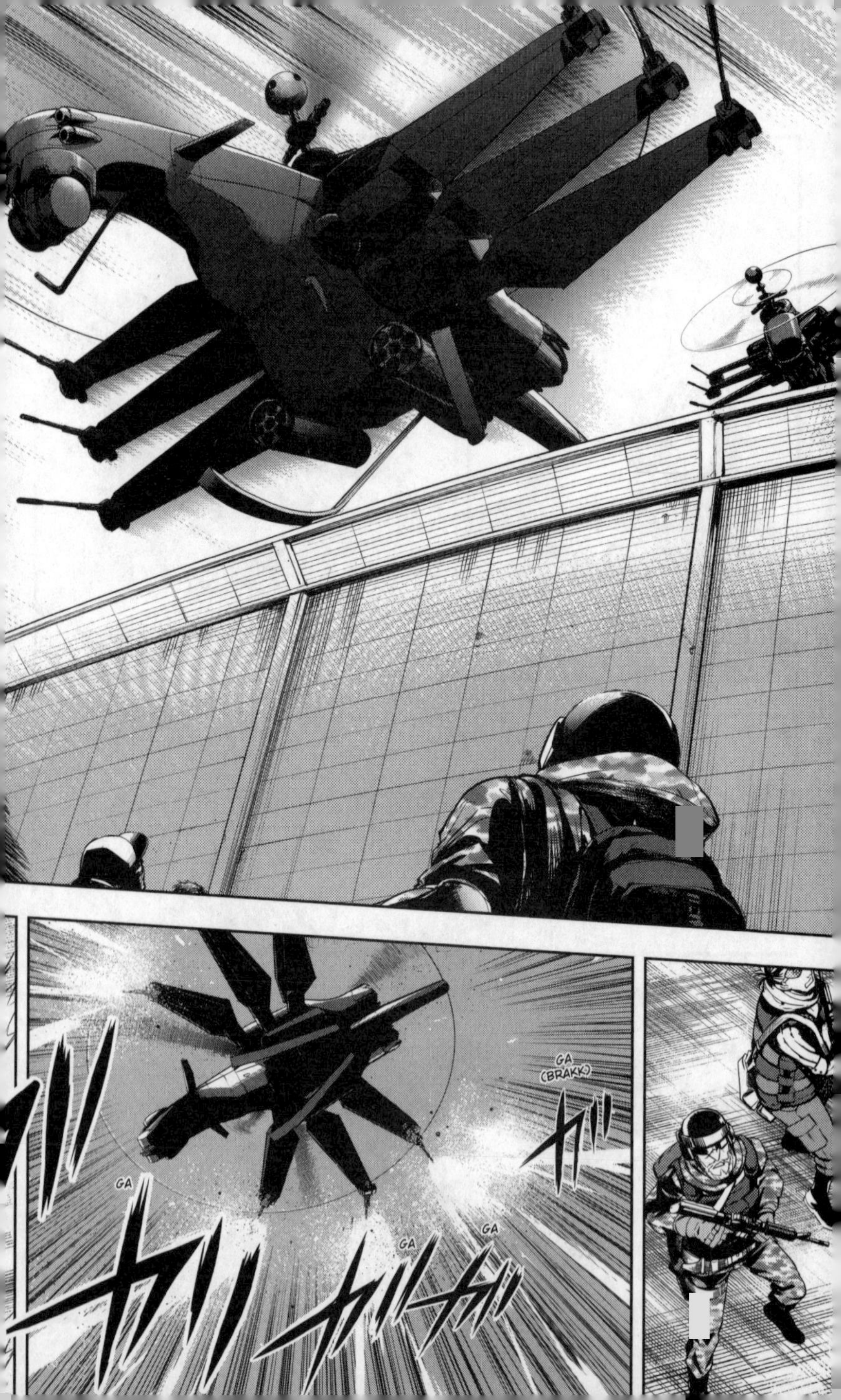
GA
(BRAKK)
GA
GA
GA

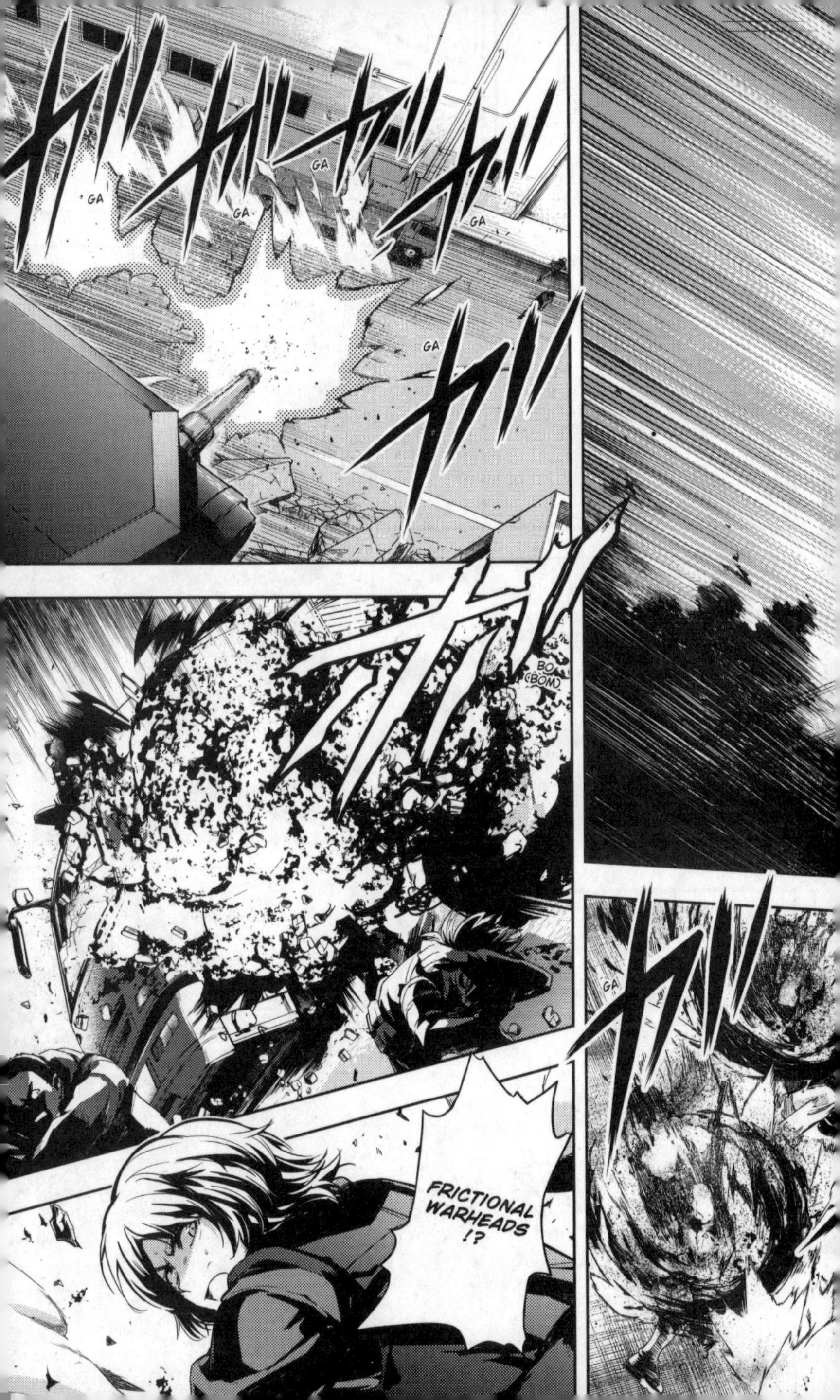
GA
GA
GA
GA
GA
BO (BOM)
GA
FRICTIONAL WARHEADS !?

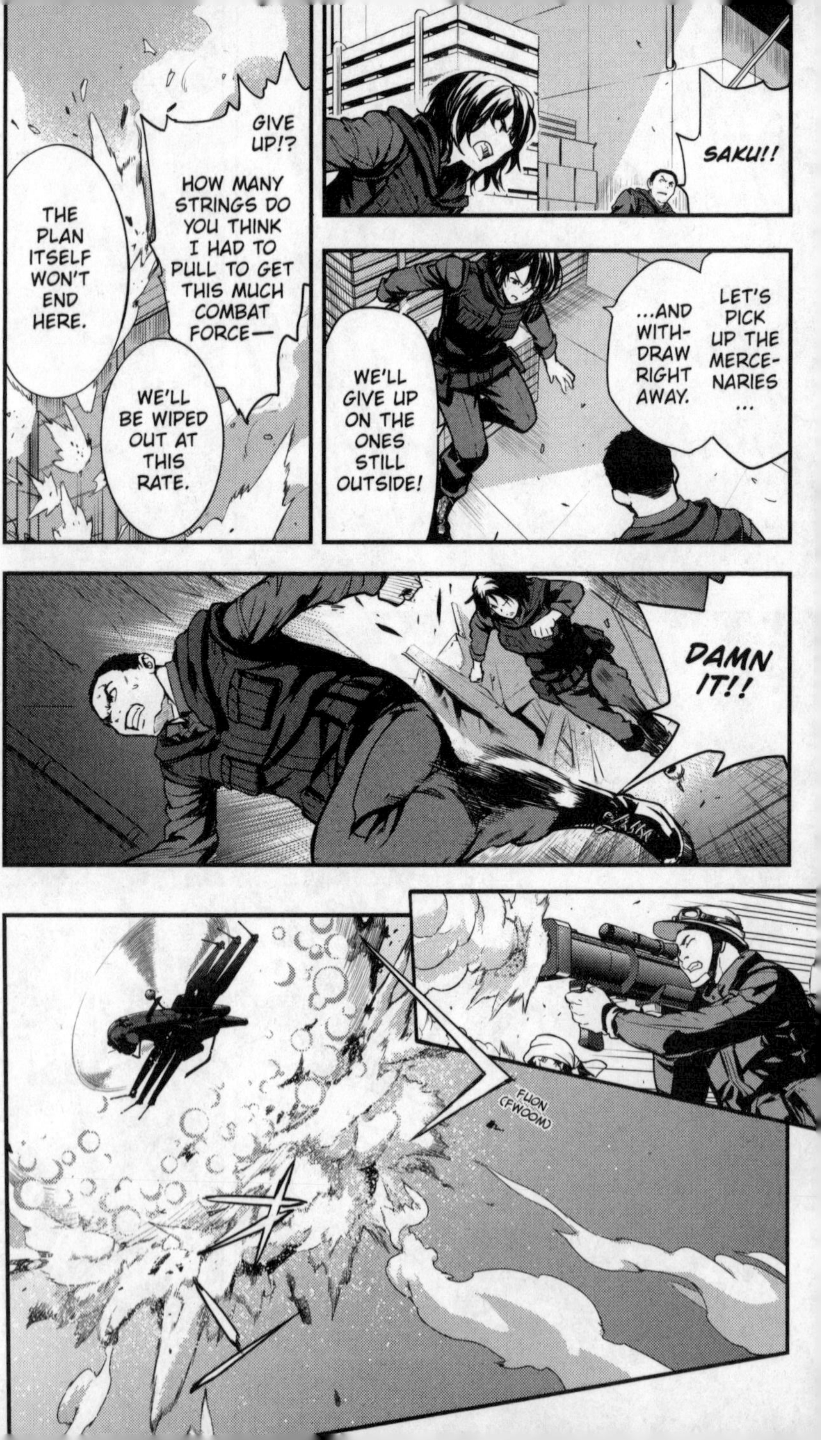
SAKU!!
LET'S PICK UP THE MERCENARIES...
...AND WITHDRAW RIGHT AWAY.
WE'LL GIVE UP ON THE ONES STILL OUTSIDE!
GIVE UP!? HOW MANY STRINGS DO YOU THINK I HAD TO PULL TO GET THIS MUCH COMBAT FORCE—
THE PLAN ITSELF WON'T END HERE.
WE'LL BE WIPED OUT AT THIS RATE.
DAMN IT!!
FUON (FWOOM)

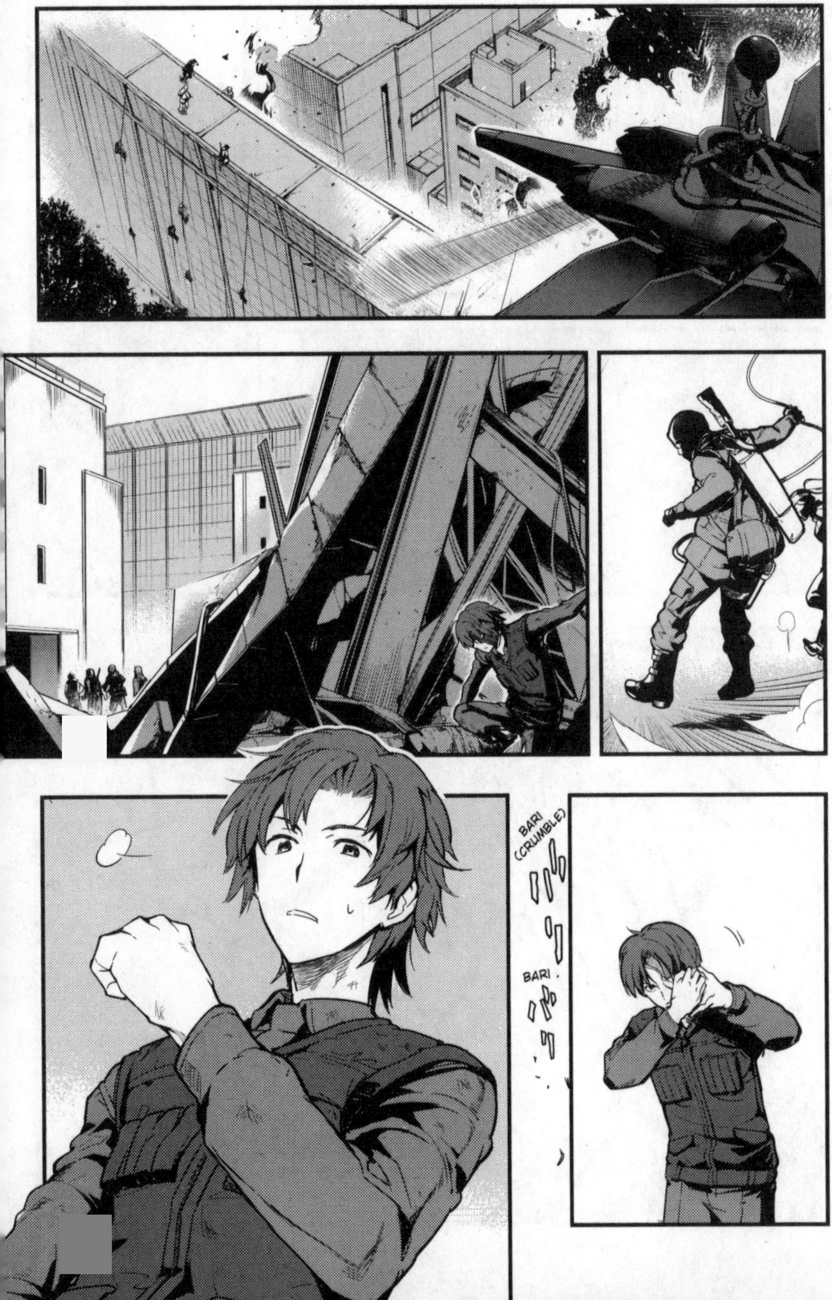
BARI
(CRUMBLE)
BARI

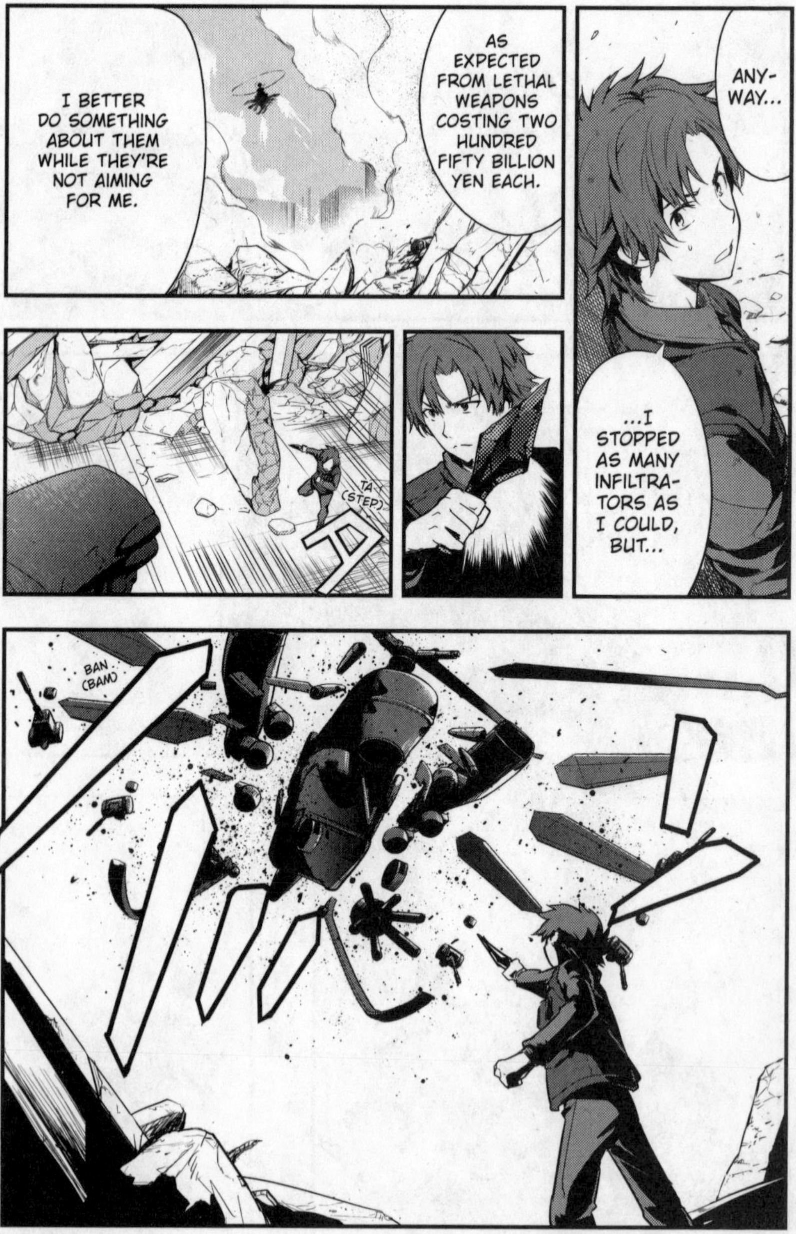
ANY-WAY...
...I STOPPED AS MANY INFILTRA-TORS AS I COULD, BUT...
AS EXPECTED FROM LETHAL WEAPONS COSTING TWO HUNDRED FIFTY BILLION YEN EACH.
I BETTER DO SOMETHING ABOUT THEM WHILE THEY'RE NOT AIMING FOR ME.
TA (STEP)
BAN (BAM)

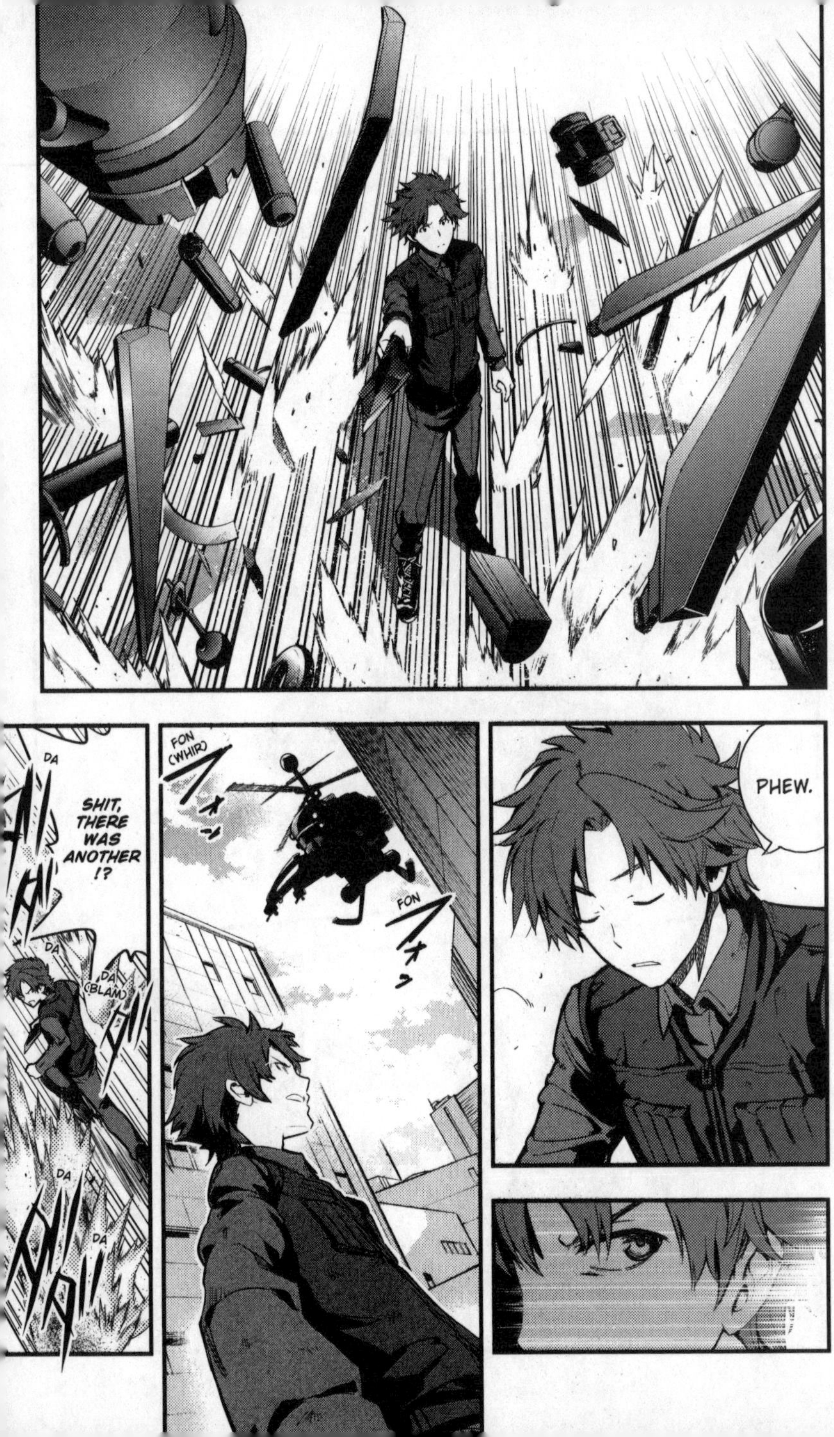
PHEW.
FON (WHIR)
FON
DA
SHIT, THERE WAS ANOTHER !?
DA
DA (BLAM)
DA
DA

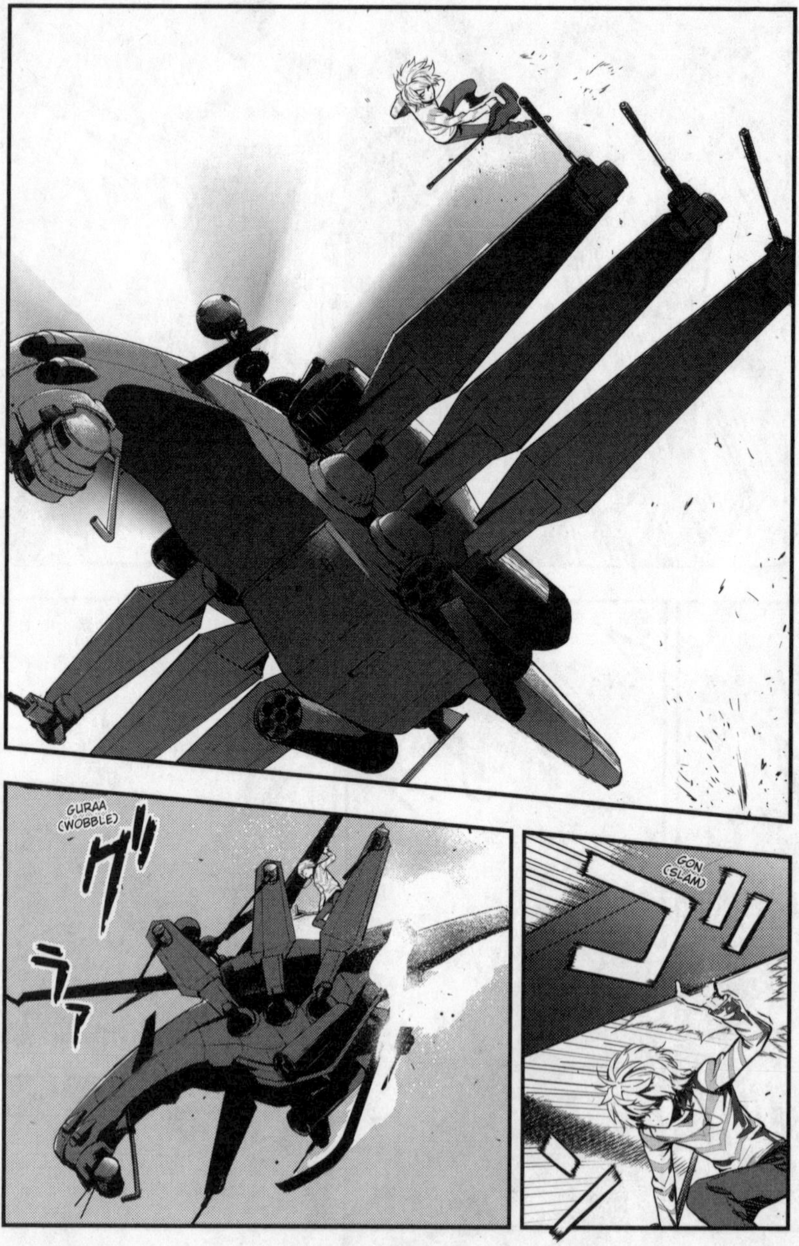
ゴッ
GON (SLAM)
グラァ
GURAA (WOBBLE)

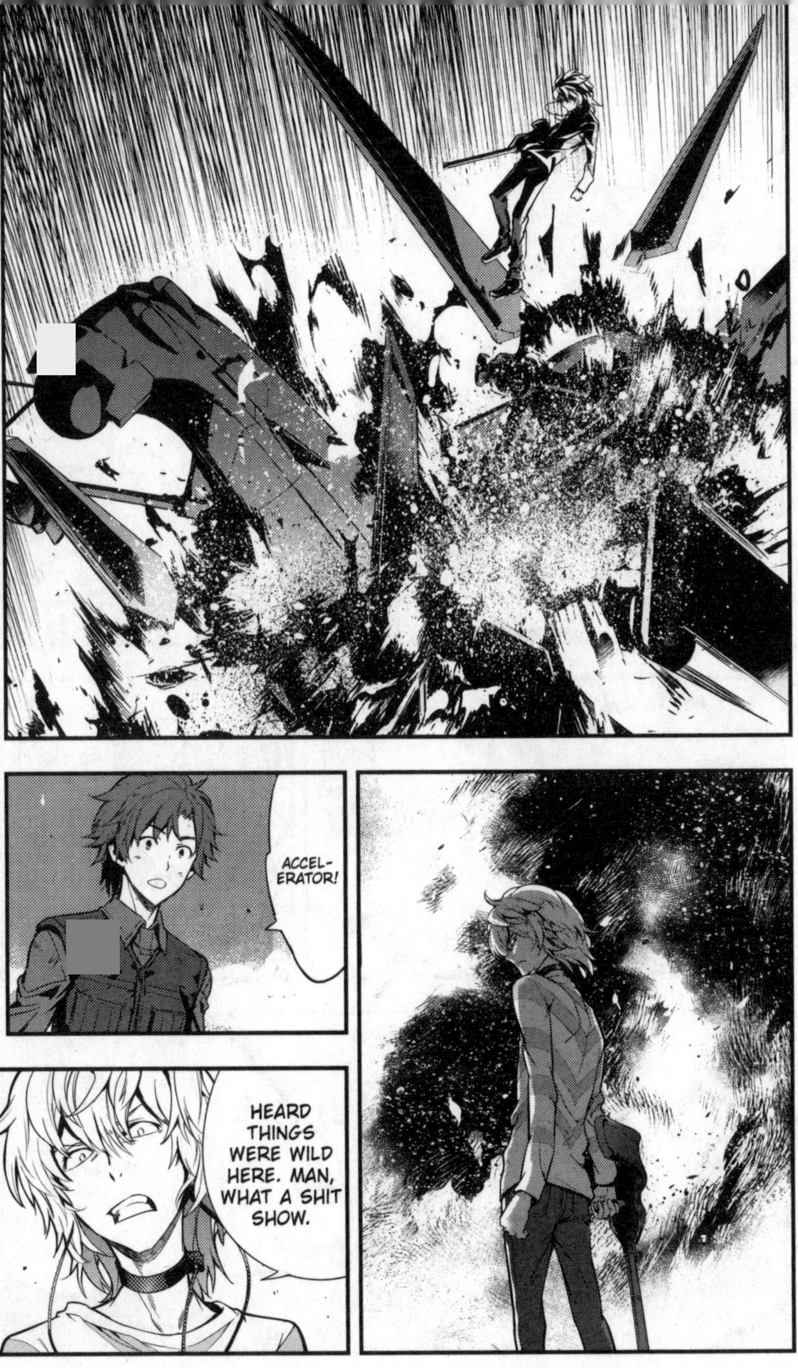
ACCEL-
ERATOR!
HEARD THINGS WERE WILD HERE. MAN, WHAT A SHIT SHOW.

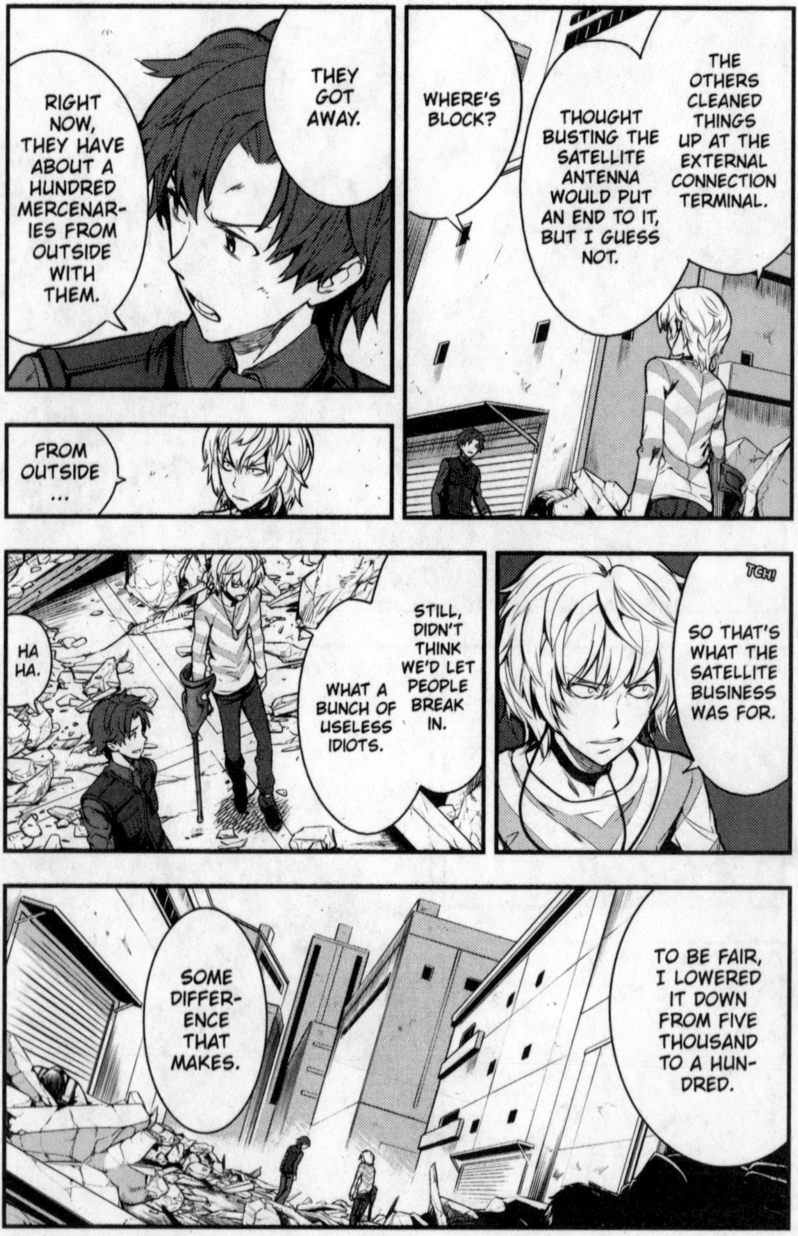
THE OTHERS CLEANED THINGS UP AT THE EXTERNAL CONNECTION TERMINAL.
THOUGHT BUSTING THE SATELLITE ANTENNA WOULD PUT AN END TO IT, BUT I GUESS NOT.
WHERE'S BLOCK?
THEY GOT AWAY.
RIGHT NOW, THEY HAVE ABOUT A HUNDRED MERCENARIES FROM OUTSIDE WITH THEM.
FROM OUTSIDE ...
TCH!
SO THAT'S WHAT THE SATELLITE BUSINESS WAS FOR.
STILL, DIDN'T THINK WE'D LET PEOPLE BREAK IN.
WHAT A BUNCH OF USELESS IDIOTS.
HA HA.
TO BE FAIR, I LOWERED IT DOWN FROM FIVE THOUSAND TO A HUNDRED.
SOME DIFFERENCE THAT MAKES.

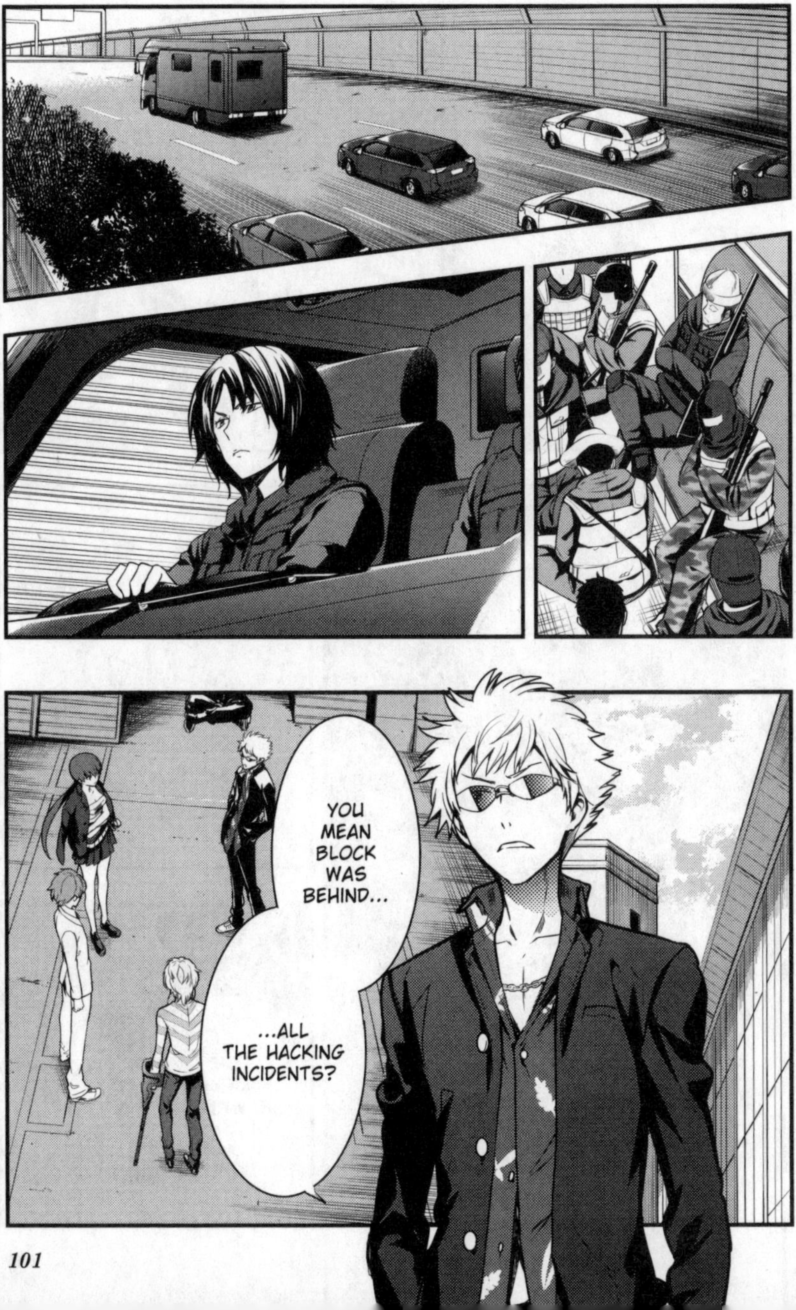
YOU MEAN BLOCK WAS BEHIND...
...ALL THE HACKING INCIDENTS?

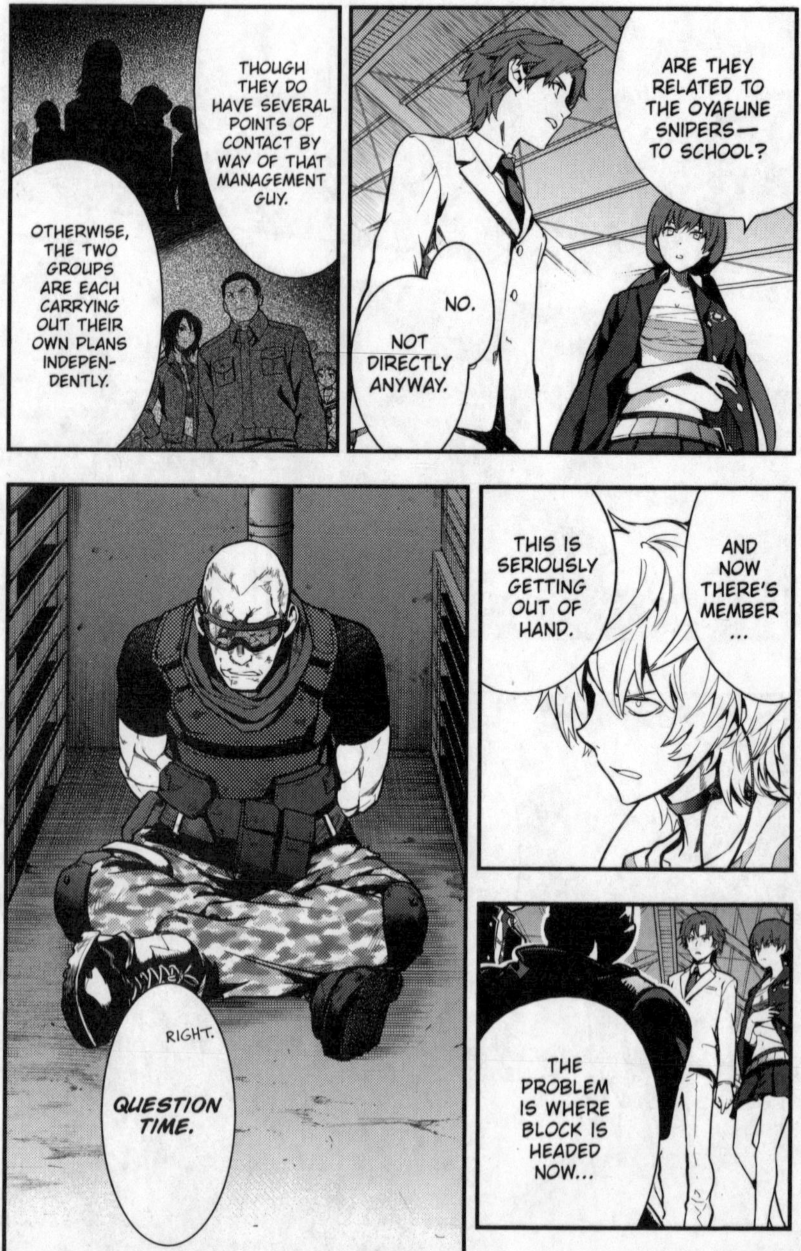

ARE THEY RELATED TO THE OYAFUNE SNIPERS— TO SCHOOL?
NO.
NOT DIRECTLY ANYWAY.
THOUGH THEY DO HAVE SEVERAL POINTS OF CONTACT BY WAY OF THAT MANAGEMENT GUY.
OTHERWISE, THE TWO GROUPS ARE EACH CARRYING OUT THEIR OWN PLANS INDEPEN-DENTLY.
AND NOW THERE'S MEMBER...
THIS IS SERIOUSLY GETTING OUT OF HAND.
THE PROBLEM IS WHERE BLOCK IS HEADED NOW...
RIGHT.
QUESTION TIME.

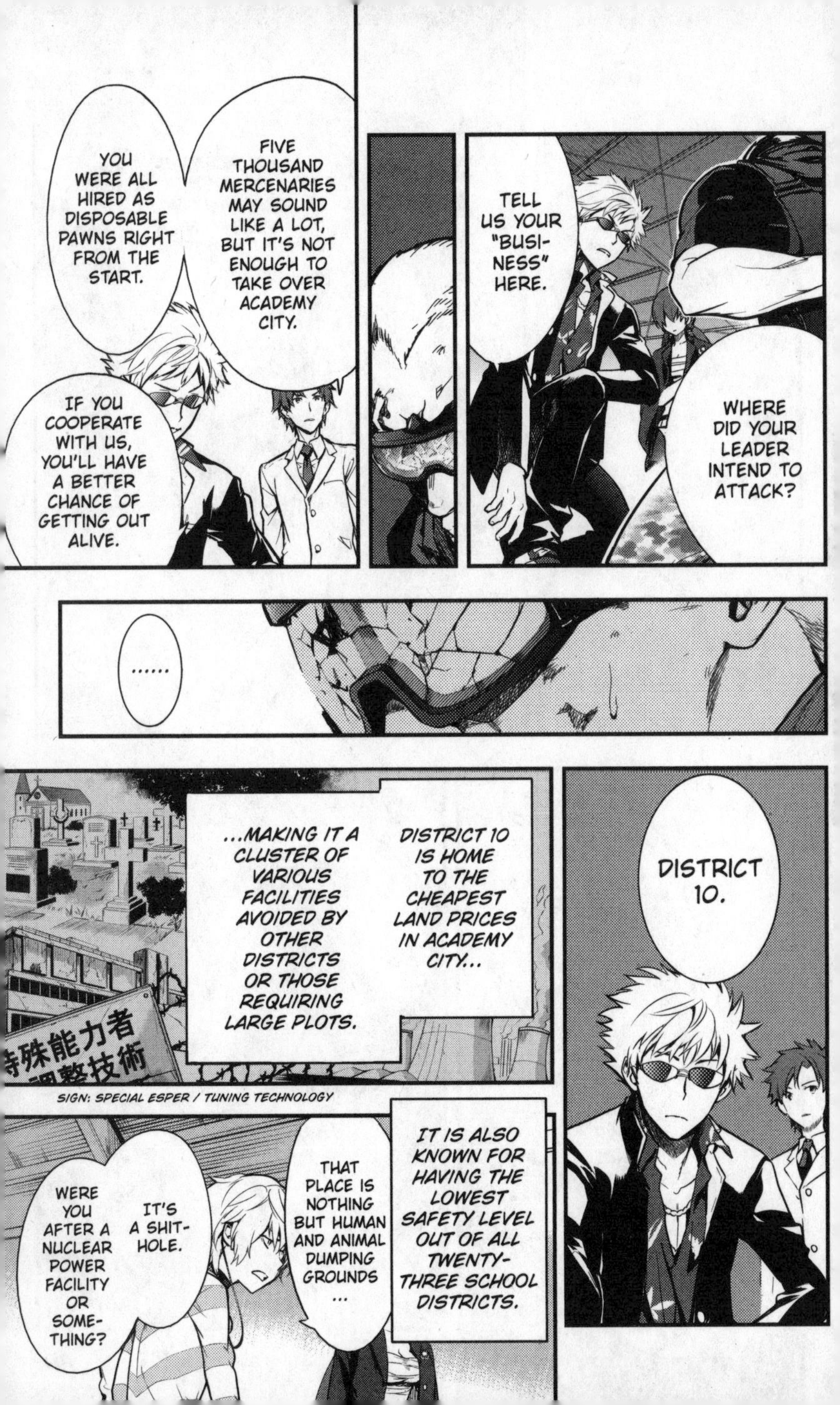

TELL US YOUR "BUSI-NESS" HERE.
WHERE DID YOUR LEADER INTEND TO ATTACK?
FIVE THOUSAND MERCENARIES MAY SOUND LIKE A LOT, BUT IT'S NOT ENOUGH TO TAKE OVER ACADEMY CITY.
YOU WERE ALL HIRED AS DISPOSABLE PAWNS RIGHT FROM THE START.
IF YOU COOPERATE WITH US, YOU'LL HAVE A BETTER CHANCE OF GETTING OUT ALIVE.
......
DISTRICT 10.
DISTRICT 10 IS HOME TO THE CHEAPEST LAND PRICES IN ACADEMY CITY...
...MAKING IT A CLUSTER OF VARIOUS FACILITIES AVOIDED BY OTHER DISTRICTS OR THOSE REQUIRING LARGE PLOTS.
特殊能力者
調整技術
SIGN: SPECIAL ESPER / TUNING TECHNOLOGY
IT IS ALSO KNOWN FOR HAVING THE LOWEST SAFETY LEVEL OUT OF ALL TWENTY-THREE SCHOOL DISTRICTS.
THAT PLACE IS NOTHING BUT HUMAN AND ANIMAL DUMPING GROUNDS...
IT'S A SHIT-HOLE.
WERE YOU AFTER A NUCLEAR POWER FACILITY OR SOME-THING?

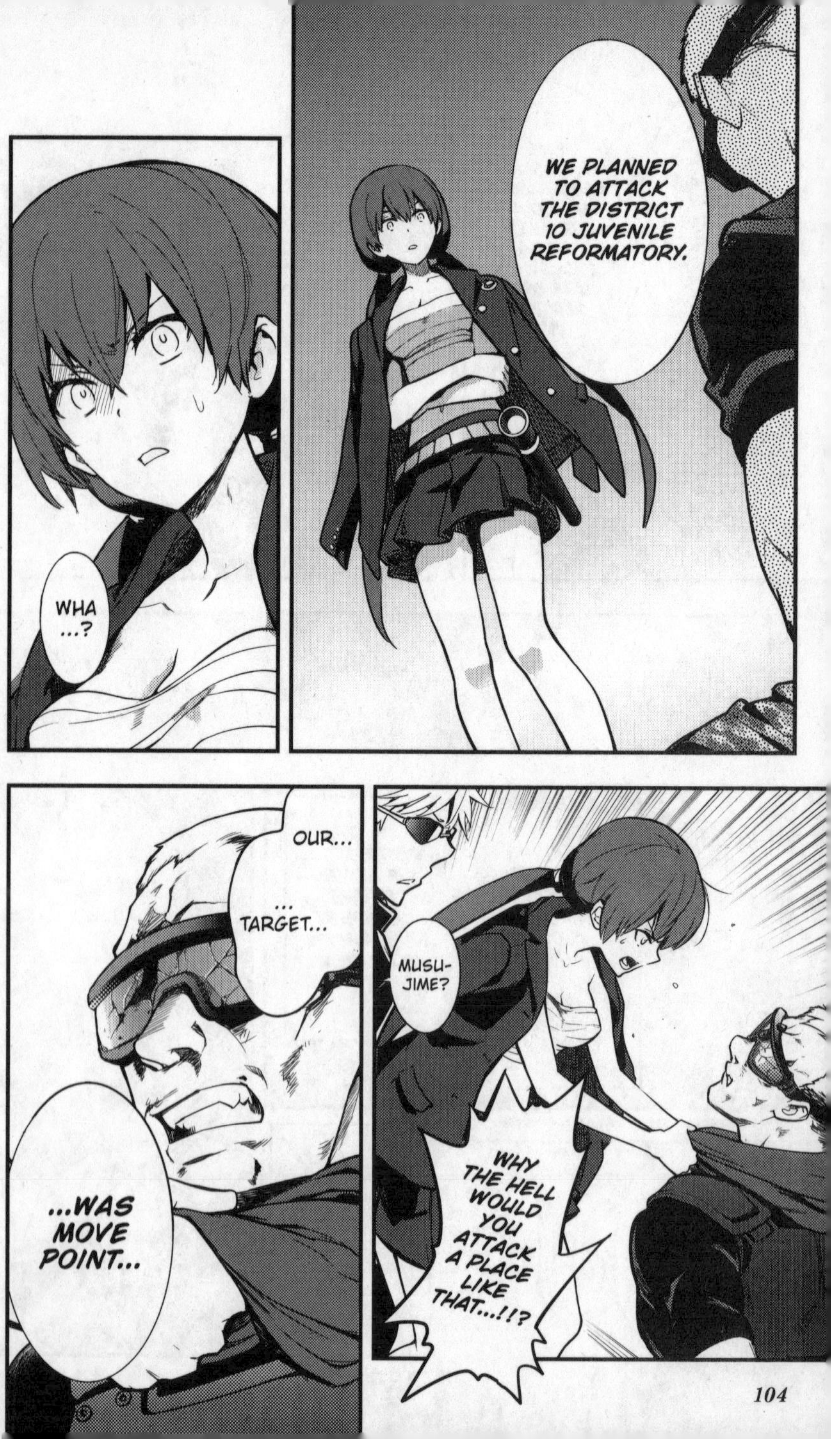
WE PLANNED TO ATTACK THE DISTRICT 10 JUVENILE REFORMATORY.
WHA ...?
MUSU-JIME?
WHY THE HELL WOULD YOU ATTACK A PLACE LIKE THAT...!!?
OUR...
... TARGET...
...WAS MOVE POINT...

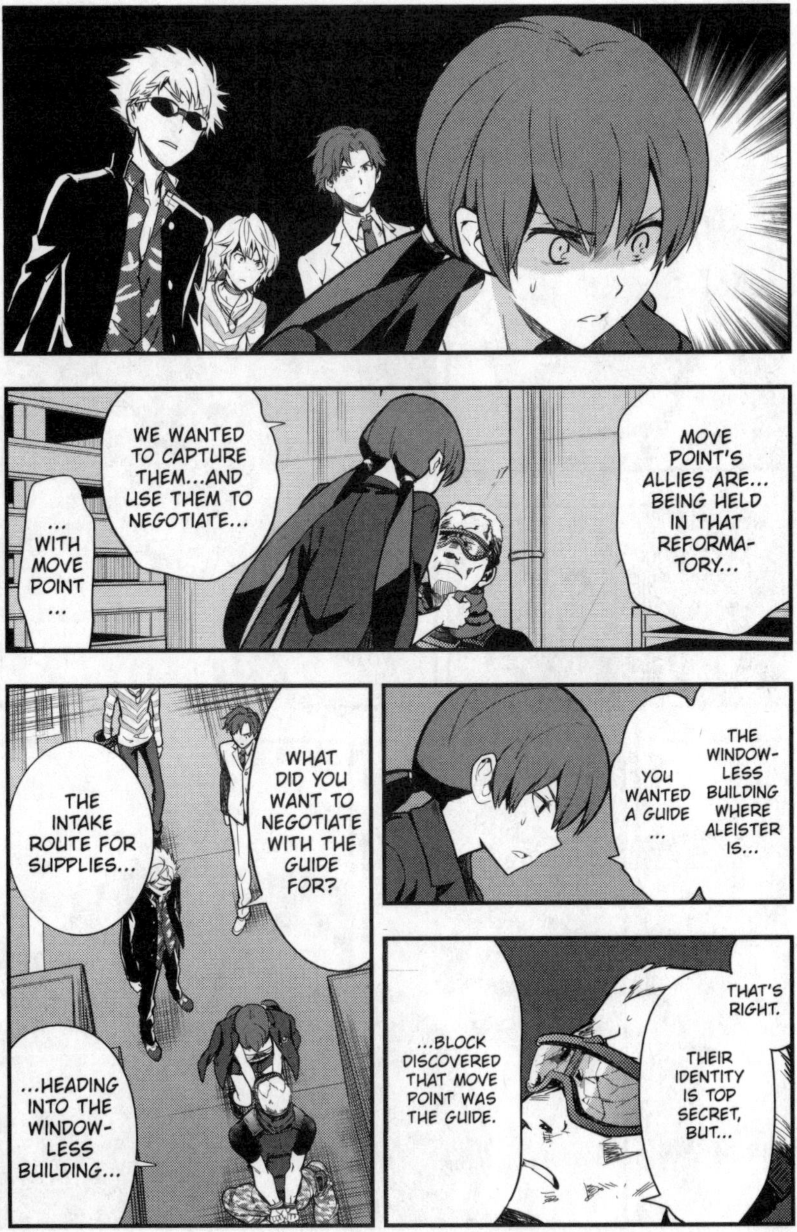
MOVE POINT'S ALLIES ARE... BEING HELD IN THAT REFORMA-TORY...
WE WANTED TO CAPTURE THEM...AND USE THEM TO NEGOTIATE...
... WITH MOVE POINT ...
THE WINDOW-LESS BUILDING WHERE ALEISTER IS...
YOU WANTED A GUIDE ...
THAT'S RIGHT.
THEIR IDENTITY IS TOP SECRET, BUT...
...BLOCK DISCOVERED THAT MOVE POINT WAS THE GUIDE.
WHAT DID YOU WANT TO NEGOTIATE WITH THE GUIDE FOR?
THE INTAKE ROUTE FOR SUPPLIES...
...HEADING INTO THE WINDOW-LESS BUILDING...

I SEE.

EVEN NUKES CAN'T DESTROY IT FROM THE OUTSIDE... BUT WHAT ABOUT THE INSIDE?

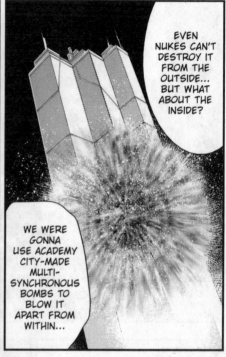

WE WERE GONNA USE ACADEMY CITY-MADE MULTI-SYNCHRONOUS BOMBS TO BLOW IT APART FROM WITHIN...

DOSA (THUD)

PARIN (CRCK)

NO...

THAT CAN'T BE...

BY THE WAY...

...DO YOU KNOW WHO'S STANDING IN FRONT OF YOU RIGHT NOW?

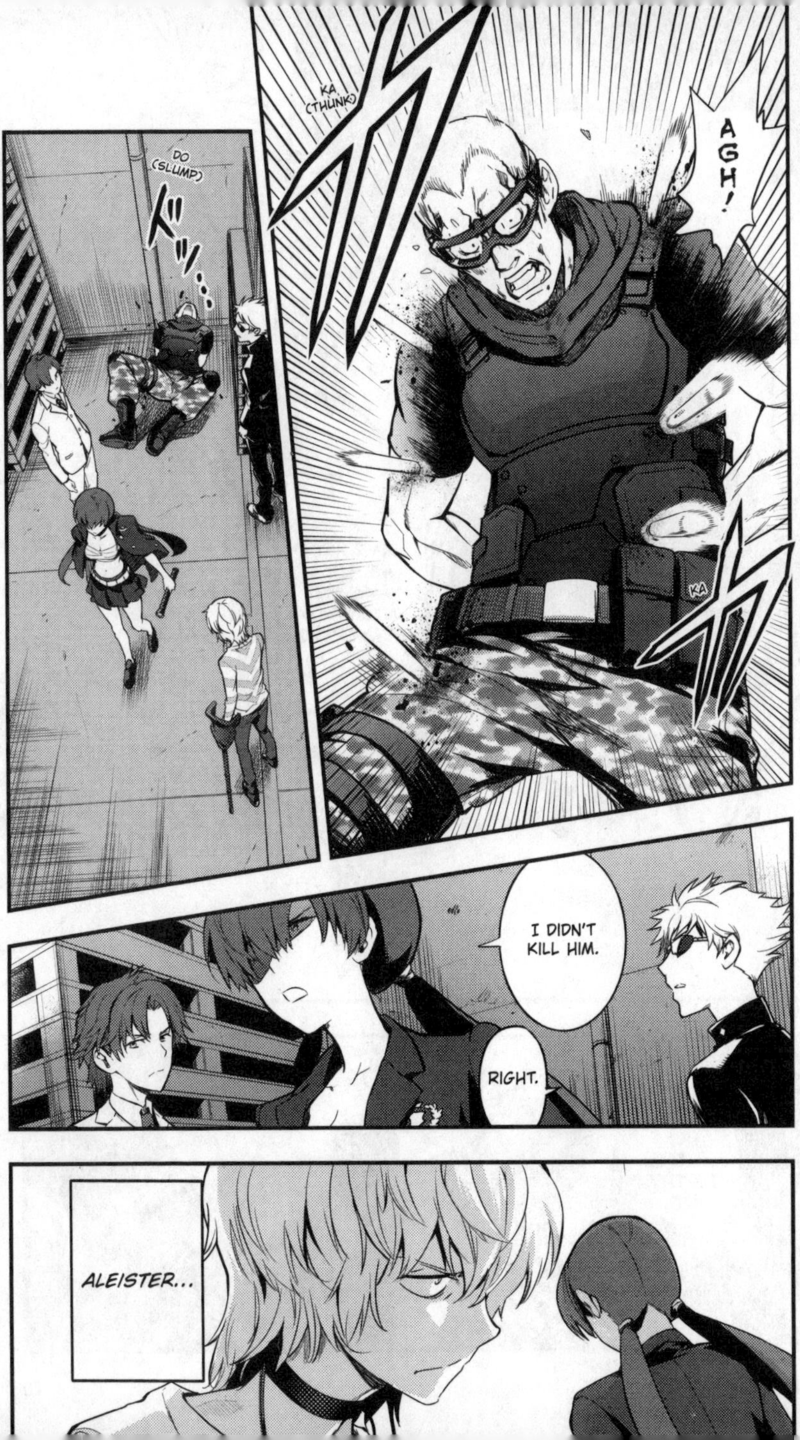
KA (THUNK)
AGH!
KA
DO (SLUMP)
ドッ…
I DIDN'T KILL HIM.
RIGHT.
ALEISTER...

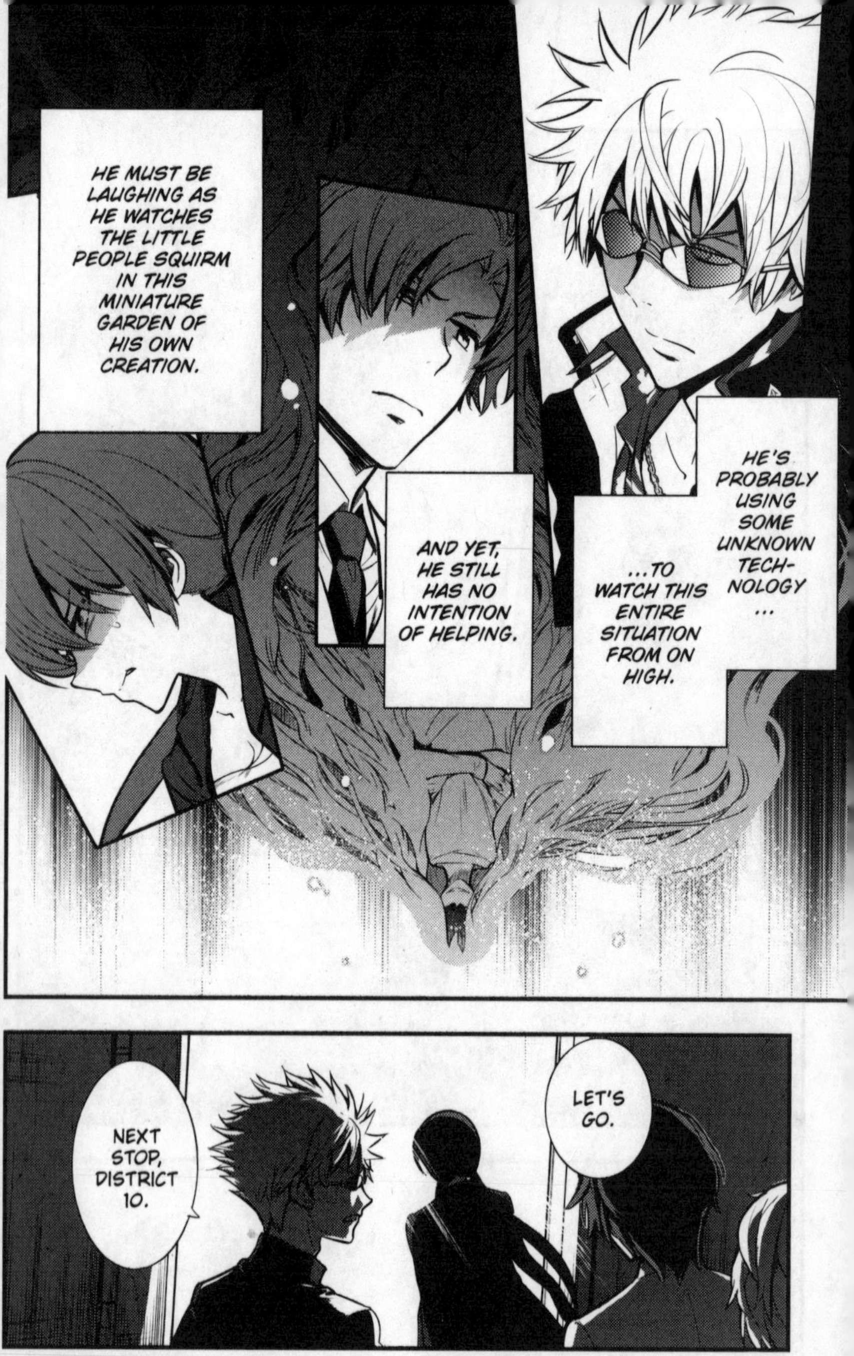
HE MUST BE LAUGHING AS HE WATCHES THE LITTLE PEOPLE SQUIRM IN THIS MINIATURE GARDEN OF HIS OWN CREATION.
HE'S PROBABLY USING SOME UNKNOWN TECH-NOLOGY ...
...TO WATCH THIS ENTIRE SITUATION FROM ON HIGH.
AND YET, HE STILL HAS NO INTENTION OF HELPING.
LET'S GO.
NEXT STOP, DISTRICT 10.

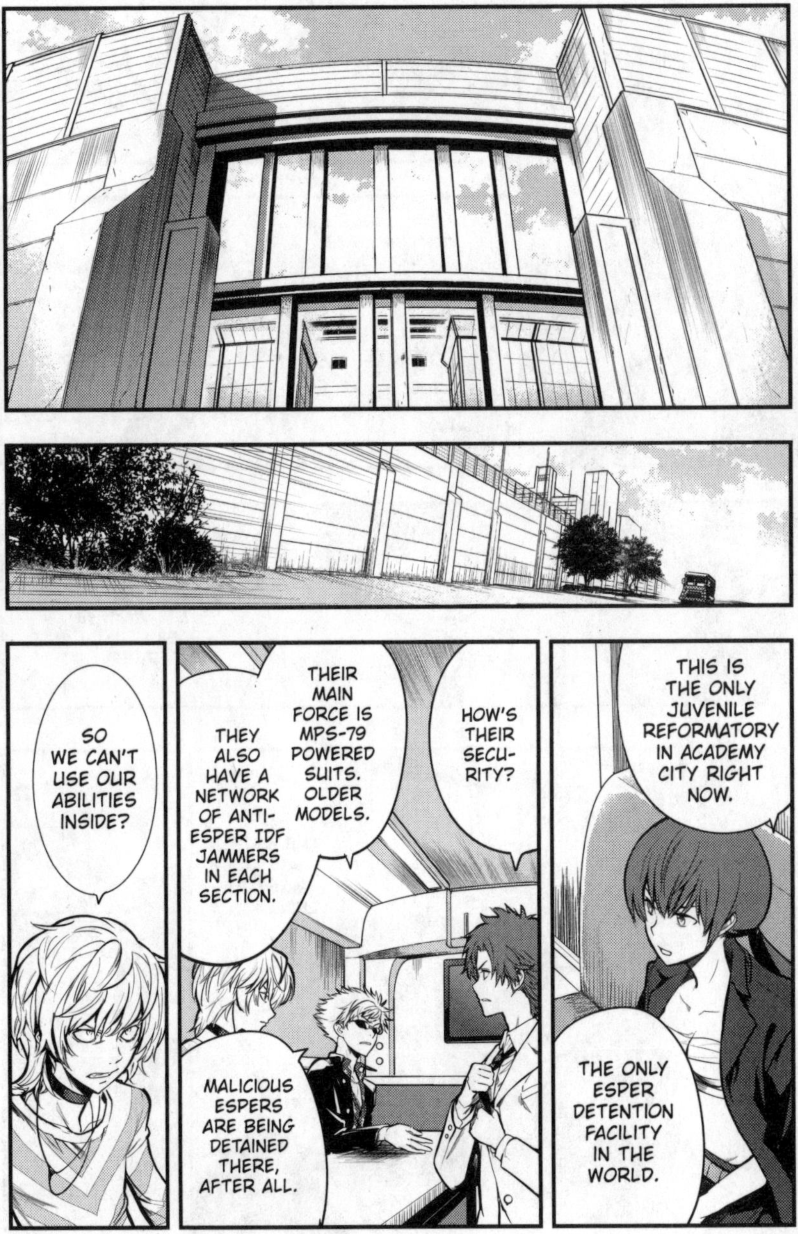
THIS IS THE ONLY JUVENILE REFORMATORY IN ACADEMY CITY RIGHT NOW.
THE ONLY ESPER DETENTION FACILITY IN THE WORLD.
HOW'S THEIR SECU-RITY?
THEIR MAIN FORCE IS MPS-79 POWERED SUITS. OLDER MODELS.
THEY ALSO HAVE A NETWORK OF ANTI-ESPER IDF JAMMERS IN EACH SECTION.
MALICIOUS ESPERS ARE BEING DETAINED THERE, AFTER ALL.
SO WE CAN'T USE OUR ABILITIES INSIDE?

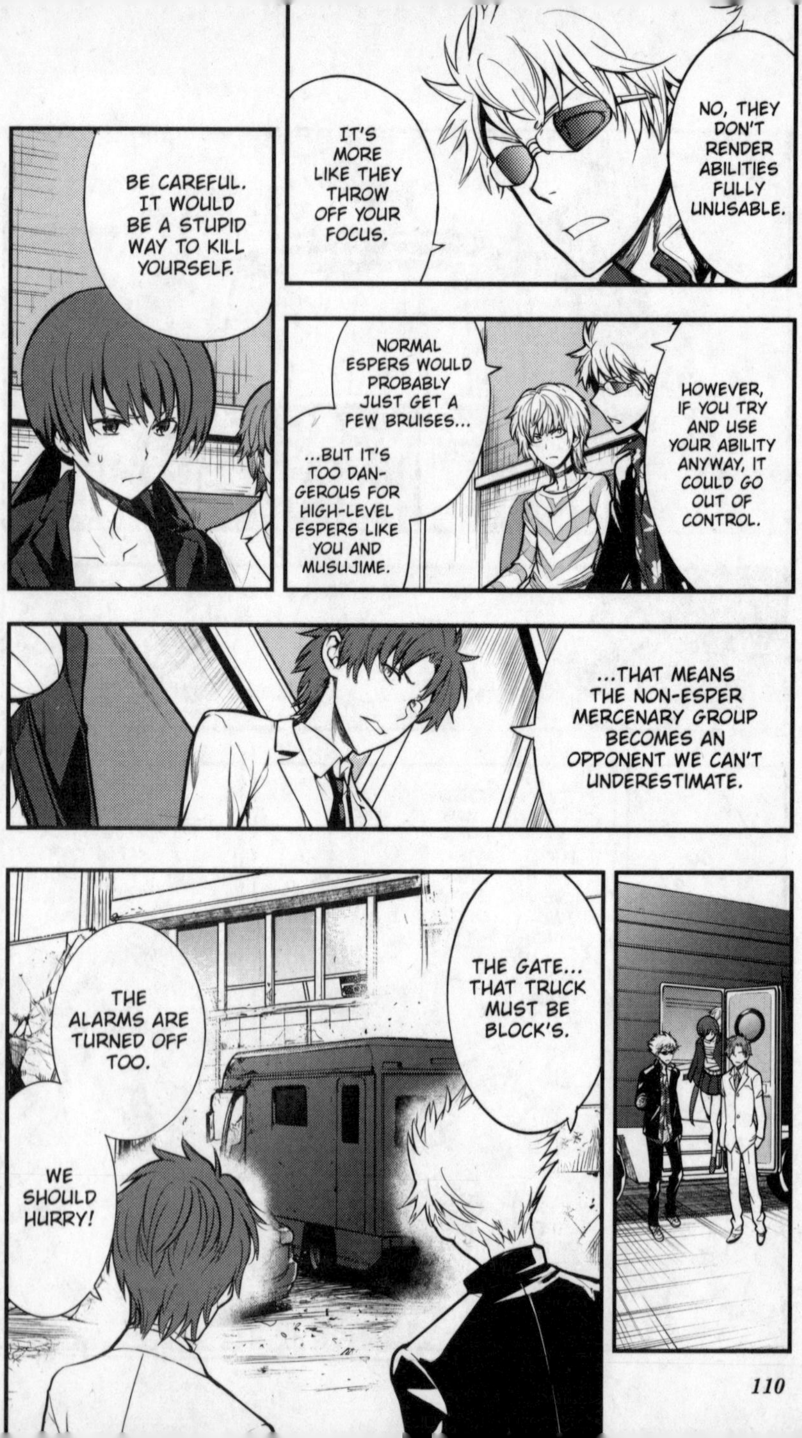
NO, THEY DON'T RENDER ABILITIES FULLY UNUSABLE.
IT'S MORE LIKE THEY THROW OFF YOUR FOCUS.
HOWEVER, IF YOU TRY AND USE YOUR ABILITY ANYWAY, IT COULD GO OUT OF CONTROL.
NORMAL ESPERS WOULD PROBABLY JUST GET A FEW BRUISES...
...BUT IT'S TOO DAN-GEROUS FOR HIGH-LEVEL ESPERS LIKE YOU AND MUSUJIME.
BE CAREFUL. IT WOULD BE A STUPID WAY TO KILL YOURSELF.
...THAT MEANS THE NON-ESPER MERCENARY GROUP BECOMES AN OPPONENT WE CAN'T UNDERESTIMATE.
THE GATE... THAT TRUCK MUST BE BLOCK'S.
THE ALARMS ARE TURNED OFF TOO.
WE SHOULD HURRY!

HIRI
(TINGLE)

ARE THOSE...

...THE IDF JAMMERS?

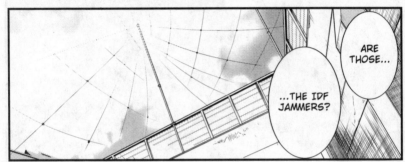

THIS IS...

...!!

THEY'RE EMITTING SPECIAL E.M. WAVES TO CREATE INVOLUNTARY DIFFUSION FIELDS.

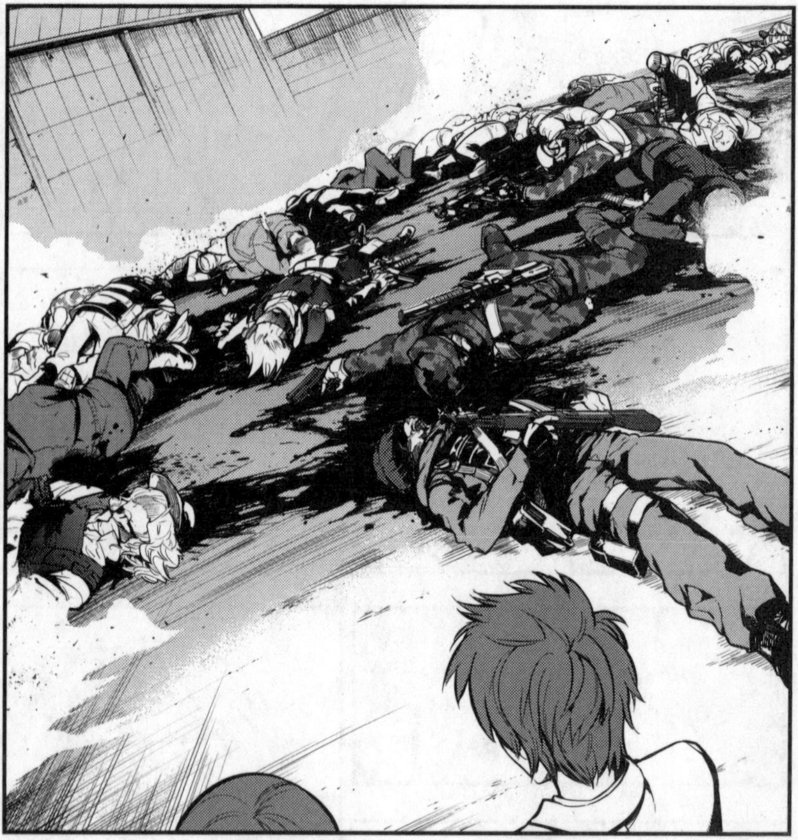

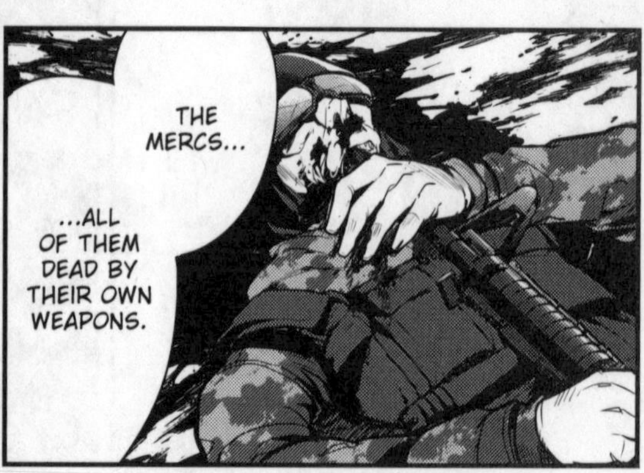
THE MERCS...
...ALL OF THEM DEAD BY THEIR OWN WEAPONS.

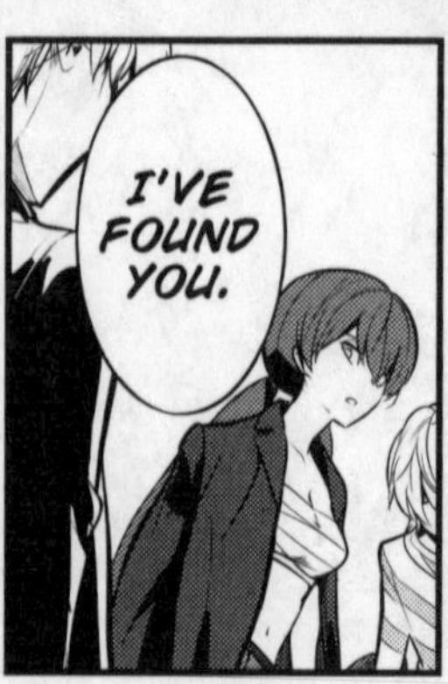
I'VE FOUND YOU.

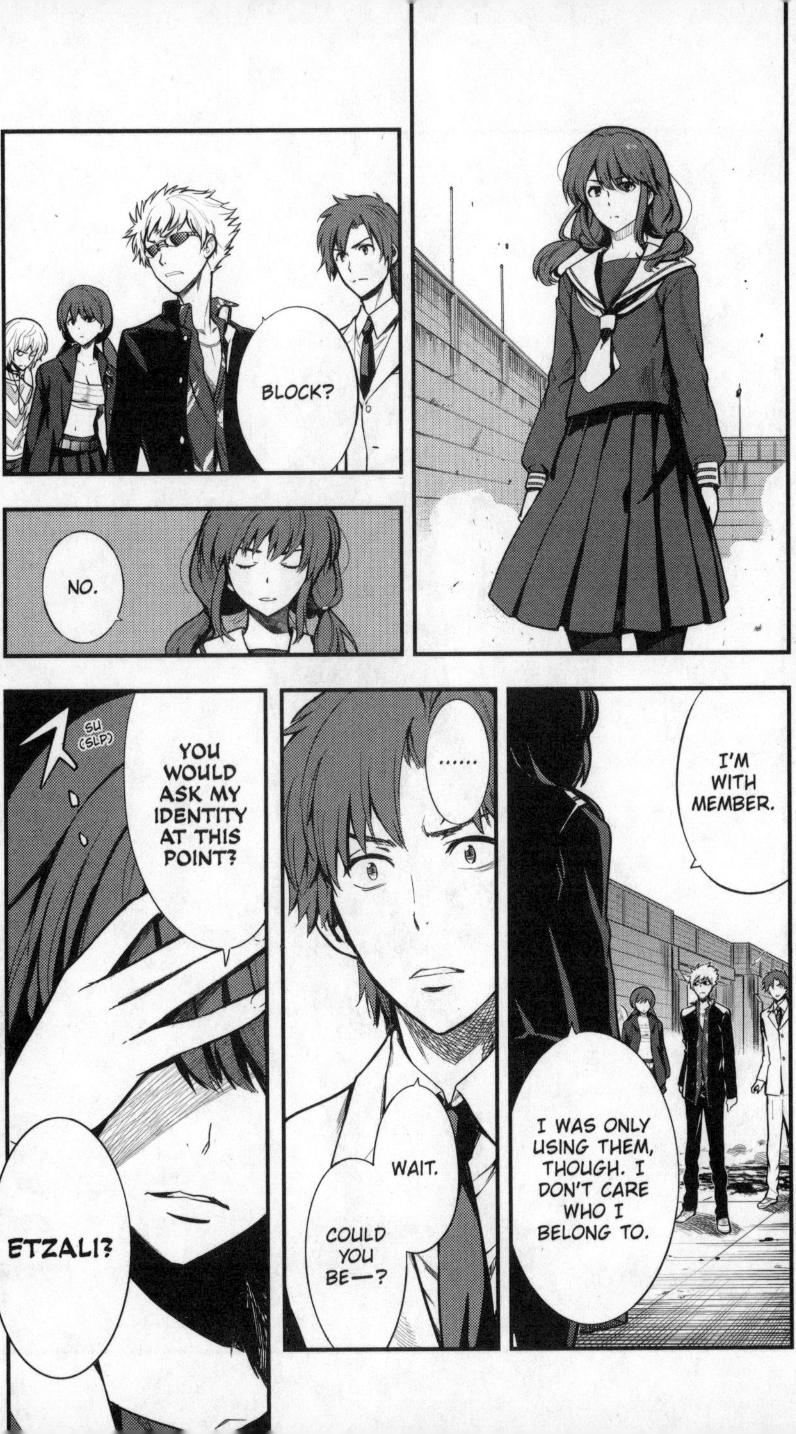
BLOCK?
NO.
I'M WITH MEMBER.
I WAS ONLY USING THEM, THOUGH. I DON'T CARE WHO I BELONG TO.
......
WAIT.
COULD YOU BE—?
SU (SLP)
YOU WOULD ASK MY IDENTITY AT THIS POINT?
ETZALI?

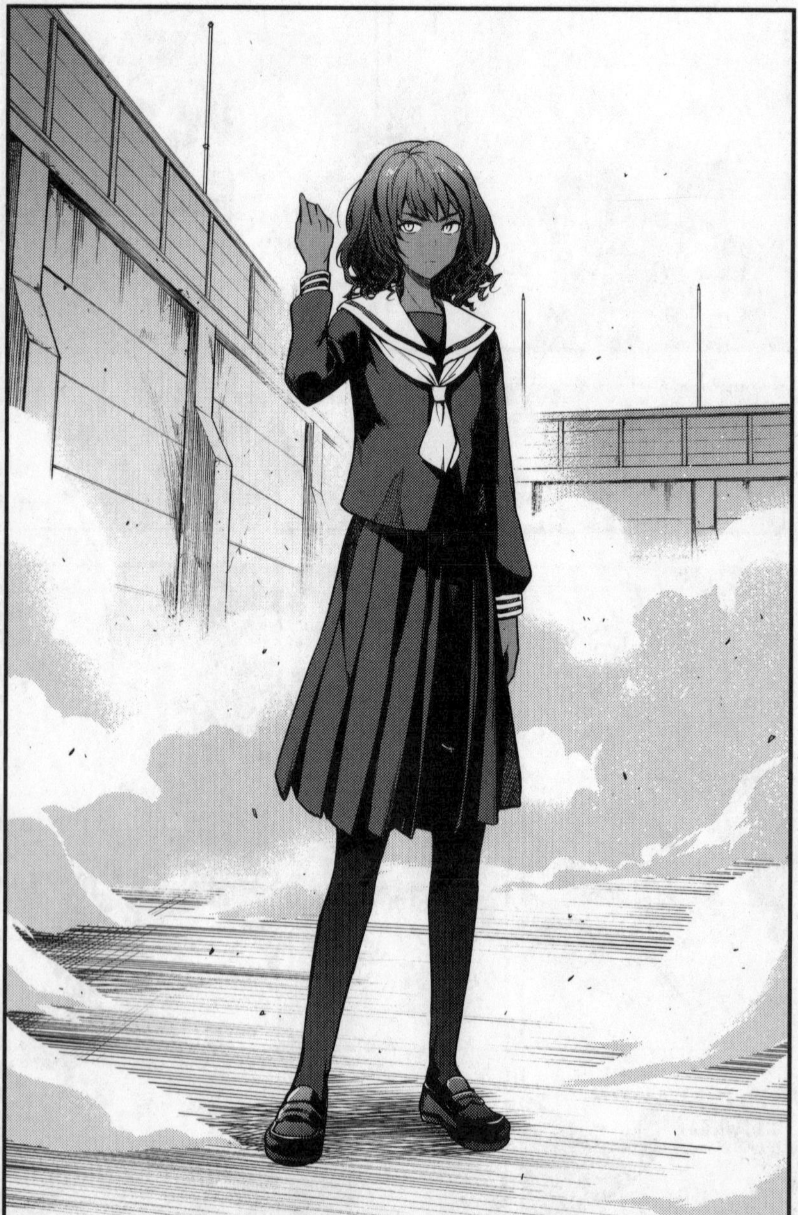

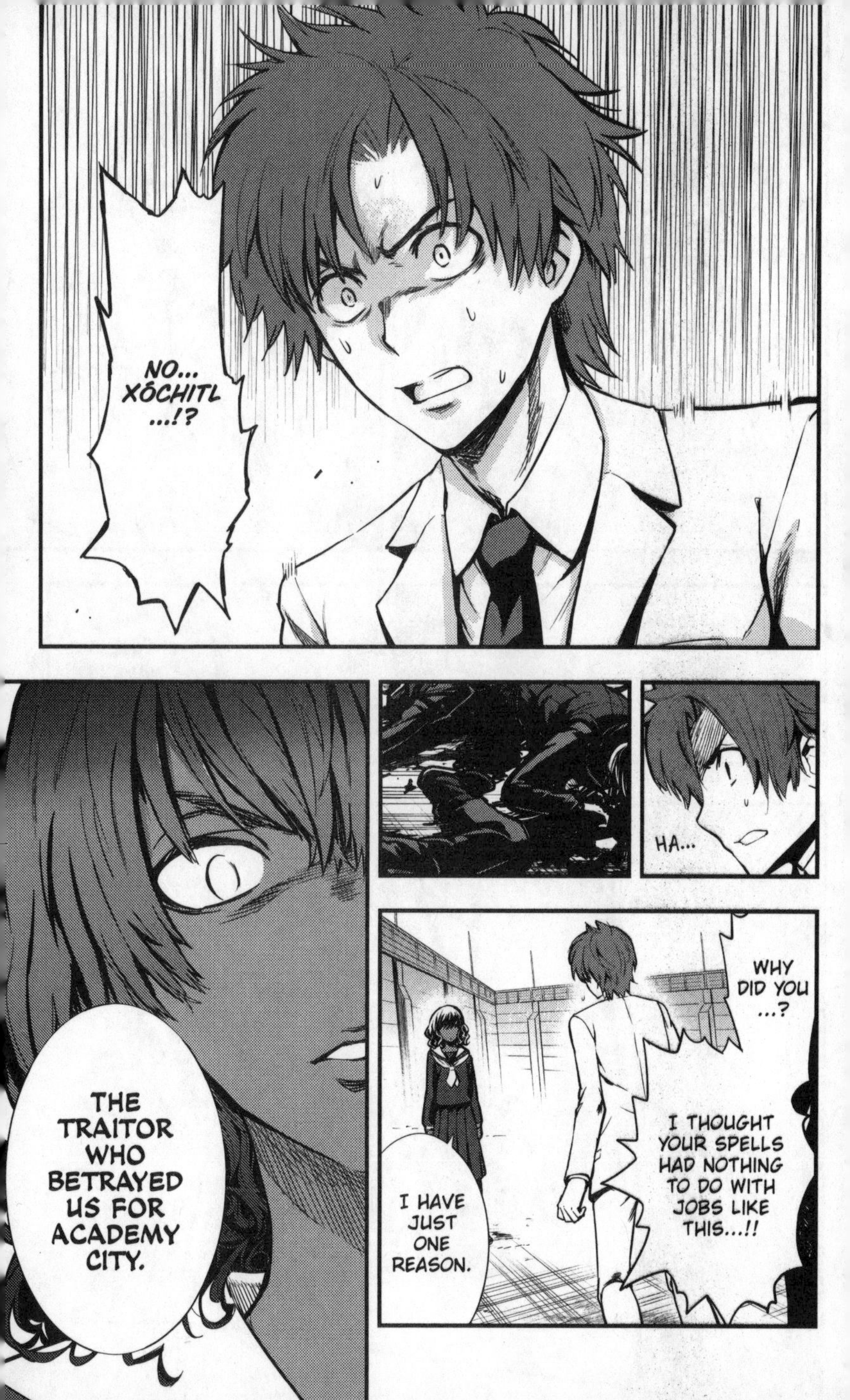
NO... XÓCHITL ...!?
HA...
WHY DID YOU ...?
I THOUGHT YOUR SPELLS HAD NOTHING TO DO WITH JOBS LIKE THIS...!!
I HAVE JUST ONE REASON.
THE TRAITOR WHO BETRAYED US FOR ACADEMY CITY.

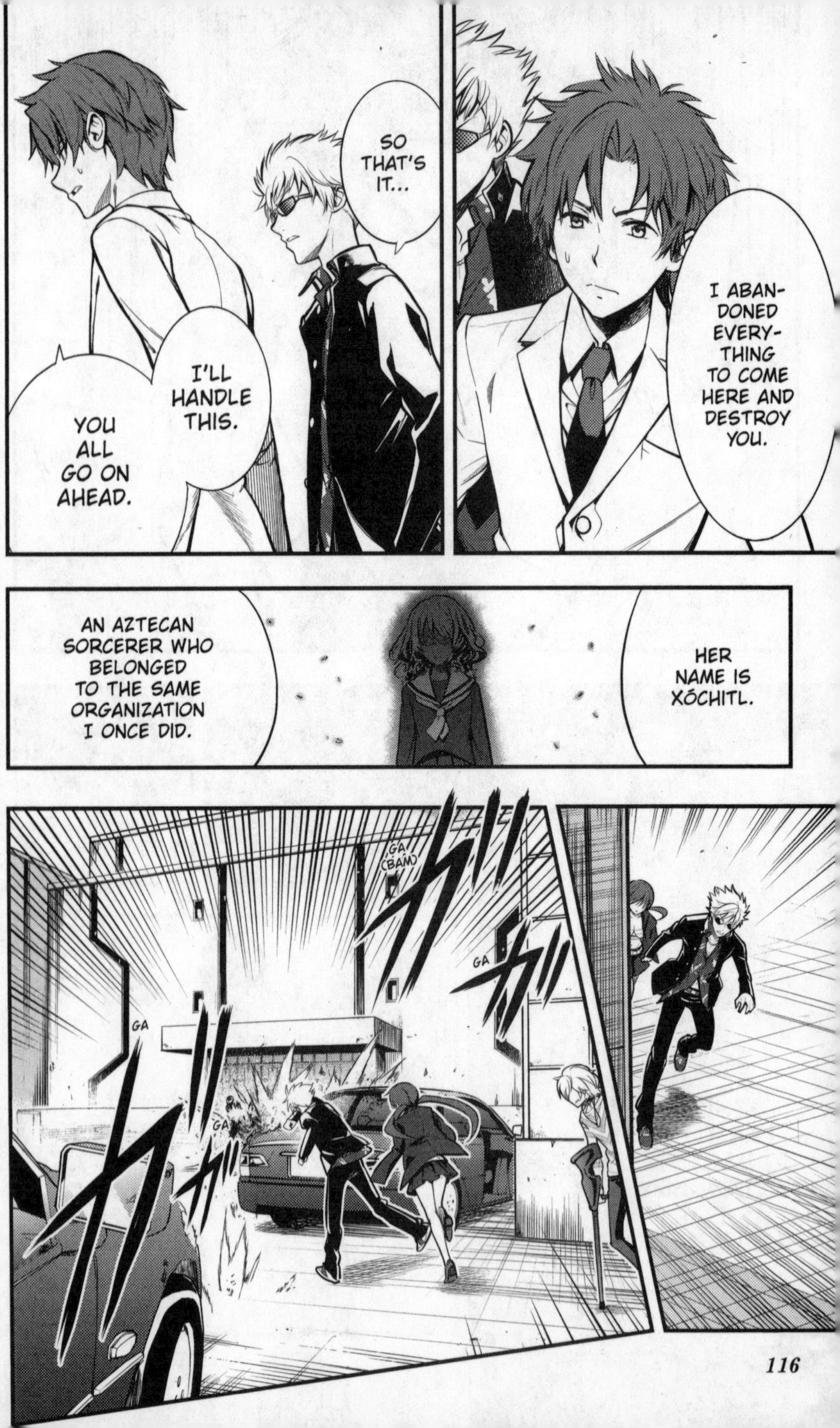
I ABAN-DONED EVERY-THING TO COME HERE AND DESTROY YOU.
SO THAT'S IT...
I'LL HANDLE THIS.
YOU ALL GO ON AHEAD.
HER NAME IS XÓCHITL.
AN AZTECAN SORCERER WHO BELONGED TO THE SAME ORGANIZATION I ONCE DID.
GA (BAM)
GA
GA
GA

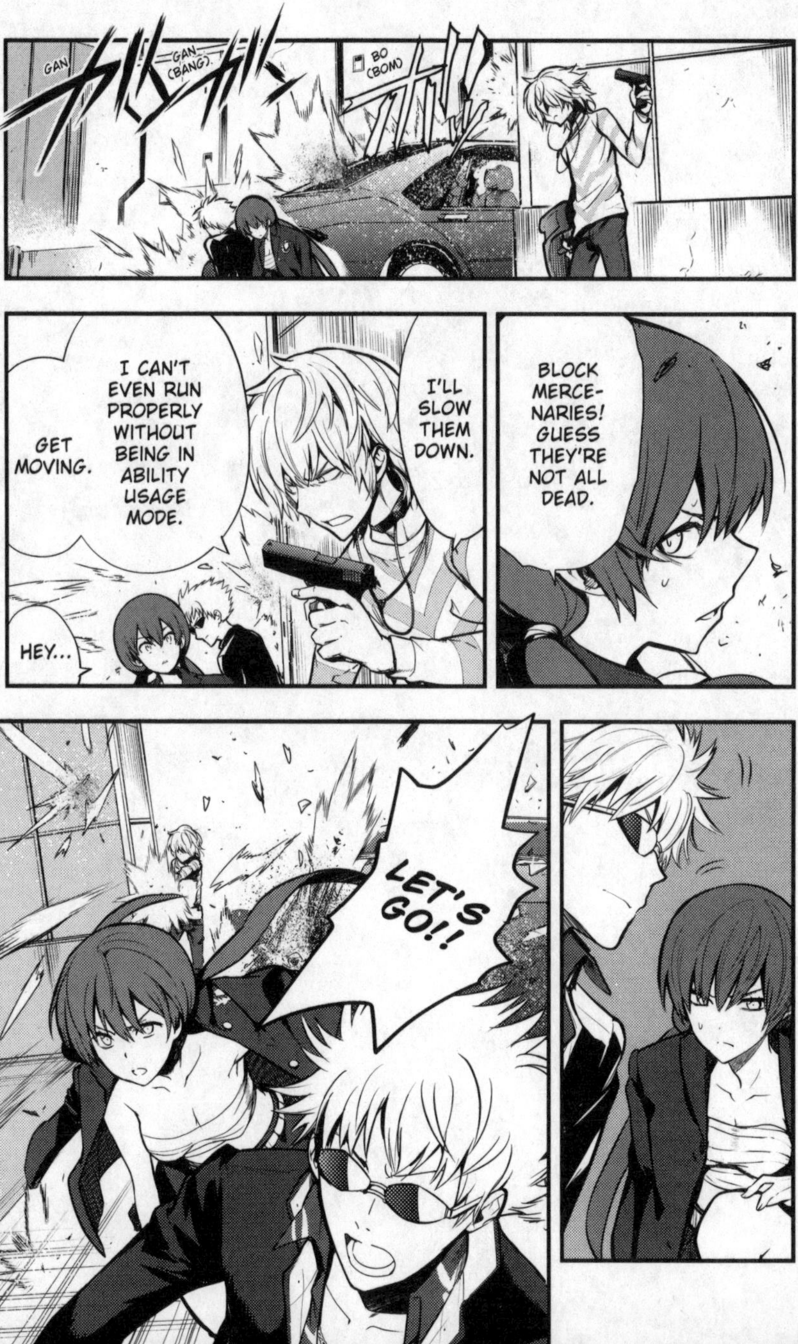

BO (BOM)
GAN (BANG)
GAN
BLOCK MERCENARIES! GUESS THEY'RE NOT ALL DEAD.
I'LL SLOW THEM DOWN.
I CAN'T EVEN RUN PROPERLY WITHOUT BEING IN ABILITY USAGE MODE.
GET MOVING.
HEY...
LET'S GO!!

# A Certain Magical Index

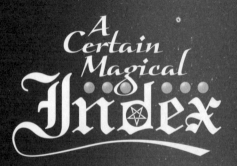

# #140 DISTRICT 10 JUVENILE REFORMATORY ①

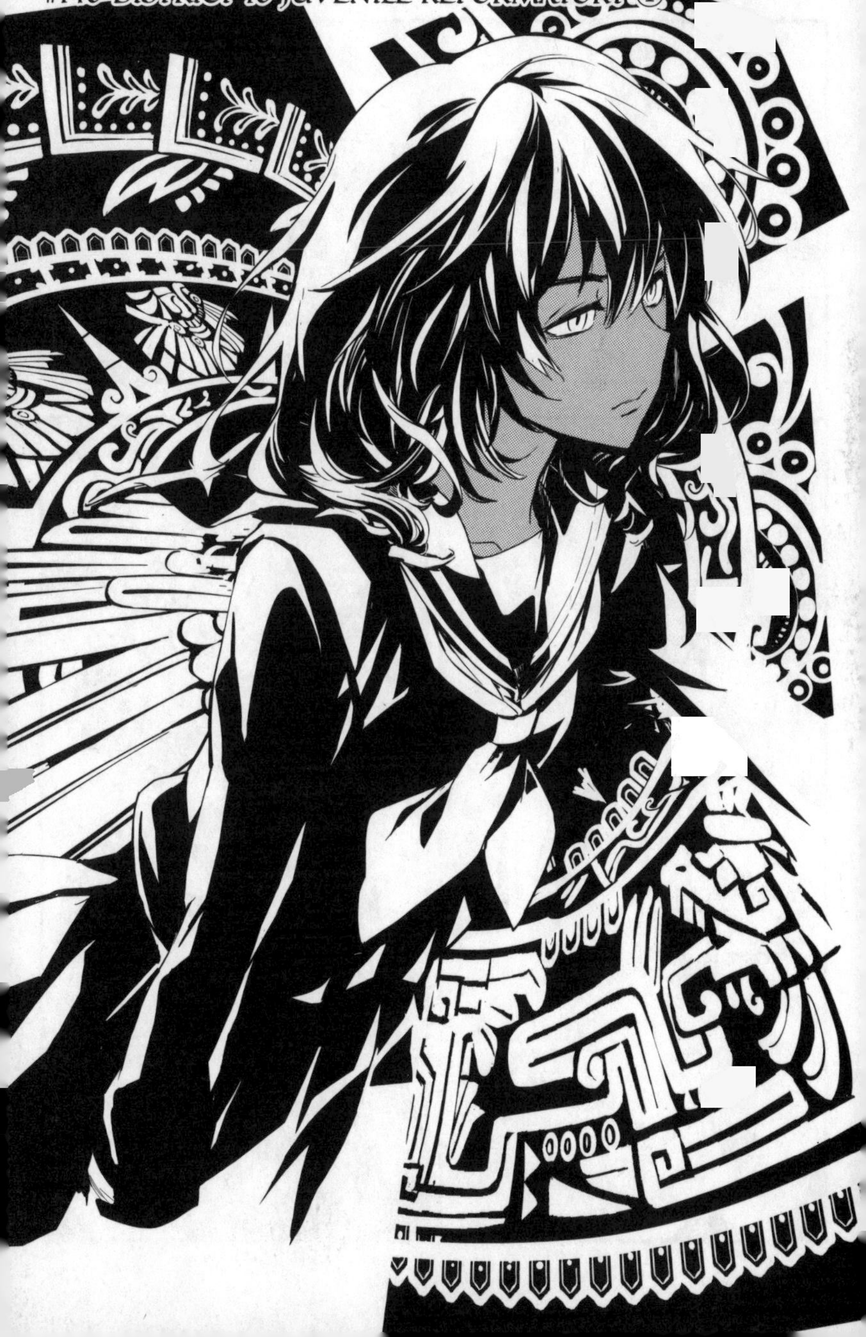

IS THAT YOUR IDEA OF COURTESY, ETZALI? CONFRONTING ME WITH A FALSE FACE?
...UNFOR-TUNATELY, I'VE TAKEN QUITE A LIKING TO THIS ONE.
AND AS SOMEONE WHO LEFT THE ORGANIZATION, I DON'T HAVE THE RIGHT TO USE THAT FACE ANYWAY.

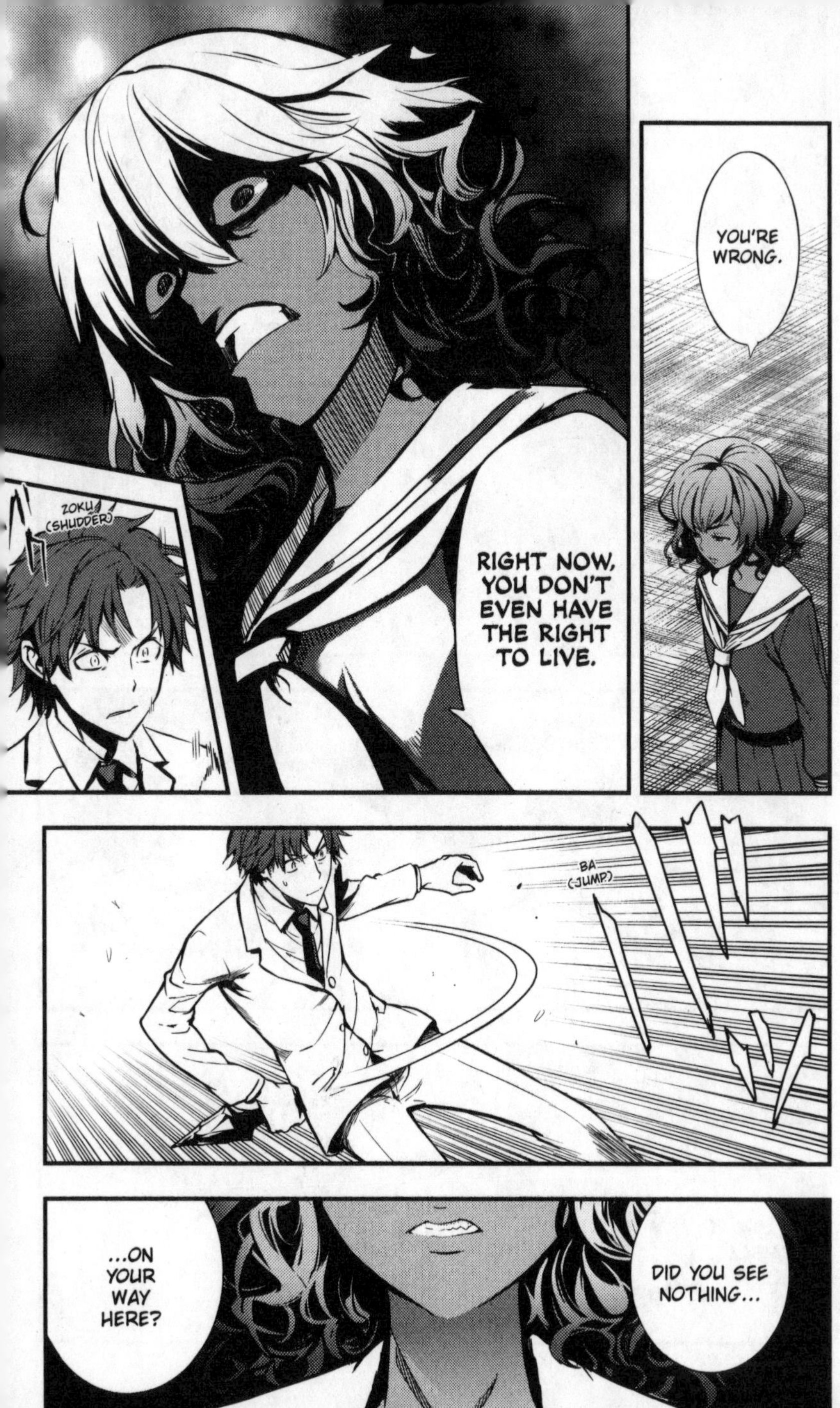

YOU'RE WRONG.
RIGHT NOW, YOU DON'T EVEN HAVE THE RIGHT TO LIVE.
ZOKU (SHUDDER)
BA (JUMP)
DID YOU SEE NOTHING...
...ON YOUR WAY HERE?

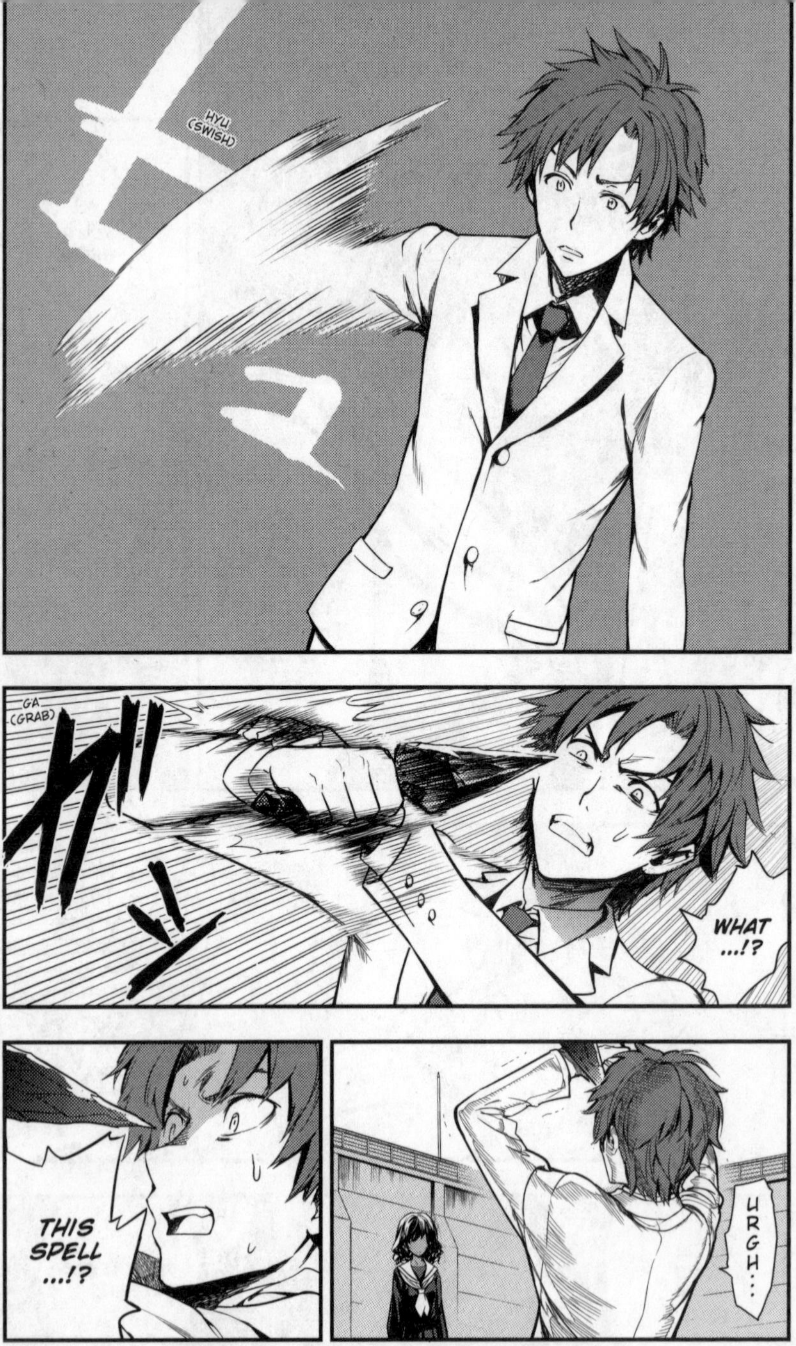
HYU
(SWISH)
GA
(GRAB)
WHAT
...!?
URGH...
THIS
SPELL
...!?

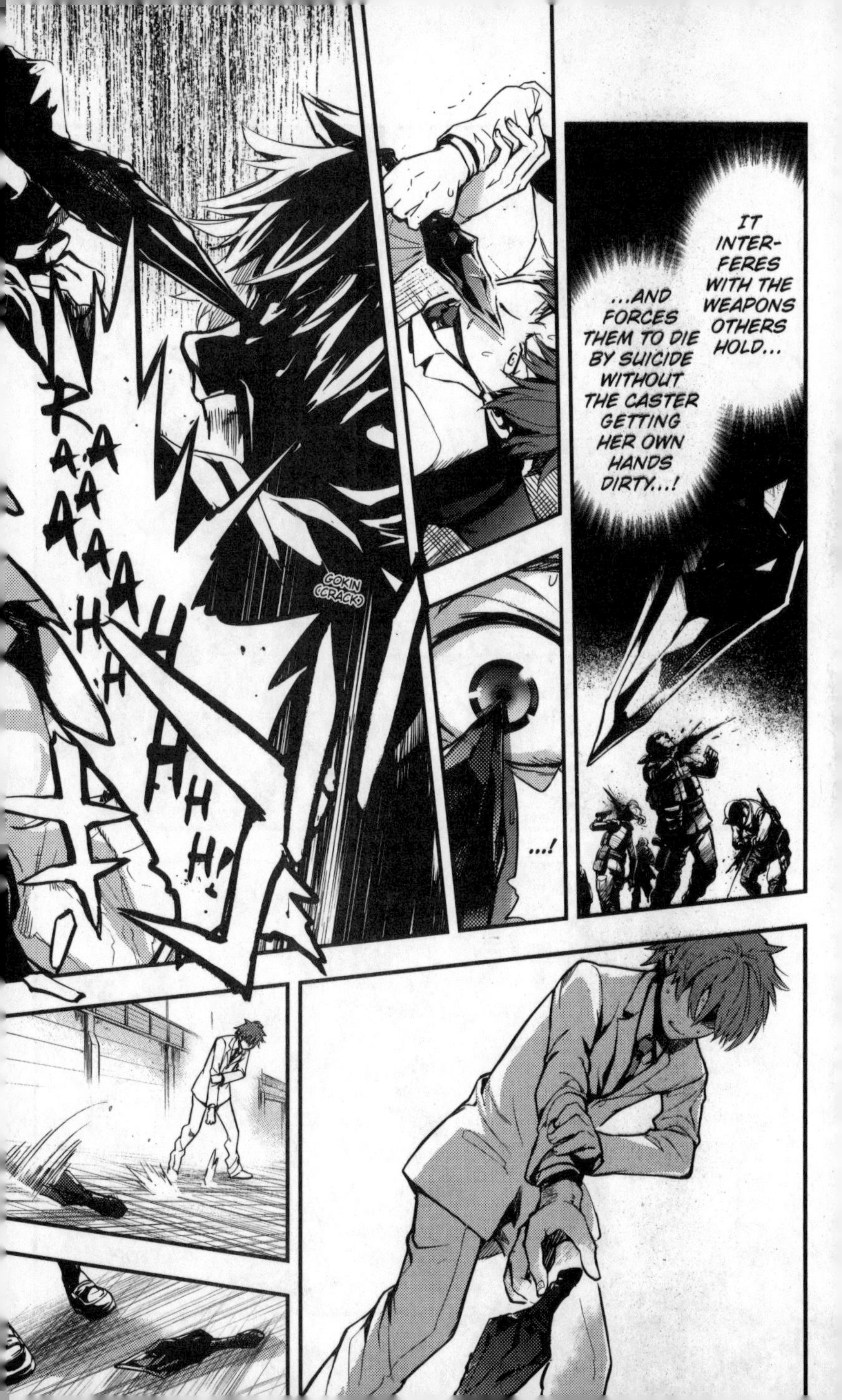
IT INTER-FERES WITH THE WEAPONS OTHERS HOLD...
...AND FORCES THEM TO DIE BY SUICIDE WITHOUT THE CASTER GETTING HER OWN HANDS DIRTY...!
...!
GOKIN (CRACK)
RAAAAAAAAHHHHHHHH!

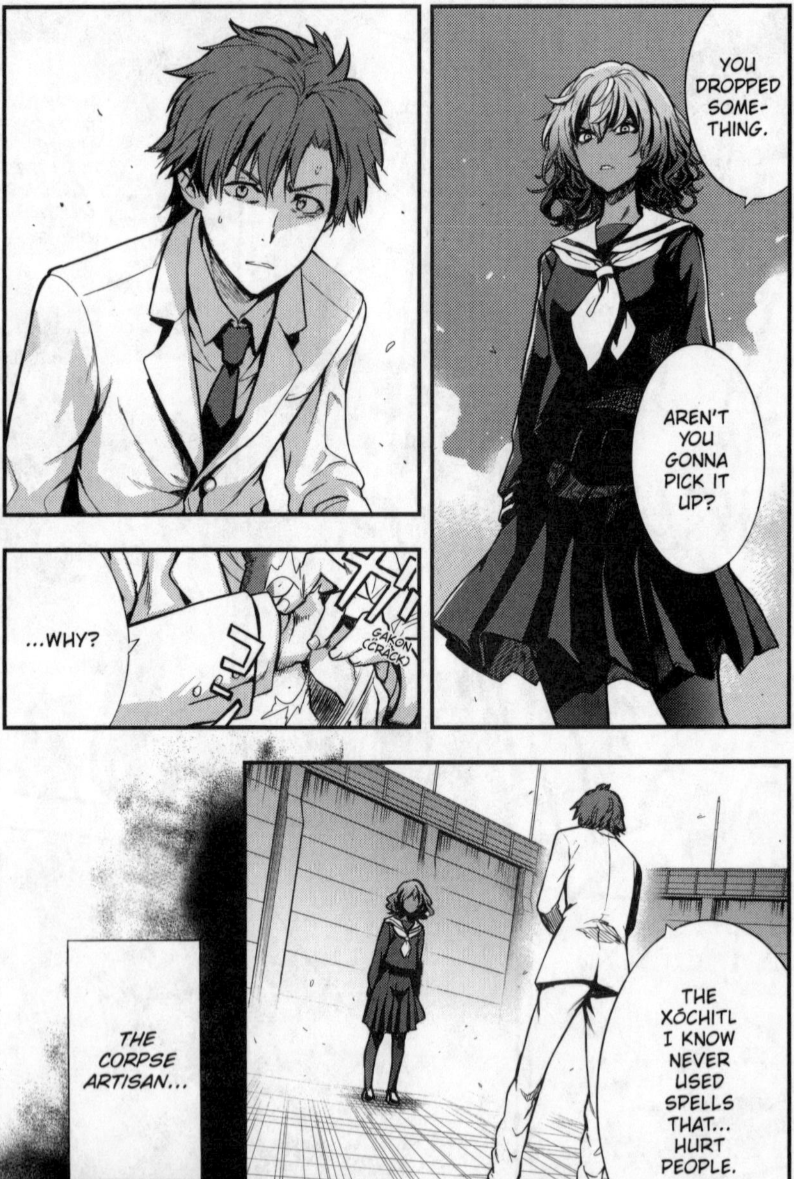
YOU DROPPED SOME-THING.
AREN'T YOU GONNA PICK IT UP?
GAKON (CRACK)
...WHY?
THE XÓCHITL I KNOW NEVER USED SPELLS THAT... HURT PEOPLE.
THE CORPSE ARTISAN...

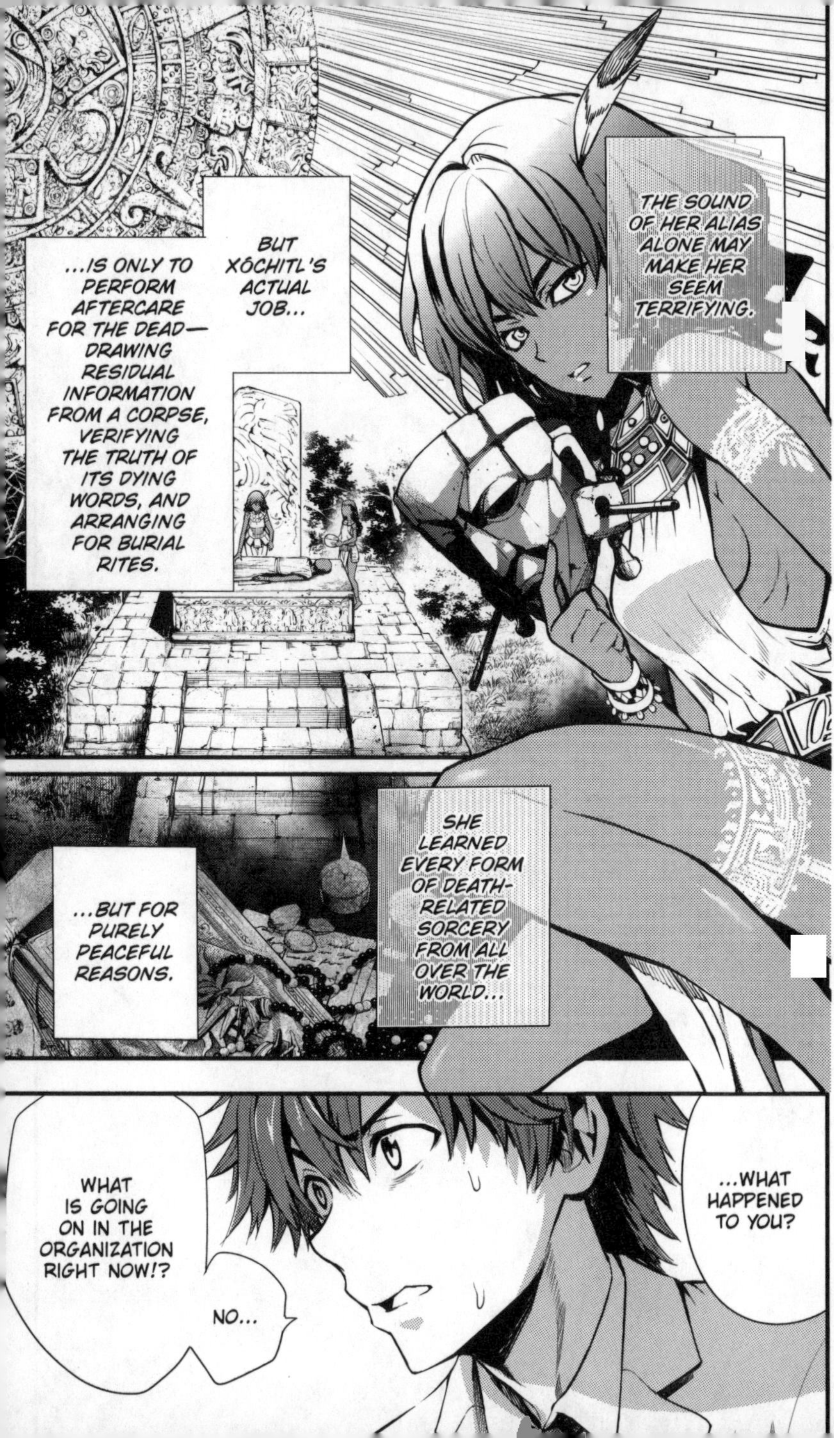
THE SOUND OF HER ALIAS ALONE MAY MAKE HER SEEM TERRIFYING.
BUT XÓCHITL'S ACTUAL JOB...
...IS ONLY TO PERFORM AFTERCARE FOR THE DEAD—DRAWING RESIDUAL INFORMATION FROM A CORPSE, VERIFYING THE TRUTH OF ITS DYING WORDS, AND ARRANGING FOR BURIAL RITES.
SHE LEARNED EVERY FORM OF DEATH-RELATED SORCERY FROM ALL OVER THE WORLD...
...BUT FOR PURELY PEACEFUL REASONS.
...WHAT HAPPENED TO YOU?
WHAT IS GOING ON IN THE ORGANIZATION RIGHT NOW!?
NO...

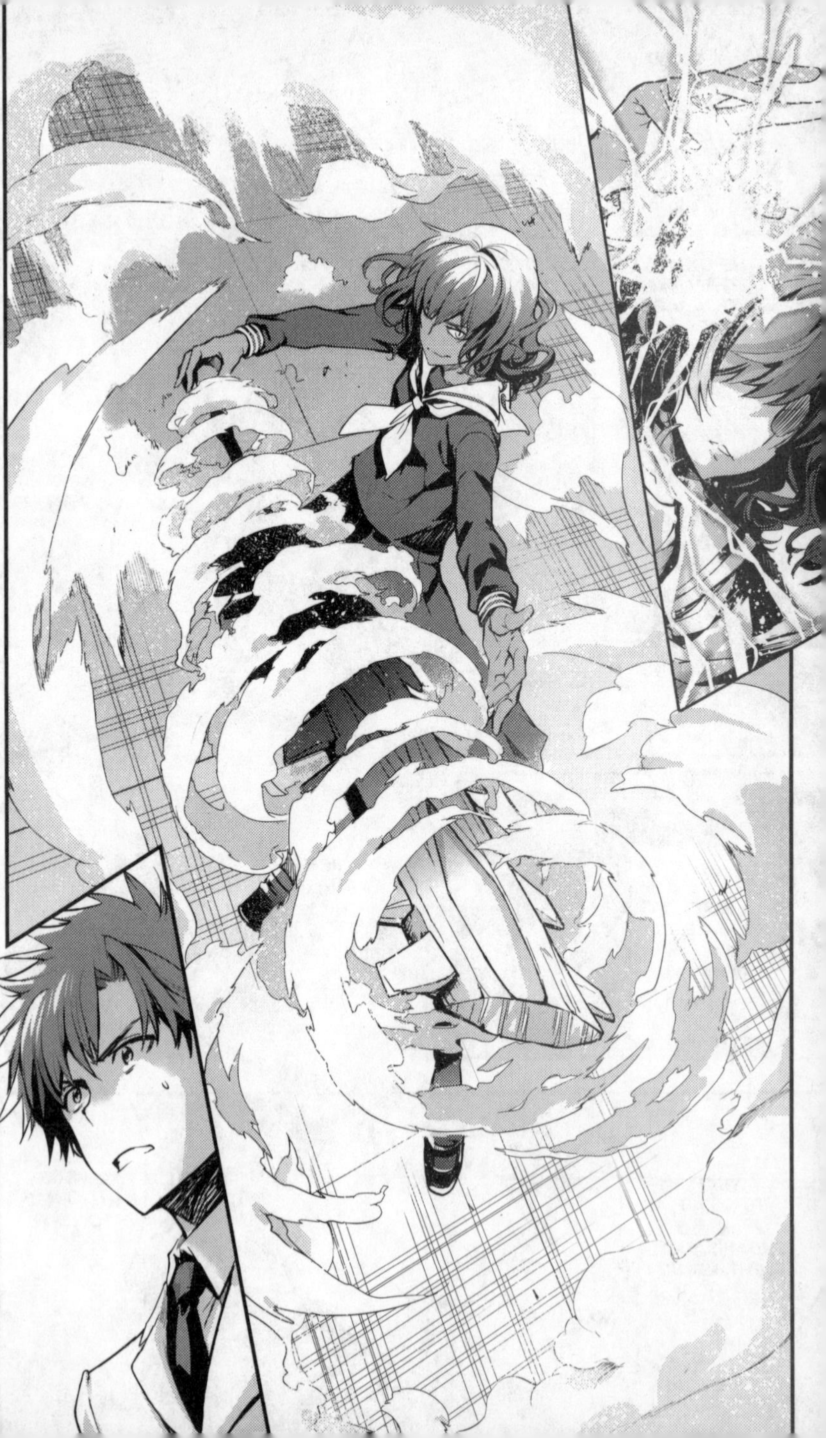

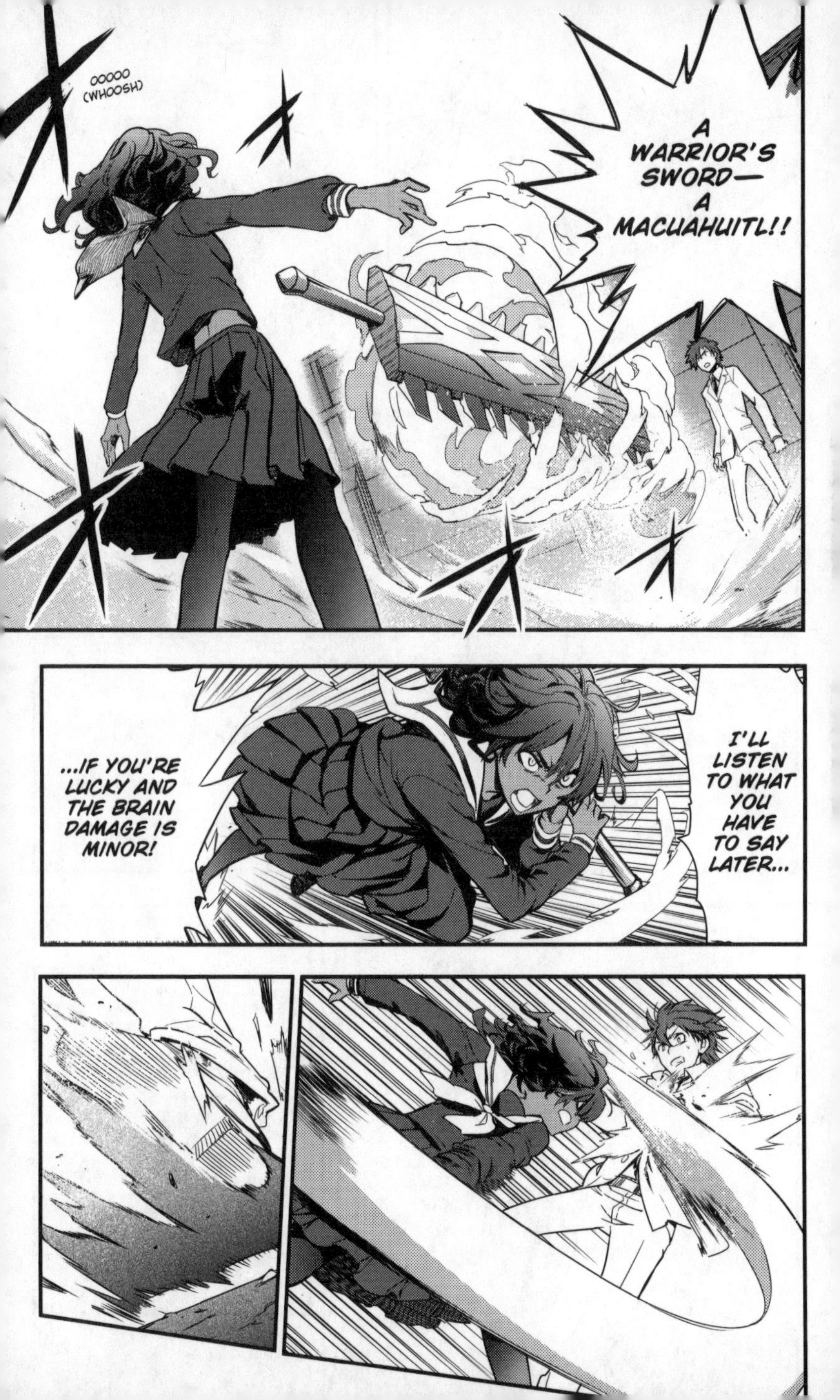
A WARRIOR'S SWORD— A MACUAHUITL!!
OOOOO (WHOOSH)
I'LL LISTEN TO WHAT YOU HAVE TO SAY LATER...
...IF YOU'RE LUCKY AND THE BRAIN DAMAGE IS MINOR!

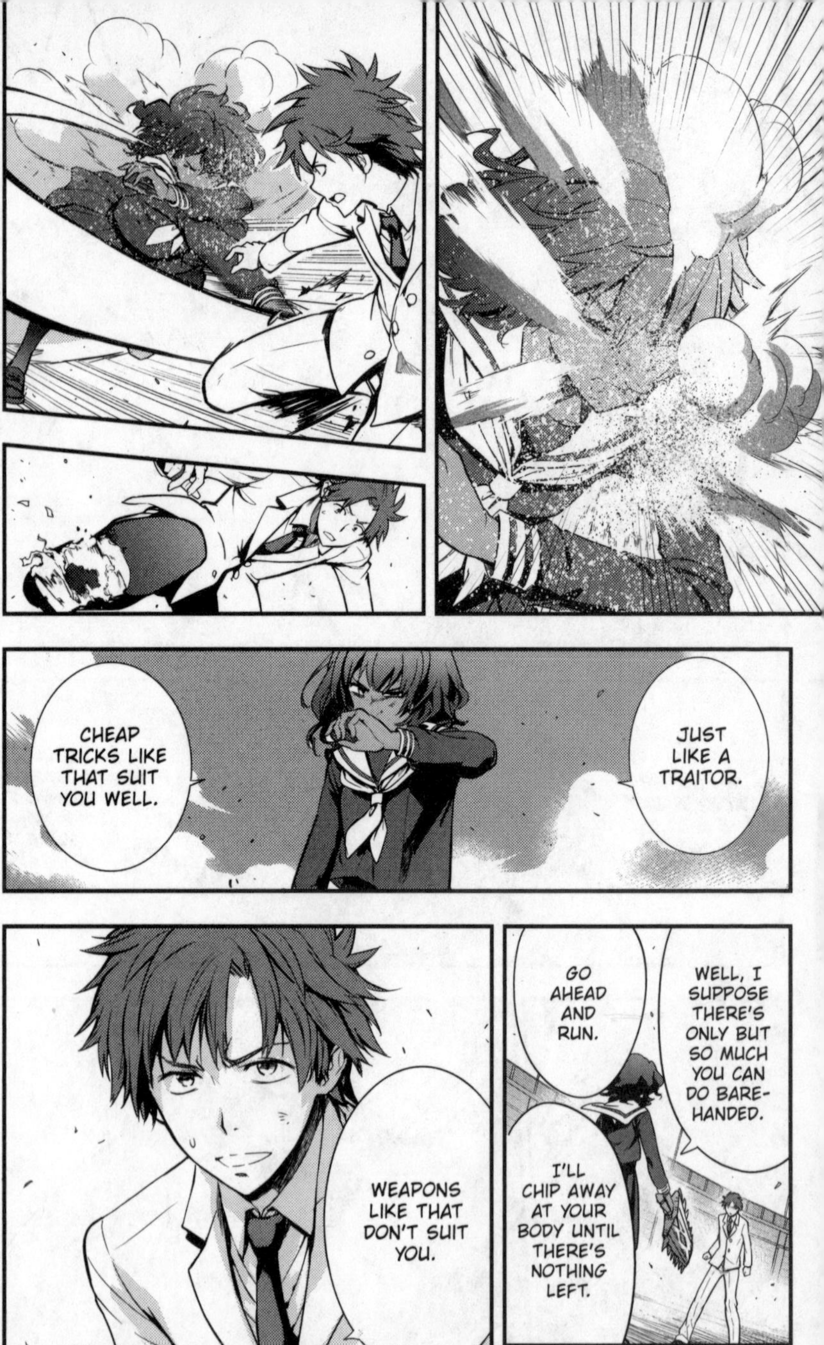
JUST LIKE A TRAITOR.
CHEAP TRICKS LIKE THAT SUIT YOU WELL.
WELL, I SUPPOSE THERE'S ONLY BUT SO MUCH YOU CAN DO BARE-HANDED.
GO AHEAD AND RUN.
I'LL CHIP AWAY AT YOUR BODY UNTIL THERE'S NOTHING LEFT.
WEAPONS LIKE THAT DON'T SUIT YOU.

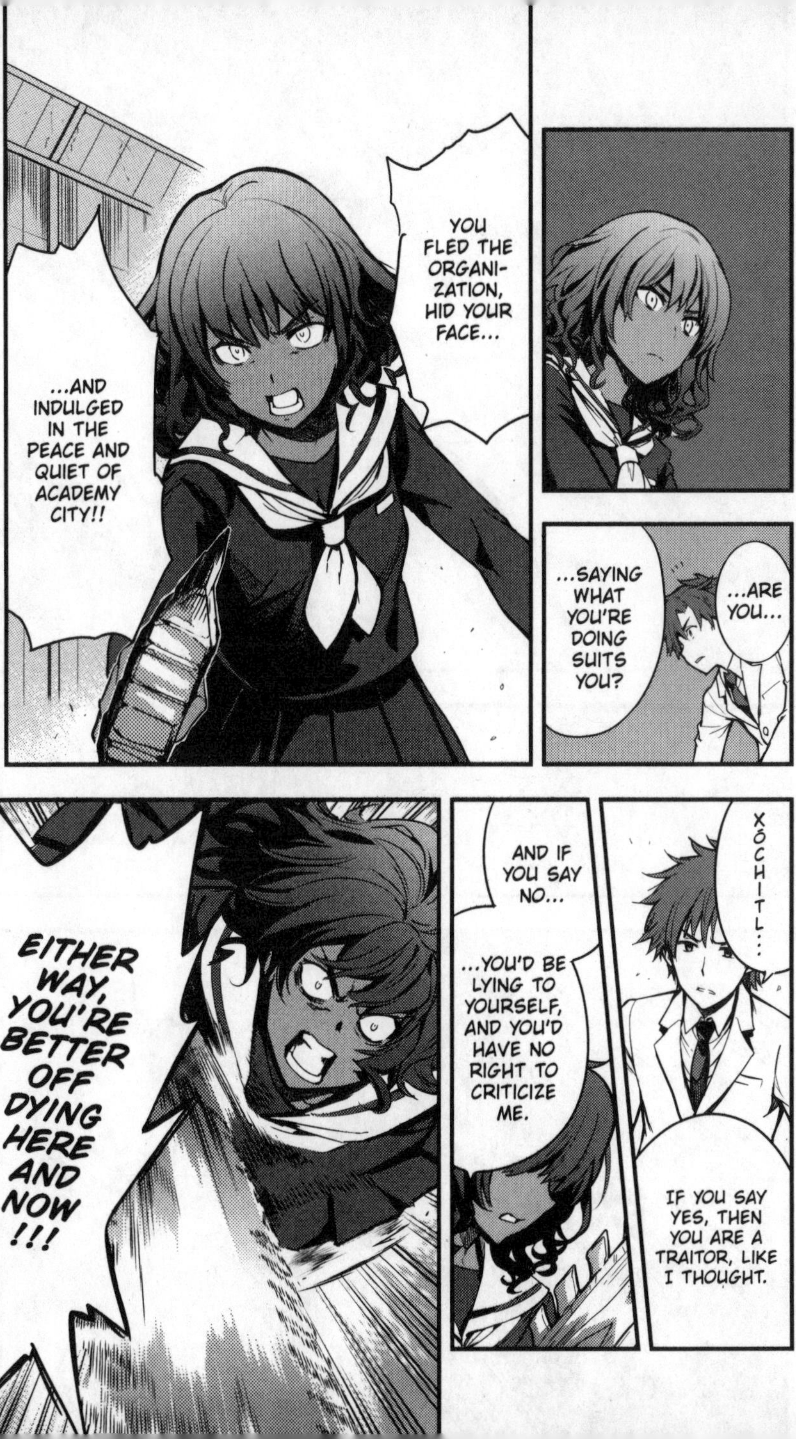
...ARE YOU...
...SAYING WHAT YOU'RE DOING SUITS YOU?
YOU FLED THE ORGANI-ZATION, HID YOUR FACE...
...AND INDULGED IN THE PEACE AND QUIET OF ACADEMY CITY!!
XÓCHITL...
IF YOU SAY YES, THEN YOU ARE A TRAITOR, LIKE I THOUGHT.
AND IF YOU SAY NO...
...YOU'D BE LYING TO YOURSELF, AND YOU'D HAVE NO RIGHT TO CRITICIZE ME.
EITHER WAY, YOU'RE BETTER OFF DYING HERE AND NOW!!!

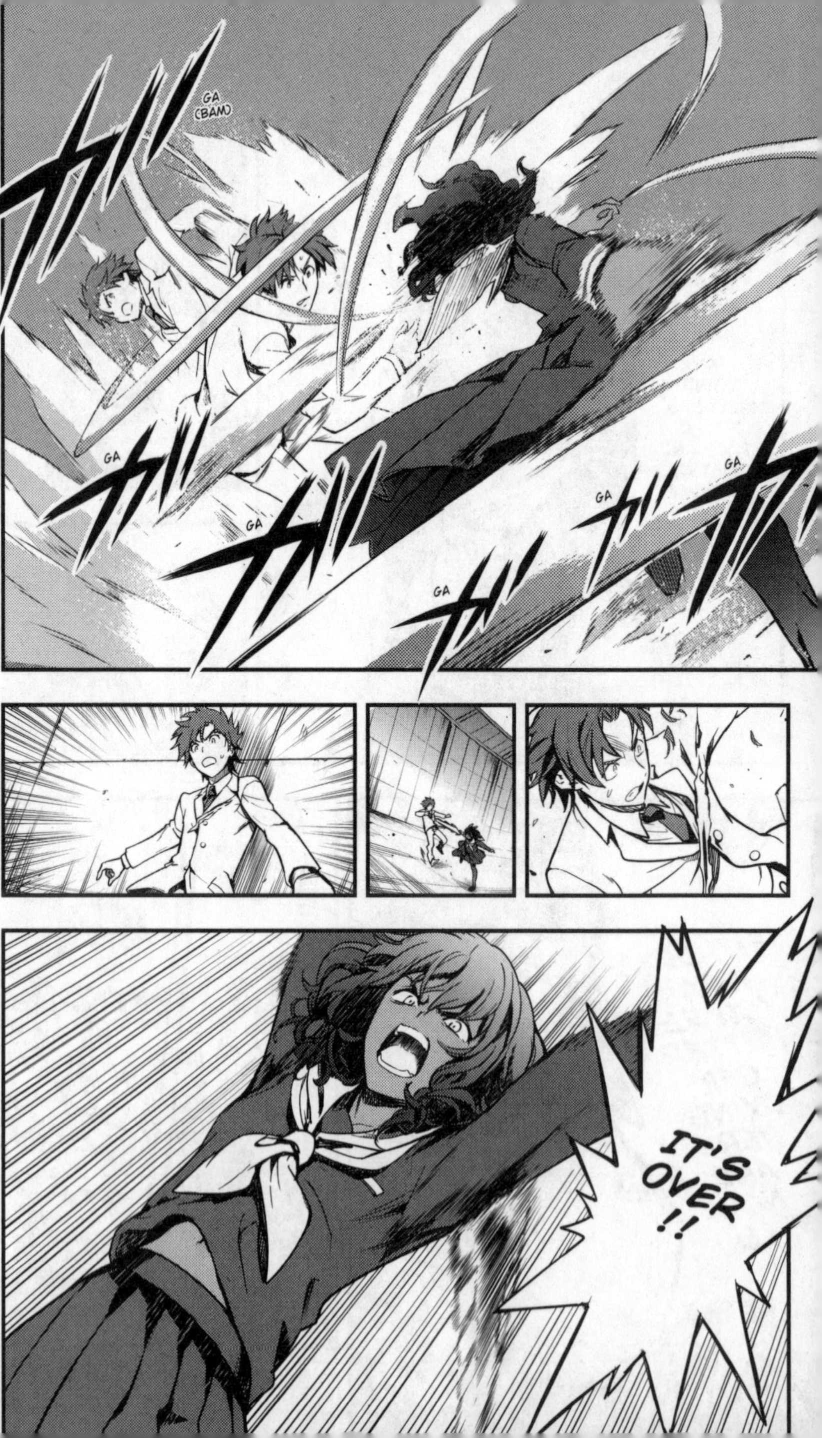
GA
(BAM)
GA
GA
GA
GA
GA
IT'S OVER!!

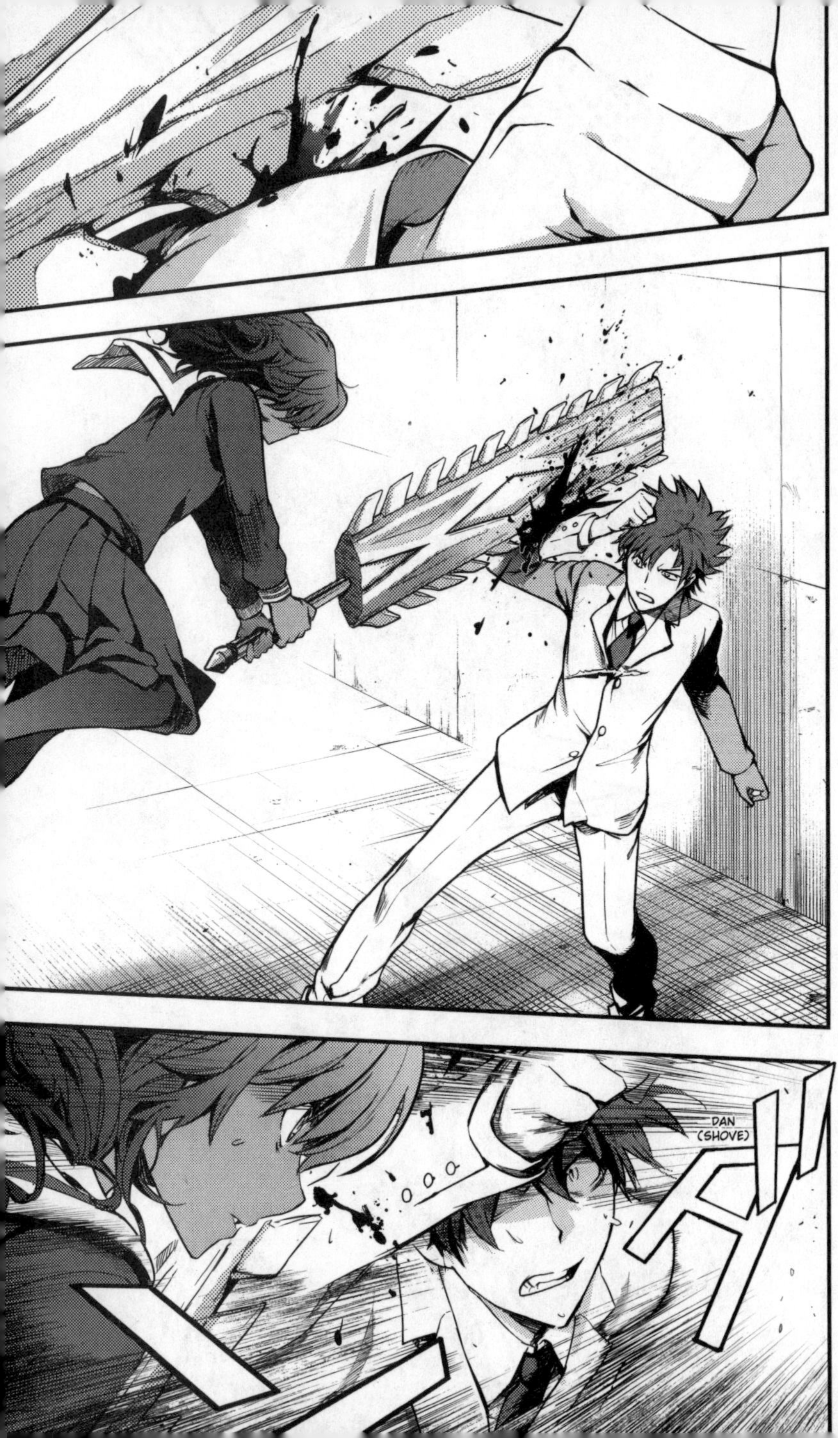
DAN
(SHOVE)

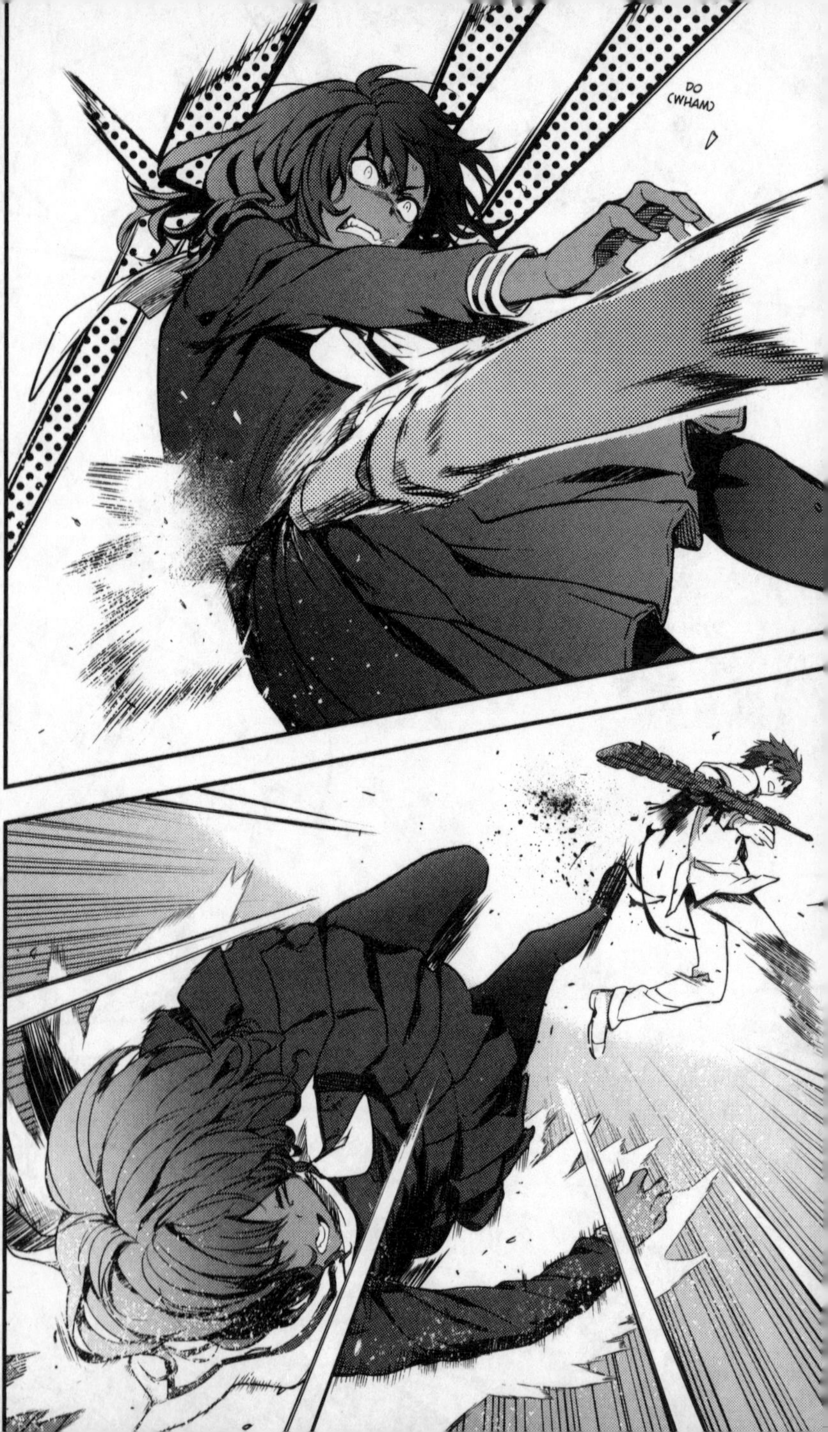
DO
(WHAM)

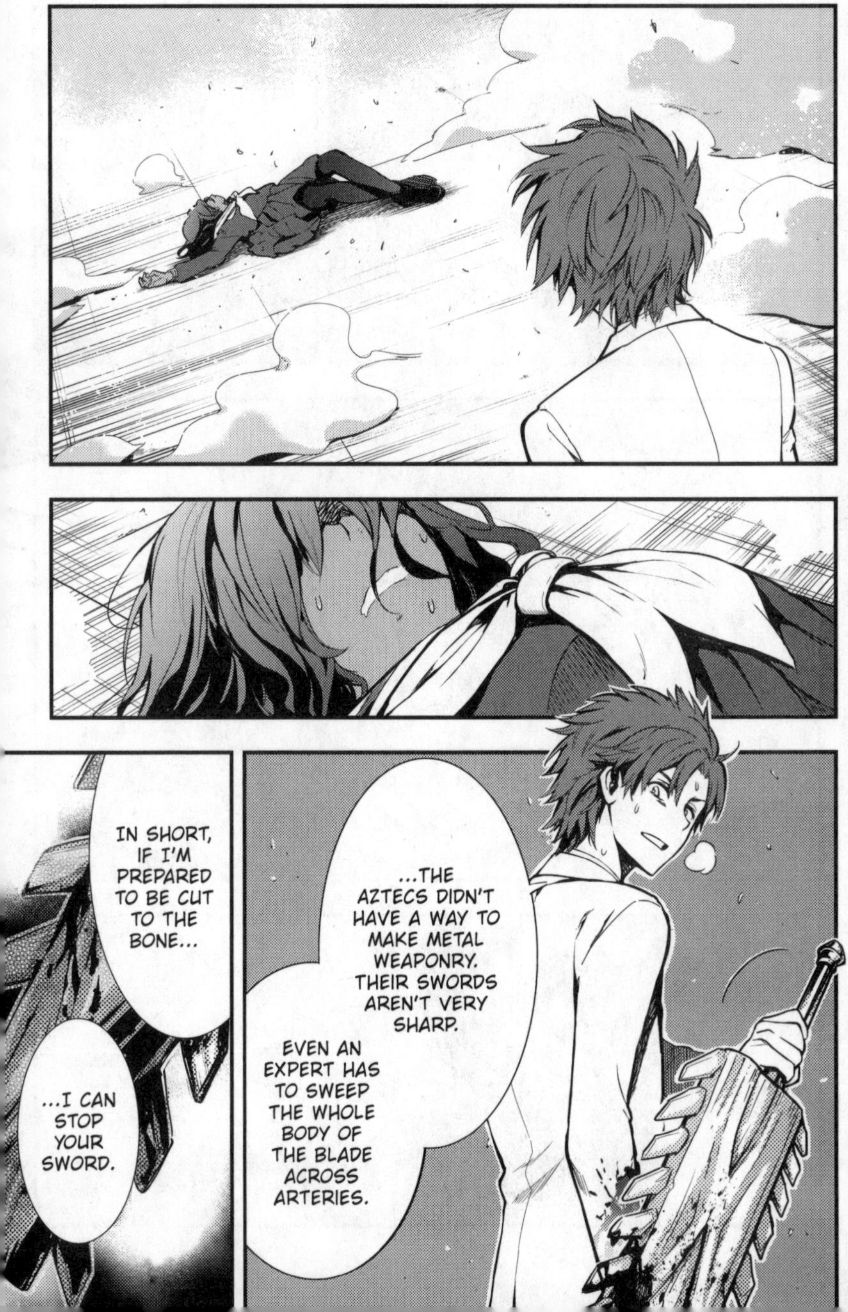
...THE AZTECS DIDN'T HAVE A WAY TO MAKE METAL WEAPONRY. THEIR SWORDS AREN'T VERY SHARP.
EVEN AN EXPERT HAS TO SWEEP THE WHOLE BODY OF THE BLADE ACROSS ARTERIES.
IN SHORT, IF I'M PREPARED TO BE CUT TO THE BONE...
...I CAN STOP YOUR SWORD.

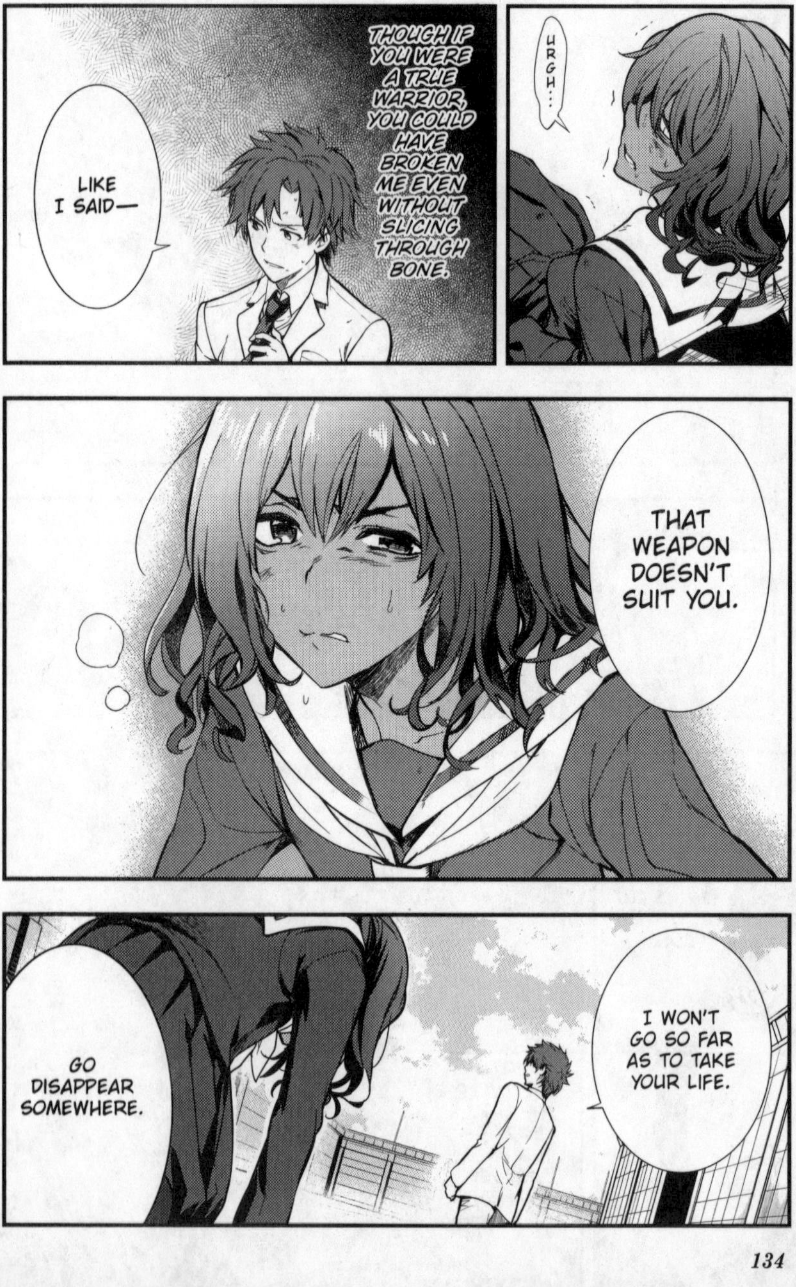
URGH...
THOUGH IF YOU WERE A TRUE WARRIOR, YOU COULD HAVE BROKEN ME EVEN WITHOUT SLICING THROUGH BONE.
LIKE I SAID—
THAT WEAPON DOESN'T SUIT YOU.
I WON'T GO SO FAR AS TO TAKE YOUR LIFE.
GO DISAPPEAR SOMEWHERE.

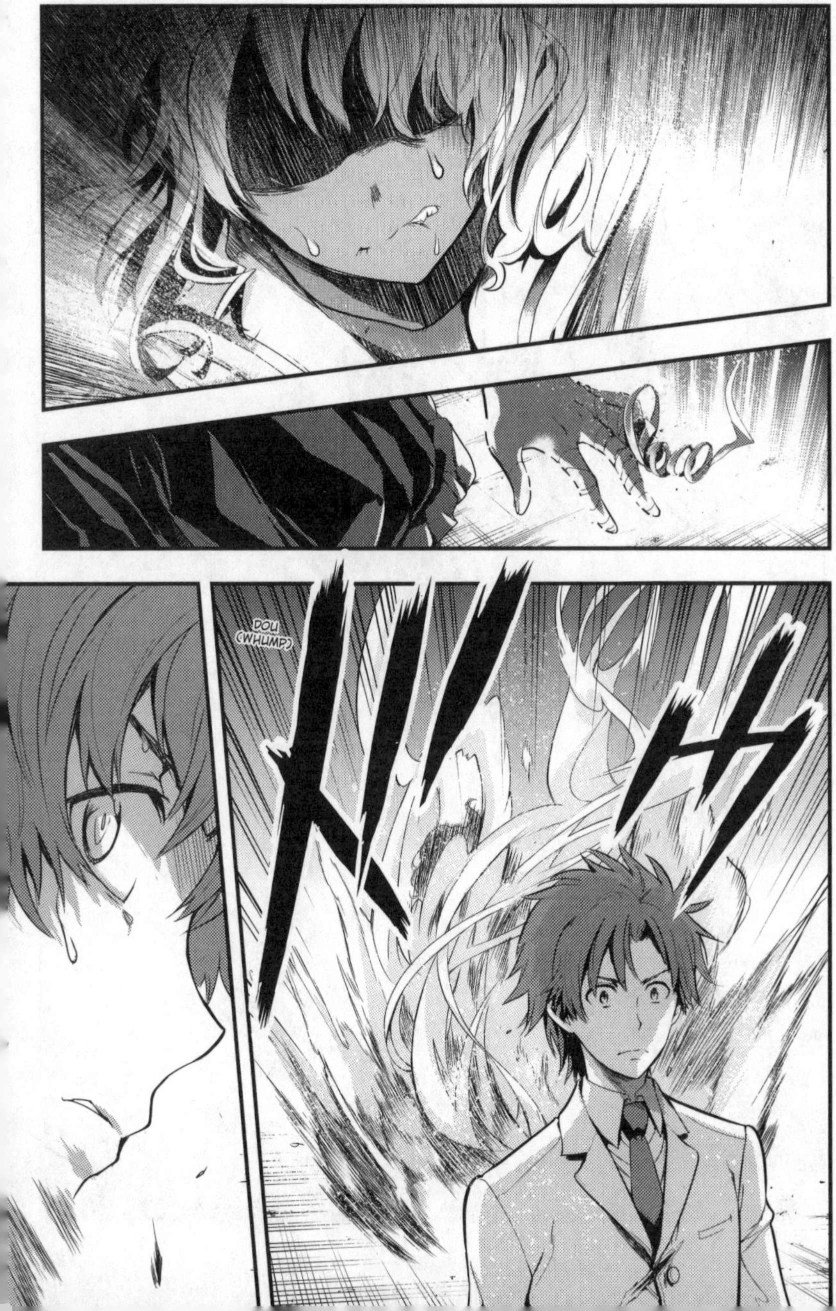
DOU
(WHUMP)

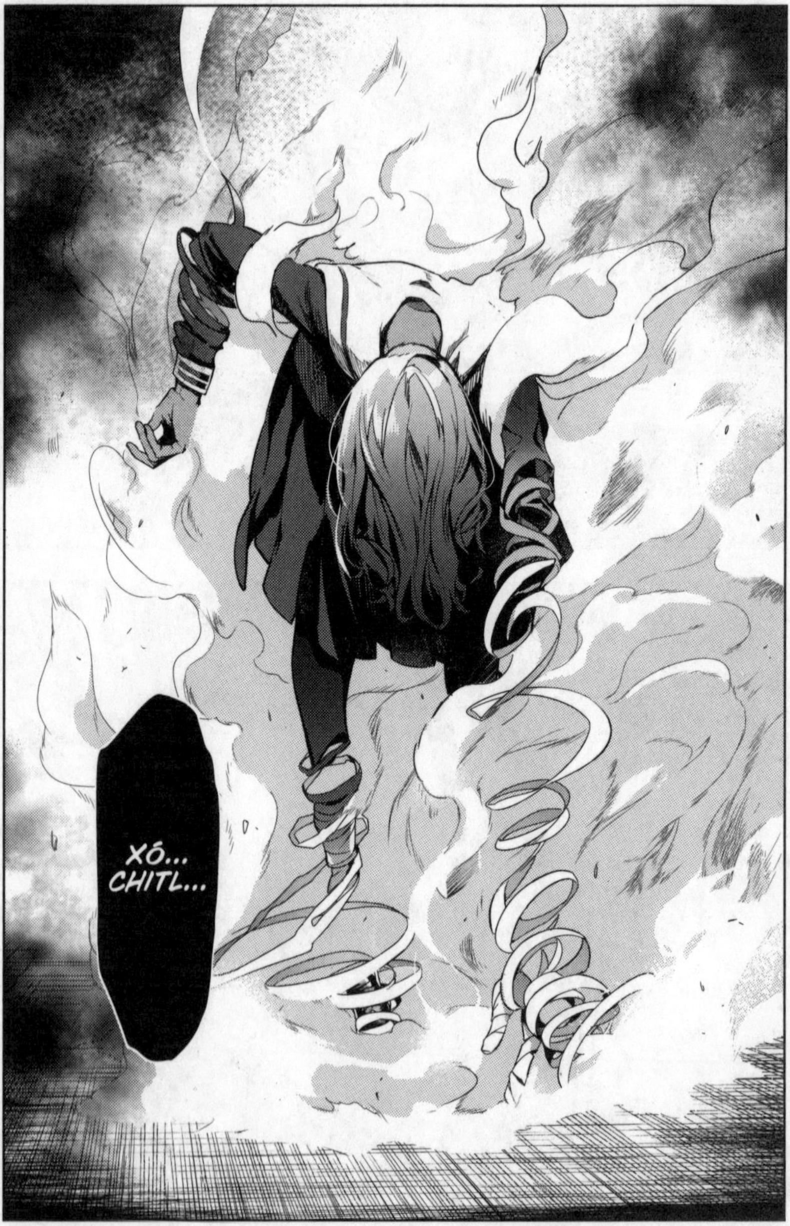
XÓ...
CHITL...

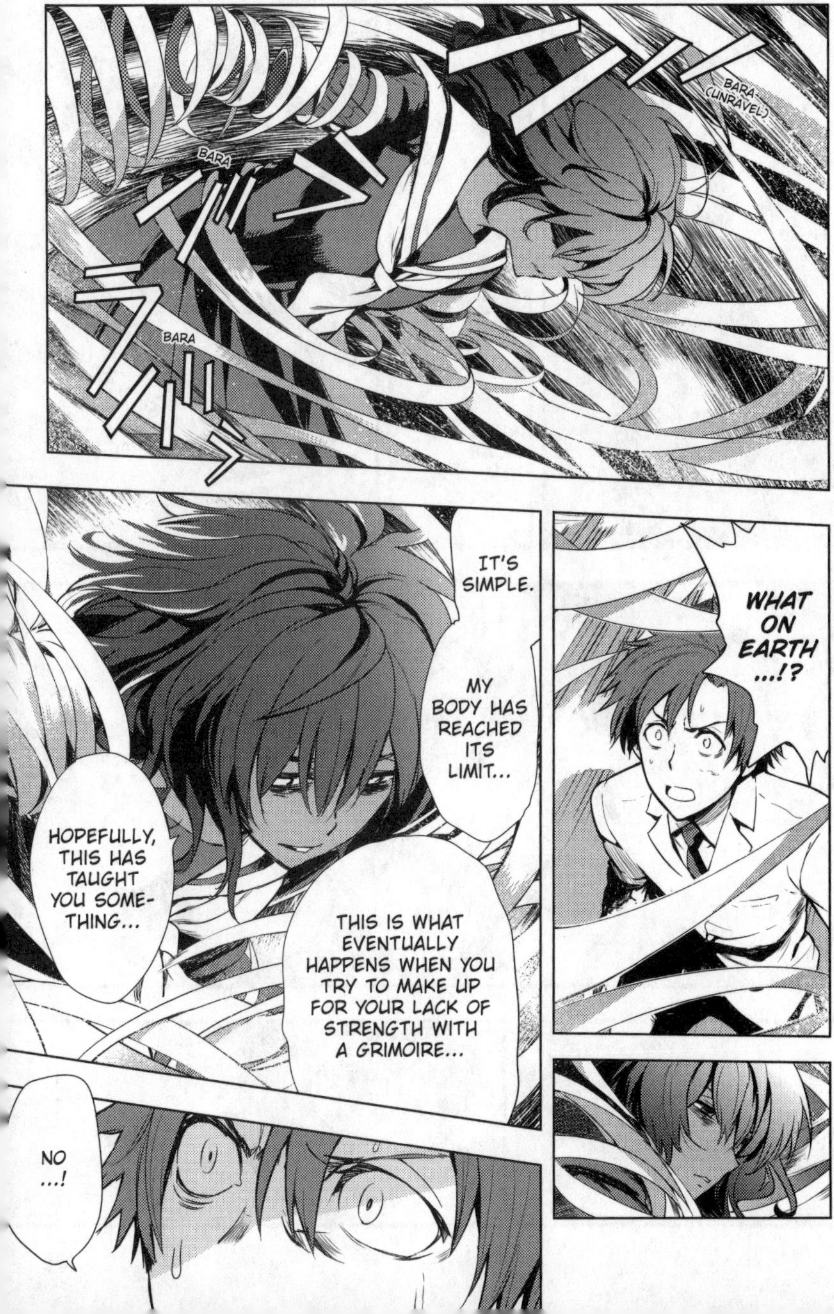
BARA (UNRAVEL)
BARA
BARA
WHAT ON EARTH ...!?
IT'S SIMPLE.
MY BODY HAS REACHED ITS LIMIT...
THIS IS WHAT EVENTUALLY HAPPENS WHEN YOU TRY TO MAKE UP FOR YOUR LACK OF STRENGTH WITH A GRIMOIRE...
HOPEFULLY, THIS HAS TAUGHT YOU SOME-THING...
NO ...!

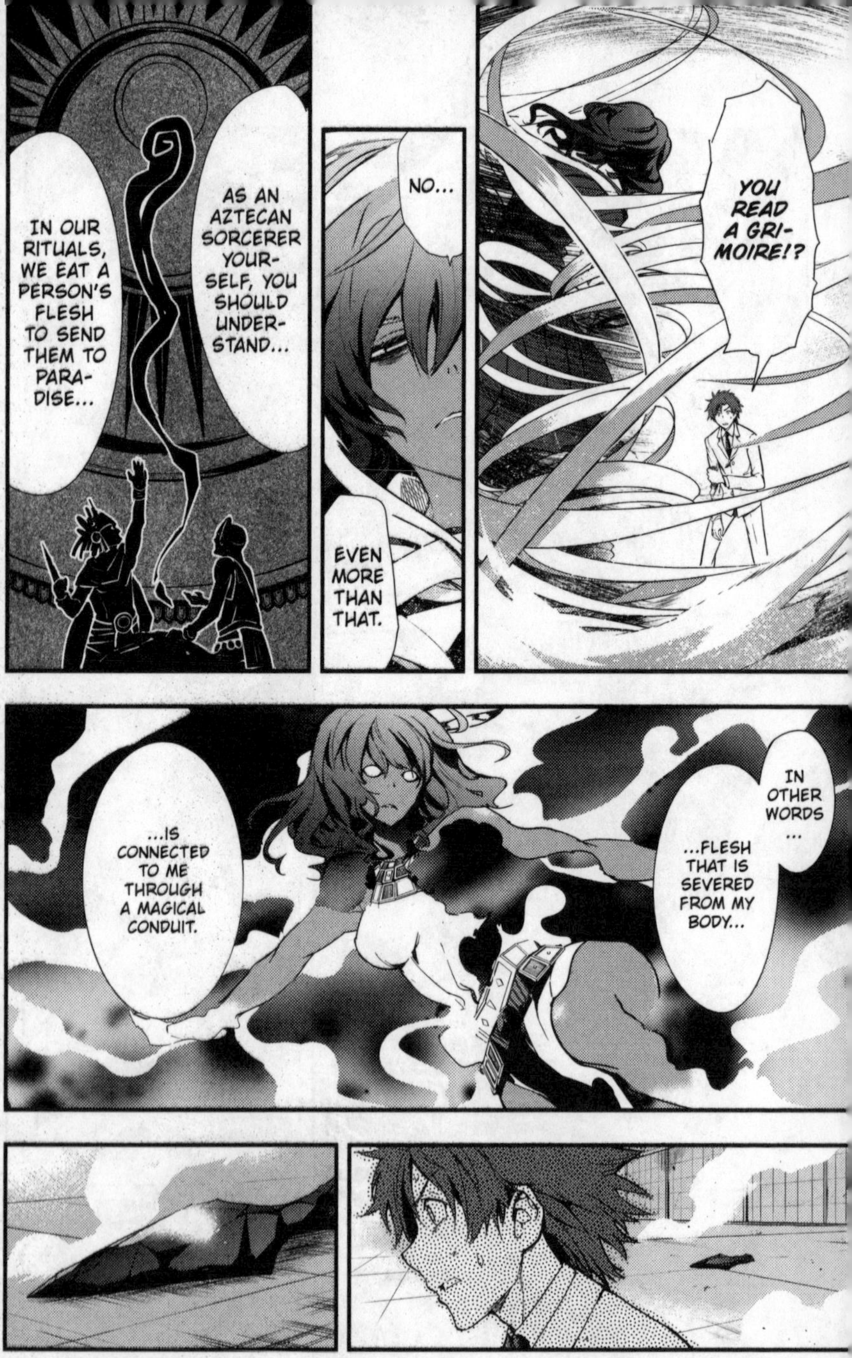
YOU READ A GRIMOIRE!?
NO...
EVEN MORE THAN THAT.
AS AN AZTECAN SORCERER YOURSELF, YOU SHOULD UNDERSTAND...
IN OUR RITUALS, WE EAT A PERSON'S FLESH TO SEND THEM TO PARADISE...
IN OTHER WORDS...
...FLESH THAT IS SEVERED FROM MY BODY...
...IS CONNECTED TO ME THROUGH A MAGICAL CONDUIT.

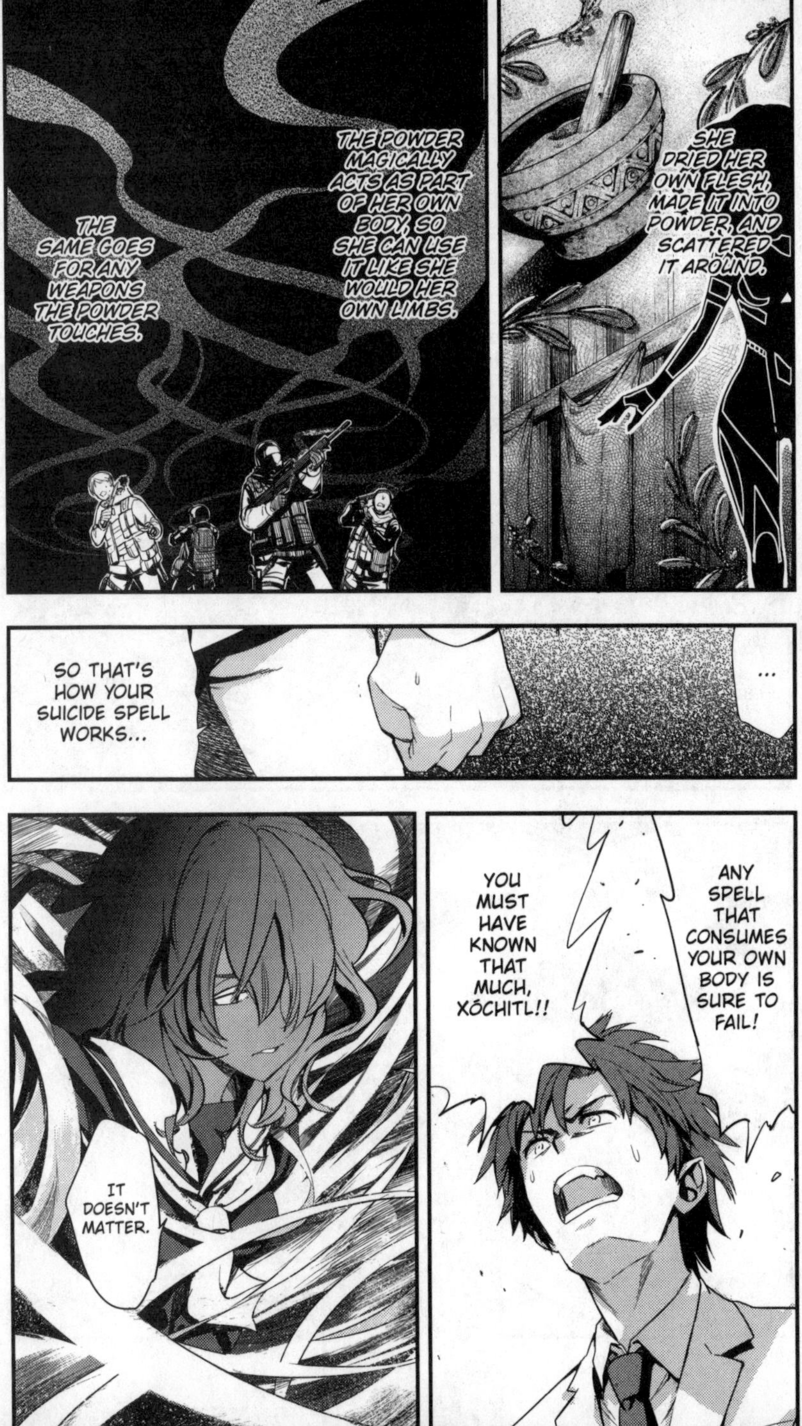
SHE DRIED HER OWN FLESH, MADE IT INTO POWDER, AND SCATTERED IT AROUND.
THE POWDER MAGICALLY ACTS AS PART OF HER OWN BODY, SO SHE CAN USE IT LIKE SHE WOULD HER OWN LIMBS.
THE SAME GOES FOR ANY WEAPONS THE POWDER TOUCHES.
...
SO THAT'S HOW YOUR SUICIDE SPELL WORKS...
ANY SPELL THAT CONSUMES YOUR OWN BODY IS SURE TO FAIL!
YOU MUST HAVE KNOWN THAT MUCH, XÓCHITL!!
IT DOESN'T MATTER.

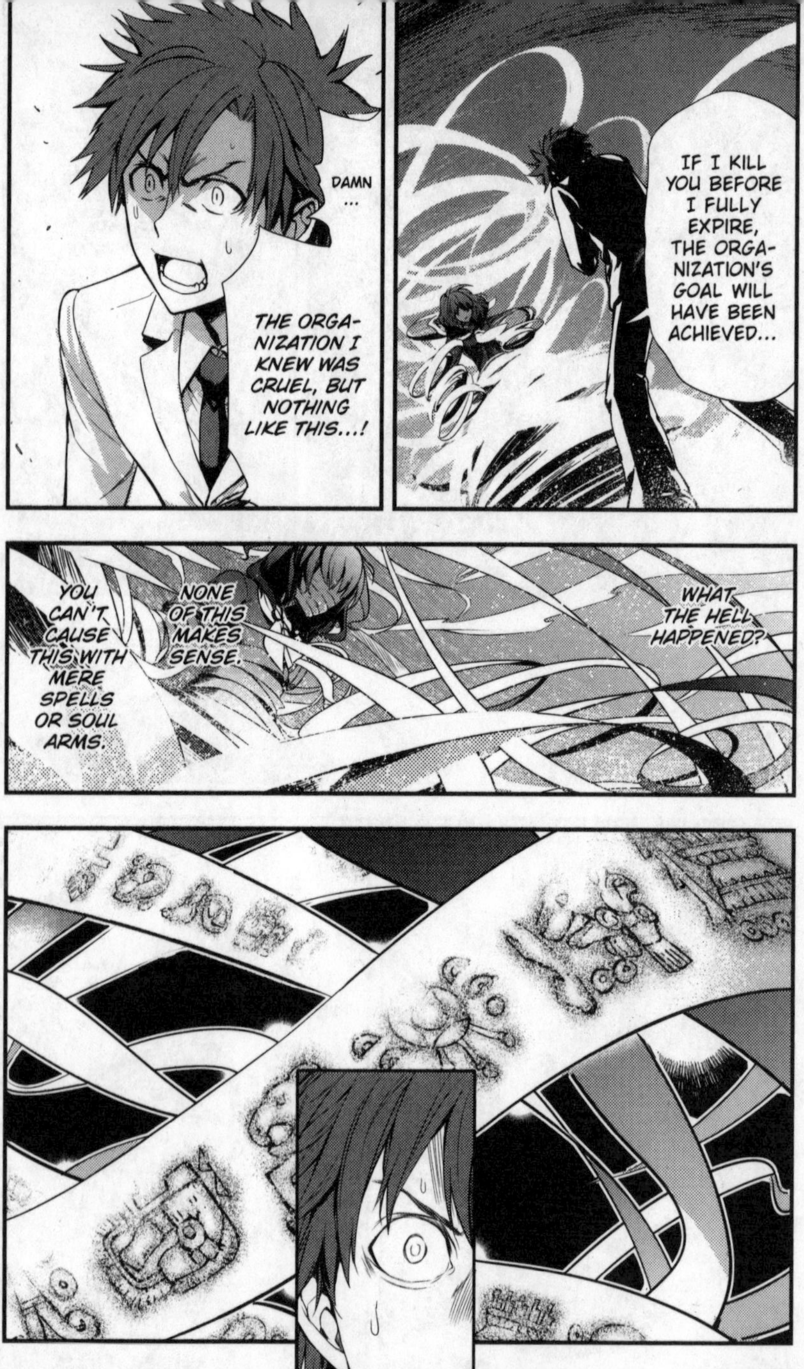
IF I KILL YOU BEFORE I FULLY EXPIRE, THE ORGA-NIZATION'S GOAL WILL HAVE BEEN ACHIEVED...
DAMN ...
THE ORGA-NIZATION I KNEW WAS CRUEL, BUT NOTHING LIKE THIS...!
WHAT THE HELL HAPPENED?
NONE OF THIS MAKES SENSE.
YOU CAN'T CAUSE THIS WITH MERE SPELLS OR SOUL ARMS.

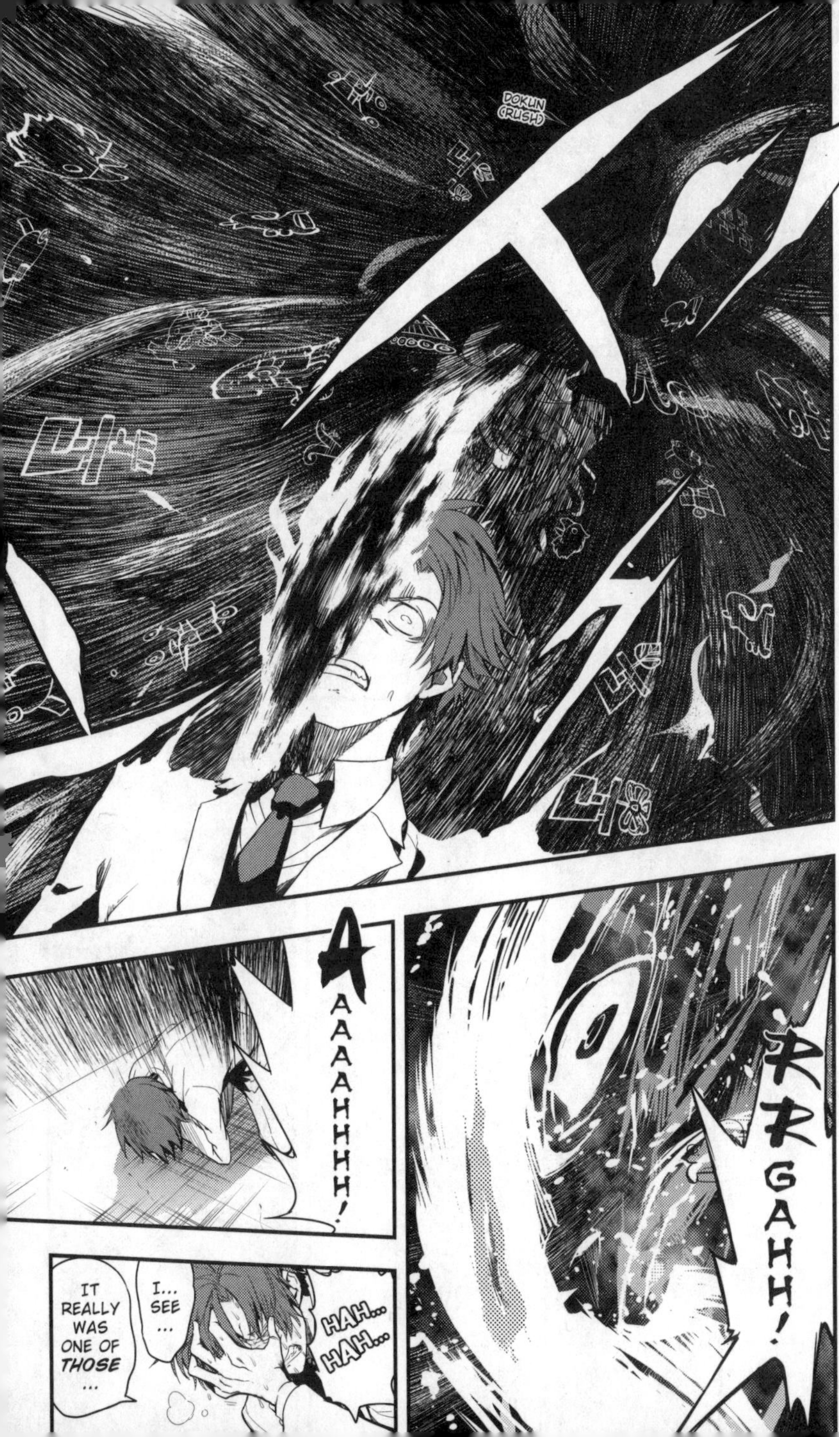
DOKUN (RUSH)
RRGAHH!
AAAAAHHHH!
HAH... HAH...
I... SEE...
IT REALLY WAS ONE OF THOSE...

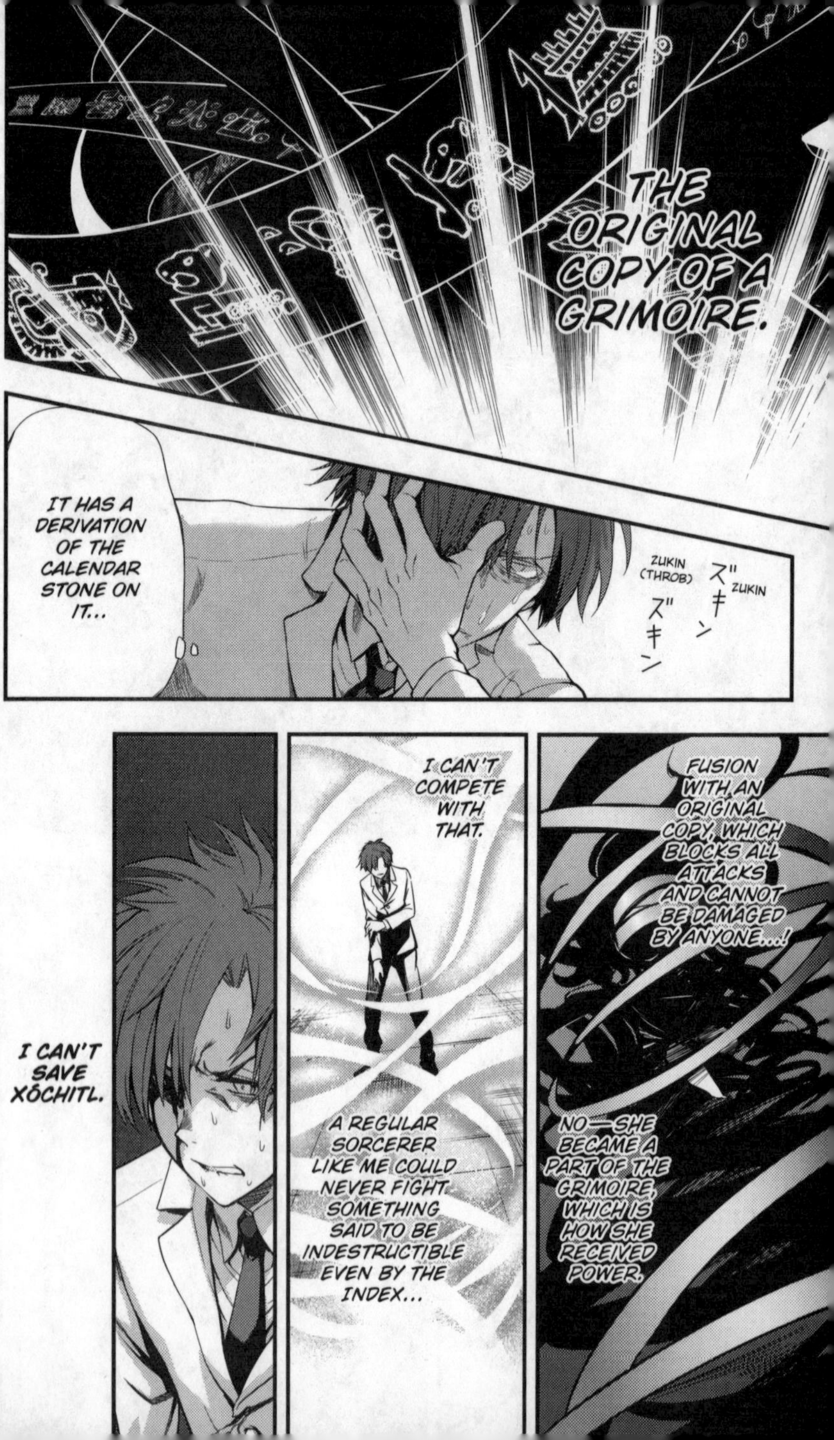
THE ORIGINAL COPY OF A GRIMOIRE.
ZUKIN (THROB) ズキン ZUKIN ズキン
IT HAS A DERIVATION OF THE CALENDAR STONE ON IT...
FUSION WITH AN ORIGINAL COPY, WHICH BLOCKS ALL ATTACKS AND CANNOT BE DAMAGED BY ANYONE...!
NO—SHE BECAME A PART OF THE GRIMOIRE, WHICH IS HOW SHE RECEIVED POWER.
I CAN'T COMPETE WITH THAT.
A REGULAR SORCERER LIKE ME COULD NEVER FIGHT SOMETHING SAID TO BE INDESTRUCTIBLE EVEN BY THE INDEX...
I CAN'T SAVE XÕCHITL.

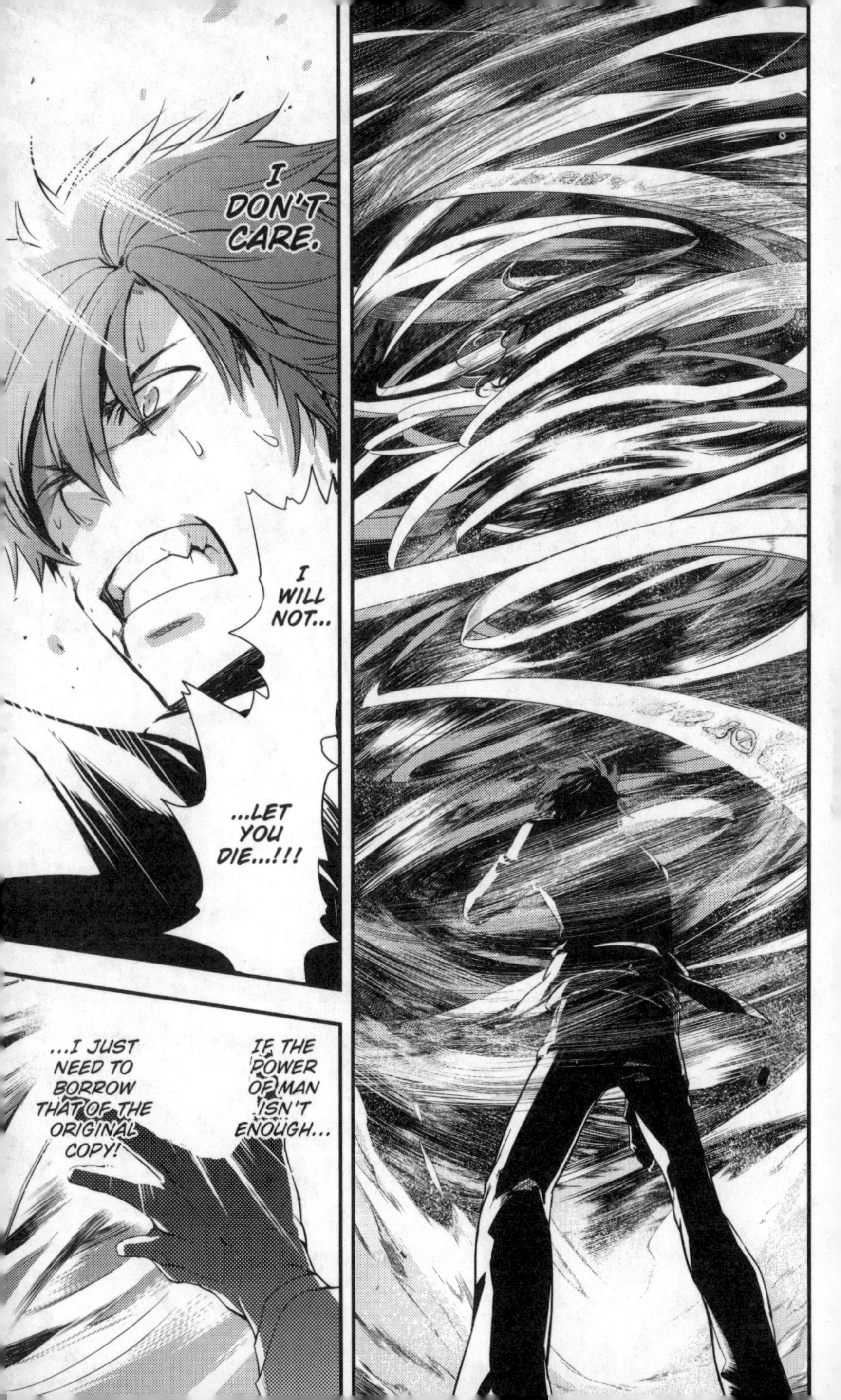
I DON'T CARE.
I WILL NOT...
...LET YOU DIE...!!!
IF THE POWER OF MAN ISN'T ENOUGH...
...I JUST NEED TO BORROW THAT OF THE ORIGINAL COPY!

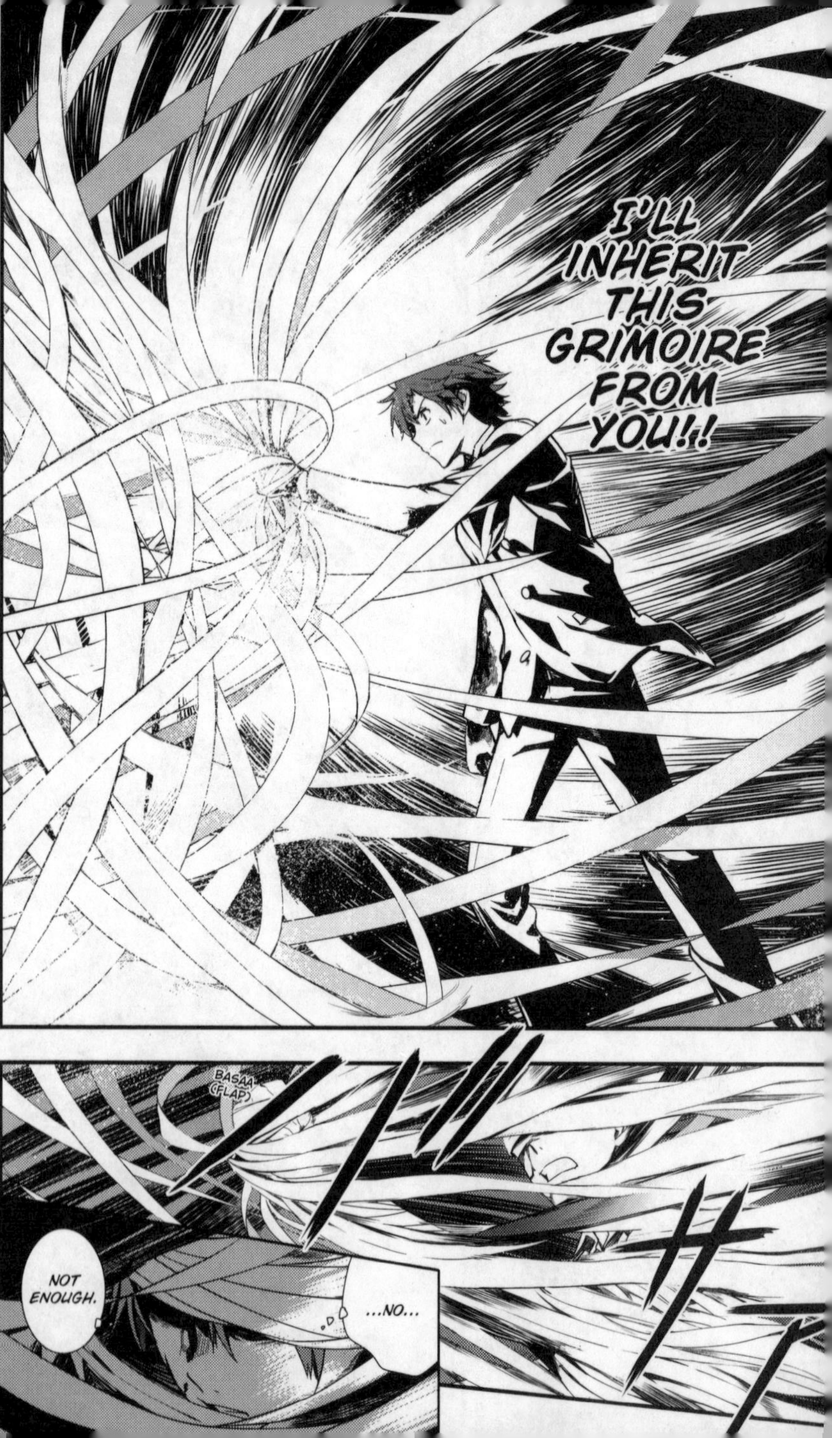
I'LL INHERIT THIS GRIMOIRE FROM YOU!!
BASAA (FLAP)
...NO...
NOT ENOUGH.

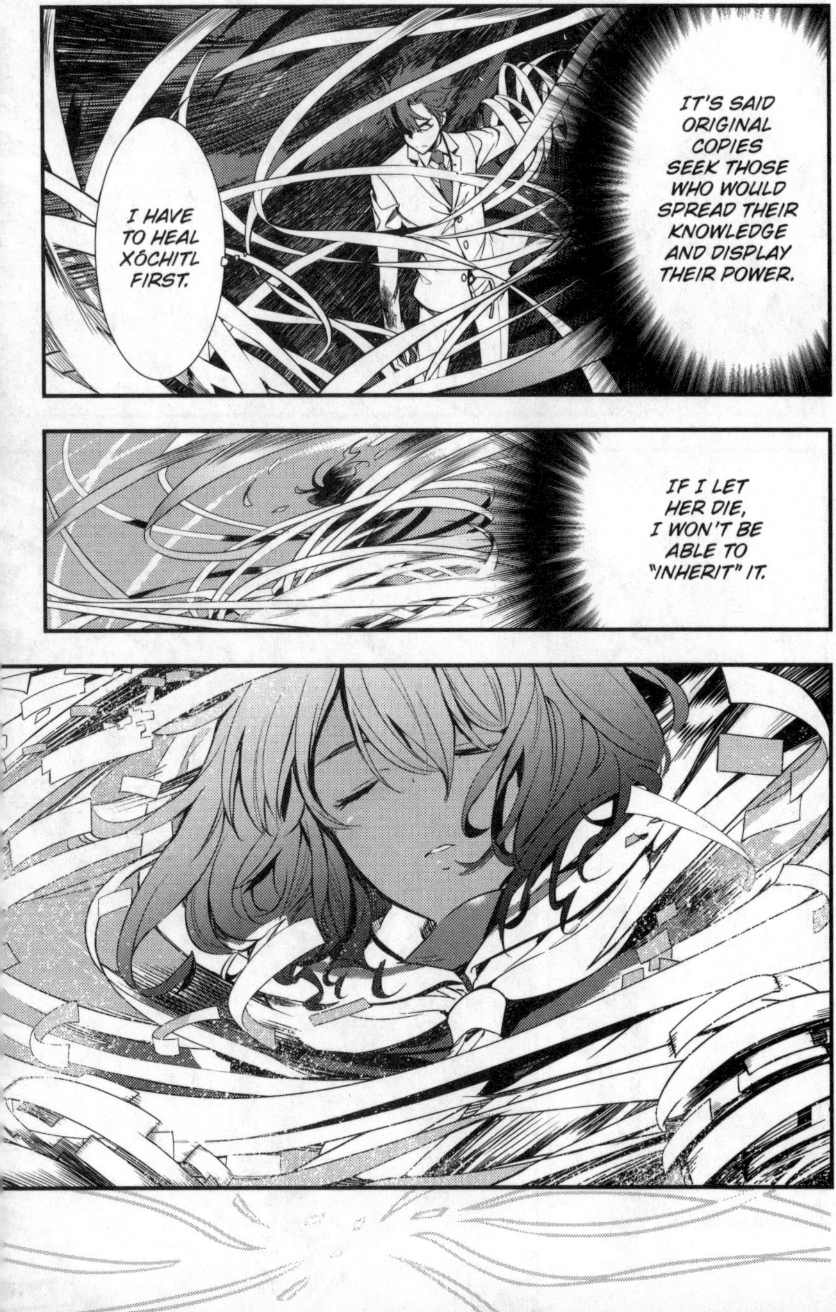
IT'S SAID ORIGINAL COPIES SEEK THOSE WHO WOULD SPREAD THEIR KNOWLEDGE AND DISPLAY THEIR POWER.
I HAVE TO HEAL XÓCHITL FIRST.
IF I LET HER DIE, I WON'T BE ABLE TO "INHERIT" IT.

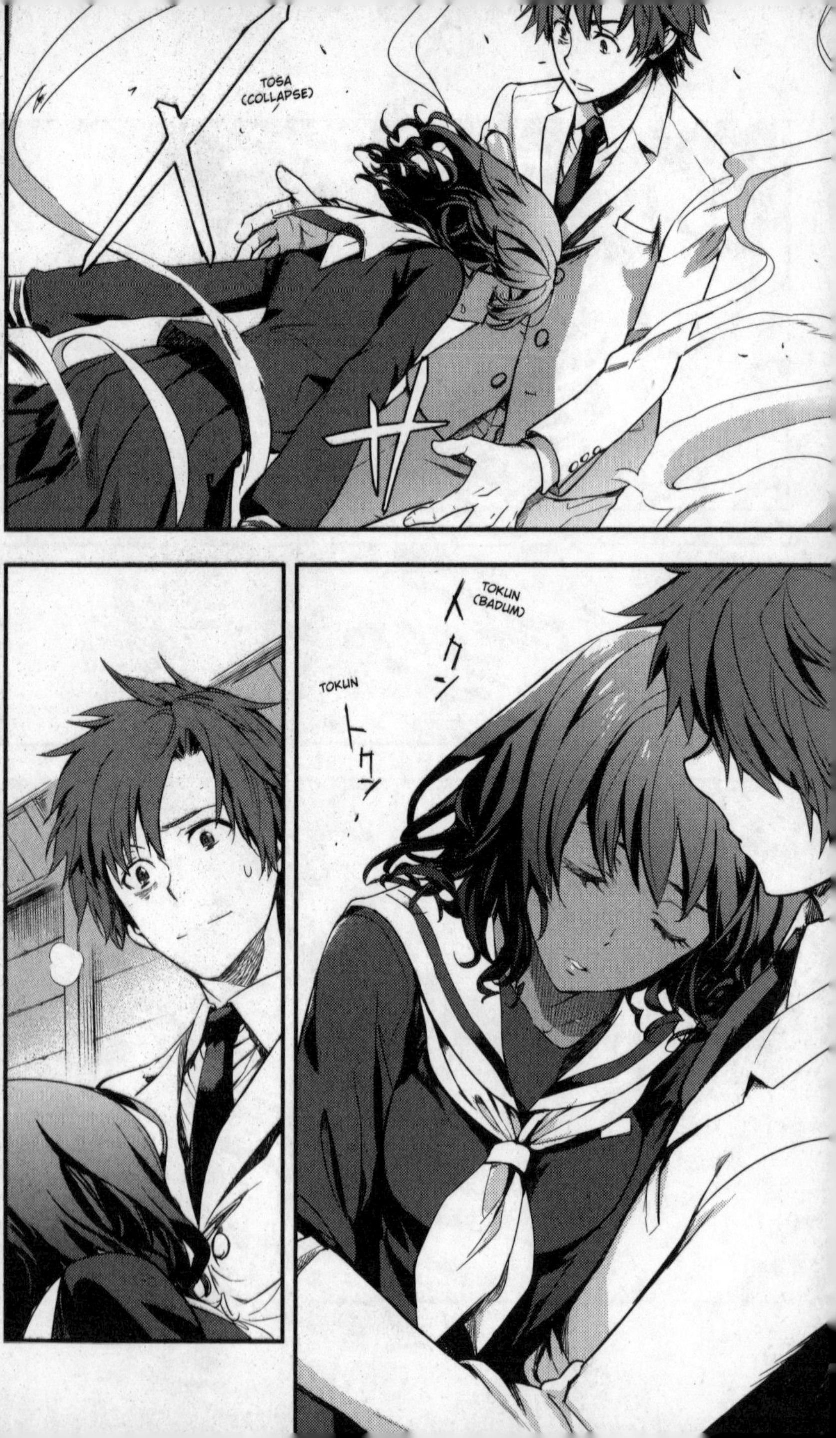
TOSA
(COLLAPSE)
TOKUN
(BADUM)
TOKUN

Transmission data from "UNDER_LINE"

Item
Shizuri Mugino (Leader)
Saiai Kinuhata
Frenda Seivelun
Rikou Takitsubo

Member
Professor (Leader)
Yoshio Baba
Xóchitl
Saraku

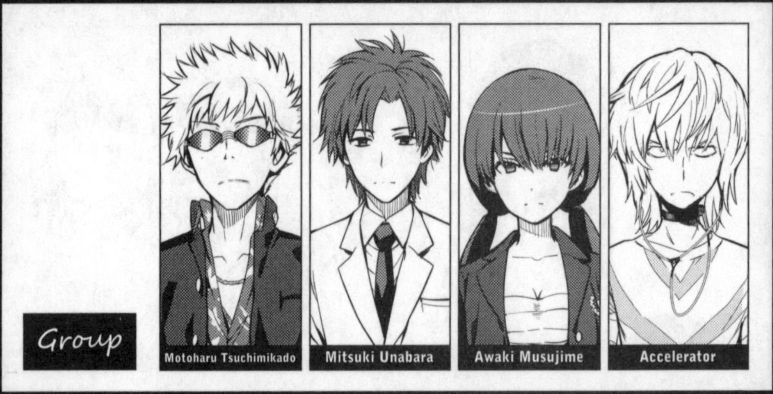
Group
Motoharu Tsuchimikado
Mitsuki Unabara
Awaki Musujime
Accelerator

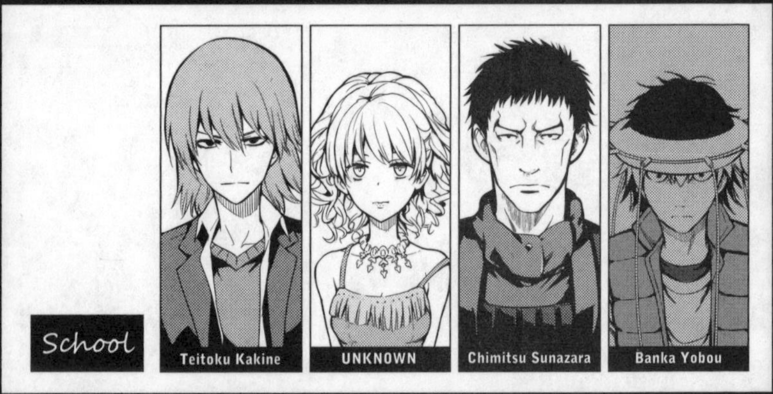
School
Teitoku Kakine
UNKNOWN
Chimitsu Sunazara
Banka Yobou

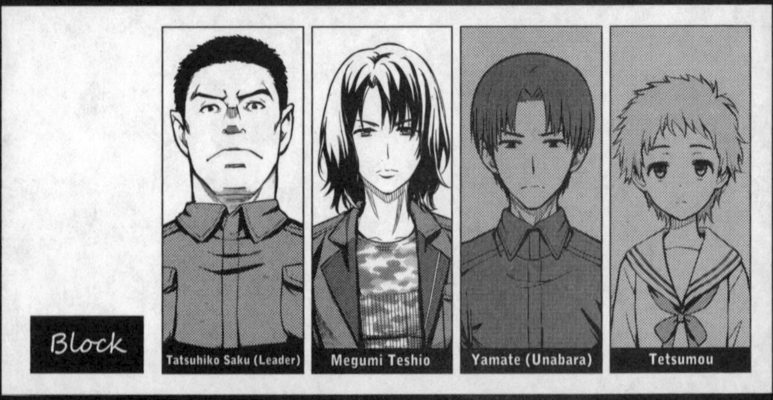
Block
Tatsuhiko Saku (Leader)
Megumi Teshio
Yamate (Unabara)
Tetsumou

# #141 DISTRICT 10 JUVENILE REFORMATORY ②

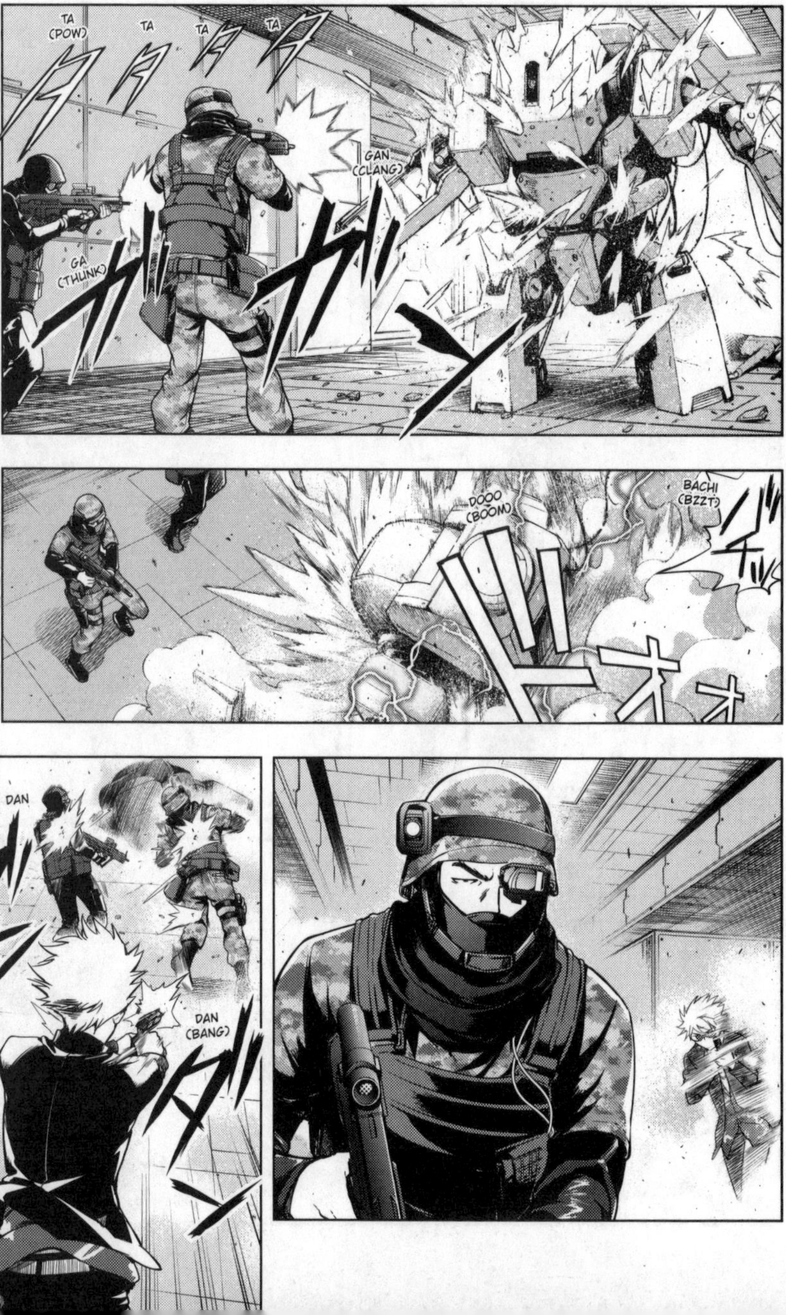
TA
TA
TA
TA (POW)
GAN (CLANG)
GA (THUNK)
BACHI (BZZT)
DOOO (BOOM)
DAN
DAN (BANG)

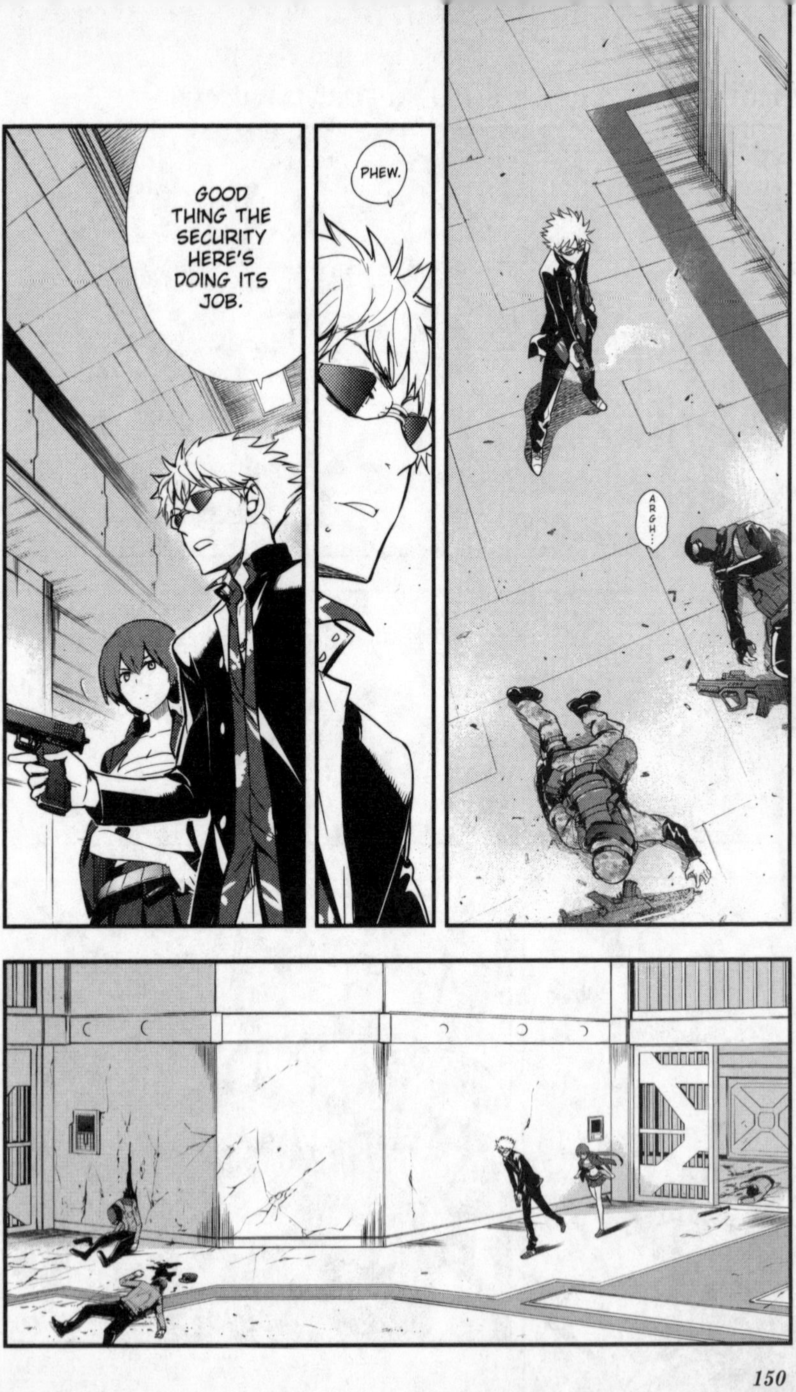
ARGH...
PHEW.
GOOD THING THE SECURITY HERE'S DOING ITS JOB.

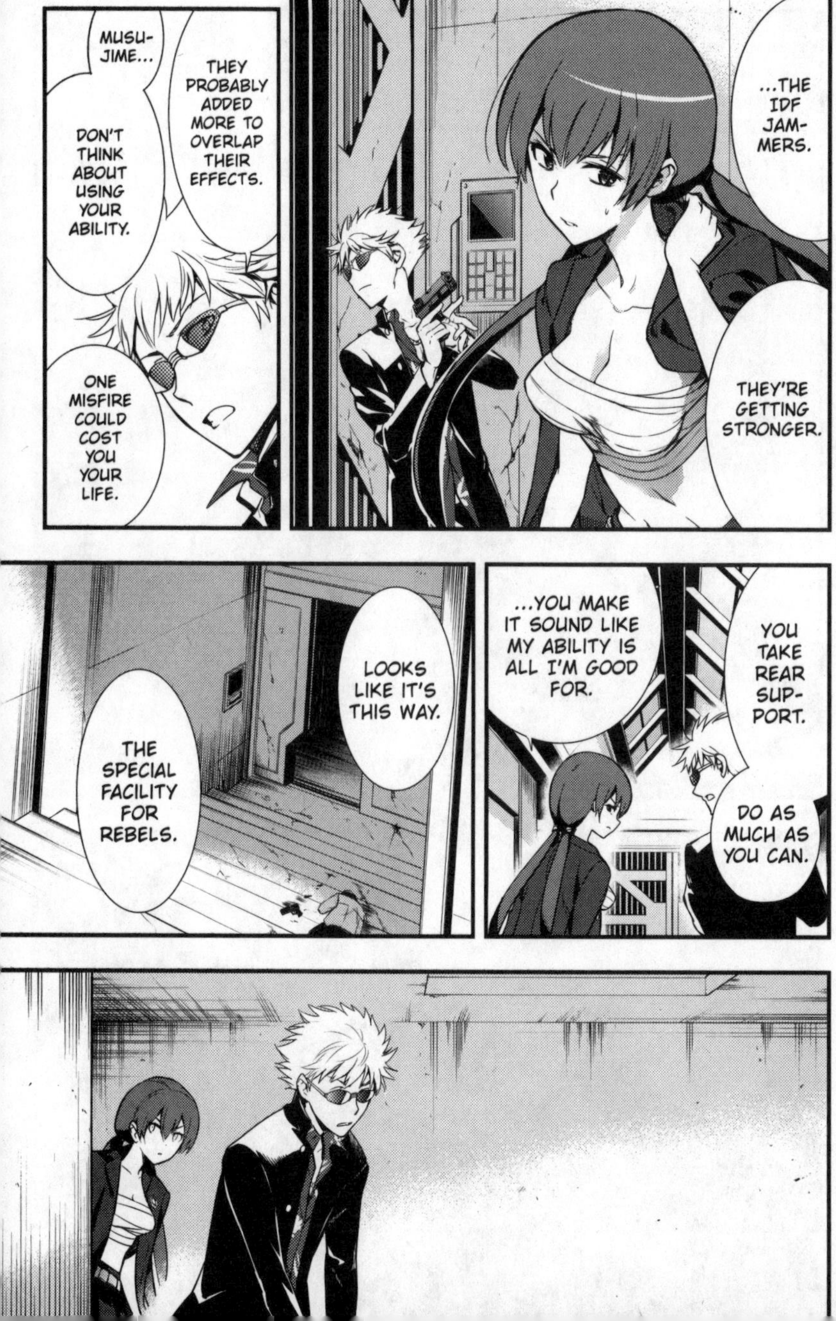
...THE IDF JAMMERS.
THEY'RE GETTING STRONGER.
THEY PROBABLY ADDED MORE TO OVERLAP THEIR EFFECTS.
MUSUJIME...
DON'T THINK ABOUT USING YOUR ABILITY.
ONE MISFIRE COULD COST YOU YOUR LIFE.
YOU TAKE REAR SUPPORT.
...YOU MAKE IT SOUND LIKE MY ABILITY IS ALL I'M GOOD FOR.
DO AS MUCH AS YOU CAN.
LOOKS LIKE IT'S THIS WAY.
THE SPECIAL FACILITY FOR REBELS.

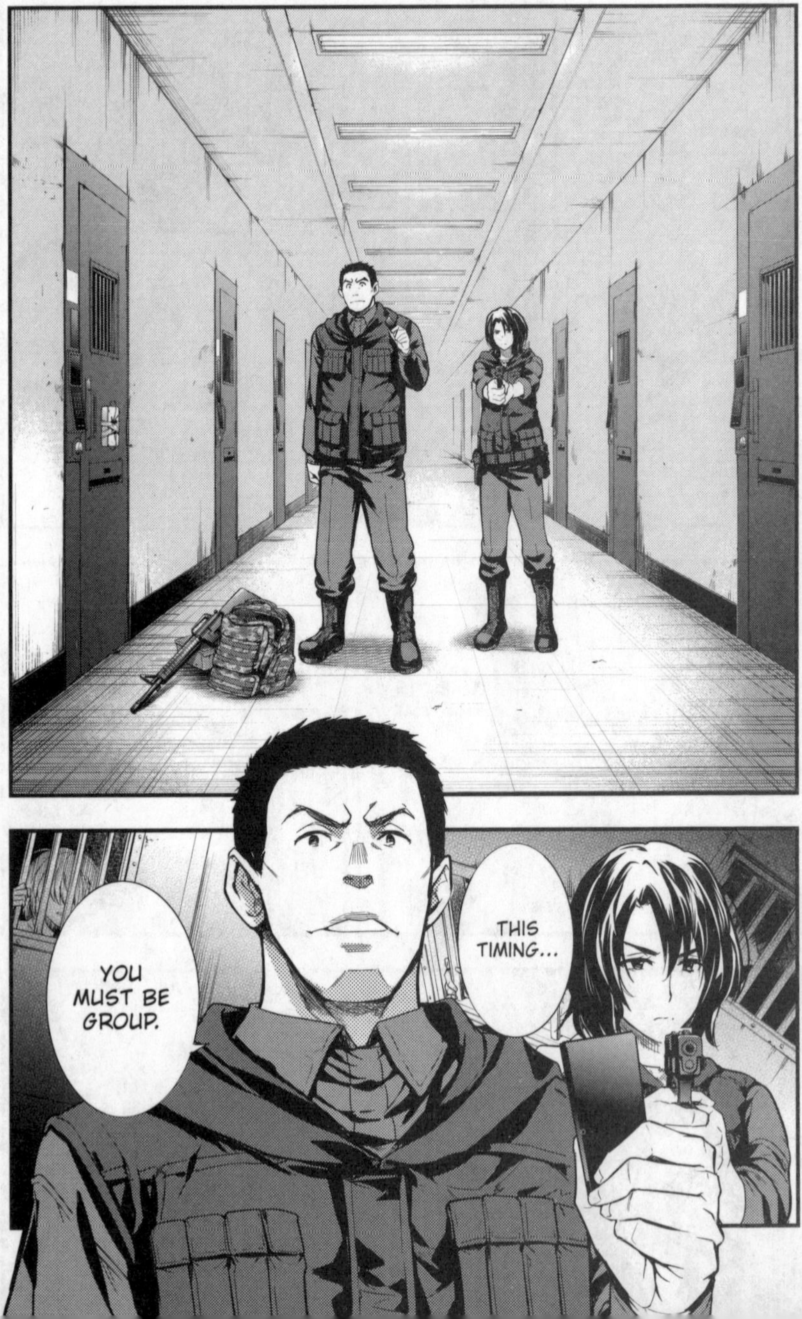
THIS TIMING...
YOU MUST BE GROUP.

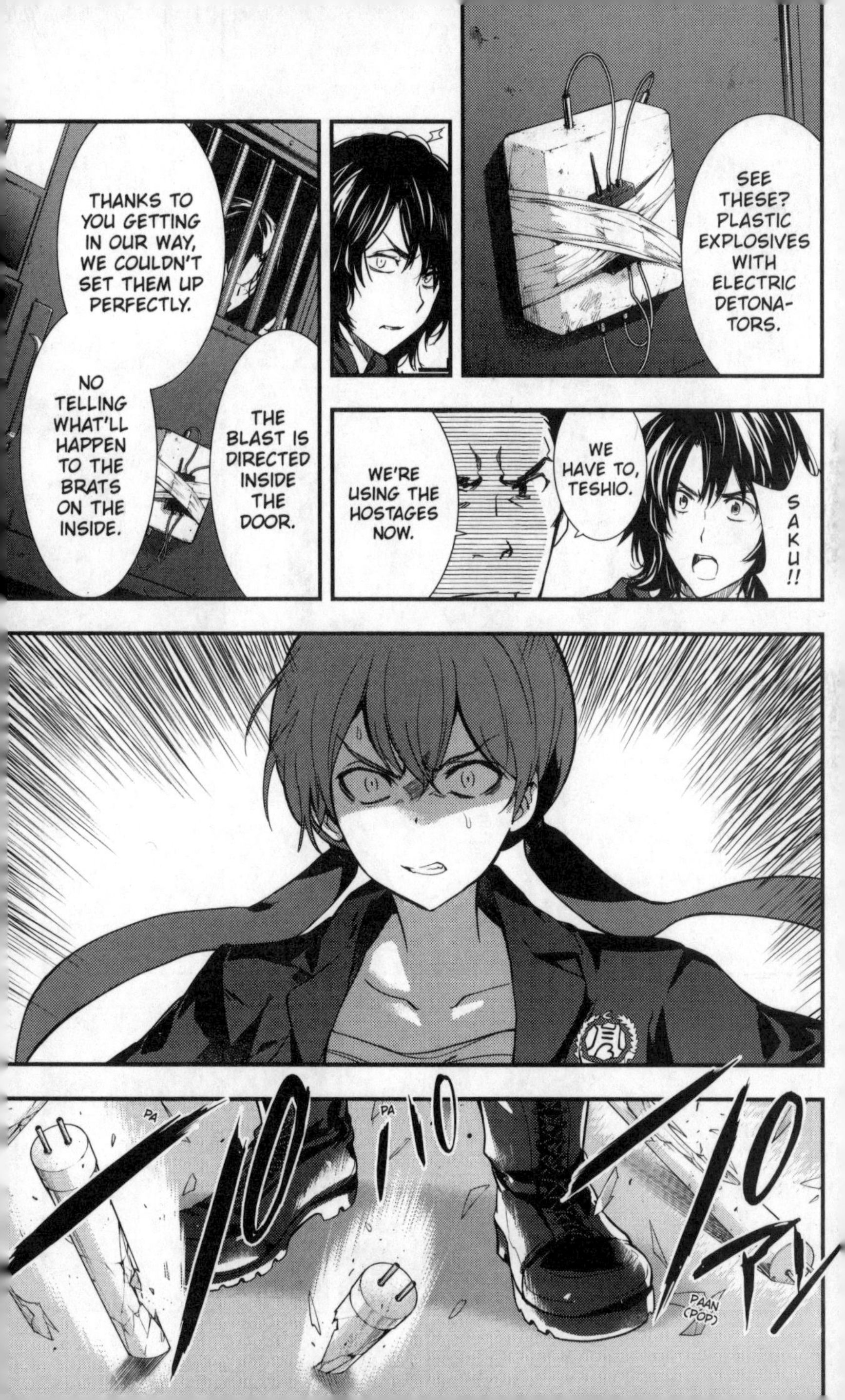
SEE THESE? PLASTIC EXPLOSIVES WITH ELECTRIC DETONATORS.
SAKU!!
WE HAVE TO, TESHIO.
WE'RE USING THE HOSTAGES NOW.
THANKS TO YOU GETTING IN OUR WAY, WE COULDN'T SET THEM UP PERFECTLY.
THE BLAST IS DIRECTED INSIDE THE DOOR.
NO TELLING WHAT'LL HAPPEN TO THE BRATS ON THE INSIDE.
PA
PA
PAAN (POP)

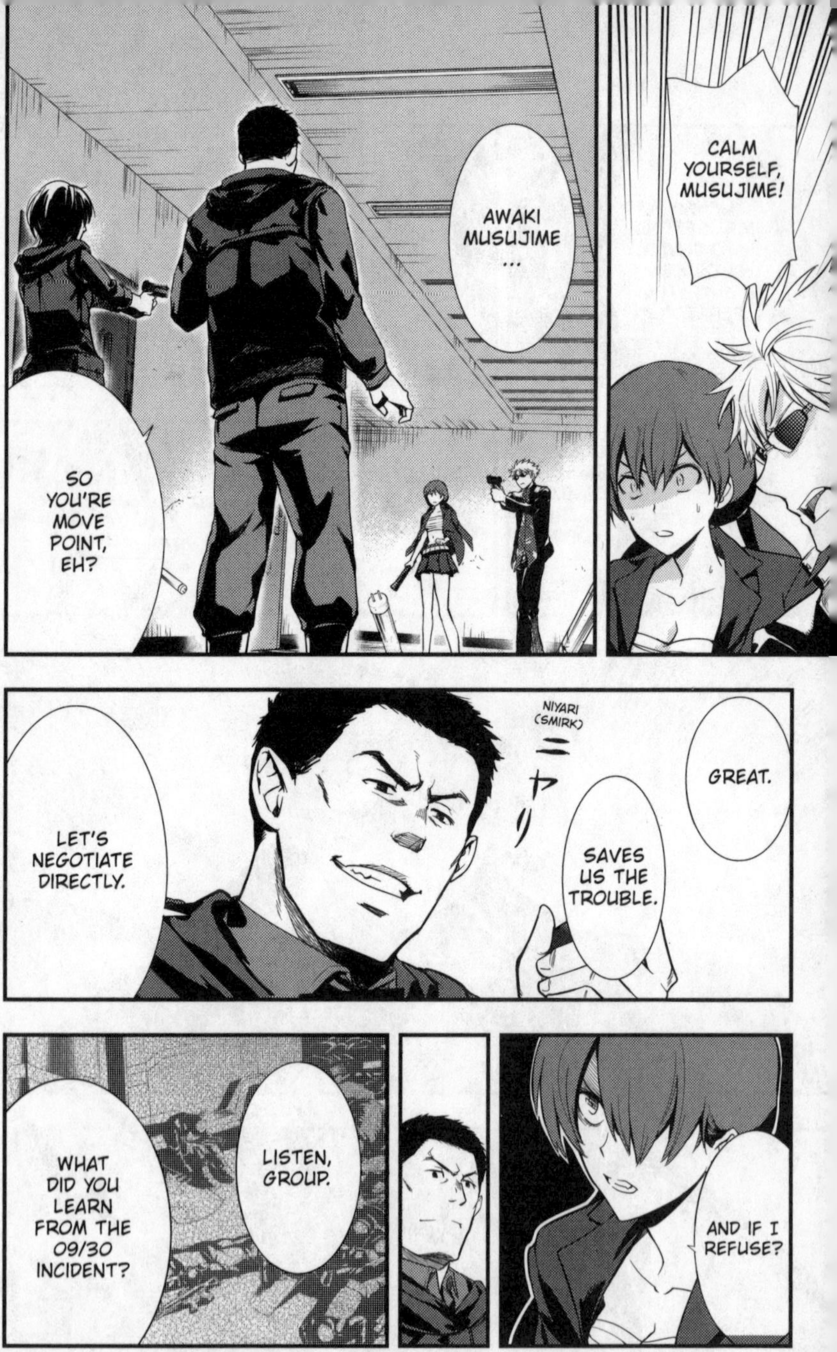
CALM YOURSELF, MUSUJIME!
AWAKI MUSUJIME ...
SO YOU'RE MOVE POINT, EH?
GREAT.
NIYARI (SMIRK)
ニヤリ
SAVES US THE TROUBLE.
LET'S NEGOTIATE DIRECTLY.
AND IF I REFUSE?
LISTEN, GROUP.
WHAT DID YOU LEARN FROM THE 09/30 INCIDENT?

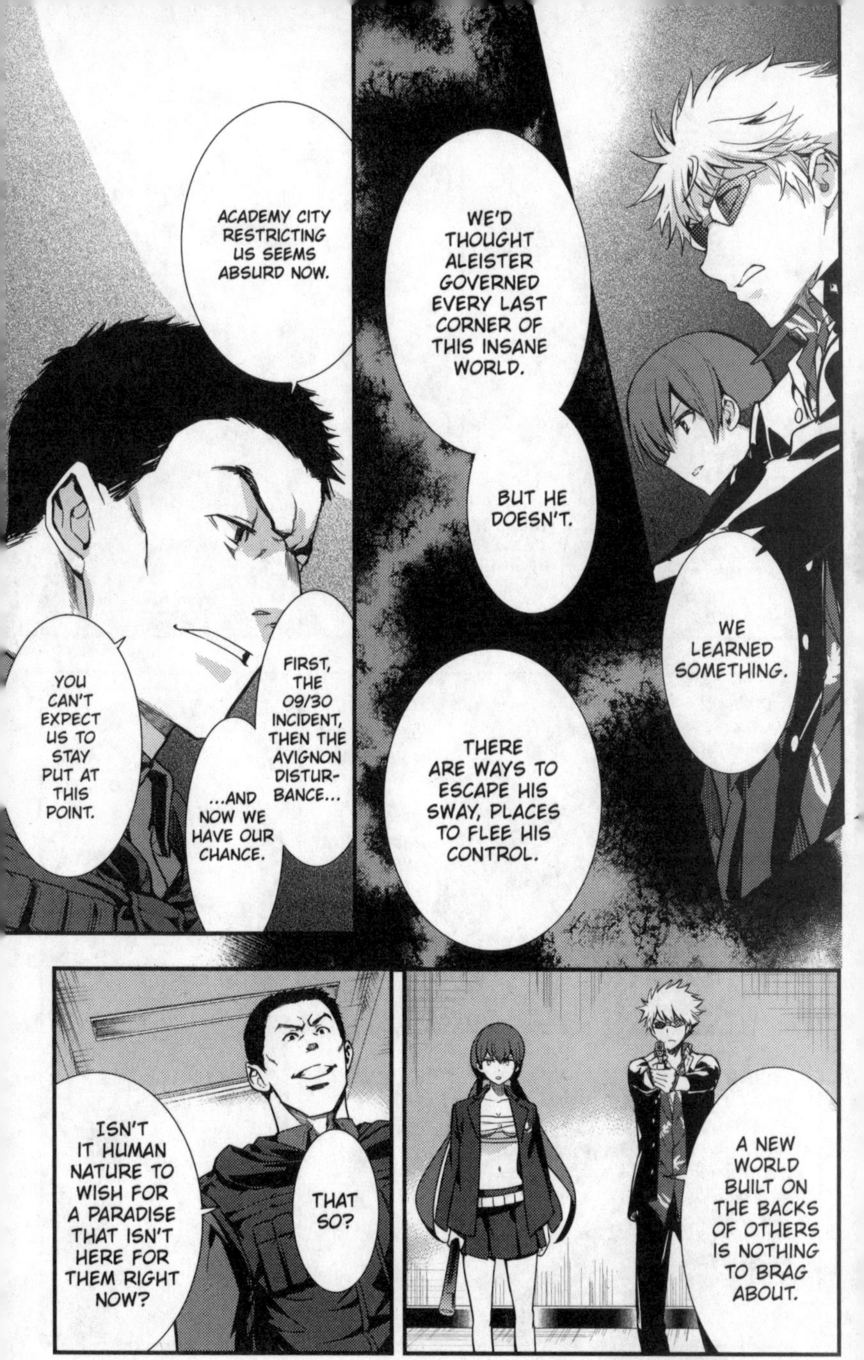
WE'D THOUGHT ALEISTER GOVERNED EVERY LAST CORNER OF THIS INSANE WORLD.
BUT HE DOESN'T.
WE LEARNED SOMETHING.
THERE ARE WAYS TO ESCAPE HIS SWAY, PLACES TO FLEE HIS CONTROL.
ACADEMY CITY RESTRICTING US SEEMS ABSURD NOW.
FIRST, THE 09/30 INCIDENT, THEN THE AVIGNON DISTUR-BANCE...
...AND NOW WE HAVE OUR CHANCE.
YOU CAN'T EXPECT US TO STAY PUT AT THIS POINT.
A NEW WORLD BUILT ON THE BACKS OF OTHERS IS NOTHING TO BRAG ABOUT.
THAT SO?
ISN'T IT HUMAN NATURE TO WISH FOR A PARADISE THAT ISN'T HERE FOR THEM RIGHT NOW?

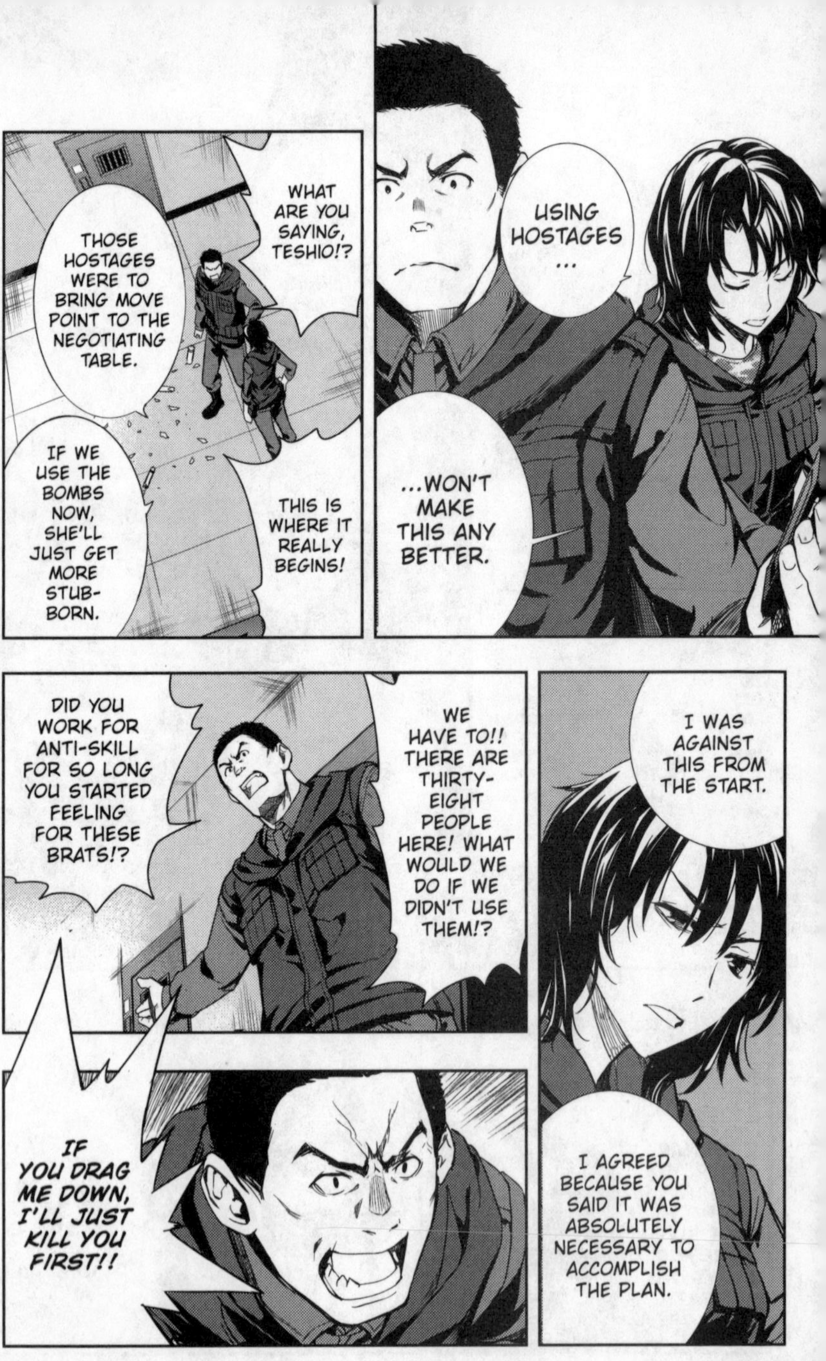
USING HOSTAGES ...
...WON'T MAKE THIS ANY BETTER.
WHAT ARE YOU SAYING, TESHIO!?
THOSE HOSTAGES WERE TO BRING MOVE POINT TO THE NEGOTIATING TABLE.
THIS IS WHERE IT REALLY BEGINS!
IF WE USE THE BOMBS NOW, SHE'LL JUST GET MORE STUB-BORN.
I WAS AGAINST THIS FROM THE START.
I AGREED BECAUSE YOU SAID IT WAS ABSOLUTELY NECESSARY TO ACCOMPLISH THE PLAN.
WE HAVE TO!! THERE ARE THIRTY-EIGHT PEOPLE HERE! WHAT WOULD WE DO IF WE DIDN'T USE THEM!?
DID YOU WORK FOR ANTI-SKILL FOR SO LONG YOU STARTED FEELING FOR THESE BRATS!?
IF YOU DRAG ME DOWN, I'LL JUST KILL YOU FIRST!!

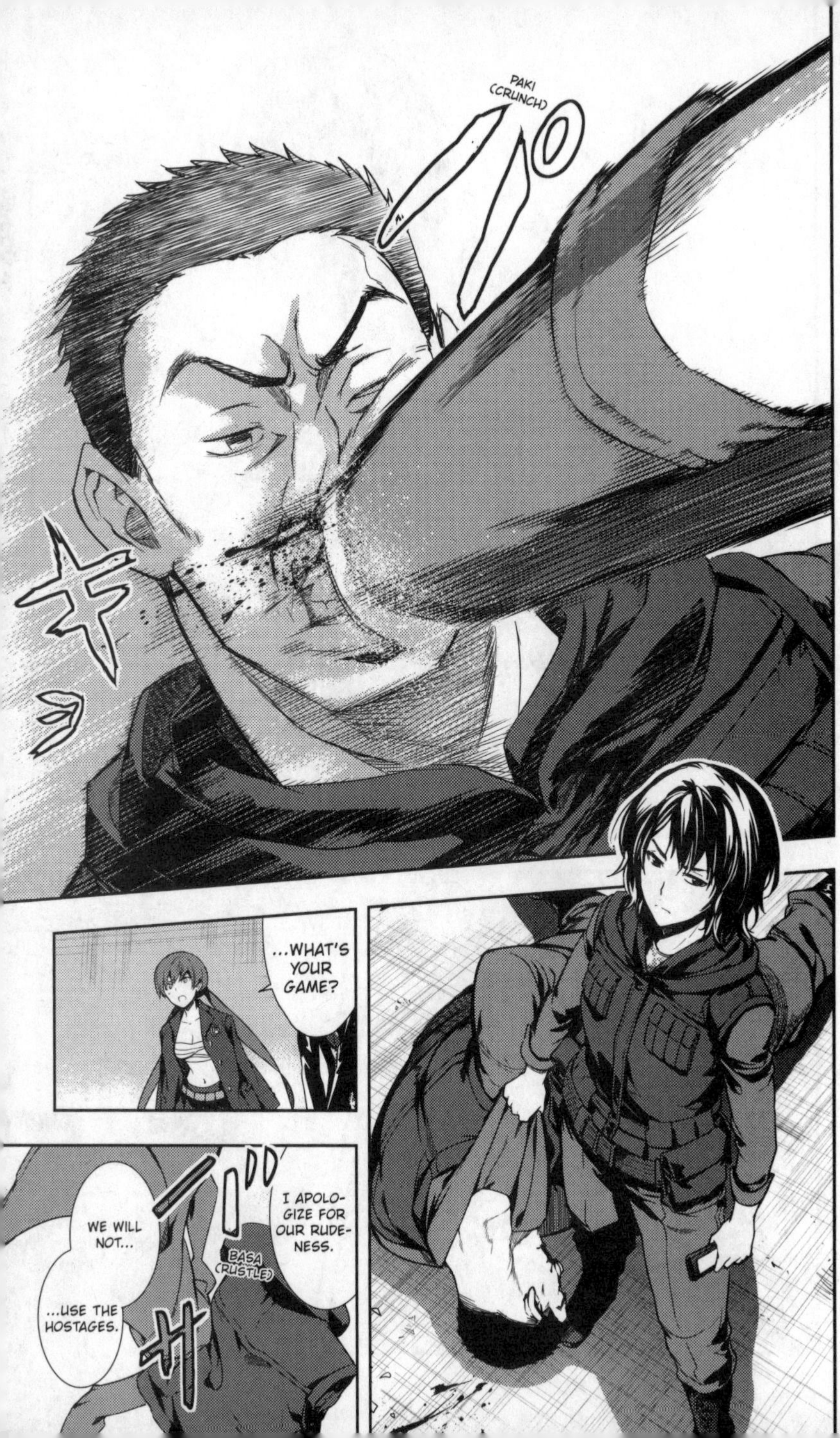
PAKI (CRUNCH)
...WHAT'S YOUR GAME?
I APOLOGIZE FOR OUR RUDENESS.
BASA (RUSTLE)
WE WILL NOT...
...USE THE HOSTAGES.

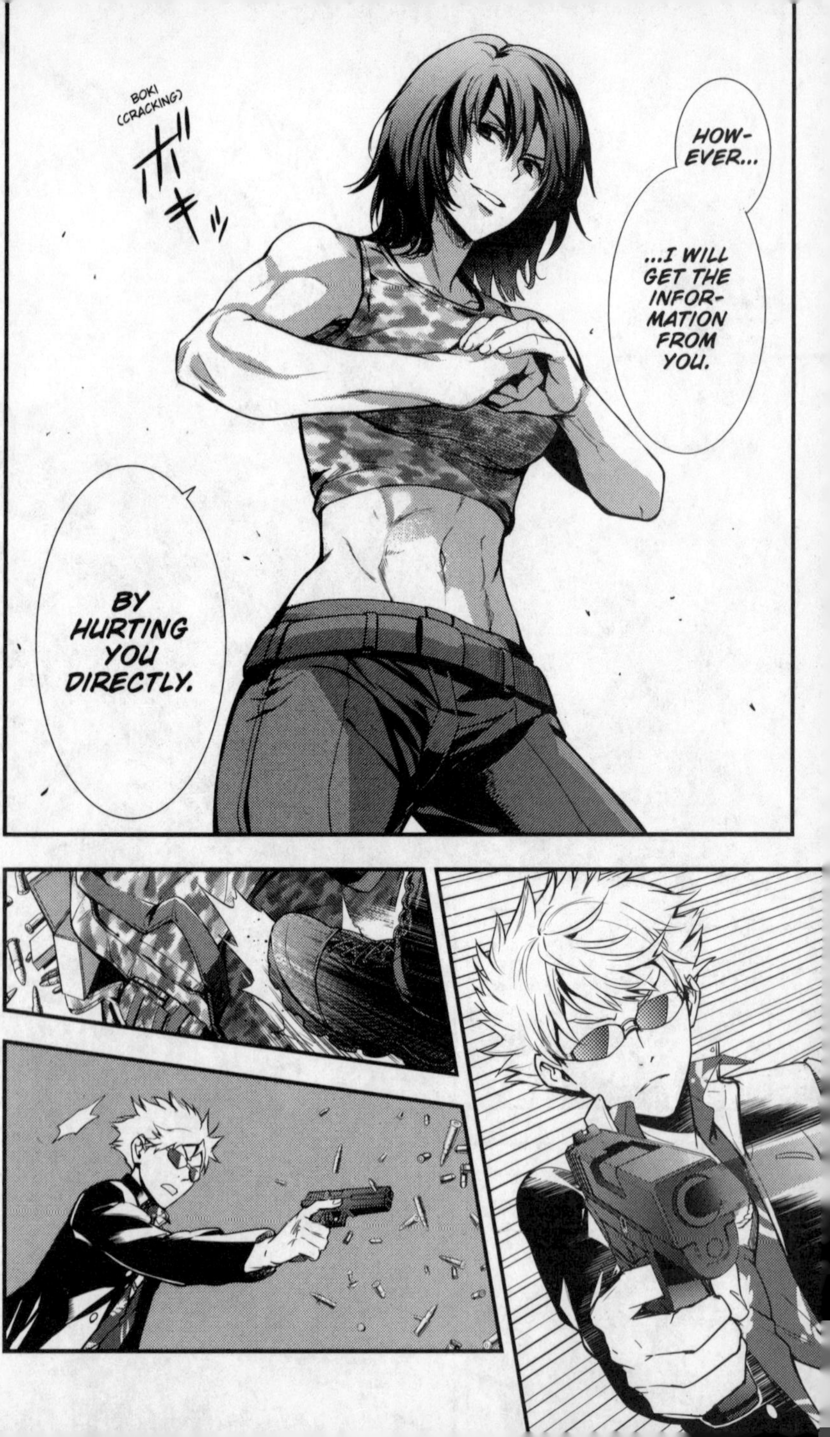
HOW-EVER...
...I WILL GET THE INFORMATION FROM YOU.
BOKI (CRACKING)
BY HURTING YOU DIRECTLY.

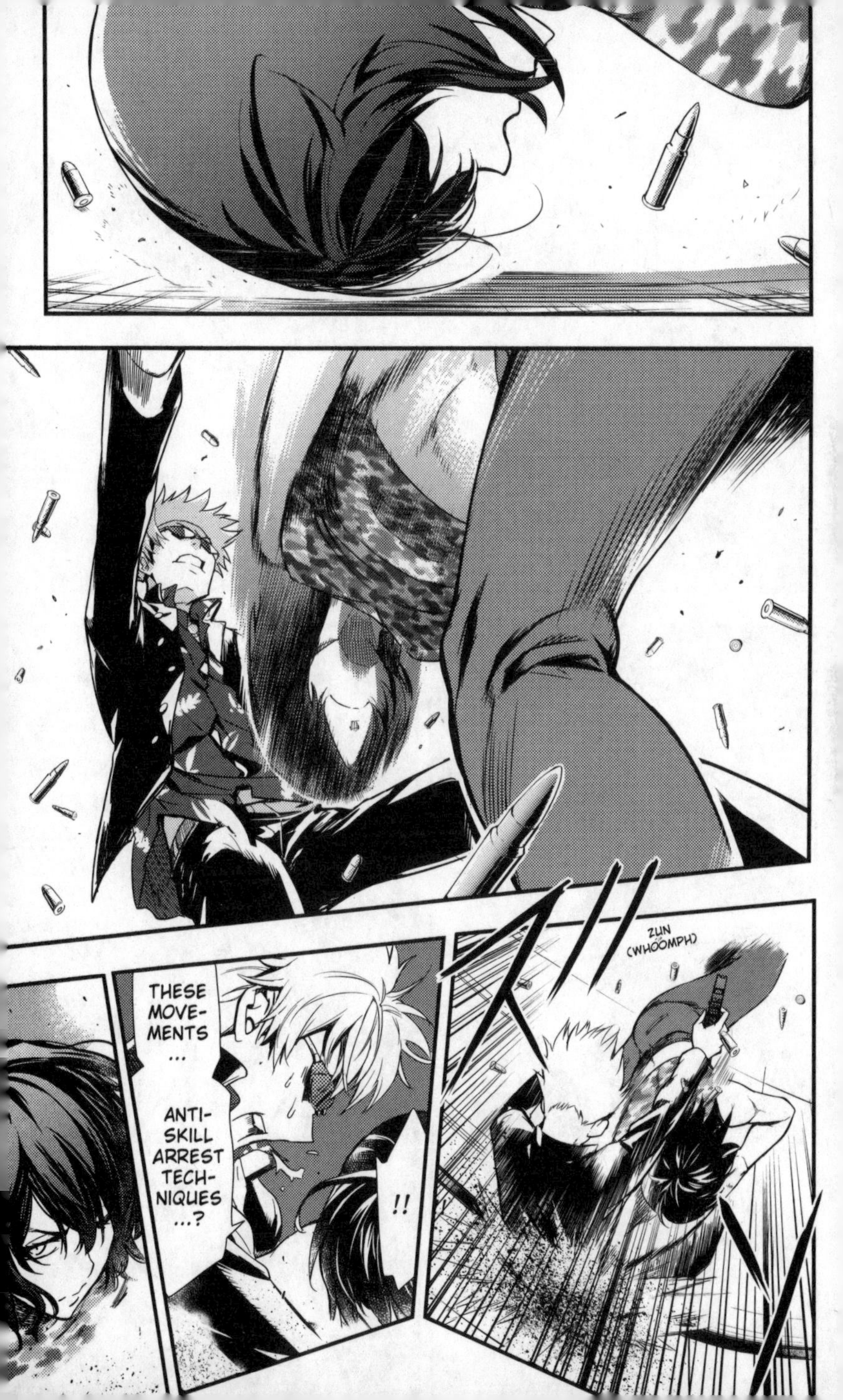

ZUN
(WHOOMPH)
THESE MOVEMENTS...
ANTI-SKILL ARREST TECHNIQUES...?
!!

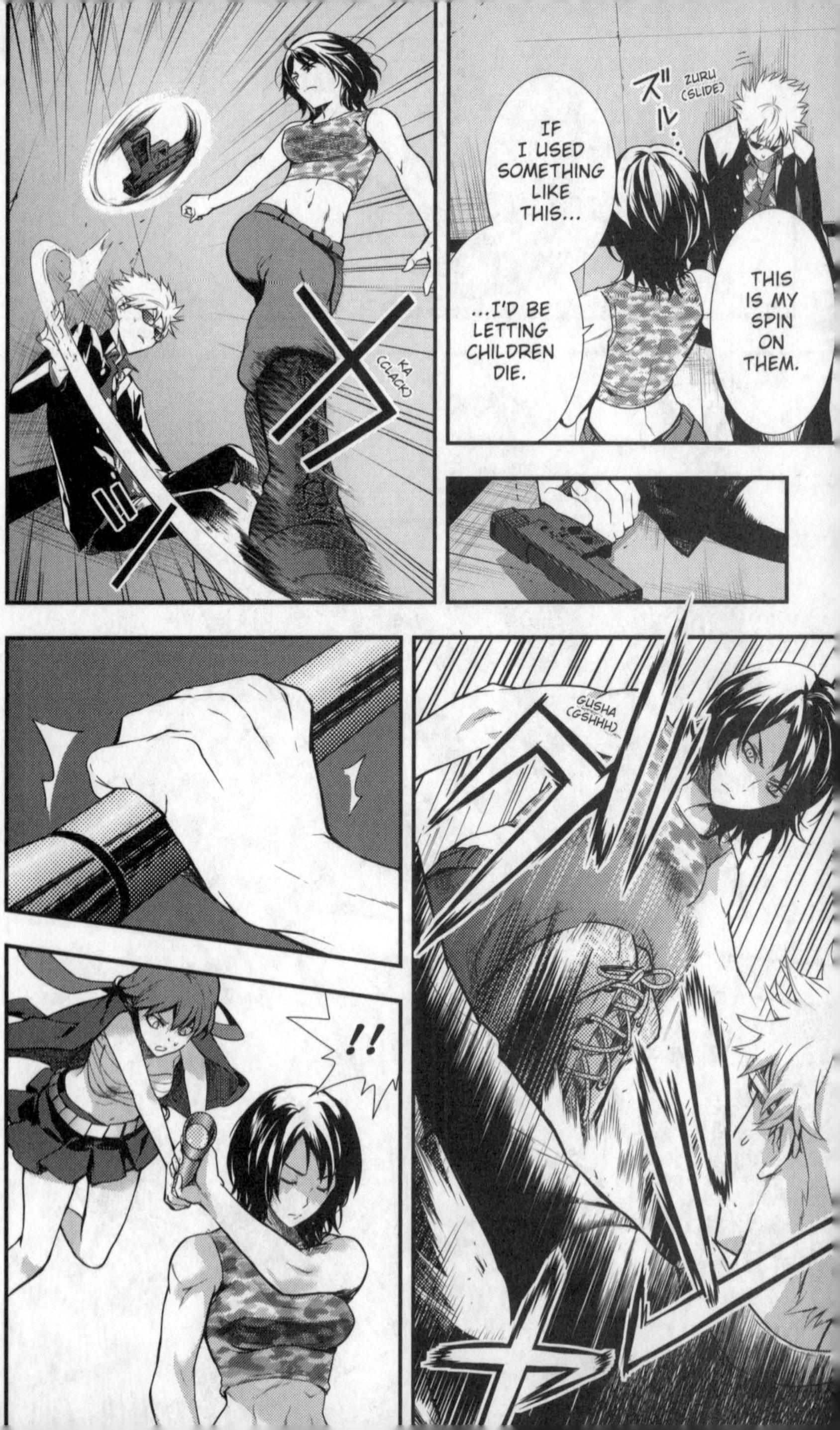

ズル…
ZURU (SLIDE)
IF I USED SOMETHING LIKE THIS...
...I'D BE LETTING CHILDREN DIE.
THIS IS MY SPIN ON THEM.
KA (CLACK)
!!
GUSHA (GSHHH)
!!

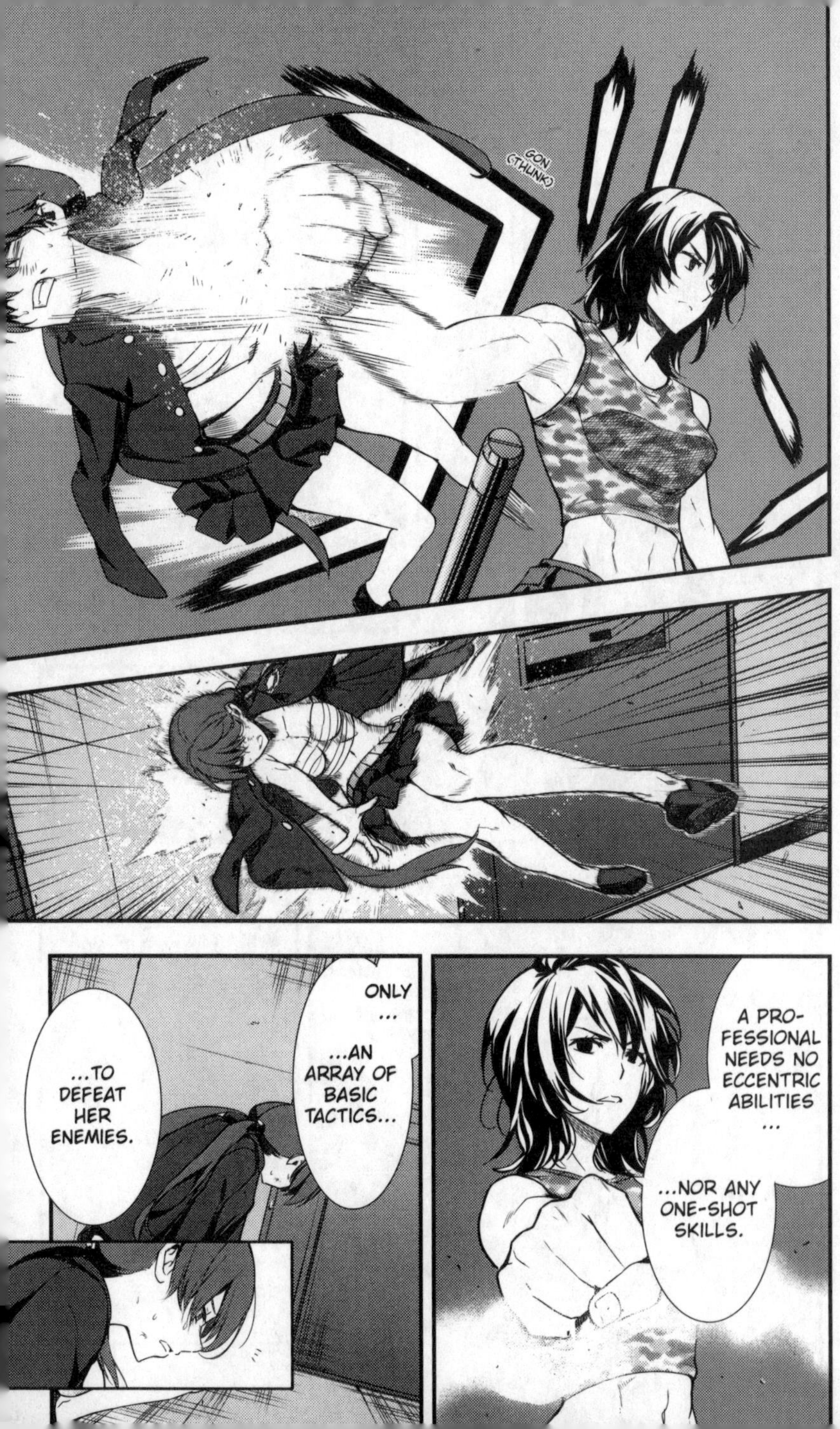
GON (THUNK)
A PROFESSIONAL NEEDS NO ECCENTRIC ABILITIES ...
...NOR ANY ONE-SHOT SKILLS.
ONLY ...
...AN ARRAY OF BASIC TACTICS...
...TO DEFEAT HER ENEMIES.

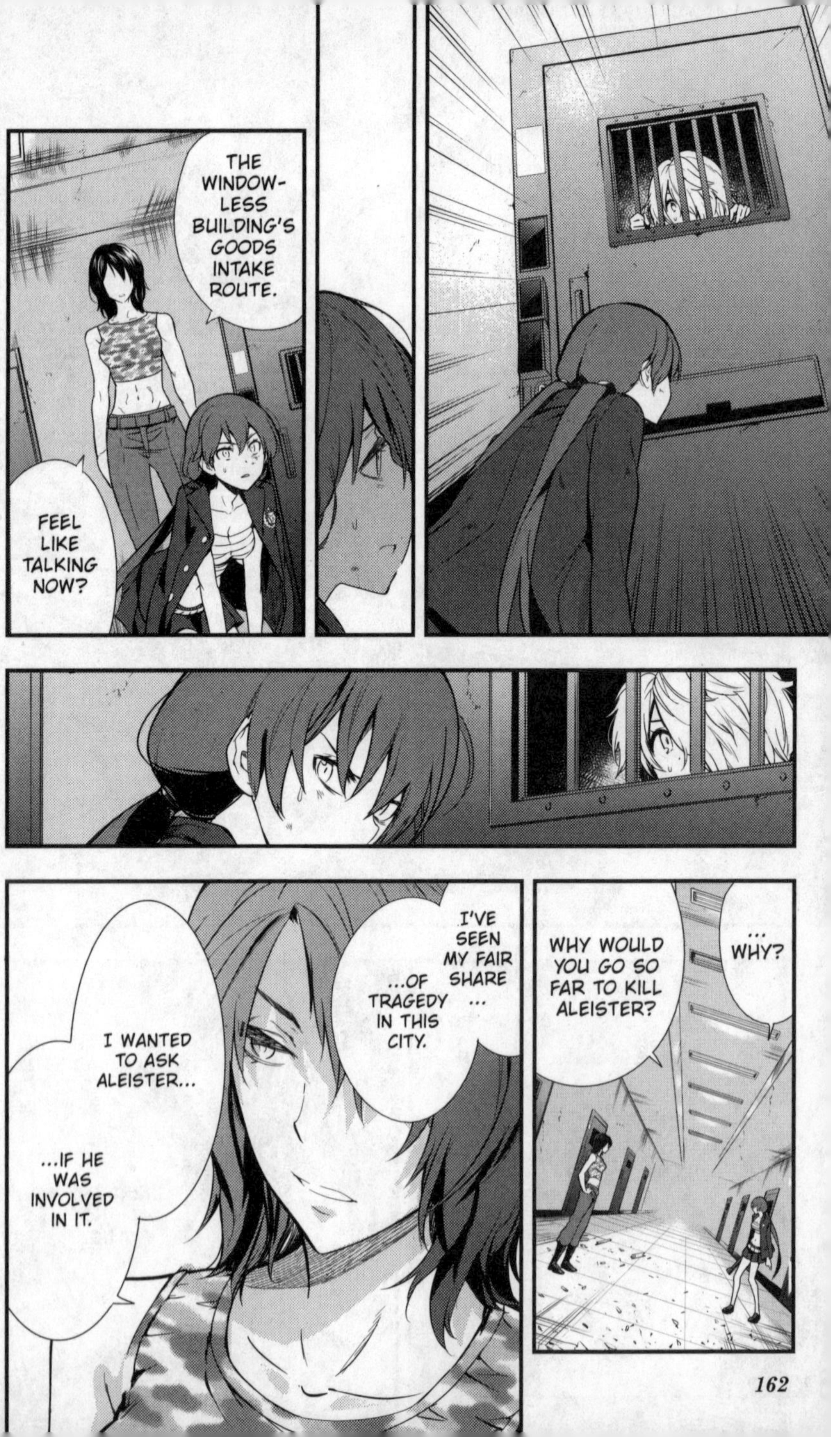
THE WINDOW-LESS BUILDING'S GOODS INTAKE ROUTE.
FEEL LIKE TALKING NOW?
...WHY?
WHY WOULD YOU GO SO FAR TO KILL ALEISTER?
I'VE SEEN MY FAIR SHARE ...
...OF TRAGEDY IN THIS CITY.
I WANTED TO ASK ALEISTER...
...IF HE WAS INVOLVED IN IT.

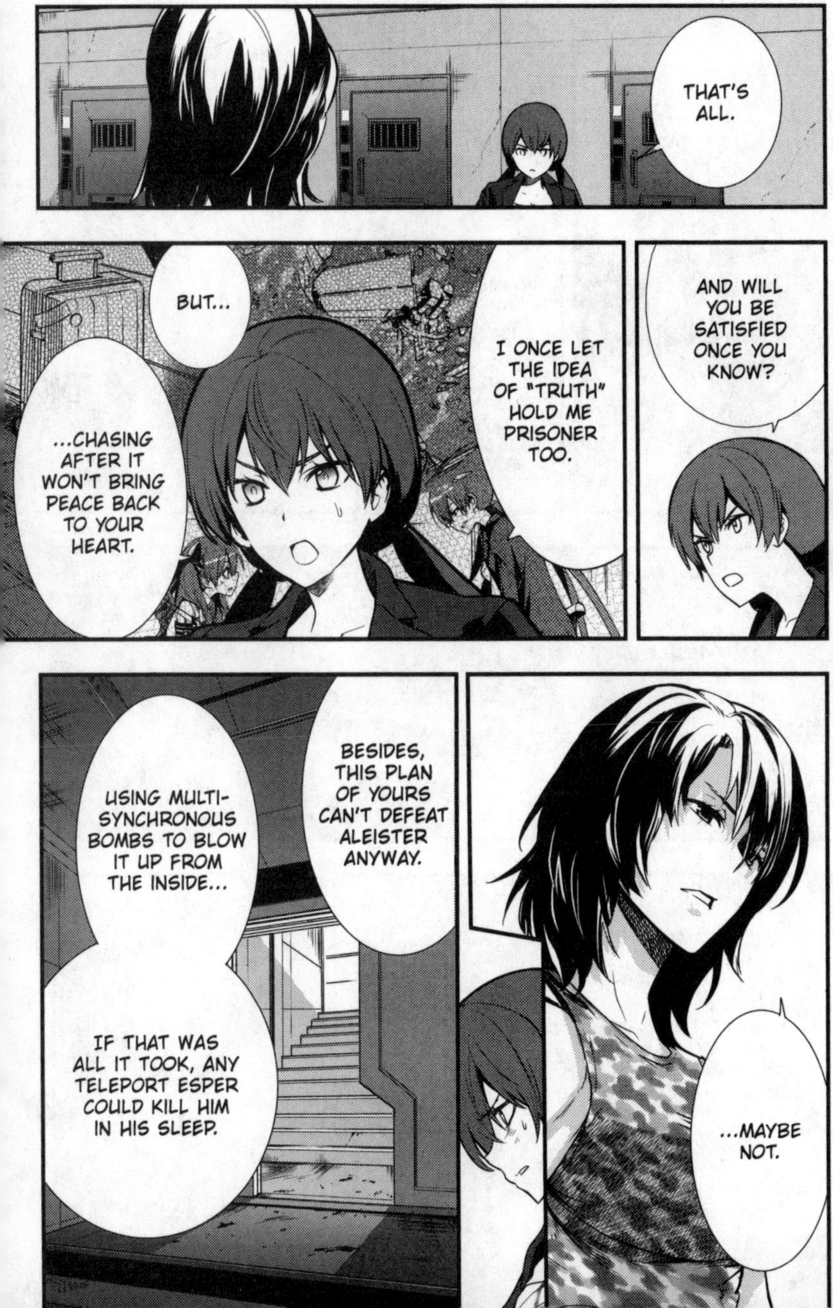
THAT'S ALL.
AND WILL YOU BE SATISFIED ONCE YOU KNOW?
I ONCE LET THE IDEA OF "TRUTH" HOLD ME PRISONER TOO.
BUT...
...CHASING AFTER IT WON'T BRING PEACE BACK TO YOUR HEART.
...MAYBE NOT.
BESIDES, THIS PLAN OF YOURS CAN'T DEFEAT ALEISTER ANYWAY.
USING MULTI-SYNCHRONOUS BOMBS TO BLOW IT UP FROM THE INSIDE...
IF THAT WAS ALL IT TOOK, ANY TELEPORT ESPER COULD KILL HIM IN HIS SLEEP.

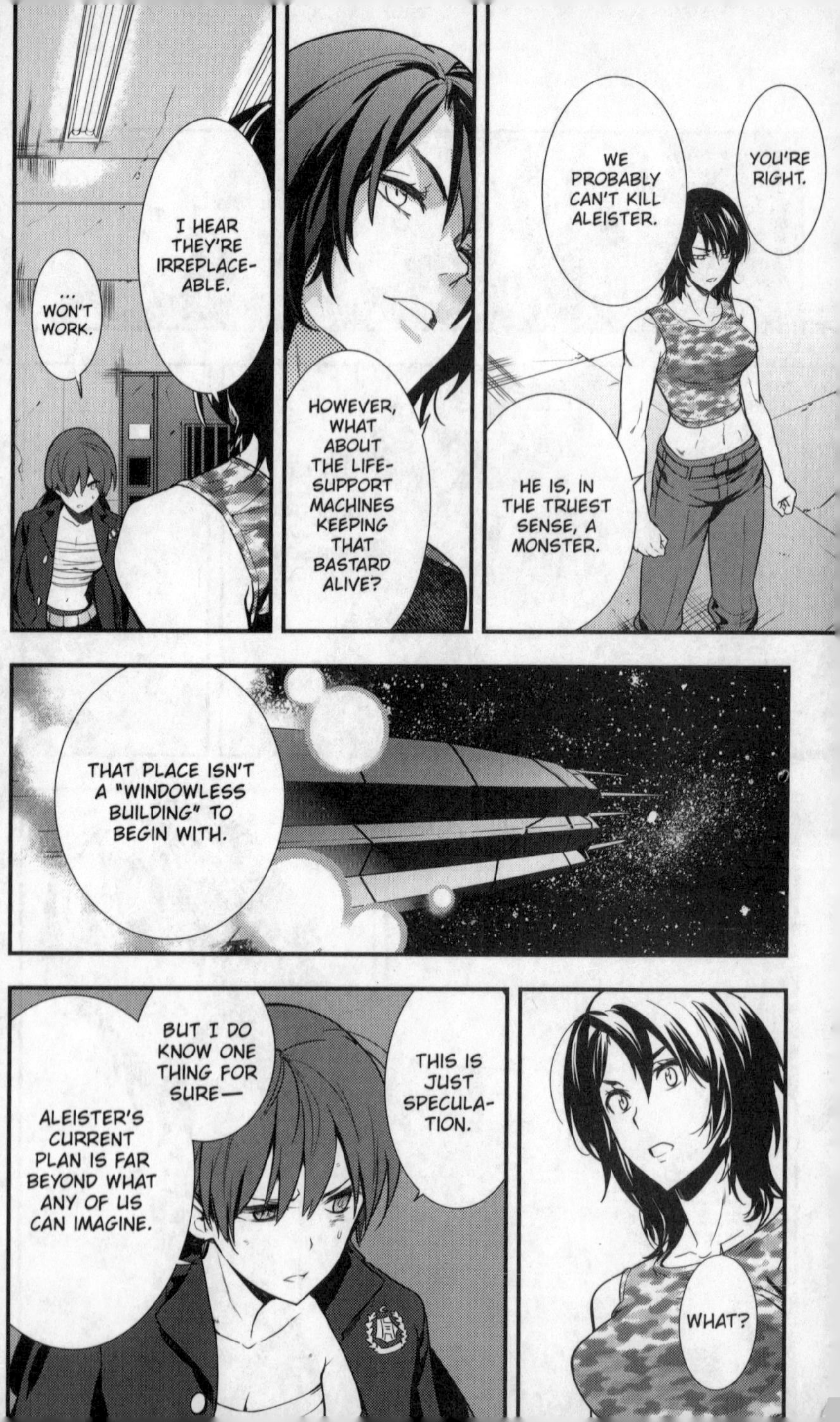
YOU'RE RIGHT.
WE PROBABLY CAN'T KILL ALEISTER.
HE IS, IN THE TRUEST SENSE, A MONSTER.
HOWEVER, WHAT ABOUT THE LIFE-SUPPORT MACHINES KEEPING THAT BASTARD ALIVE?
I HEAR THEY'RE IRREPLACEABLE.
...WON'T WORK.
THAT PLACE ISN'T A "WINDOWLESS BUILDING" TO BEGIN WITH.
WHAT?
THIS IS JUST SPECULATION.
BUT I DO KNOW ONE THING FOR SURE—
ALEISTER'S CURRENT PLAN IS FAR BEYOND WHAT ANY OF US CAN IMAGINE.

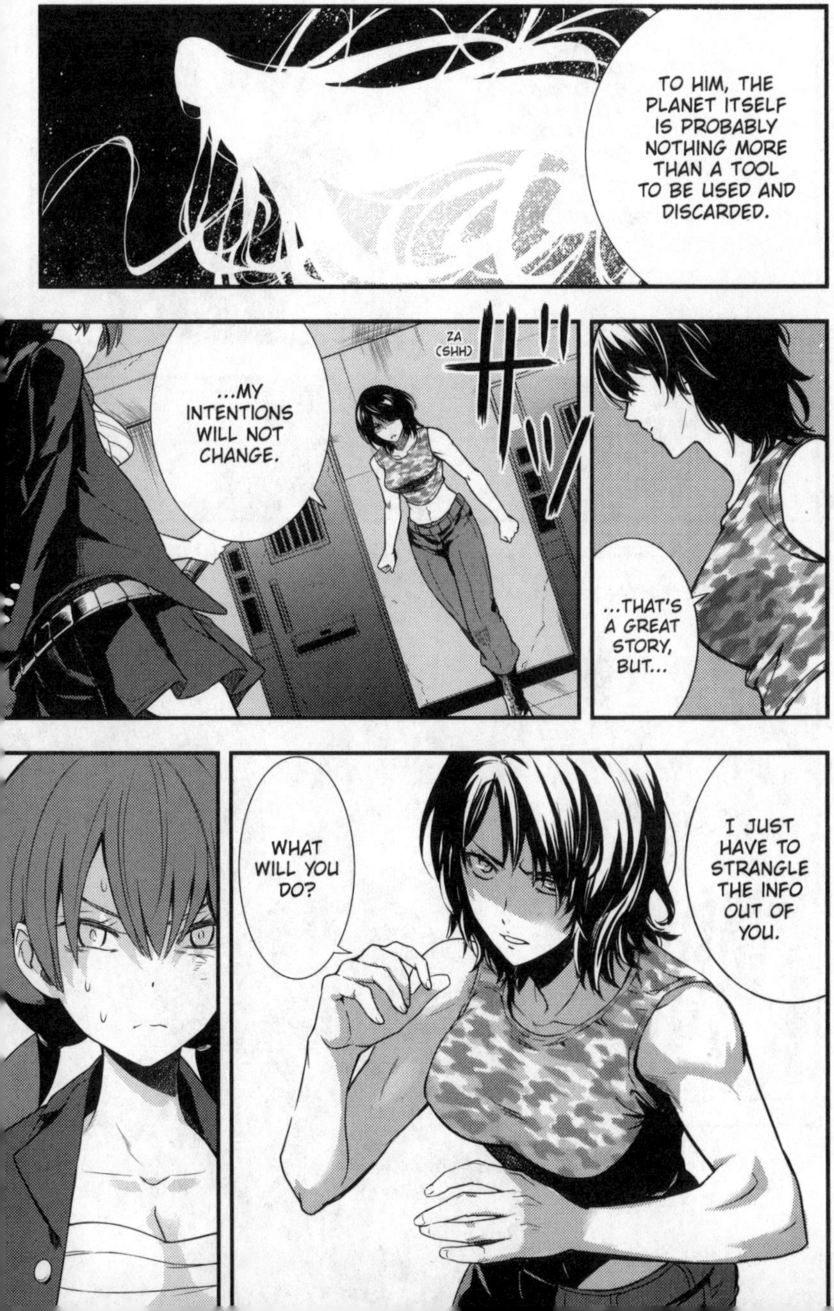
TO HIM, THE PLANET ITSELF IS PROBABLY NOTHING MORE THAN A TOOL TO BE USED AND DISCARDED.
...THAT'S A GREAT STORY, BUT...
ZA (SHH)
...MY INTENTIONS WILL NOT CHANGE.
I JUST HAVE TO STRANGLE THE INFO OUT OF YOU.
WHAT WILL YOU DO?

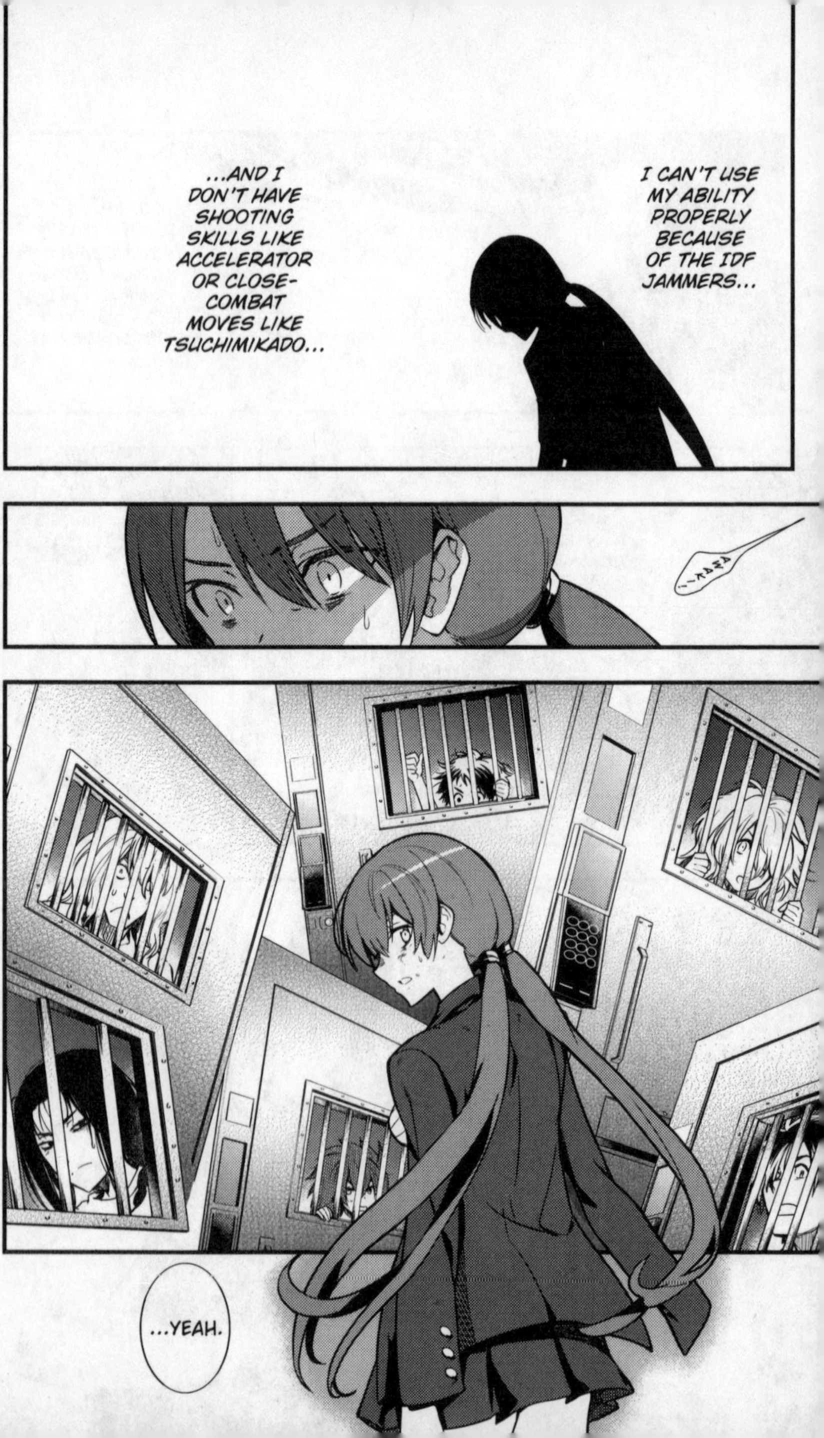
I CAN'T USE MY ABILITY PROPERLY BECAUSE OF THE IDF JAMMERS...
...AND I DON'T HAVE SHOOTING SKILLS LIKE ACCELERATOR OR CLOSE-COMBAT MOVES LIKE TSUCHIMIKADO...
...YEAH.

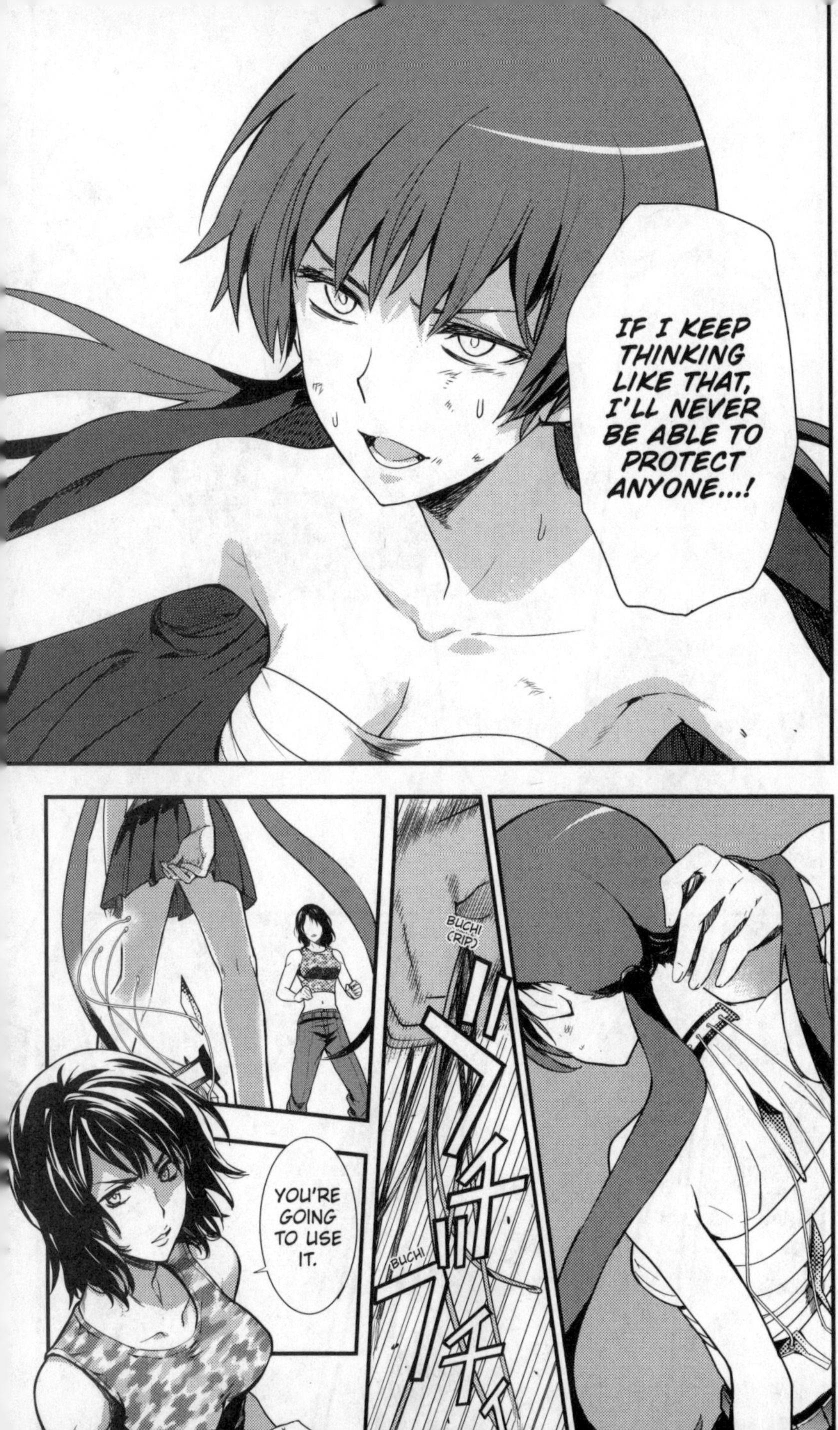
IF I KEEP THINKING LIKE THAT, I'LL NEVER BE ABLE TO PROTECT ANYONE...!
BUCHI (RIP)
BUCHI
YOU'RE GOING TO USE IT.

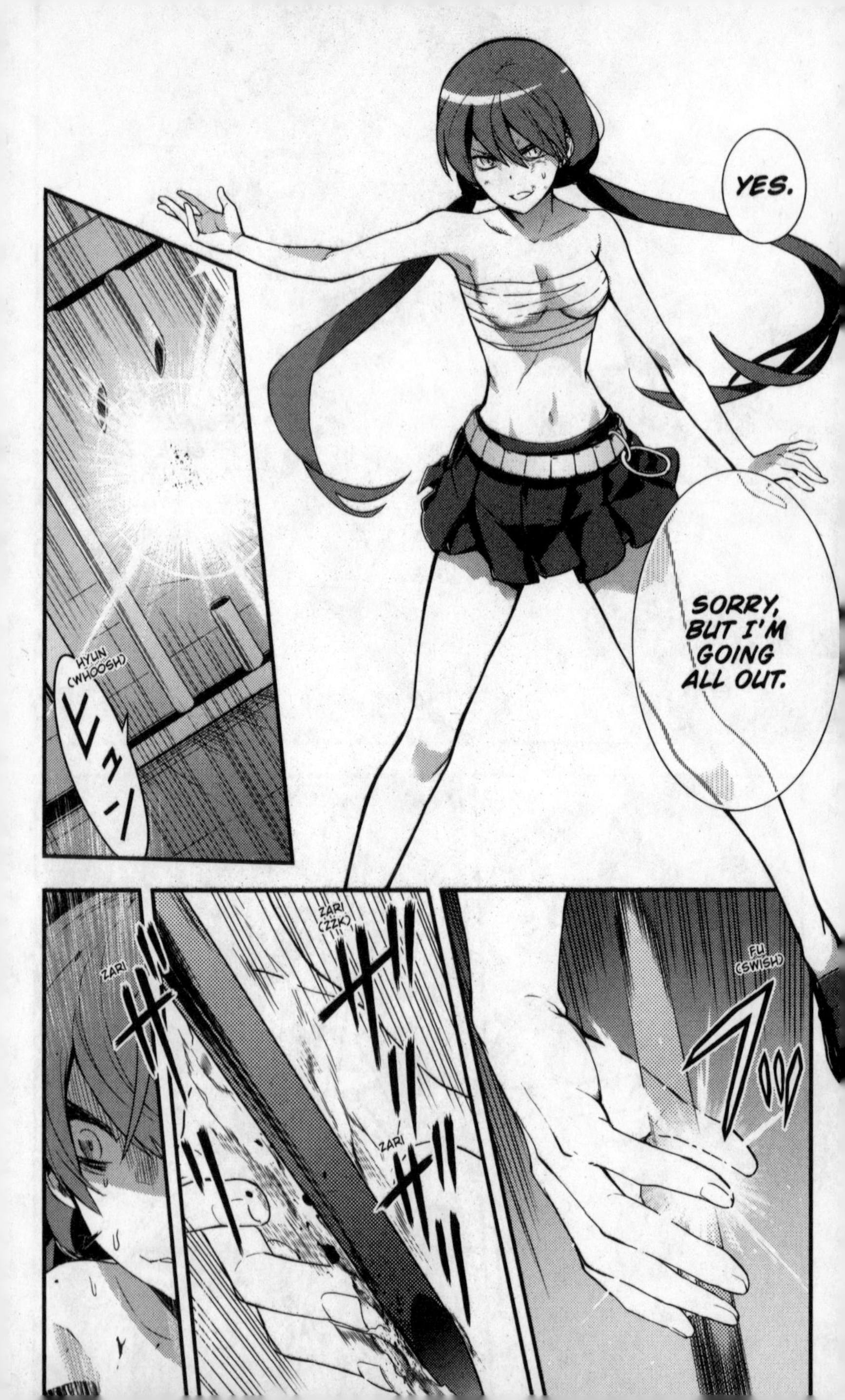

YES.
SORRY, BUT I'M GOING ALL OUT.
HYUN (WHOOSH)
FU (SWISH)
ZARI (ZZK)
ZARI
ZARI

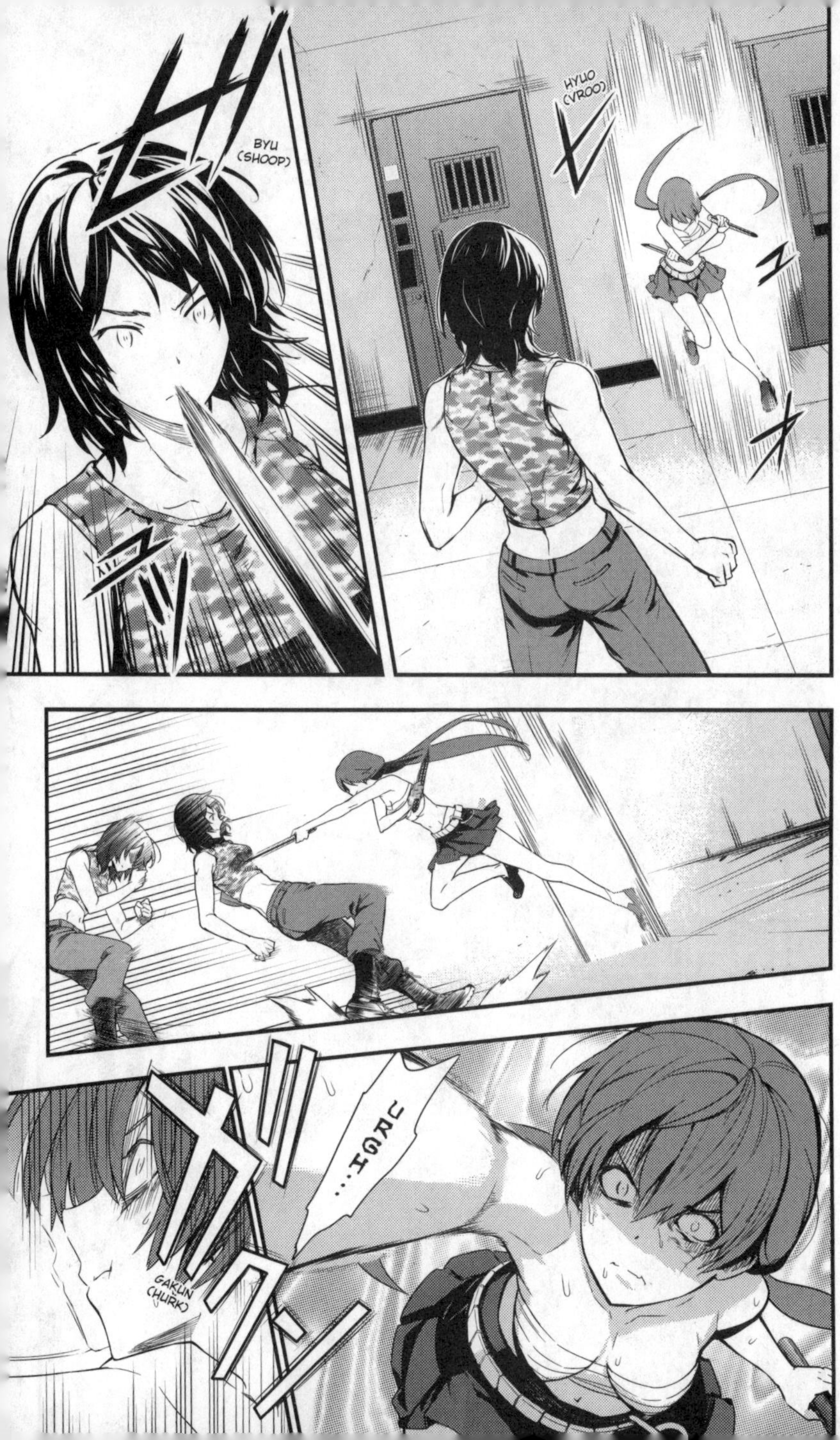
HYUO
(VROO)
BYU
(SHOOP)
URGH...
GAKUN
(HURK)

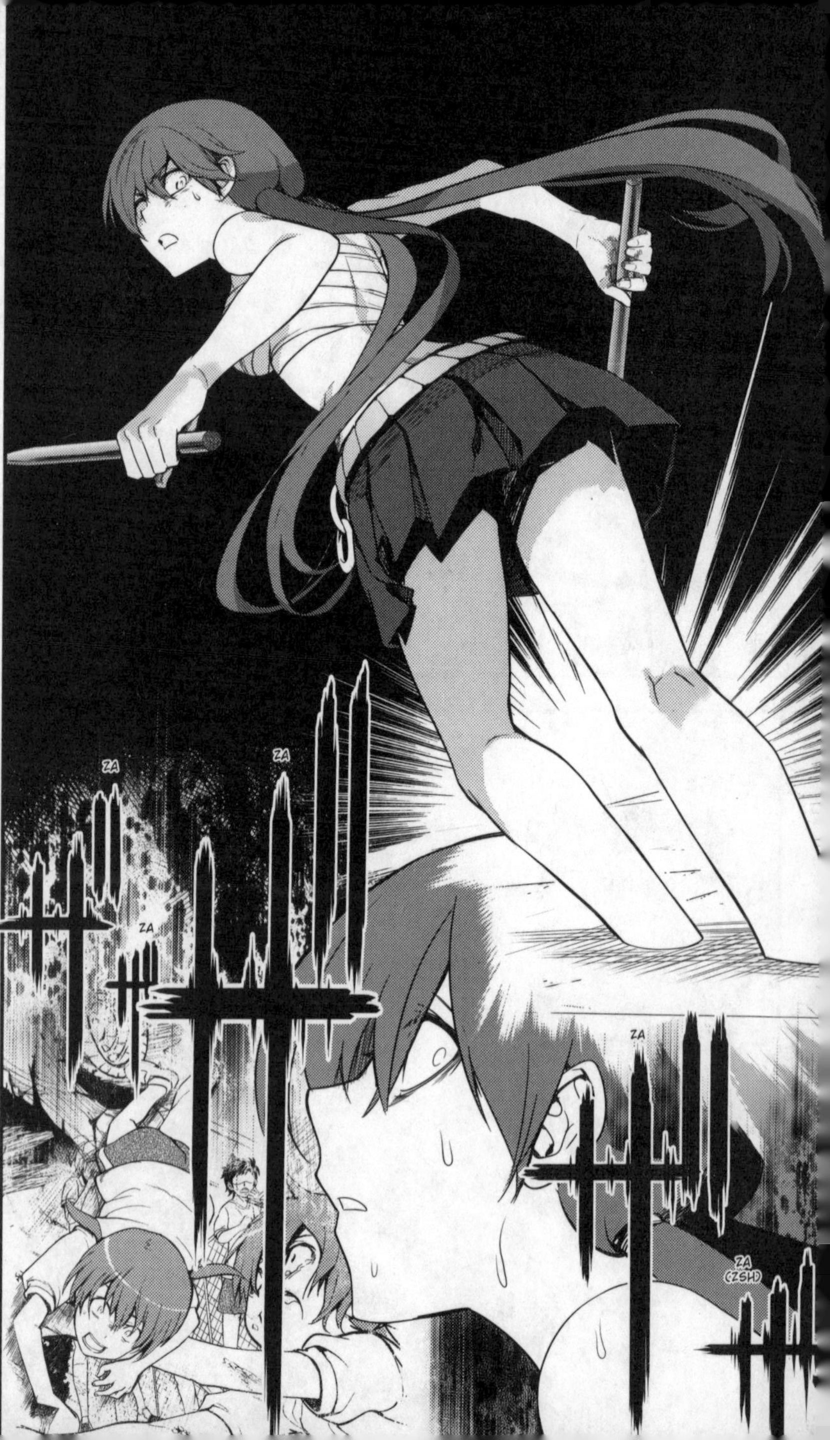
ZA
ZA
ZA
ZA
ZA
CZSHD

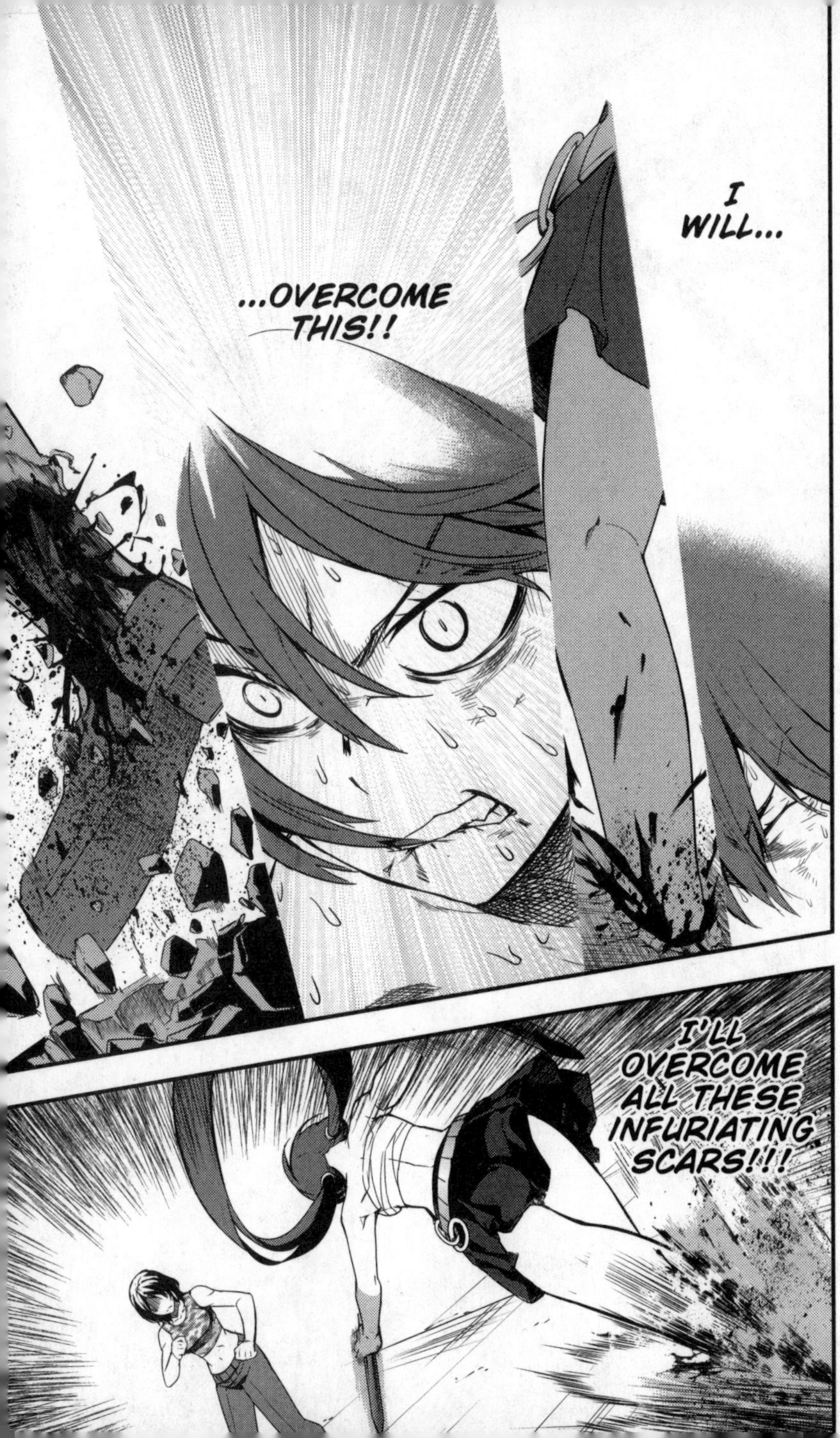
I WILL...
...OVERCOME THIS!!
I'LL OVERCOME ALL THESE INFURIATING SCARS!!!

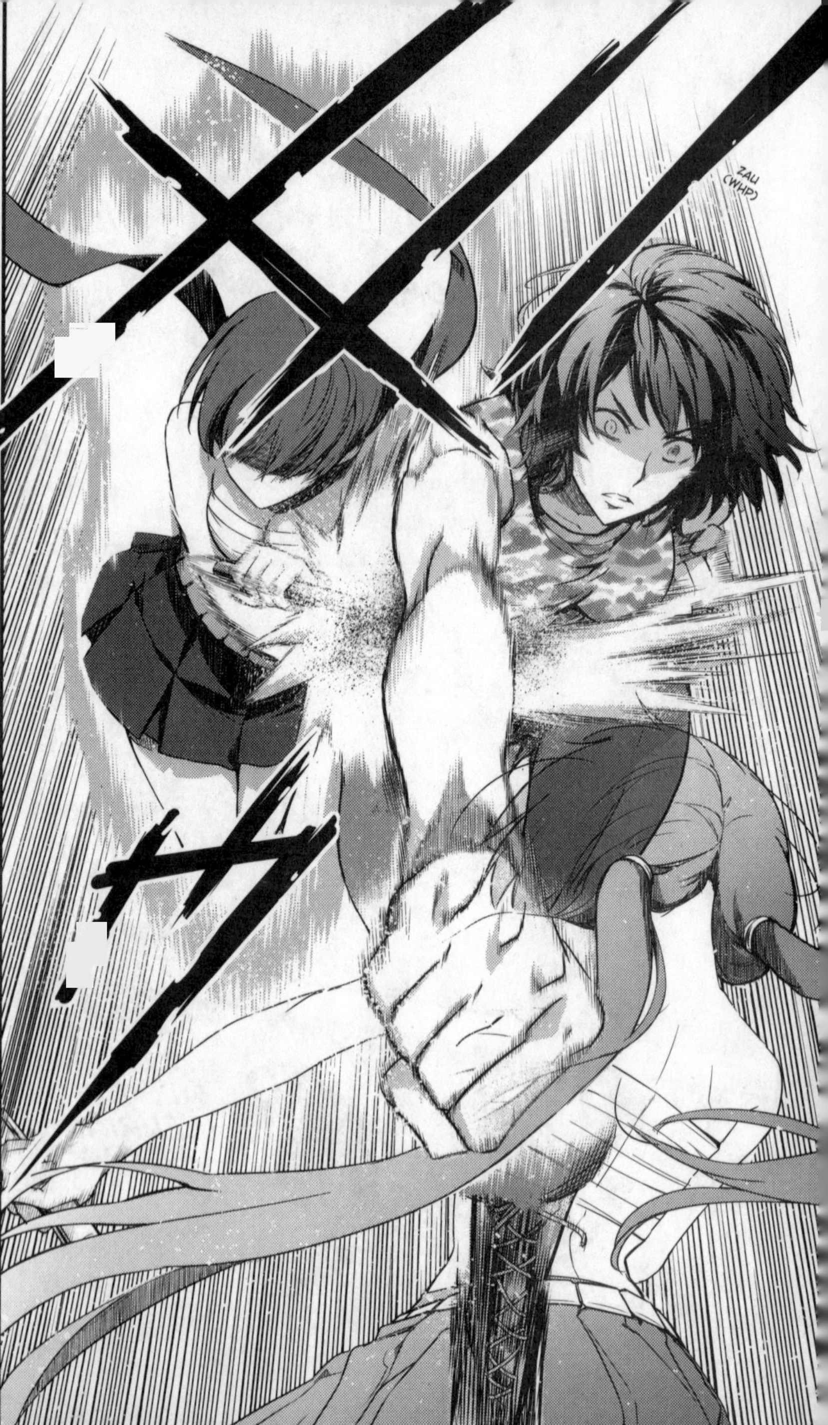
ZAU
(WHP)

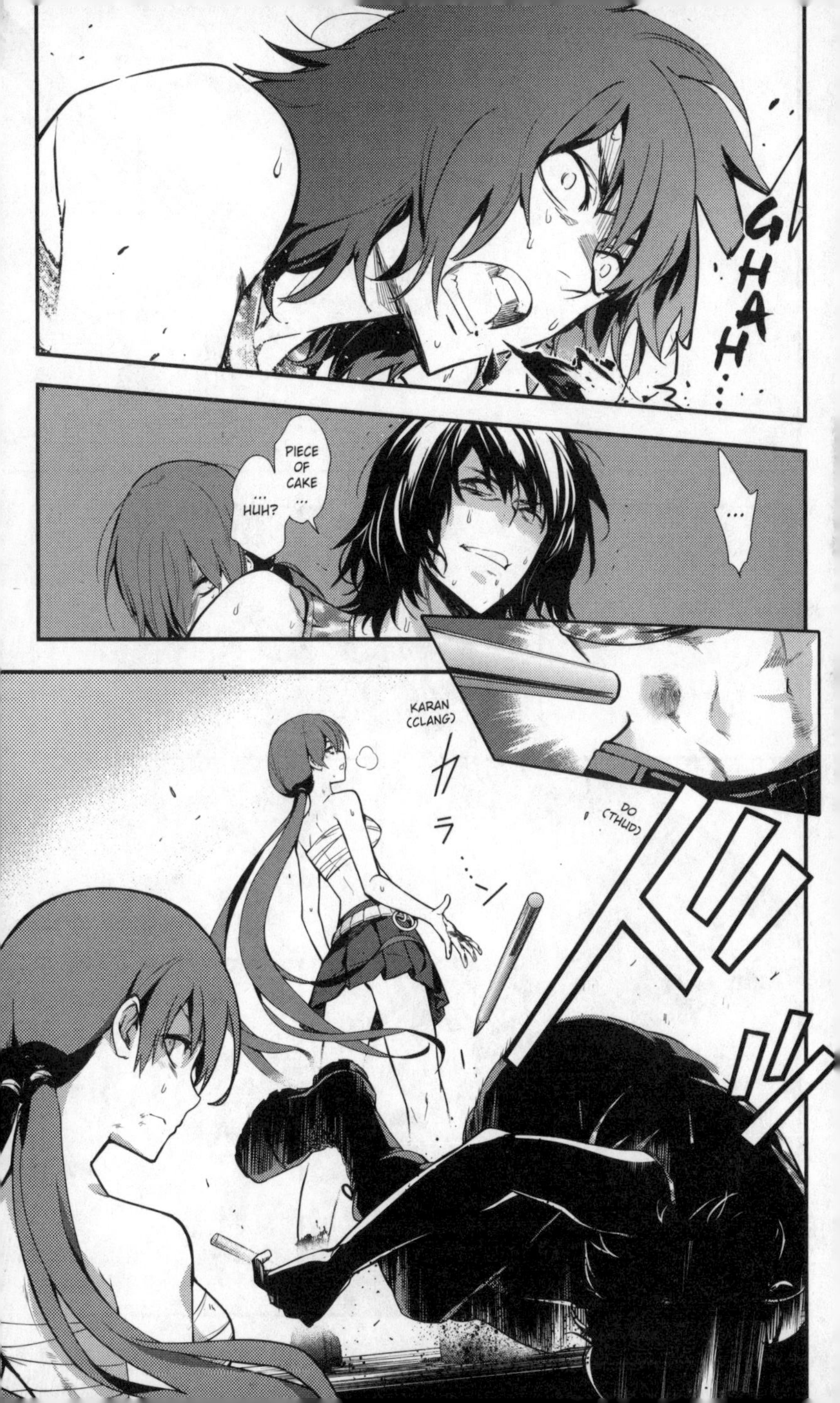
GHAH...
...
PIECE OF CAKE... ...HUH?
DO (THUD)
KARAN (CLANG)

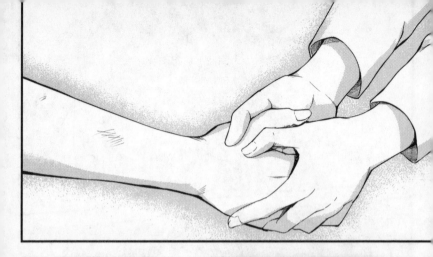

YES.

GOOD NOW?

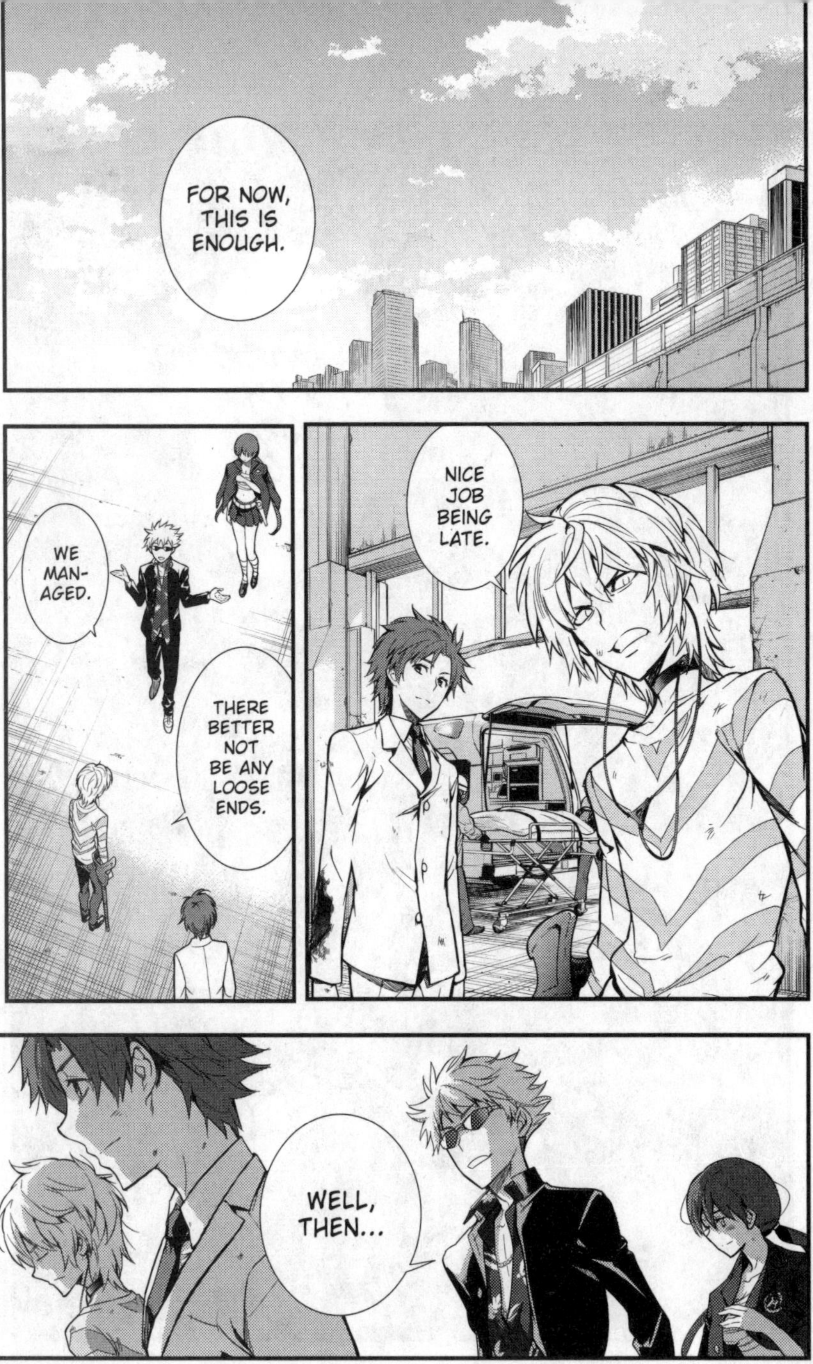
FOR NOW, THIS IS ENOUGH.
NICE JOB BEING LATE.
WE MAN-AGED.
THERE BETTER NOT BE ANY LOOSE ENDS.
WELL, THEN...

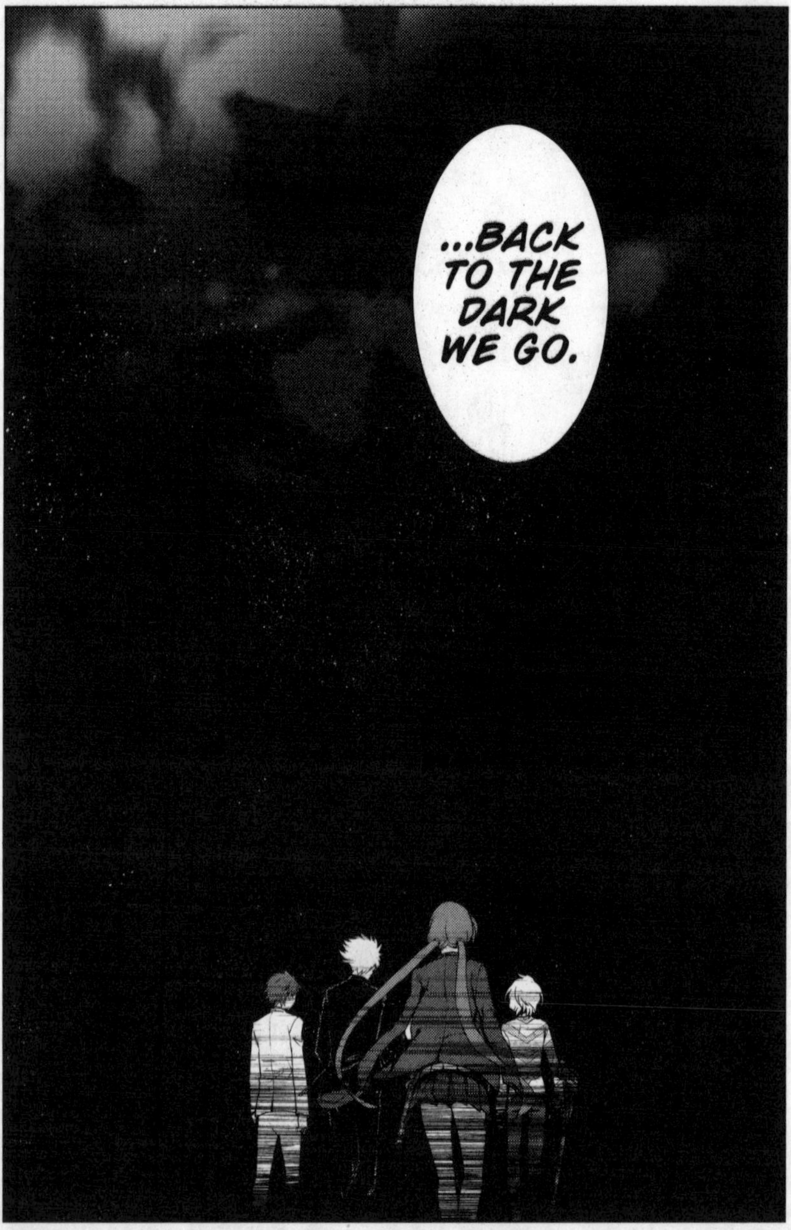
...BACK TO THE DARK WE GO.

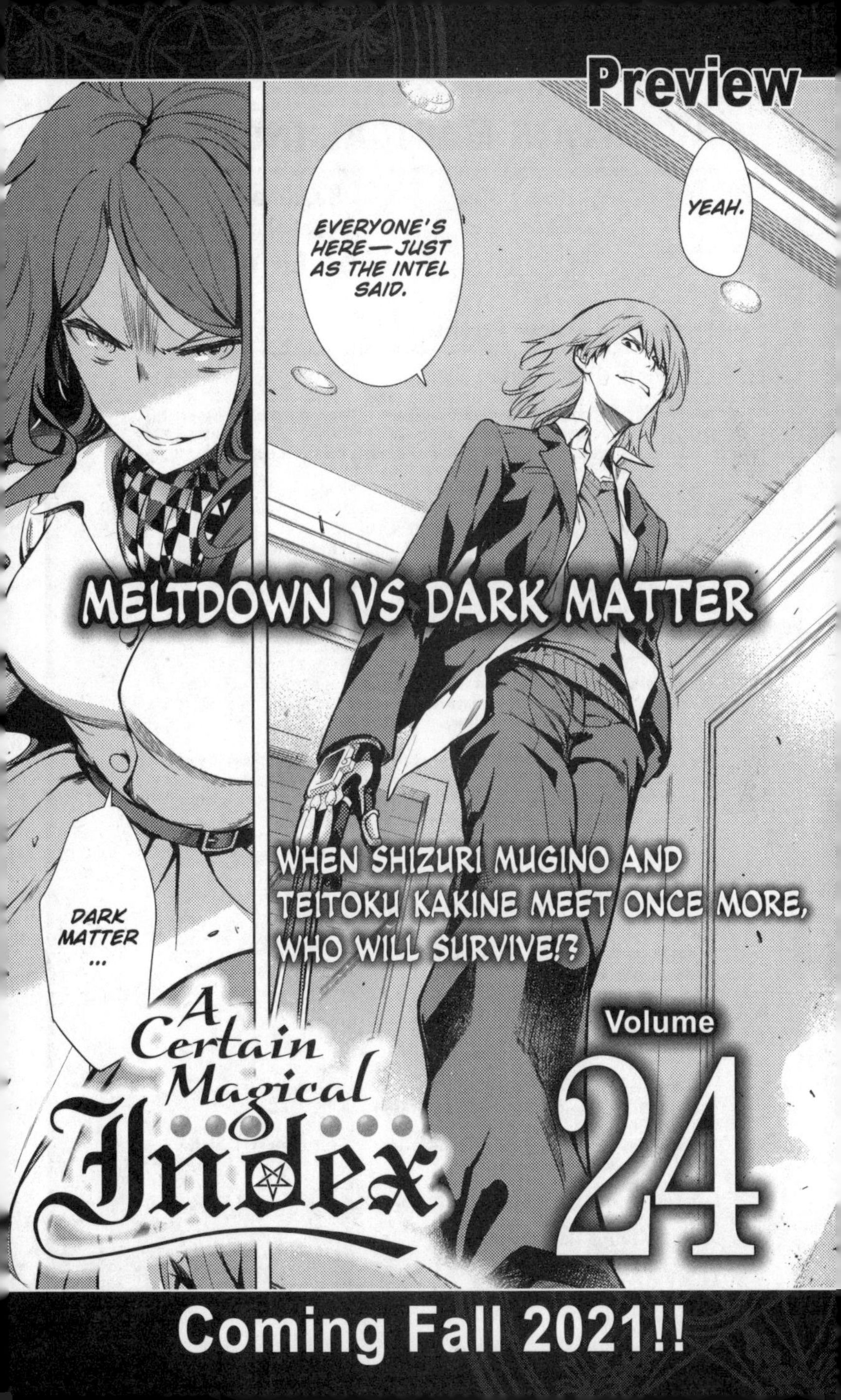
Preview
YEAH.
EVERYONE'S HERE—JUST AS THE INTEL SAID.
DARK MATTER...
MELTDOWN VS DARK MATTER
WHEN SHIZURI MUGINO AND TEITOKU KAKINE MEET ONCE MORE, WHO WILL SURVIVE!?
A Certain Magical Index
Volume 24
Coming Fall 2021!!

# A CERTAIN MAGICAL INDEX ㉓

**Kazuma Kamachi**
**Kiyotaka Haimura**
**Chuya Kogino**

**Translation: Andrew Prowse**

**Lettering: Phil Christie**

TOARU MAJYUTSU NO INDEX Vol. 23
© 2019 Kazuma Kamachi
© 2019 Chuya Kogino / SQUARE ENIX CO., LTD.
Licensed by KADOKAWA CORPORATION ASCII MEDIA WORKS
First published in Japan in 2019 by SQUARE ENIX CO., LTD.
English translation rights arranged with SQUARE ENIX CO., LTD.
and Yen Press, LLC through Tuttle-Mori Agency, Inc.

English translation © 2021 by SQUARE ENIX CO., LTD.

Yen Press
150 West 30th Street, 19th Floor
New York, NY 10001

Visit us at yenpress.com
facebook.com/yenpress
twitter.com/yenpress
yenpress.tumblr.com
instagram.com/yenpress

First Yen Press Edition: May 2021

Yen Press is an imprint of Yen Press, LLC.
The Yen Press name and logo are trademarks of Yen Press, LLC.

The publisher is not responsible for websites (or their content) that are not owned by the publisher.

Library of Congress Control Number: 2015373809

ISBN: 978-1-9753-1698-3 (paperback)

10 9 8 7 6 5 4 3 2 1

BVG

Printed in the United States of America